SAGA OF THE SWAMP THING BOOK THREE

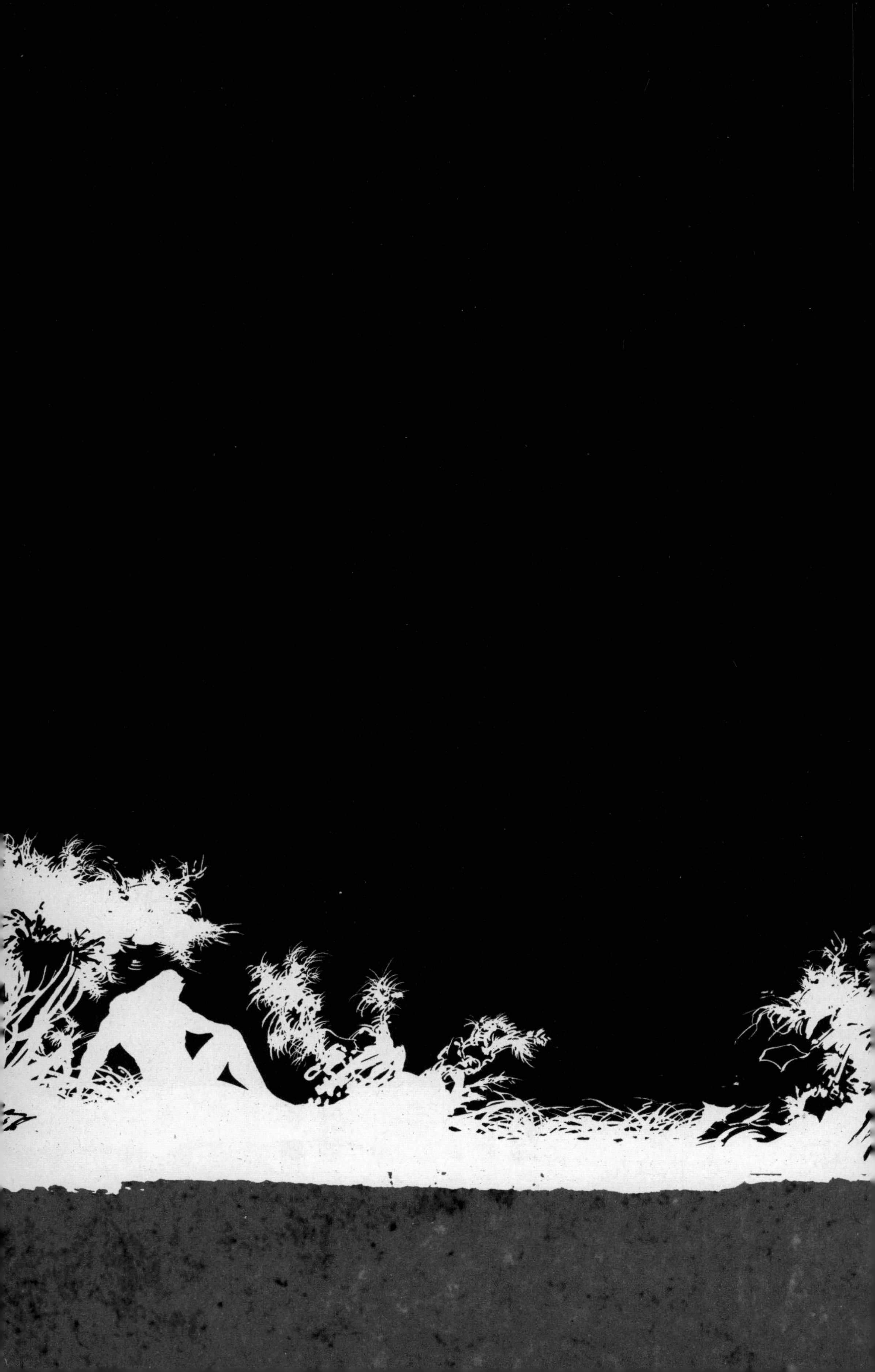

Original Series Cover Art by Stephen Bissette · John Totleben

Original Series Cover Color by Tatjana Wood

Swamp Thing created by Len Wein and Bernie Wrightson

SAGA OF THE
SWAMP THING
BOOK THREE

Karen Berger Editor – Original Series
Scott Nybakken Editor
Robbin Brosterman Design Director – Books
Louis Prandi Publication Design

Hank Kanalz Senior VP – Vertigo & Integrated Publishing

Diane Nelson President
Dan DiDio and Jim Lee Co-Publishers
Geoff Johns Chief Creative Officer
John Rood Executive VP – Sales, Marketing & Business Development
Amy Genkins Senior VP – Business & Legal Affairs
Nairi Gardiner Senior VP – Finance
Jeff Boison VP – Publishing Planning
Mark Chiarello VP – Art Direction & Design
John Cunningham VP – Marketing
Terri Cunningham VP – Editorial Administration
Alison Gill Senior VP – Manufacturing & Operations
Jay Kogan VP – Business & Legal Affairs, Publishing
Jack Mahan VP – Business Affairs, Talent
Nick Napolitano VP – Manufacturing Administration
Sue Pohja VP – Book Sales
Courtney Simmons Senior VP – Publicity
Bob Wayne Senior VP – Sales

Cover pencils by Stephen Bissette.
Cover inks by John Totleben.
Cover color by Allen Passalaqua.
Color reconstruction on selected interior pages by Drew Moore.

DC Comics
1700 Broadway, New York, NY 10019
A Warner Bros. Entertainment Company.
Printed in the USA. Second Printing.
ISBN: 978-1-4012-2767-8

Library of Congress Cataloging-in-Publication Data

Moore, Alan, 1953-
 Saga of the Swamp Thing. Book three / Alan Moore,
Stephen Bissette, John Totleben.
  p. cm.
 "Originally published as The Saga of the Swamp
Thing 35-38 and Swamp Thing 39-42."
 ISBN 978-1-4012-2767-8 (alk. paper)
 1. Graphic novels. I. Bissette, Stephen. II. Totleben,
John. III. Title.
 PN6728.S93M645 2012
 741.5'973–dc23
                                          2012033186

SUSTAINABLE FORESTRY INITIATIVE

Certified Chain of Custody
Promoting Sustainable Forestry
www.sfiprogram.org
SFI-01042
APPLIES TO TEXT STOCK ONLY

Cursed Earth & Uneasy Riders

It begins with fires raging underground, and it ends with a burning mansion.

The fires are still burning beneath the soil — in real life, as in these pages — but as for the plantation and the ashes of its gutted mansion... well, that's something we left behind us long ago.

Let's sift through the ashes together, shall we?

Gathered herein, between two covers, is the end of our initial arc of Swamp Thing stories, the conclusion of our collective breaking of new ground with the two-part "The Nukeface Papers" and the beginning of a more self-conscious travelogue of cursed turf that Alan dubbed "American Gothic."

This span of stories — originally published as *The Saga of the Swamp Thing* #35-38 and *Swamp Thing* #39-42 (1985) — encompassed a major shift in the creative collaboration that Alan Moore, John Totleben, Rick Veitch and I enjoyed back in the "salad days" working under the steady hand of editor Karen Berger. It was our second major shift, planned as an ending of sorts and a new beginning.

The plan, as Alan put it at the time, was to shift gears into something different, "a kind of Ramsey Campbell version of *Easy Rider*." For a multitude of reasons, John and I let Alan and Karen know we were going to leave the series with *Swamp Thing* #50, if we could last that long. Rick Veitch would take over the regular pencilling of the series at that point. Alan pondered the various plot suggestions that John and I had sent him since we'd begun our collaboration, including story ideas that our friends had tossed into the ring (read on), and charted a best-case scenario of how to work that untidy mass of story ideas, characters and notions into a cohesive tapestry that would culminate in something special.

Alan's revisionist 1980s *Easy Rider* began with "Growth Patterns" (*The Saga of the Swamp Thing* #37), which introduced John Constantine as a character. John Totleben and I had introduced Constantine's face in the background of a panel in an earlier issue (see issue #25, page 21, panel 2) — a cameo prompted by our mutual affection for Sting of The Police. Meshing Sting's mug (and a bit of his Aceface persona from the movie *Quadrophenia*) with elements of punk fatalism, Michael Moorcock's Jerry Cornelius character, and the grand tradition of occult detectives dating back to Margery Lawrence's Mile Pennoyer and Seabury Quinn's Jules de Grandin, Alan then concocted the John Constantine we know and love. Fellow traveler (and Kubert School alumni) Rick Veitch was the first to pencil the real John Constantine in "Growth Patterns," so he too is a key element in the character's creation.

"Growth Patterns" was the beginning of "American Gothic," and of John Constantine, and of Vertigo — but it's not the beginning of the collected edition you're about to read.

***

It begins with a resurrected script, and it ends with the resurrected dead.

Resurrection is a common theme in horror, and it applies on multiple levels to the stories that follow.

Collectively, we were exhausted but still high on our previous run of issues, the epic arc that began with "Love and Death" and ended with the double-sized "Down Amongst the Dead Men" — capped off with my personal favorite of all of our efforts, the brief respite granted to our put-upon lovers Abby and Swamp Thing entitled "The Rites of Spring." That issue was sparked by a postcard I'd mailed to Alan amid our steady exchange of lengthy letters and longer phone calls. As we were working on "Down Amongst the Dead Men," I had written a very short postcard to Alan saying, "If Abby were a real woman, what we've put her through would have landed her in an asylum by now. Why don't we give Alec and Abby a break and just spend a quiet day in the swamps with them, let them relax and enjoy one another?" From that Alan forged something extraordinary, and John and I did our best to do his script for "The Rites of Spring" justice.

Unknown to our growing readership, Alan had already worked similar magic on one of John Totleben's character concepts. From a list of story springboards that John and I had earlier mailed to Marty Pasko (the previous writer on *The Saga of the Swamp*

Thing) and subsequently mailed to Alan, Alan took an immediate shine to John's idea for a toxic waste–drinking wino dubbed "Nukeface."

John had created Nukeface in the late 1970s while he shared a house in Dover, New Jersey with myself, Rick Veitch and Tom Yeates, the original artist on *The Saga of the Swamp Thing*. Among John's doodles and sketches was the visage of a rather pudgy, ill-looking hobo with a smile on his face and glinting eyes glowering from cinder-hole sockets. He seemed like an affable enough fellow, but he looked downright lethal. John labeled this sketch "Nukeface," and we had a laugh — but we never forgot about it.

Once Tom Yeates landed the art chores for DC's revived Swamp Thing title, John was right there, assisting Tom sans credit from its second issue. Of all of us, John was the one with the deepest affinity and affection for Len Wein and Berni Wrightson's original Swamp Thing, and as soon as Tom knew he had the gig we began brainstorming possibilities for the character. John's ideas were the best of all.

When editor Len Wein chose John and I as the new art team with issue #16 (1983), he was looking at two sets of sample pages we'd auditioned with that featured John's toxic wino. I pencilled a set of pages that John inked involving an outsized mutant frog, and John pencilled a few pages that I inked featuring Nukeface kindly offering Swamp Thing a drink of steaming swill from a rusty soup can. Those pages got us the job, but Nukeface remained gainfully unemployed. John's bigger ideas — including the notion of visualizing Swamp Thing as less of a pitiful man trapped in a monstrous body and more of a completely plant-based being — weren't embraced until Alan was brought in to take over scripting duties, and the same was true for Nukeface.

In the meantime, John and I had fabricated another proposed story for a possible Swamp Thing scenario based on the real-life subterranean hell of a town in John's home state of Pennsylvania. Founded in 1866, Centralia, PA was a coal mining town (not to be confused with Centralia, Illinois, infamous for a 1947 coal

mine explosion that claimed the lives of over 100 miners), and like most mining towns it had suffered its share of tragedies, including cave-ins, mine fires, labor strife and worse. Cursed by a Catholic priest in the 19th century — "One day this town will be erased from the face of the earth!" — Centralia was literally damned to hell when an underground mine fire erupted in 1962. It spread unchecked through the extensive network of tunnels underlying the town, and it continues to burn to this day. Working from reports of accidents in 1981 involving a boy being rescued from a fiery pit that opened up in his yard and residents being hospitalized after inhaling deadly fumes, John and I researched the disaster as best we could in that pre-internet era and mailed all that we could find to Alan.

Things have only gotten worse for Centralia since "The Nukeface Papers" was published in 1985. All efforts to extinguish the fires have ended in failure, and after three decades the subterranean inferno fulfilled the priest's curse — following years of government-sponsored relocation efforts, the state invoked eminent domain in 1992 to condemn the entire town and evacuate its remaining population. Today, only nine die-hard residents remain. [1]

Alan originally scripted Part One of "The Nukeface Papers" for *The Saga of the Swamp Thing* #29, completing the full script and delivering it a couple of days ahead of deadline to our new editor Karen Berger, who had assumed editorial duties with issue #25. Karen made the tough call — correctly, we reluctantly agreed — to shelve the script for future use, requiring Alan to quickly write a new issue from scratch in only two days. She felt that a less funereal and a more suspenseful story — something that moved with more urgency than "The Nukeface Papers" — was essential for the book at that juncture, so Alan superhumanly hammered out "Love and Death" in one marathon push, keeping us on schedule and redirected with what I still think is our strongest dose of horror in the entire run. Meanwhile, "The Nukeface Papers" lay quietly in Karen's files. It didn't malinger there for long.

As horror comics scholars and fans like

Bob Heer have pointed out over the years, there was a precursor to "The Nukeface Papers." Steve Ditko had illustrated a pre-Comics Code story (writer unknown) entitled "Doom in the Air" (published in *The Thing* #14, Charlton Comics, 1954). Narratively, the two stories are completely unlike one another. "Doom in the Air" involves a victim of premature burial resurrected by an atomic bomb test. He becomes an ambulatory radioactive nightmare, his mere proximity lethal to all. The story ends with the irradiated, undead man climbing aboard a train, intent on revenge "if it takes me to the ends of the Earth!" This final panel resonates eerily with the final page of "The Nukeface Papers," though none of us had ever laid eyes on Ditko's *The Thing* story before sending our own wayward toxic hobo on his merry way.[2]

One other thing: all those newspaper clippings I pasted into the pencilled pages weren't pulled from an archive of similarly themed stories. I took them solely from my daily newspaper during the eight or nine weeks I spent pencilling those two issues, and I didn't have to look hard to find them. Accidents, nuclear power controversies, toxic and nuclear waste spills, leakages and cover-ups were a constant in the news.

These horrors overlapped into my own neck of the woods as well. John, Rick, Tom Yeates and I were still living in Dover when the March 1979 accident at the Three Mile Island nuclear power plant near Harrisburg, Pennsylvania occurred. News of the escalating situation prompted John and I to plot an escape route from New Jersey to Vermont using John's car should the worst happen. Vermont's own Yankee nuclear power plant is also less than a half an hour from the Wilmington, Vermont home in which I drew "The Nukeface Papers," and it too was (and still is) constantly in the news.

Weirder still, I almost drove into a toxic cloud while transporting the original boards of "The Nukeface Papers." While working on the second part of the story, I drove from Wilmington to nearby Greenfield, Massachusetts to photocopy the pencils I was about to express-mail to Karen that very day. As I drove down the Mohawk Trail to my destination, a dark cloud began rising over the village. Smoke? As I went from the photocopy shop to the post office, it was evident that people were becoming increasingly alarmed by something. I learned that a train had derailed on the west side of Greenfield, and a tank car of dangerous chemicals was burning. After mailing the pages, I fled Greenfield and upon my return home I rang Karen with the tale.

Karen paused and said, "Maybe you should have mailed the pages from a different post office."

Nukeface, come home.

***

It begins with torn papers, and it ends with torn tickets.

Alan, John and I had planned and plotted the water vampire story which ran in #38 and #39 months before, when we were fully enjoying the heat of our team's chemistry. I still feel a strong sentimental attachment to that two-parter, based as it was on one of the Marty Pasko/Tom Yeates stories that predated our run ("The Town Has Turned to Blood," from *The Saga of the Swamp Thing* #3, July 1982). Marty and Tom had resolved their tale of the punk vampire-infested town of Rosewood, Illinois by demolishing a nearby dam and letting the tsunami of running water conveniently dissolve the bloodsuckers; the three of us were going to go back to Rosewood to reveal how the vampires had mutated to continue un-life as the biggest leeches in the pond. We were very much looking forward to doing it.

I have fond memories of Alan's and John's visit to my Vermont home at that time. Alan, John and I worked out the details for this tale of the aquatic undead as we wandered the dirt roads near my home, with my very wee daughter Maia happily chattering between us. Maia was enjoying holding my hand and Alan's hand, occasionally picking her feet up off the ground and swinging between us, shouting "Wheeeee!" Meanwhile, we three grown men worked out the physiology and life cycle of amphibious vampires and how they might be exterminated. Alan recalled details of Richard Matheson's classic novel *I Am Legend*, how exposure of a vampire's hermetic interior to oxygen via staking prompted their disintegration, and we were off and running. Maia blithely ignored this grim conversation and savored another swing. "Wheeeee!"

Alas, by the time the storyline was finally

eady to go, I was so late in turning in the first pages of part one ("Still Waters") that Karen had no choice but to replace me with Stan Woch — who did an absolutely terrific job — and put me to work pencilling part two ("Fish Story") to keep us all on schedule. Properly chastised and briefly reinvigorated (in part by my own anger and frustration with the never-ending battle with deadlines), I poured my all into "Fish Story" and issue #40's "The Curse," which was based in part on another of the story proposals that John and I had submitted to Alan and Karen.

My contribution to "The Curse" grew out of a pitch I'd made to *Heavy Metal* magazine in 1980: an article about the failed career of a completely fictional science fiction author I'd invented named Curtis Slarch, illustrated with finished paintings for imaginary book jackets, including the "forgotten" 1960 Slarch novella *Lunia Bridge*. John Workman liked my paintings but didn't think the article format worked, so it was declined and relegated to my reject files. From that filed 1980 proposal, here's the synopsis of *Lunia Bridge*:

> "... [the] prologue introduces Lunia, a female star being who... establishes a psychic bond with a man of Earth... his terran biology distorts the alien influence of Lunia's lunar female cycles into lycanthropy. The resulting bloodbath leads our werewolf hero to self-exile in the wilds of Canada, where he and (vicariously) Lunia find fulfillment in experiencing the 'bestial self' given full reign."

It was a simple tweak to suggest that we cook up a more direct incarnation linking the female menstrual cycle with the cycle of the moon and lycanthropy for our take on the werewolf archetype. Alan made it work beautifully, wedding that conceit with a backwoods portrait of spousal abuse, generational stigmatization of "the curse" and an individual woman's plight in his final script.

Incredible as it seems today, "The Curse" kicked up a little storm of controversy. In that pre-Vertigo era, many observers (including Marvel's then-editor-in-chief) blasted the issue as an offense to the industry. Code or no Code, menstruation was still a major taboo. From another quarter came the even more flabbergasting claim that "The Curse" was dated because there was no more domestic abuse in our nation... heated up the title's letter column.[3]

Coming up with a fresh visual approach to werewolf transformation was a challenge. Alan settled on what you see here as the wolf within sheds its human sheath like a snake sheds its skin, and at the time we thought it was an original approach. Once we saw Neil Jordan's inventive movie *The Company of Wolves* (U.K. premiere September 1984; U.S. premiere: April 1985) we were somewhat dispirited, but we'd done our best. The only aspect of pencilling the issue that I balked at (but carried on drawing under orders from both Alan and Karen) was the notion of an American supermarket manager being stupid enough to mount a display of kitchen knives for sale with the blades pointing outward. As the son of a grocery store owner, having stocked shelves and worked in retail since the age of six, I knew better — but I buttoned my lip and stuck to the script.

I wish I'd stuck to the script with the same level of fidelity for the final chapter of our two-part voodoo/zombie story, "Strange Fruit." I still think I botched page 20 of that chapter — between my getting fancy with Alan's straightforward six-panel grid layout and guest inker Ron Randall subtly misinterpreting my pencils, an important aspect of the story went missing from the reprinted versions of the page. The key image in the penultimate panel is of the actor Billy thinking that his skin has been flayed off; in the original comic book his chest and arms were correctly colored as flayed flesh, but when the page was prepped for reprinting those areas were mistakenly recolored to be the same brown skin tone as his face — something that, I'm glad to say, has finally been corrected in this new hardcover edition.

I also wish I could say that "Southern Change" and "Strange Fruit" now seem dated to me. They were written and drawn only a decade after studios like Paramount Pictures had scored at the box office with movies like *The Legend of Nigger Charley* (1972), *The Soul of Nigger Charley* (1973), *Mandingo* (1975) and its sequel *Drum* (1976) — titles I can't imagine being tolerated in a newspaper ad or on a multiplex marquee today. The plantation setting and gothic scenario Alan created for our two-part story were fueled as much by the fresh memory of those cinematic extremes as by the shameful American history behind them. Given the blatantly racist rhetoric openly broadcast today as we move into the second year in office for the first African-American president ever elected, these two chapters of "American Gothic" are unfortunately as timely as ever.

By this point, I was having much less fun with *Swamp Thing*. My first wife Marlene and I had a new baby on the way, and to say that it was tough juggling the demands of drawing a monthly comic and raising a family would be an understatement. I love the ending of "Strange Fruit" — the zombie who finds coffin-like comfort working the ticket booth in a grindhouse theater (its walls adorned with paste-ups I lovingly put together with photocopies from my own exploitation movie pressbook collection) — but I must note that it still resonates with the reality of what I was feeling at the time. Unlike the zombie ticket seller, I wasn't happy feeling boxed in.

Although Alan had conscientiously incorporated as many story ideas from John and I as he could, the reality was that his careful planning and plotting for "American Gothic" meant that the entire year (and more) ahead was completely mapped out, and the schedule for producing issues was set in stone. Combined with my eternal inability to crank out 23 pages in as many days, this unforgiving series of deadlines meant that stories like issue #45's "Ghost Dance" — which grew out of a suggestion by my good friend Jim Wheelock to set a ghost story in California's infamous "Winchester Mystery House" — had to be illustrated by others.

Furthermore, while I struggled to keep pace with *Swamp Thing*'s schedule, Alan could, of course, script many, many more comic book pages than either John or I could ever draw (including stories for other series — his collaboration with Dave Gibbons on the seminal *Watchmen* was then getting underway). As much as I enjoyed seeing him stretch his wings creatively on projects outside of *Swamp Thing*, it was a bit like being a branch-bound caterpillar watching a butterfly already free of his cocoon soar.

After two years of non-stop work, I had learned a great deal from Alan, John and Rick, and from our editors Len and Karen — and as the deadlines loomed for the final chapters of "American Gothic," I was aching to apply that knowledge to something beyond its boundaries.

But that's another story.

***

Enough of what was happening then, and what wasn't, can't or shouldn't be said.

All that matters is what was done, what was written, what was drawn — all that you're about to read.

The ashes may be cool, but the abandoned plantation furrows are still fertile, and ash is an excellent fertilizer — as long as Nukeface hasn't tainted it.

These seeds are still vital; a little attention, a little water, and green shoots can still be coaxed out of them.

But be careful. The subterranean embers still smolder beneath our feet.

It begins with fires raging underground, and it ends with a burning mansion...

— Stephen R. Bissette
The Mountains of Madness, Vermont
March 2010

[1] There have since been numerous books written and at least one film made about the Centralia underground fires. See Chris Perkel and Georgie Roland's documentary *The Town That Was: A True Story* (2007) and read *Unseen Danger: A Tragedy of People, Government and the Centralia Mine Fire* by David DeKok (1986, revised edition 2000), *The Day the Earth Caved In: An American Mining Tragedy* by Joan Quigley (2007) and *Fire Underground: The Ongoing Tragedy of the Centralia Mine Fire by David DeKok (2009)*.

[2] See Bob Heer's essay "It Stalks the Public Domain — Doom in the Air" from Steve Ditko's Comics Weblog, May 20, 2009 (http://ditko.blogspot.com/2009/05/it-stalks-public-domain-doom-in-air.html).

[3] The letters, and Alan's reply, were published in *Swamp Thing* #46. Also see pgs. 36-37 of Martin Cannon's Critics' Choice *Files Magazine Spotlight: Swamp Thing: Green Mansion* (1987, Psi Fi Movie Press, Inc.) for a strong opinion on "The Curse" that reflects some of the industry views on the issue at the time.

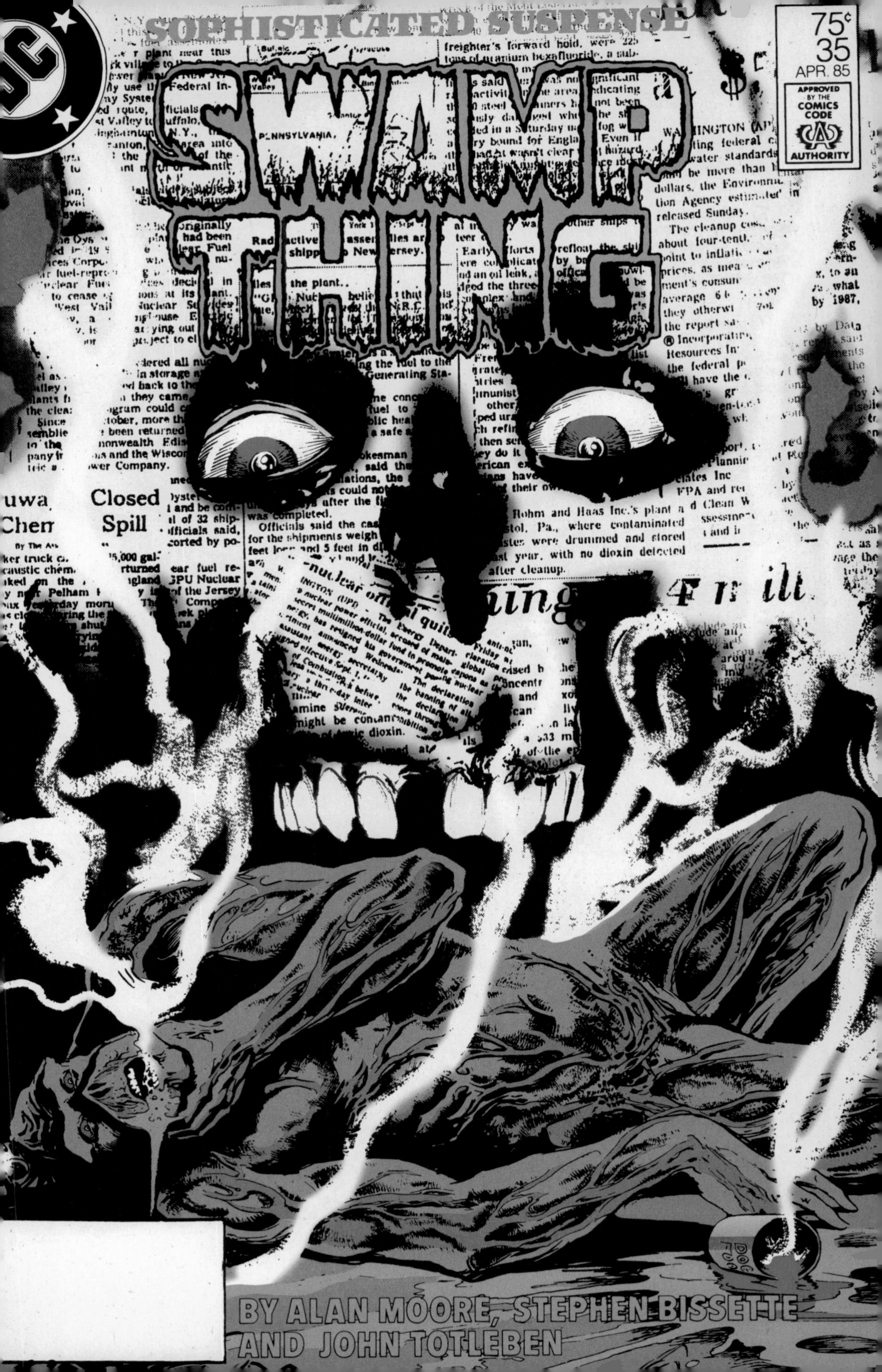
SOPHISTICATED SUSPENSE
SWAMP THING
75¢
35
APR. 85
APPROVED BY THE COMICS CODE AUTHORITY
BY ALAN MOORE, STEPHEN BISSETTE AND JOHN TOTLEBEN

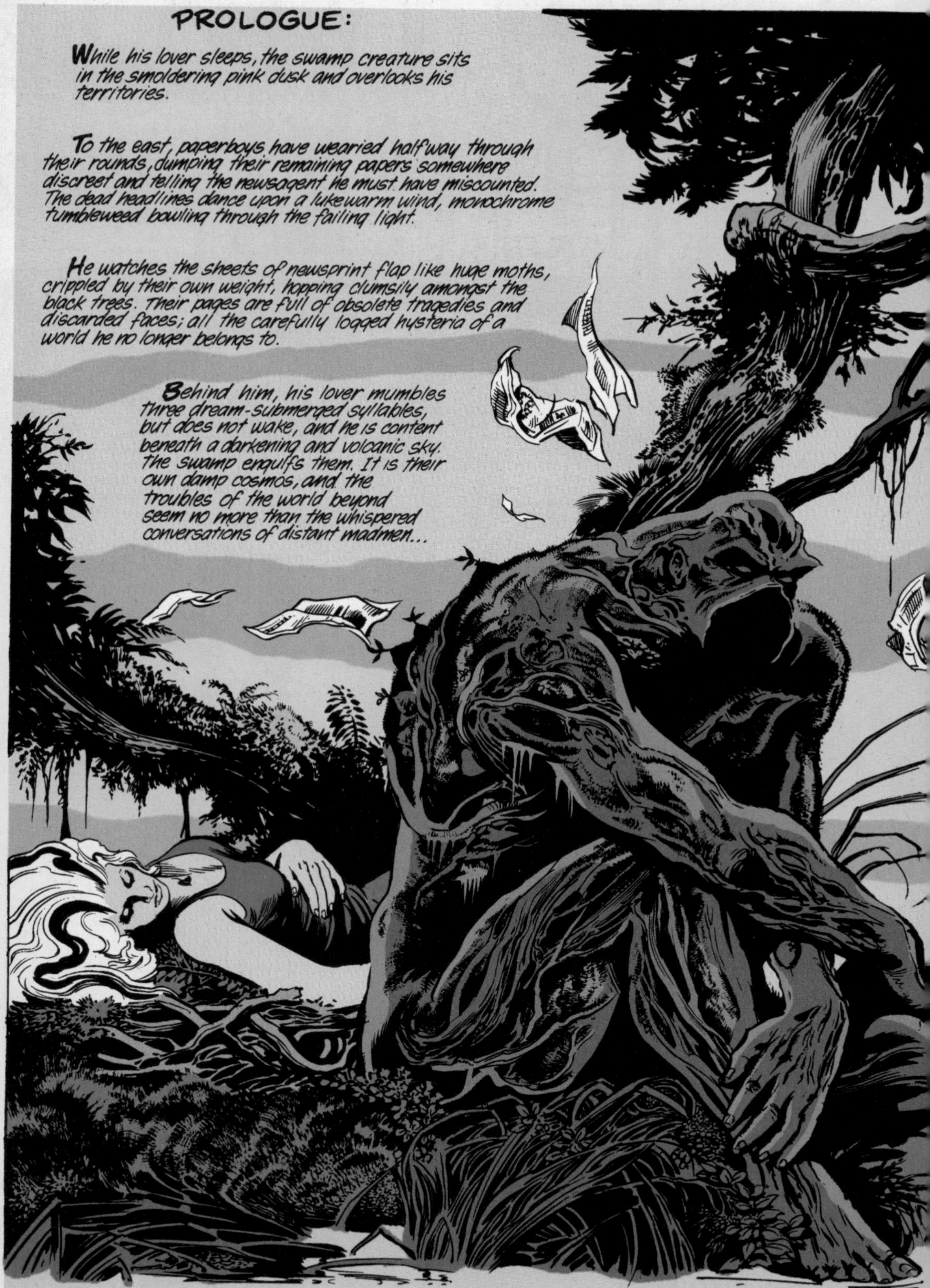
PROLOGUE:
While his lover sleeps, the swamp creature sits in the smoldering pink dusk and overlooks his territories.
To the east, paperboys have wearied halfway through their rounds, dumping their remaining papers somewhere discreet and telling the newsagent he must have miscounted. The dead headlines dance upon a lukewarm wind, monochrome tumbleweed bowling through the failing light.
He watches the sheets of newsprint flap like huge moths, crippled by their own weight, hopping clumsily amongst the black trees. Their pages are full of obsolete tragedies and discarded faces; all the carefully logged hysteria of a world he no longer belongs to.
Behind him, his lover mumbles three dream-submerged syllables, but does not wake, and he is content beneath a darkening and volcanic sky. The swamp engulfs them. It is their own damp cosmos, and the troubles of the world beyond seem no more than the whispered conversations of distant madmen...

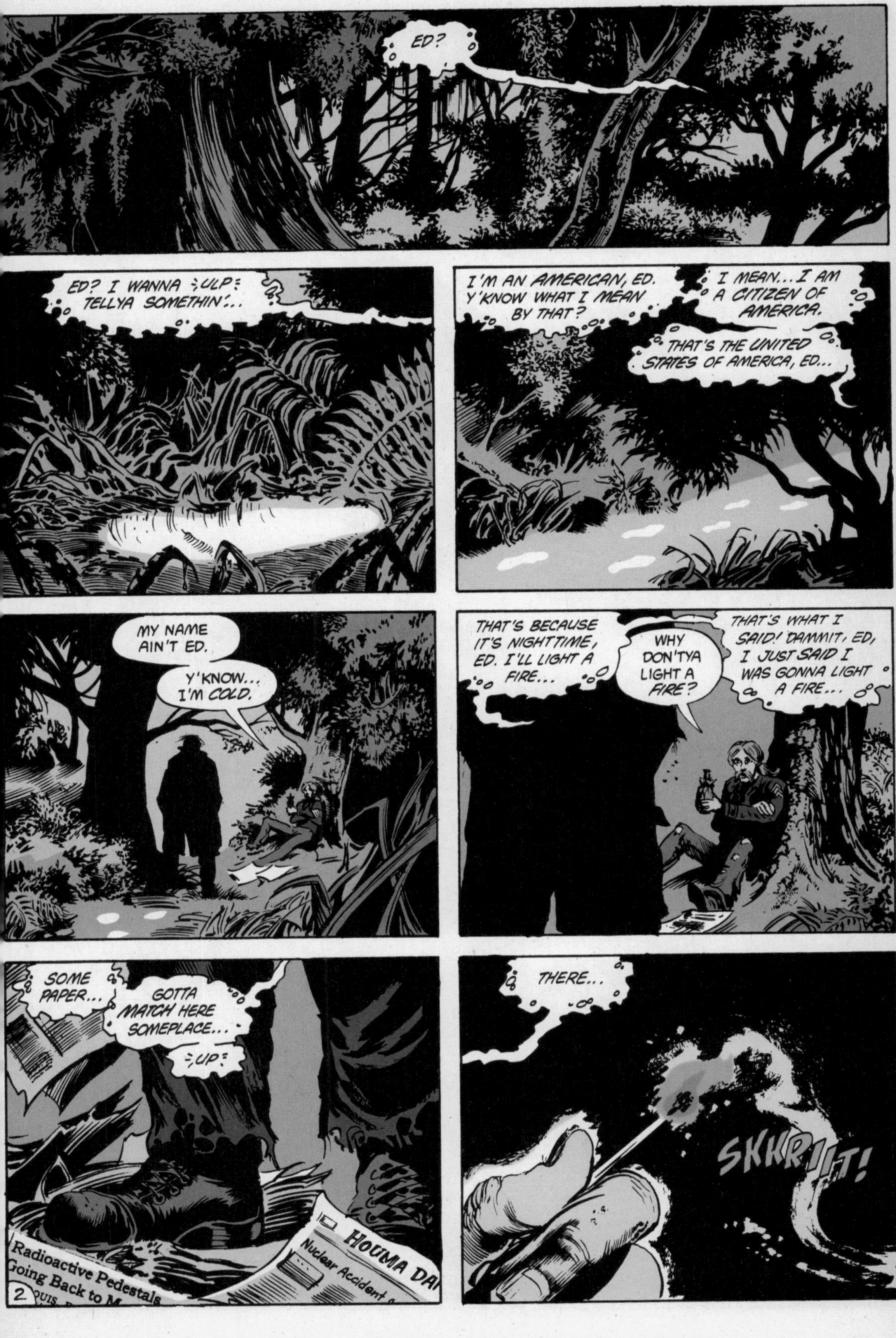
ED?
ED? I WANNA -ULP- TELLYA SOMETHIN'...
I'M AN AMERICAN, ED. Y'KNOW WHAT I MEAN BY THAT?
I MEAN... I AM A CITIZEN OF AMERICA.
THAT'S THE UNITED STATES OF AMERICA, ED...
MY NAME AIN'T ED.
Y'KNOW... I'M COLD.
THAT'S BECAUSE IT'S NIGHTTIME, ED. I'LL LIGHT A FIRE...
WHY DON'TYA LIGHT A FIRE?
THAT'S WHAT I SAID! DAMMIT, ED, I JUST SAID I WAS GONNA LIGHT A FIRE...
SOME PAPER...
GOTTA MATCH HERE SOMEPLACE...
-UP-
Radioactive Pedestals
Nuclear Accident
THERE...
SKKRIIT!

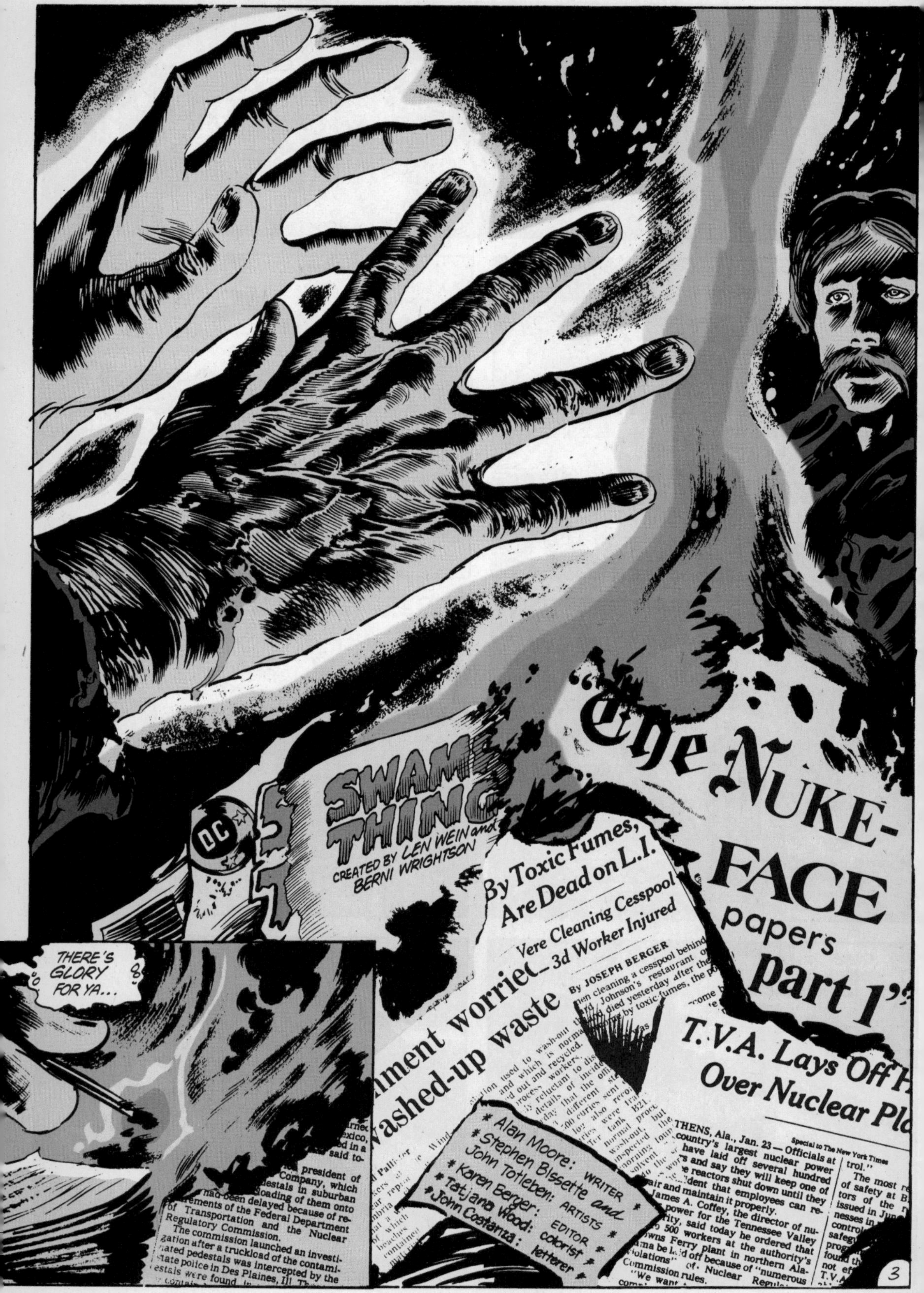
"The Nuke-Face papers part 1"
SWAMP THING
CREATED BY LEN WEIN and BERNI WRIGHTSON
By Toxic Fumes, Are Dead on L.I.
Vere Cleaning Cesspool 3d Worker Injured
By JOSEPH BERGER
ment worriec
washed-up waste
T.V.A. Lays Off
Over Nuclear Pl
THERE'S GLORY FOR YA...
* Alan Moore: WRITER
* Stephen Bissette and John Totleben: ARTISTS *
* Karen Berger: EDITOR *
* Tatjana Wood: colorist *
* John Costanza: letterer *
3

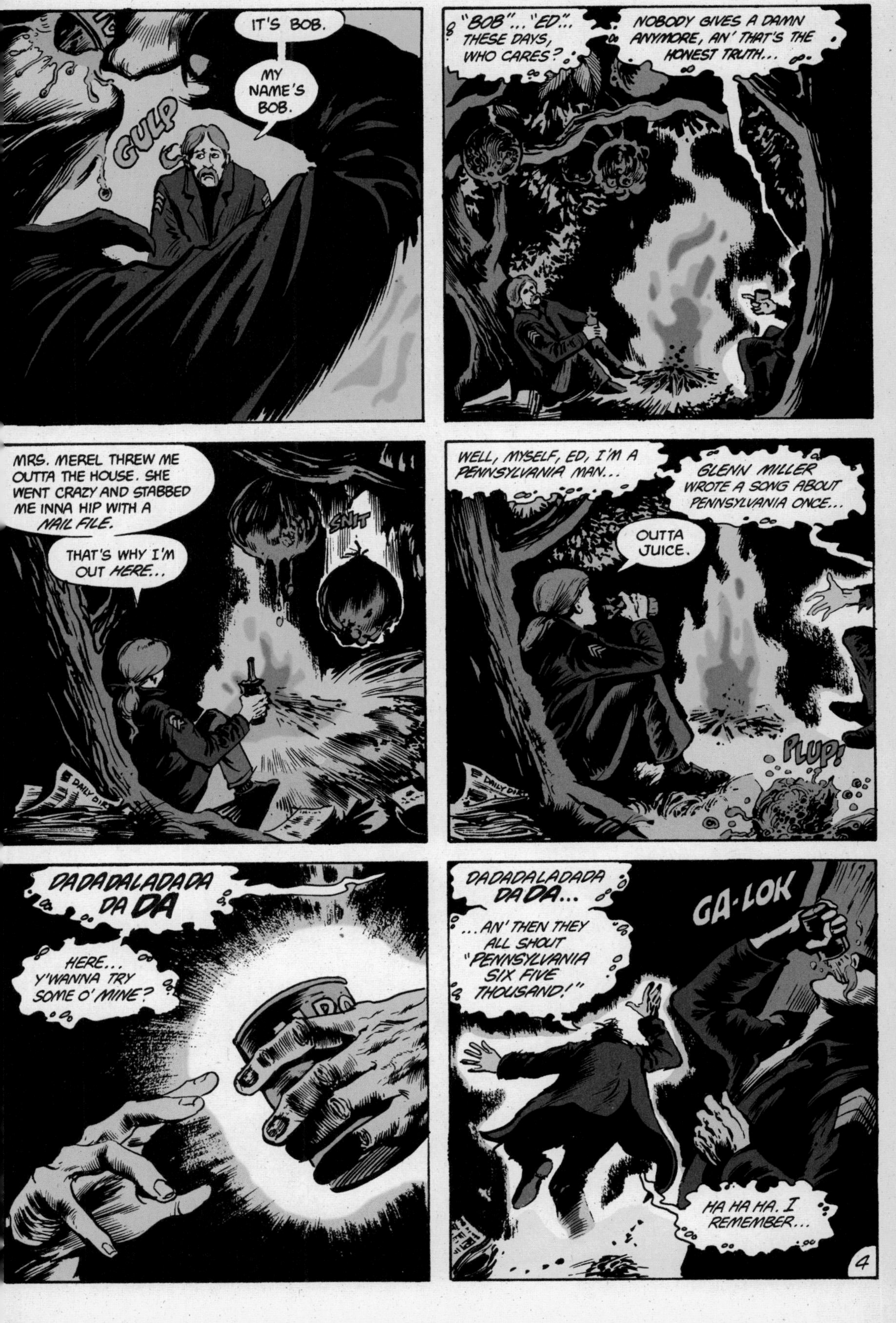
IT'S BOB.
MY NAME'S BOB.
GULP
"BOB"... "ED"... THESE DAYS, WHO CARES?
NOBODY GIVES A DAMN ANYMORE, AN' THAT'S THE HONEST TRUTH...
MRS. MEREL THREW ME OUTTA THE HOUSE. SHE WENT CRAZY AND STABBED ME INNA HIP WITH A NAIL FILE.
THAT'S WHY I'M OUT HERE...
SNIT
WELL, MYSELF, ED, I'M A PENNSYLVANIA MAN...
GLENN MILLER WROTE A SONG ABOUT PENNSYLVANIA ONCE...
OUTTA JUICE.
PLUP!
DADADALADADA DA DA
HERE... Y'WANNA TRY SOME O' MINE?
DADADALADADA DA DA...
...AN' THEN THEY ALL SHOUT "PENNSYLVANIA SIX FIVE THOUSAND!"
GA-LOK
HA HA HA. I REMEMBER...
4

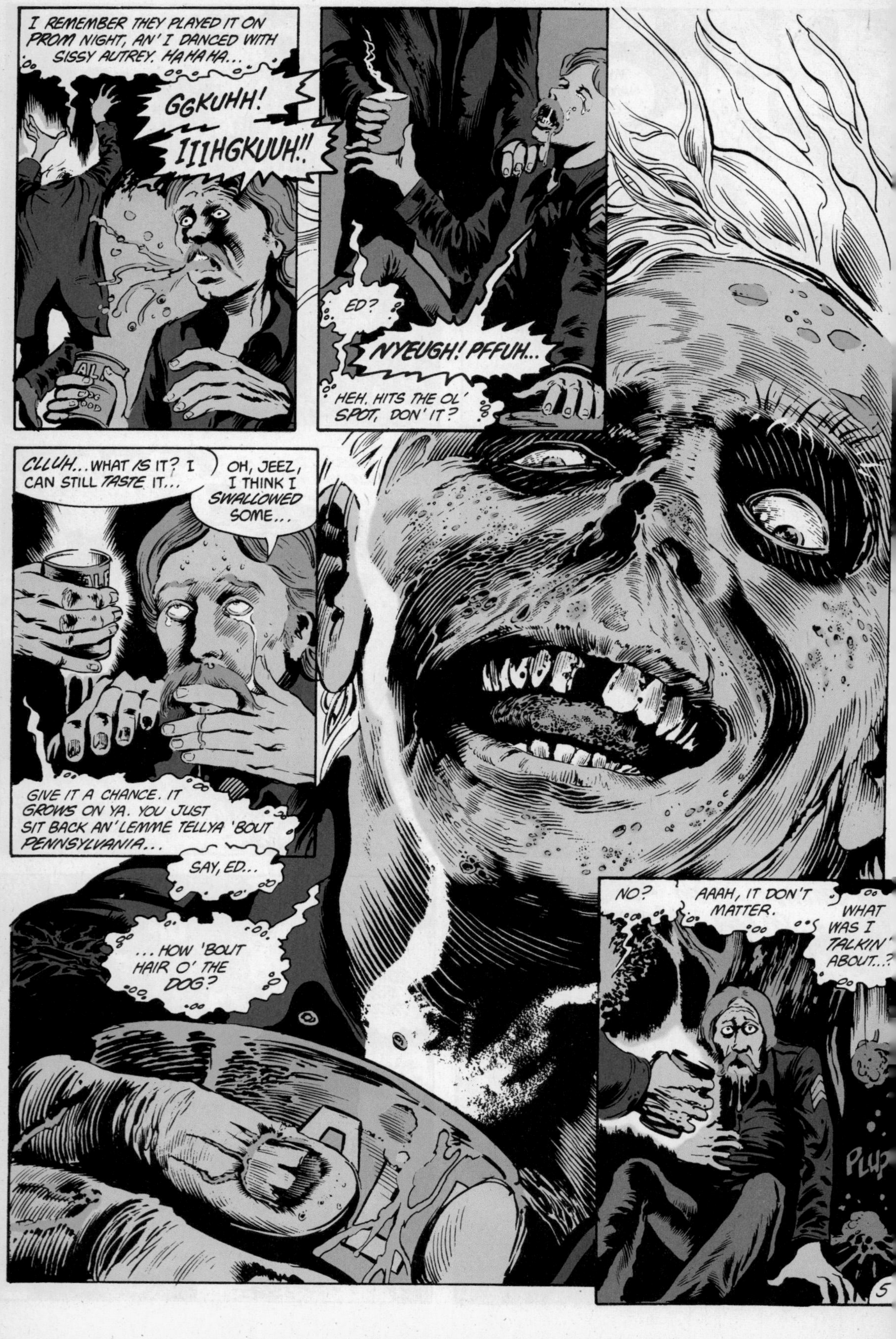
I REMEMBER THEY PLAYED IT ON PROM NIGHT, AN' I DANCED WITH SISSY AUTREY. HA HA HA...
GGKUHH!
IIIHGKUUH!!
ED?
NYEUGH! PFFUH...
HEH. HITS THE OL' SPOT, DON' IT?
CLLUH... WHAT IS IT? I CAN STILL TASTE IT...
OH, JEEZ, I THINK I SWALLOWED SOME...
GIVE IT A CHANCE. IT GROWS ON YA. YOU JUST SIT BACK AN' LEMME TELLYA 'BOUT PENNSYLVANIA...
SAY, ED...
...HOW 'BOUT HAIR O' THE DOG?
NO?
AAAH, IT DON'T MATTER.
WHAT WAS I TALKIN' ABOUT...?
PLUP
5

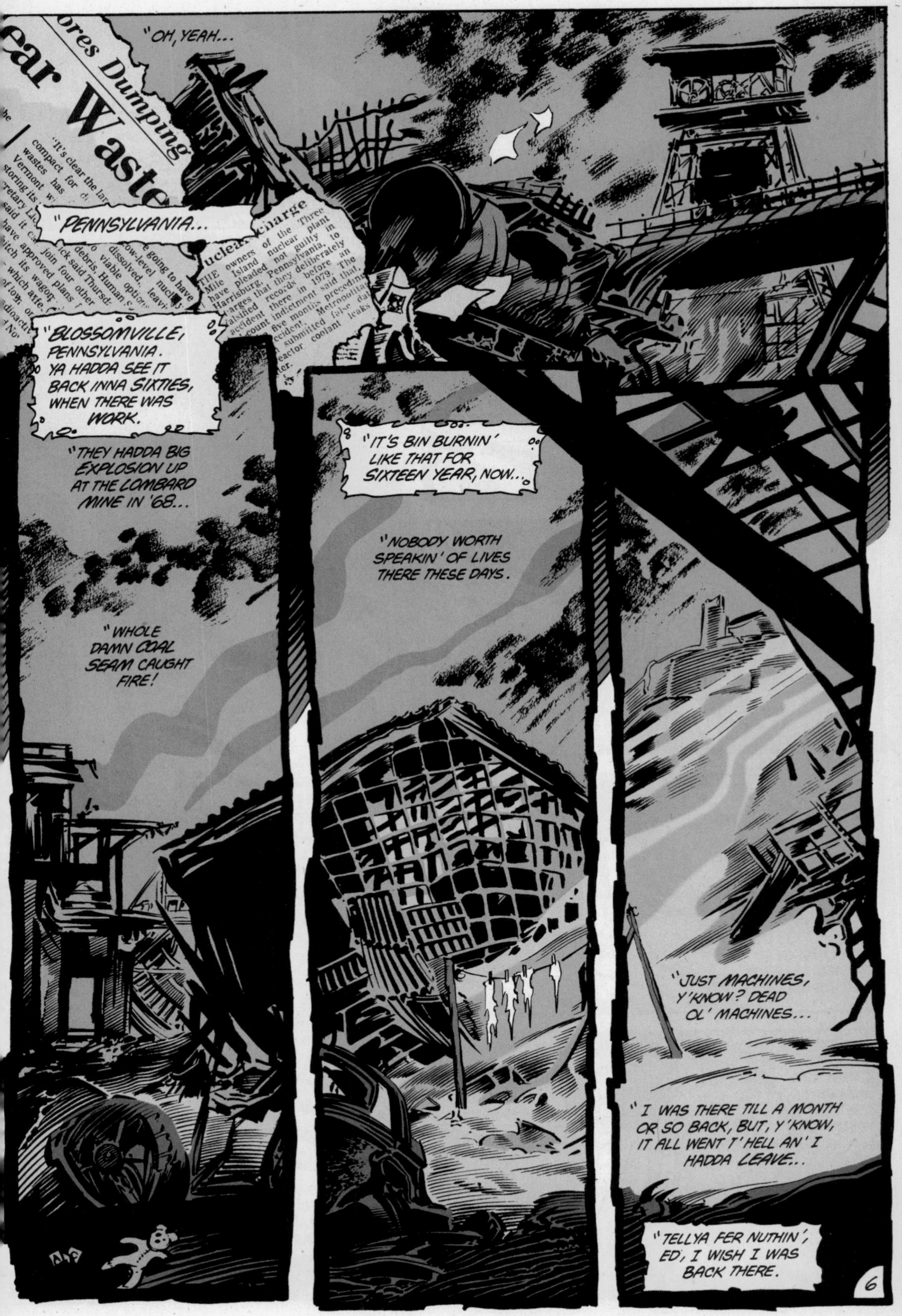
"OH, YEAH...
"PENNSYLVANIA...
"BLOSSOMVILLE, PENNSYLVANIA. YA HADDA SEE IT BACK INNA SIXTIES, WHEN THERE WAS WORK.
"THEY HADDA BIG EXPLOSION UP AT THE COMBARD MINE IN '68...
"WHOLE DAMN COAL SEAM CAUGHT FIRE!
"IT'S BIN BURNIN' LIKE THAT FOR SIXTEEN YEAR, NOW...
"NOBODY WORTH SPEAKIN' OF LIVES THERE THESE DAYS.
"JUST MACHINES, Y'KNOW? DEAD OL' MACHINES...
"I WAS THERE TILL A MONTH OR SO BACK, BUT, Y'KNOW, IT ALL WENT T' HELL AN' I HADDA LEAVE...
"TELLYA FER NUTHIN', ED, I WISH I WAS BACK THERE.
6

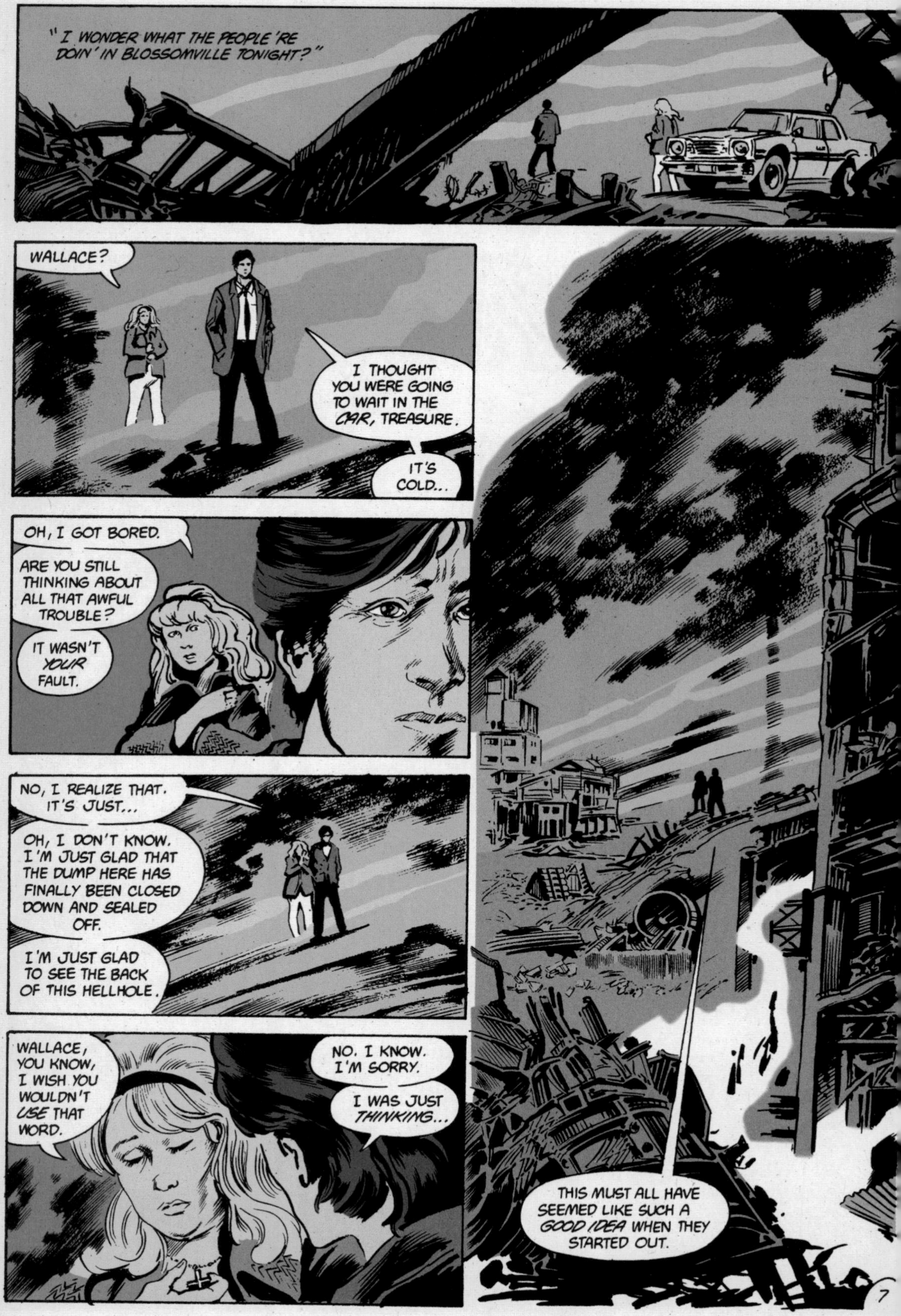
"I WONDER WHAT THE PEOPLE 'RE DOIN' IN BLOSSOMVILLE TONIGHT?"
WALLACE?
I THOUGHT YOU WERE GOING TO WAIT IN THE CAR, TREASURE.
IT'S COLD...
OH, I GOT BORED.
ARE YOU STILL THINKING ABOUT ALL THAT AWFUL TROUBLE?
IT WASN'T YOUR FAULT.
NO, I REALIZE THAT. IT'S JUST...
OH, I DON'T KNOW. I'M JUST GLAD THAT THE DUMP HERE HAS FINALLY BEEN CLOSED DOWN AND SEALED OFF.
I'M JUST GLAD TO SEE THE BACK OF THIS HELLHOLE.
WALLACE, YOU KNOW, I WISH YOU WOULDN'T USE THAT WORD.
NO. I KNOW. I'M SORRY.
I WAS JUST THINKING...
THIS MUST ALL HAVE SEEMED LIKE SUCH A GOOD IDEA WHEN THEY STARTED OUT.
7

THE *STRIPMINES* WERE ALL USED UP AND EMPTY, AND NOBODY BUT THE BUMS AND WINOS EVER CAME NEAR. IT WAS AN IDEAL PLACE TO DUMP THE, Y'KNOW, THE...

THE STUFF.

THE STUFF. YEAH.

THE COMPANY WAS STICKING IT IN THE *SLAG PITS* UNDER THE OLD *LOMBARD MINE*. IT WAS SAFE DOWN THERE! THEY DID *TESTS!*

WALLACE, I *KNOW* YOU! YOU WOULDN'T BE *INVOLVED* IF IT WAS SOMETHING THAT COULD *HURT* PEOPLE.

NO. NO, OF COURSE I WOULDN'T.

BUT THEN THOSE *TRAMPS*, THOSE *BUMS*...THEY ALL STARTED *VANISHING*...

WALLACE, YOU *KNOW* HOW DERELICTS ARE. THOSE POOR MEN, THEY GET *LOST*, THEY LEAVE THE *AREA*...

IT'S GOD'S WILL. YOU CAN'T BLAME YOURSELF.

SAY, DID I TELL YOU ABOUT THAT THING I HEARD THOSE *KIDS* SAY? ABOUT ONE OF THOSE OLD MEN THAT *VANISHED?*

THEY SAID HE WAS "*OUT ON A BENDER WITH NUKEFACE.*"

WHAT DOES THAT *MEAN*, DO YOU THINK?

I DON'T KNOW.

C'MON...IT'S GETTING COLDER. LET'S GET BACK IN THE *CAR*.

THE COMPANY WANTS US IN *LOUISIANA* BY *NOON TOMORROW*...

Nuclear Panel Votes For Proposal to Start 3 Mile Island Plant

By JANE PERLEZ
Special to The New York Times

WASHINGTON, Jan. 26 — The Nuclear Regulatory Commission has...

"O' COURSE, EVERYBODY LEFT BLOSSOMVILLE IN THE END..."

8

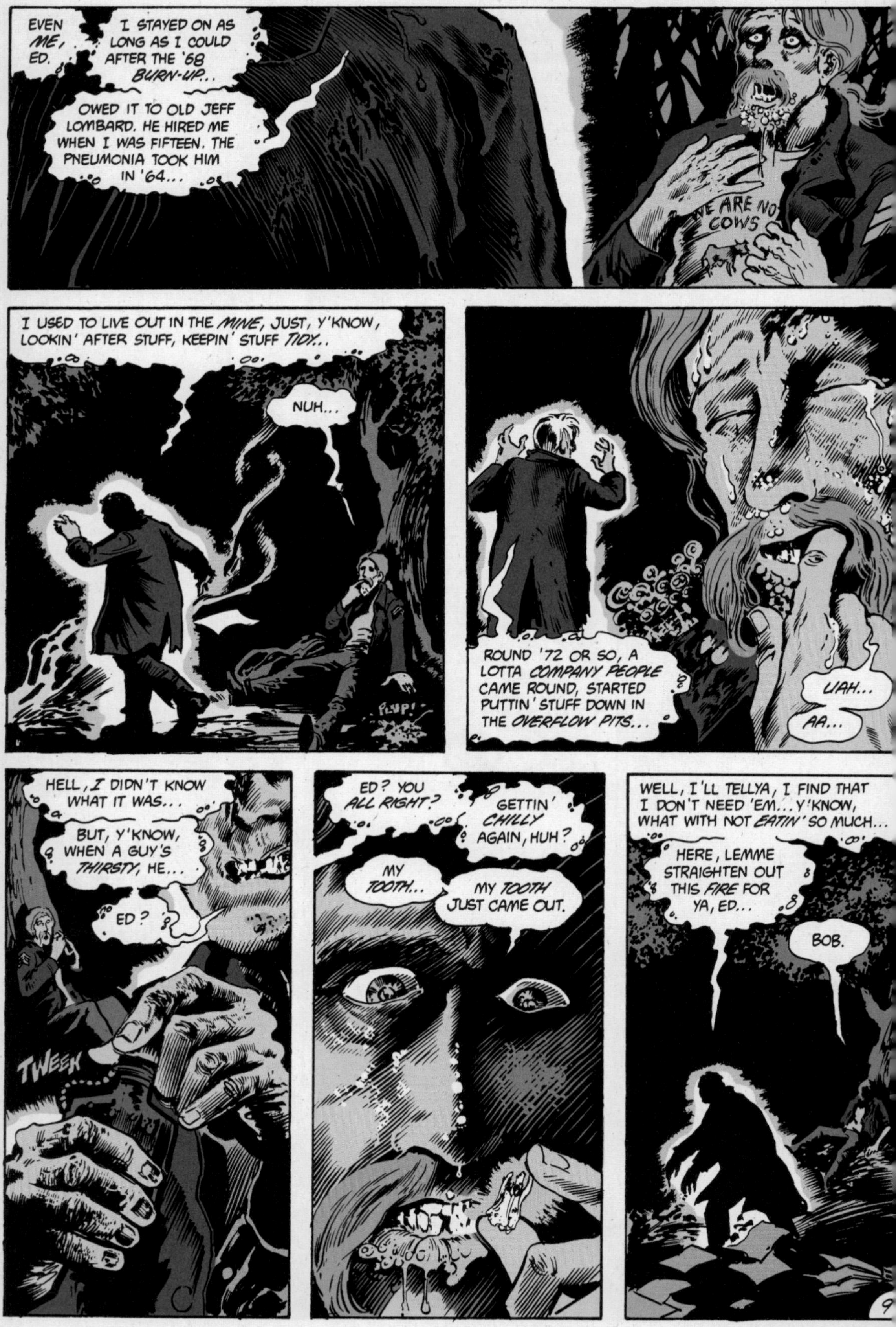
EVEN ME, ED.
I STAYED ON AS LONG AS I COULD AFTER THE '68 BURN-UP...
OWED IT TO OLD JEFF LOMBARD. HE HIRED ME WHEN I WAS FIFTEEN. THE PNEUMONIA TOOK HIM IN '64...
WE ARE NO COWS
I USED TO LIVE OUT IN THE MINE, JUST, Y'KNOW, LOOKIN' AFTER STUFF, KEEPIN' STUFF TIDY...
NUH...
PLUP!
ROUND '72 OR SO, A LOTTA COMPANY PEOPLE CAME ROUND, STARTED PUTTIN' STUFF DOWN IN THE OVERFLOW PITS...
UAH...
AA...
HELL, I DIDN'T KNOW WHAT IT WAS...
BUT, Y'KNOW, WHEN A GUY'S THIRSTY, HE...
ED?
TWEEK
ED? YOU ALL RIGHT?
GETTIN' CHILLY AGAIN, HUH?
MY TOOTH...
MY TOOTH JUST CAME OUT.
WELL, I'LL TELLYA, I FIND THAT I DON'T NEED 'EM... Y'KNOW, WHAT WITH NOT EATIN' SO MUCH...
HERE, LEMME STRAIGHTEN OUT THIS FIRE FOR YA, ED...
BOB.
9

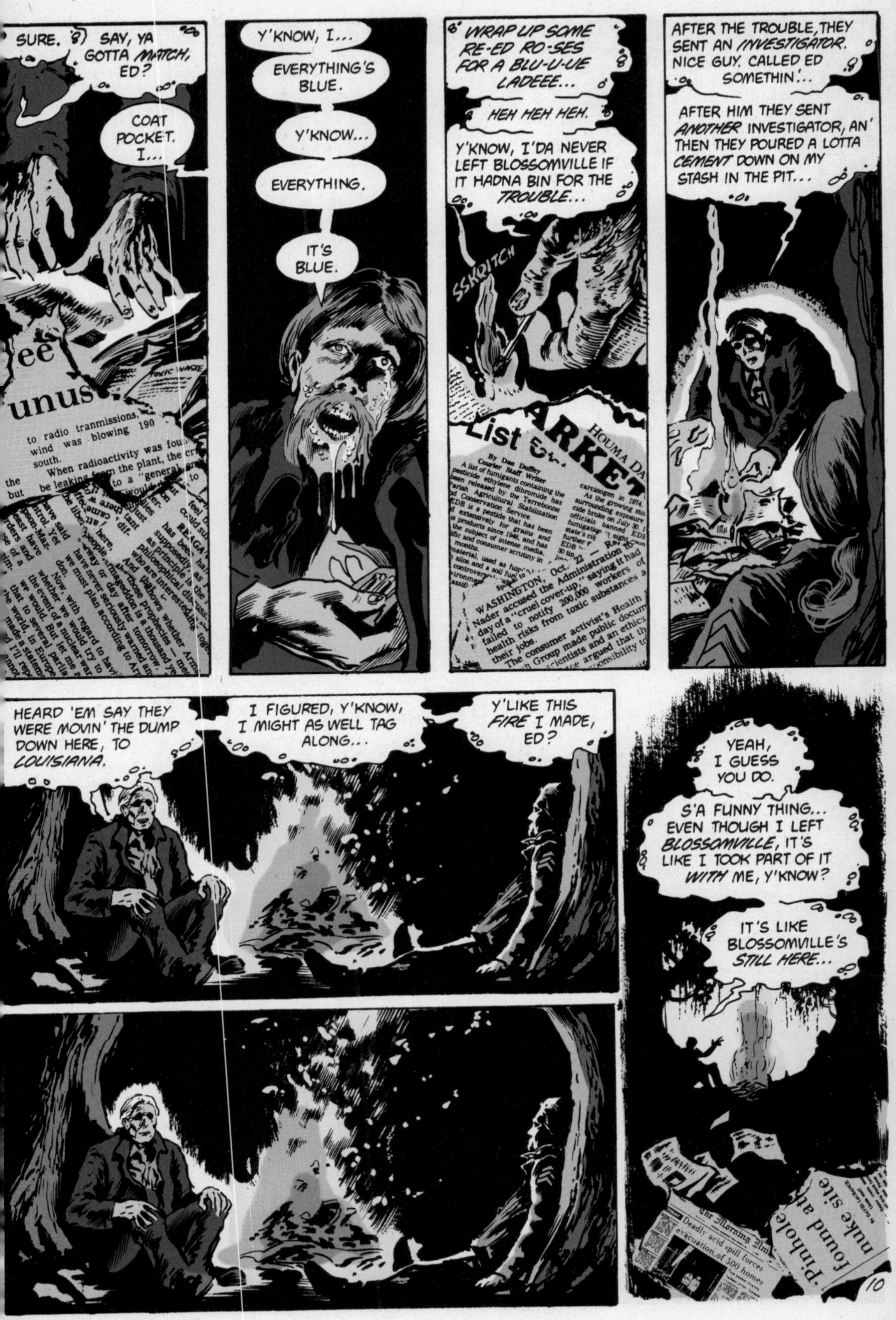
SURE. SAY, YA GOTTA MATCH, ED?
COAT POCKET. I...
Y'KNOW, I...
EVERYTHING'S BLUE.
Y'KNOW...
EVERYTHING.
IT'S BLUE.
WRAP UP SOME RE-ED RO-SES FOR A BLU-U-UE LADEEE...
HEH HEH HEH.
Y'KNOW, I'DA NEVER LEFT BLOSSOMVILLE IF IT HADNA BIN FOR THE TROUBLE...
SSKRITCH
AFTER THE TROUBLE, THEY SENT AN INVESTIGATOR. NICE GUY. CALLED ED SOMETHIN'...
AFTER HIM THEY SENT ANOTHER INVESTIGATOR, AN' THEN THEY POURED A LOTTA CEMENT DOWN ON MY STASH IN THE PIT...
HEARD 'EM SAY THEY WERE MOVIN' THE DUMP DOWN HERE, TO LOUISIANA.
I FIGURED, Y'KNOW, I MIGHT AS WELL TAG ALONG...
Y'LIKE THIS FIRE I MADE, ED?
YEAH, I GUESS YOU DO.
S'A FUNNY THING... EVEN THOUGH I LEFT BLOSSOMVILLE, IT'S LIKE I TOOK PART OF IT WITH ME, Y'KNOW?
IT'S LIKE BLOSSOMVILLE'S STILL HERE...
Deadly acid spill forces evacuation of 500 homes
Pinhole found at nuke site
10

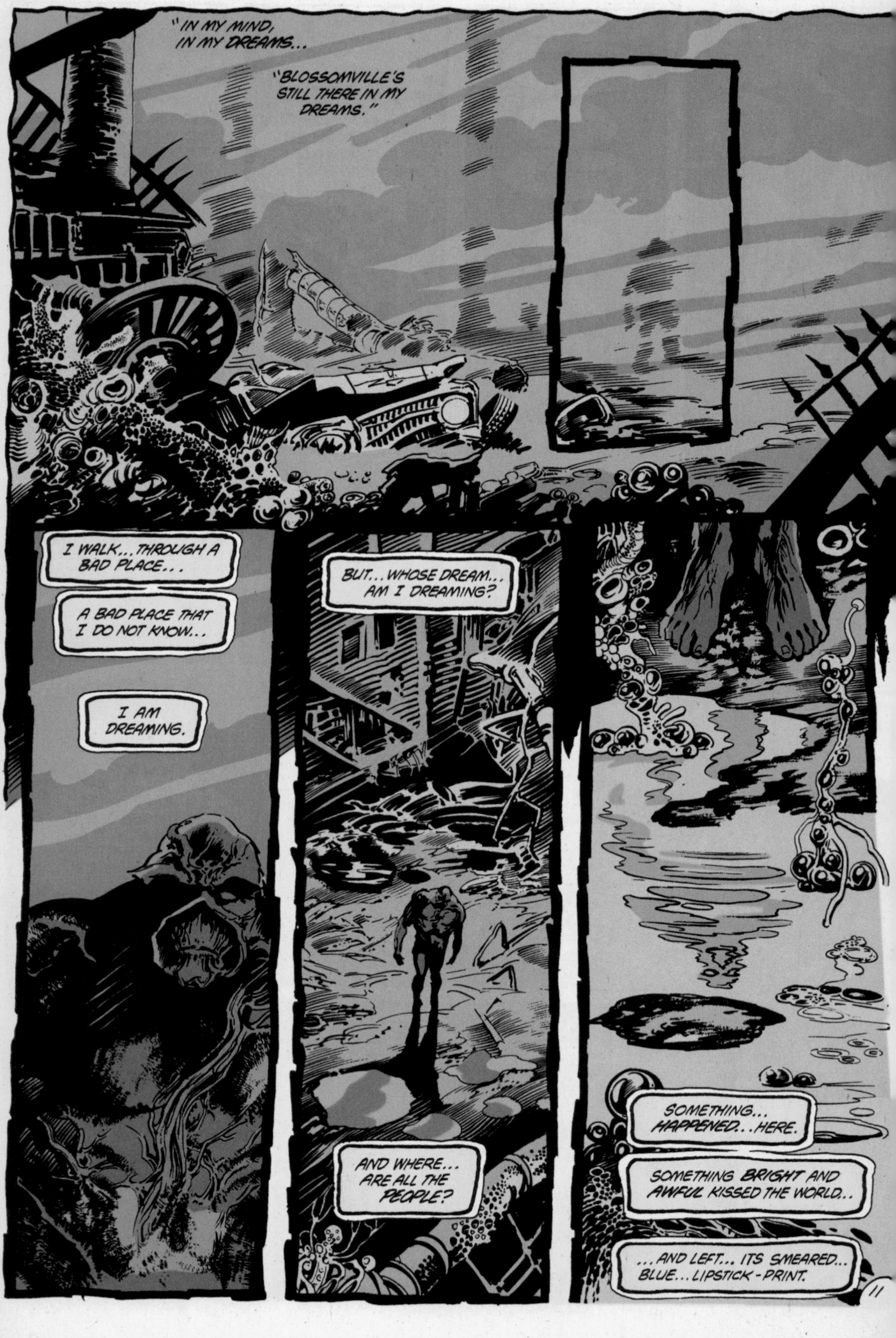
"IN MY MIND, IN MY DREAMS...
"BLOSSOMVILLE'S STILL THERE IN MY DREAMS."
I WALK... THROUGH A BAD PLACE...
A BAD PLACE THAT I DO NOT KNOW...
I AM DREAMING.
BUT... WHOSE DREAM... AM I DREAMING?
AND WHERE... ARE ALL THE PEOPLE?
SOMETHING... HAPPENED... HERE.
SOMETHING BRIGHT AND AWFUL KISSED THE WORLD...
...AND LEFT... ITS SMEARED... BLUE... LIPSTICK-PRINT.
11

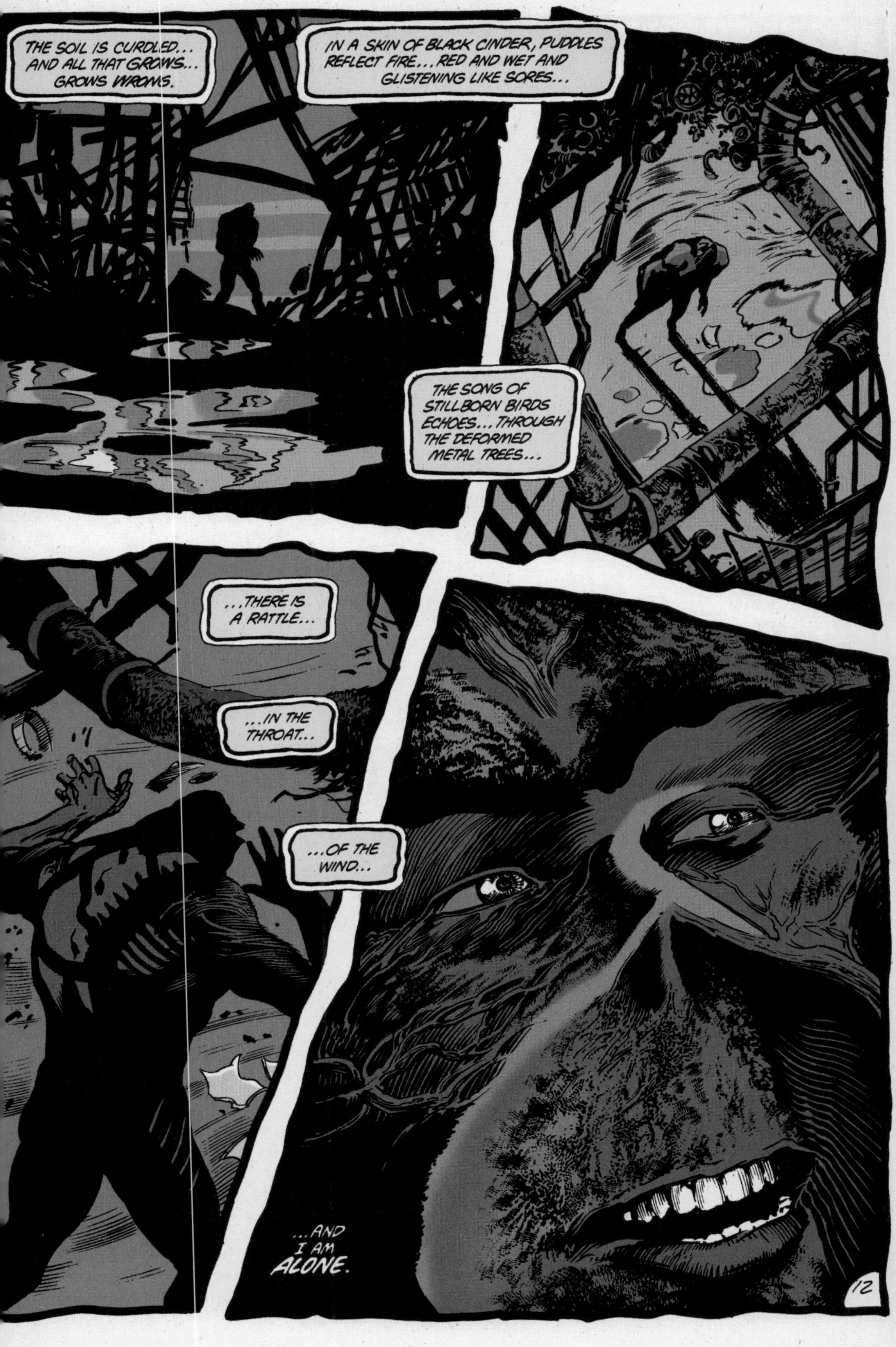
THE SOIL IS CURDLED... AND ALL THAT GROWS... GROWS WRONG.
IN A SKIN OF BLACK CINDER, PUDDLES REFLECT FIRE... RED AND WET AND GLISTENING LIKE SORES...
THE SONG OF STILLBORN BIRDS ECHOES... THROUGH THE DEFORMED METAL TREES...
...THERE IS A RATTLE...
...IN THE THROAT...
...OF THE WIND...
...AND I AM ALONE.
12

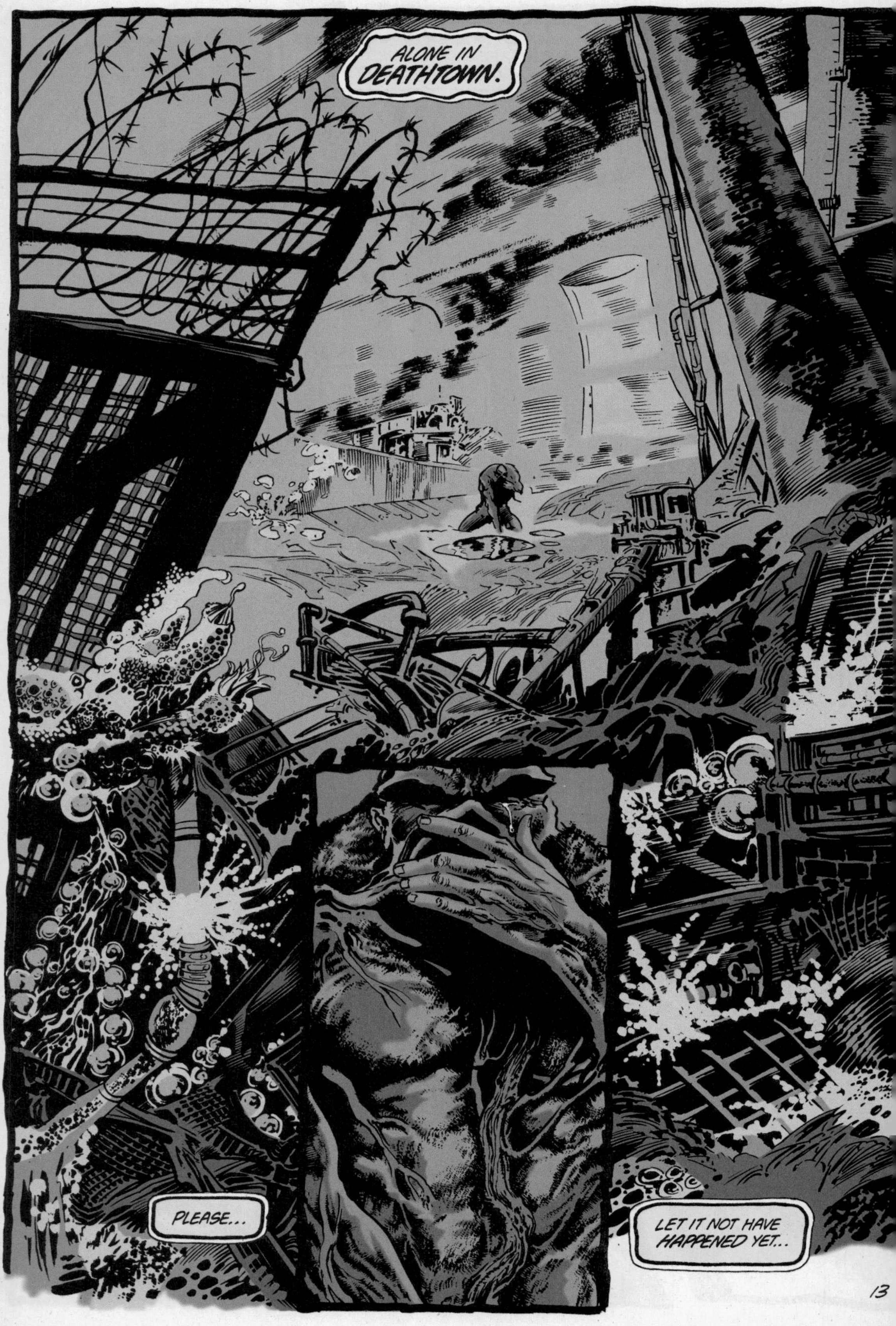
ALONE IN DEATHTOWN.
PLEASE...
LET IT NOT HAVE HAPPENED YET...

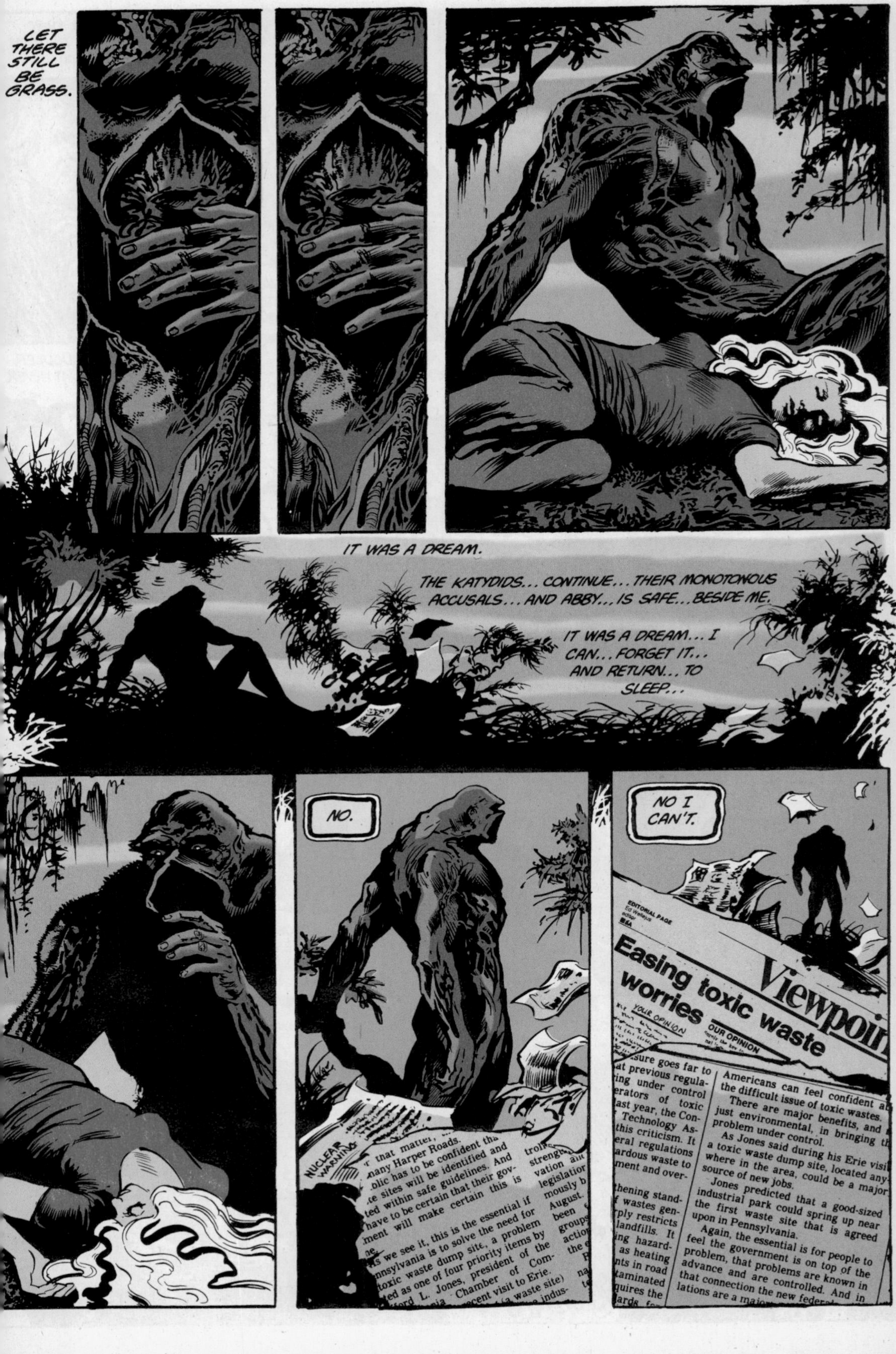
LET THERE STILL BE GRASS.
IT WAS A DREAM.
THE KATYDIDS... CONTINUE... THEIR MONOTONOUS ACCUSALS... AND ABBY... IS SAFE... BESIDE ME.
IT WAS A DREAM... I CAN... FORGET IT... AND RETURN... TO SLEEP...
NO.
NO I CAN'T.
NUCLEAR WARNING
EDITORIAL PAGE
Easing toxic waste worries
YOUR OPINION
OUR OPINION

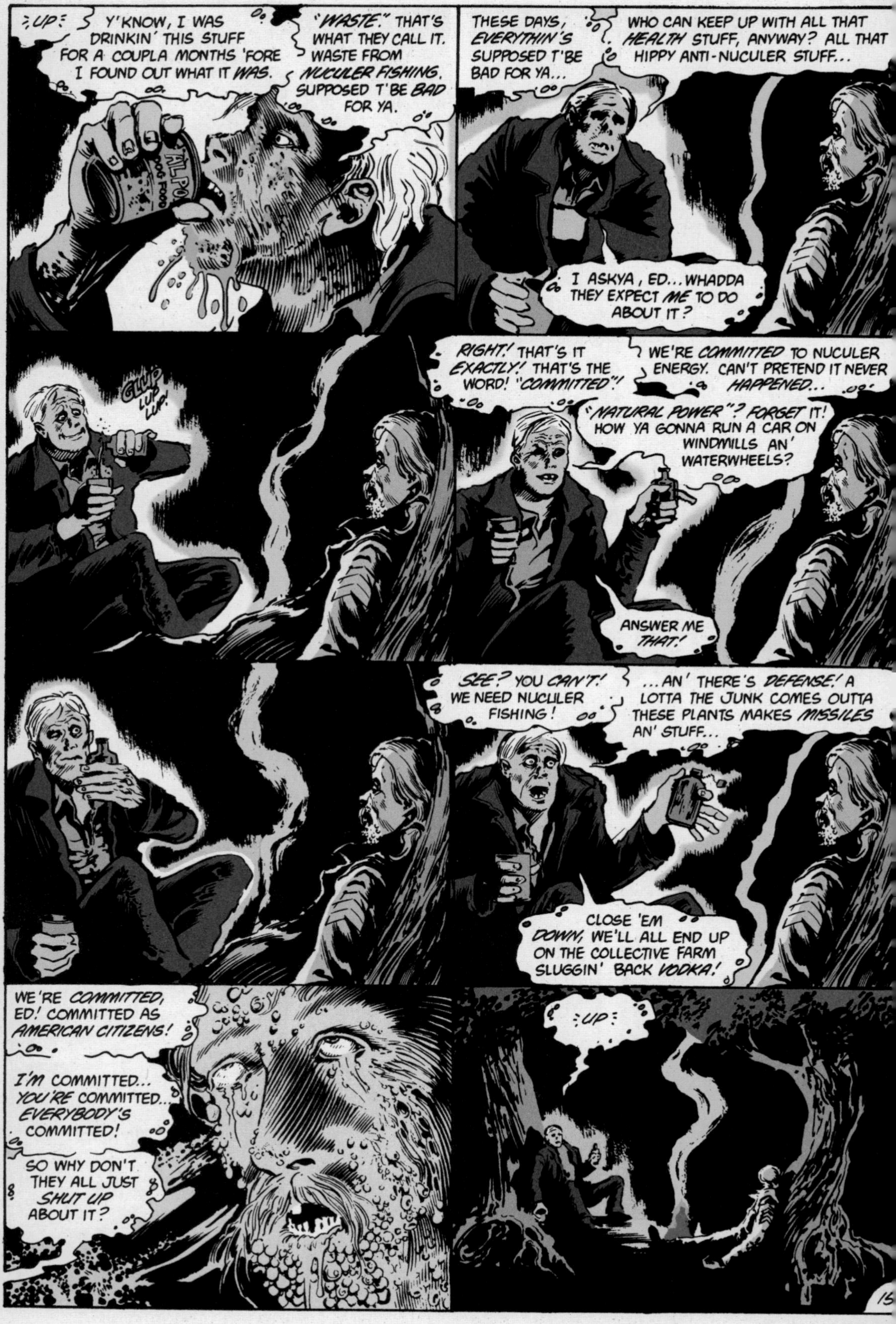
UP
Y'KNOW, I WAS DRINKIN' THIS STUFF FOR A COUPLA MONTHS 'FORE I FOUND OUT WHAT IT WAS.
"WASTE." THAT'S WHAT THEY CALL IT. WASTE FROM NUCULER FISHING. SUPPOSED T'BE BAD FOR YA.
ALPO DOG FOOD
THESE DAYS, EVERYTHIN'S SUPPOSED T'BE BAD FOR YA...
WHO CAN KEEP UP WITH ALL THAT HEALTH STUFF, ANYWAY? ALL THAT HIPPY ANTI-NUCULER STUFF...
I ASKYA, ED... WHADDA THEY EXPECT ME TO DO ABOUT IT?
GLUP LUP LUP
RIGHT! THAT'S IT EXACTLY! THAT'S THE WORD! "COMMITTED"!
WE'RE COMMITTED TO NUCULER ENERGY. CAN'T PRETEND IT NEVER HAPPENED...
"NATURAL POWER"? FORGET IT! HOW YA GONNA RUN A CAR ON WINDMILLS AN' WATERWHEELS?
ANSWER ME THAT!
SEE? YOU CAN'T! WE NEED NUCULER FISHING!
...AN' THERE'S DEFENSE! A LOTTA THE JUNK COMES OUTTA THESE PLANTS MAKES MISSILES AN' STUFF...
CLOSE 'EM DOWN, WE'LL ALL END UP ON THE COLLECTIVE FARM SLUGGIN' BACK VODKA!
WE'RE COMMITTED, ED! COMMITTED AS AMERICAN CITIZENS!
I'M COMMITTED... YOU'RE COMMITTED... EVERYBODY'S COMMITTED!
SO WHY DON'T THEY ALL JUST SHUT UP ABOUT IT?
UP
15

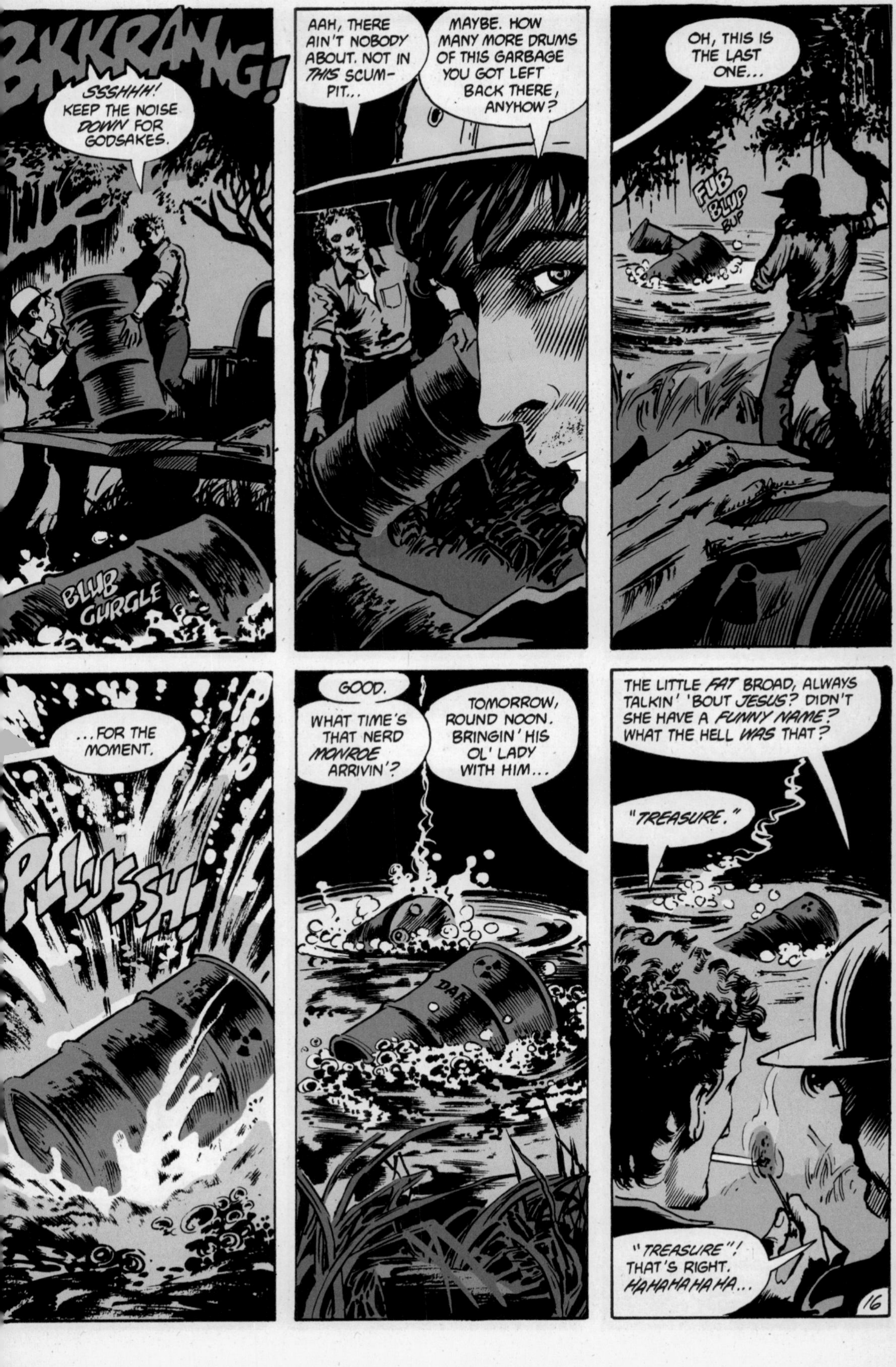
BKKRANNG!
SSSHHH! KEEP THE NOISE DOWN FOR GODSAKES.
BLUB GURGLE
AAH, THERE AIN'T NOBODY ABOUT. NOT IN THIS SCUM-PIT...
MAYBE. HOW MANY MORE DRUMS OF THIS GARBAGE YOU GOT LEFT BACK THERE, ANYHOW?
OH, THIS IS THE LAST ONE...
FUB BLUP BUP
...FOR THE MOMENT.
PLLUSSH!
GOOD.
WHAT TIME'S THAT NERD MONROE ARRIVIN'?
TOMORROW, ROUND NOON. BRINGIN' HIS OL' LADY WITH HIM...
THE LITTLE FAT BROAD, ALWAYS TALKIN' 'BOUT JESUS? DIDN'T SHE HAVE A FUNNY NAME? WHAT THE HELL WAS THAT?
"TREASURE."
"TREASURE"! THAT'S RIGHT. HAHAHAHAHA...
16

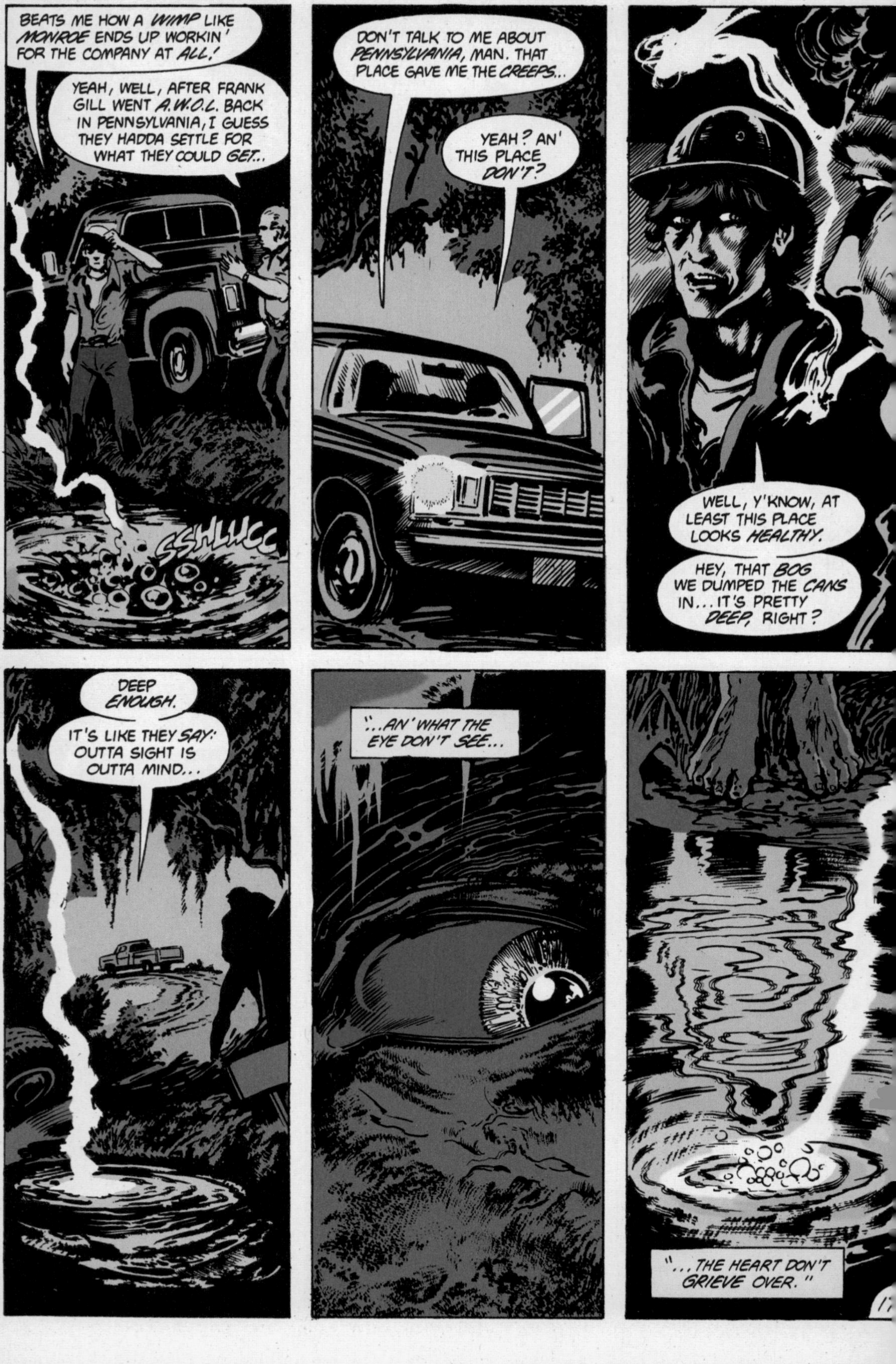
BEATS ME HOW A WIMP LIKE MONROE ENDS UP WORKIN' FOR THE COMPANY AT ALL!
YEAH, WELL, AFTER FRANK GILL WENT A.W.O.L. BACK IN PENNSYLVANIA, I GUESS THEY HADDA SETTLE FOR WHAT THEY COULD GET...
SSHLUCC
DON'T TALK TO ME ABOUT PENNSYLVANIA, MAN. THAT PLACE GAVE ME THE CREEPS...
YEAH? AN' THIS PLACE DON'T?
WELL, Y'KNOW, AT LEAST THIS PLACE LOOKS HEALTHY.
HEY, THAT BOG WE DUMPED THE CANS IN... IT'S PRETTY DEEP, RIGHT?
DEEP ENOUGH.
IT'S LIKE THEY SAY: OUTTA SIGHT IS OUTTA MIND...
"...AN' WHAT THE EYE DON'T SEE...
"...THE HEART DON'T GRIEVE OVER."

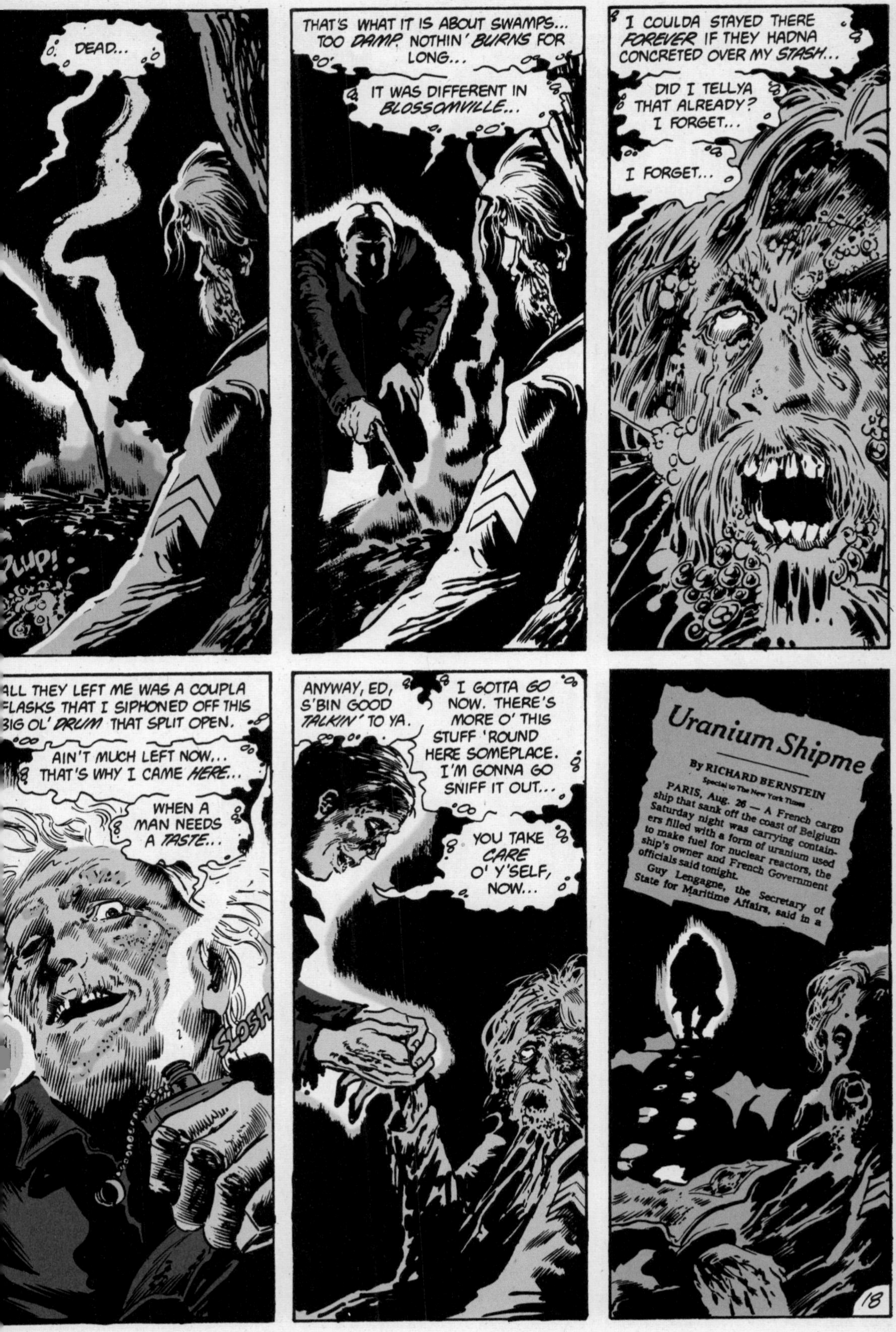
DEAD...
THAT'S WHAT IT IS ABOUT SWAMPS... TOO DAMP. NOTHIN' BURNS FOR LONG...
IT WAS DIFFERENT IN BLOSSOMVILLE...
I COULDA STAYED THERE FOREVER IF THEY HADNA CONCRETED OVER MY STASH...
DID I TELLYA THAT ALREADY? I FORGET...
I FORGET...
PLUP!
ALL THEY LEFT ME WAS A COUPLA FLASKS THAT I SIPHONED OFF THIS BIG OL' DRUM THAT SPLIT OPEN.
AIN'T MUCH LEFT NOW... THAT'S WHY I CAME HERE...
WHEN A MAN NEEDS A TASTE...
SLOSH
ANYWAY, ED, S'BIN GOOD TALKIN' TO YA.
I GOTTA GO NOW. THERE'S MORE O' THIS STUFF 'ROUND HERE SOMEPLACE. I'M GONNA GO SNIFF IT OUT...
YOU TAKE CARE O' Y'SELF, NOW...
Uranium Shipme
By RICHARD BERNSTEIN
Special to The New York Times
PARIS, Aug. 26 — A French cargo ship that sank off the coast of Belgium Saturday night was carrying containers filled with a form of uranium used to make fuel for nuclear reactors, the ship's owner and French Government officials said tonight.
Guy Lengagne, the Secretary of State for Maritime Affairs, said in a
18

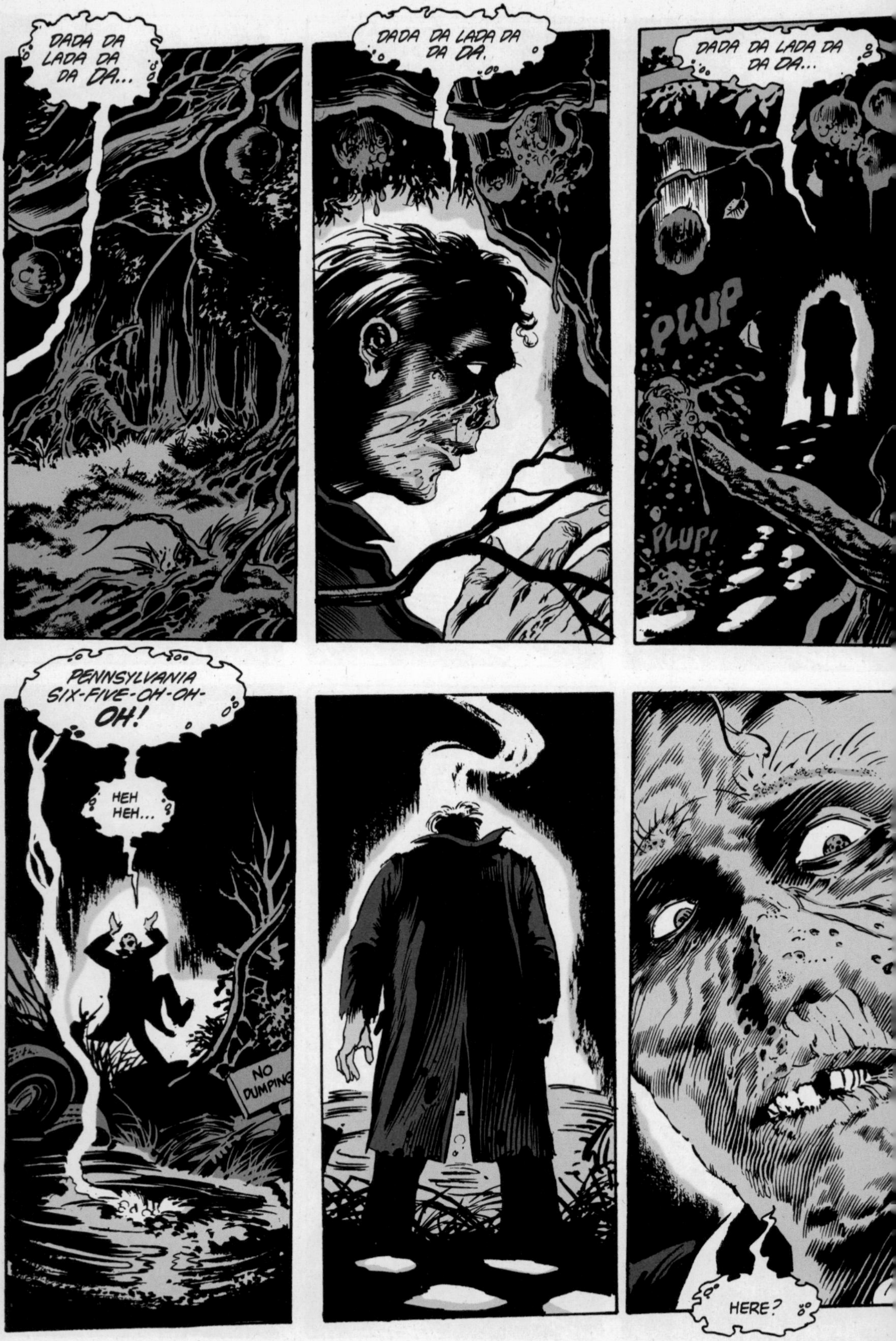
DADA DA
LADA DA
DA DA...
DADA DA LADA DA
DA DA.
DADA DA LADA DA
DA DA...
PLUP
PLUP!
PENNSYLVANIA
SIX-FIVE-OH-OH-
OH!
HEH
HEH...
NO
DUMPING
HERE?

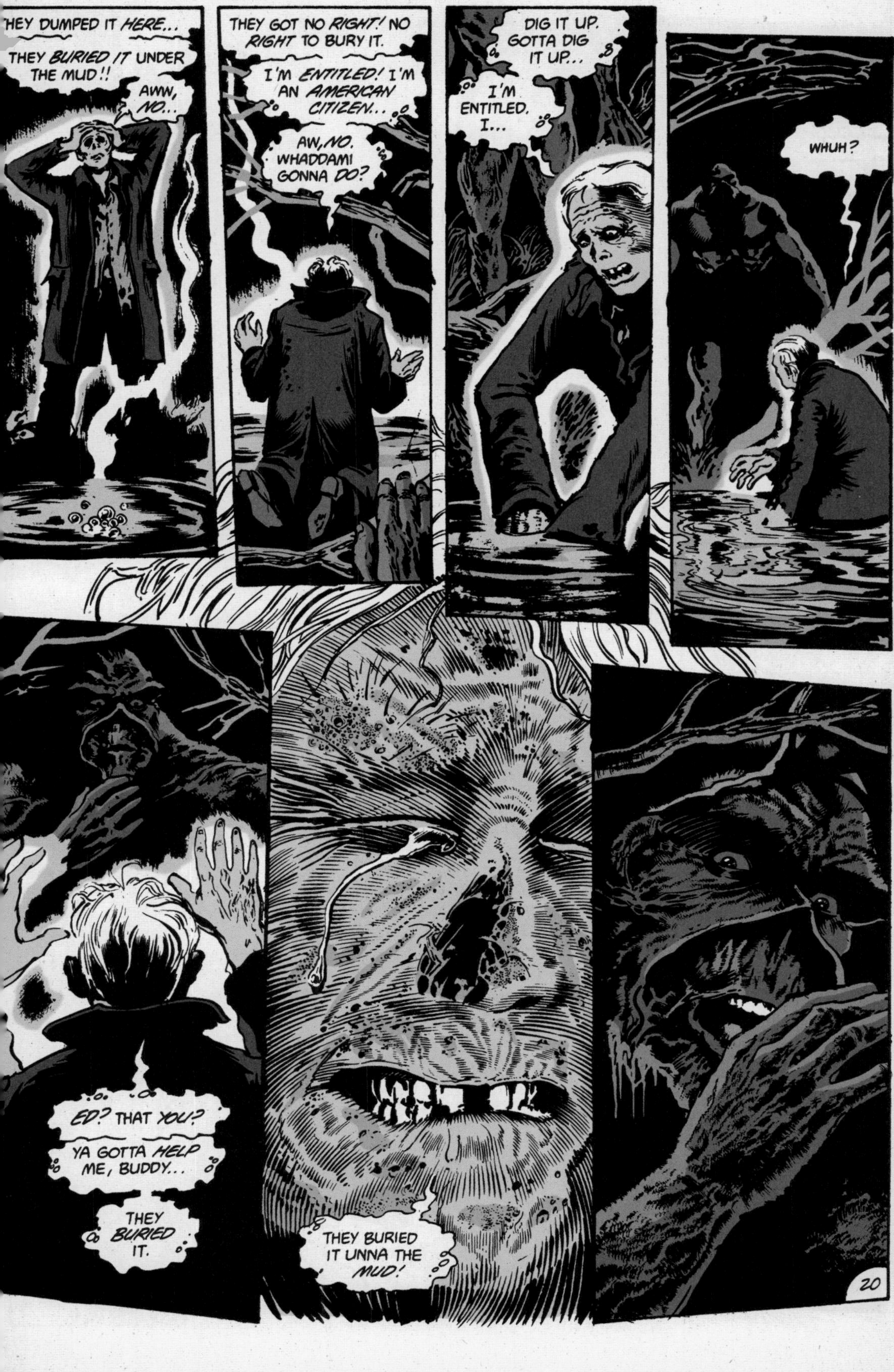
HEY DUMPED IT HERE...
THEY BURIED IT UNDER THE MUD!!
AWW, NO...
THEY GOT NO RIGHT! NO RIGHT TO BURY IT.
I'M ENTITLED! I'M AN AMERICAN CITIZEN...
AW, NO. WHADDAMI GONNA DO?
DIG IT UP. GOTTA DIG IT UP...
I'M ENTITLED. I...
WHUH?
ED? THAT YOU?
YA GOTTA HELP ME, BUDDY...
THEY BURIED IT.
THEY BURIED IT UNNA THE MUD!
20

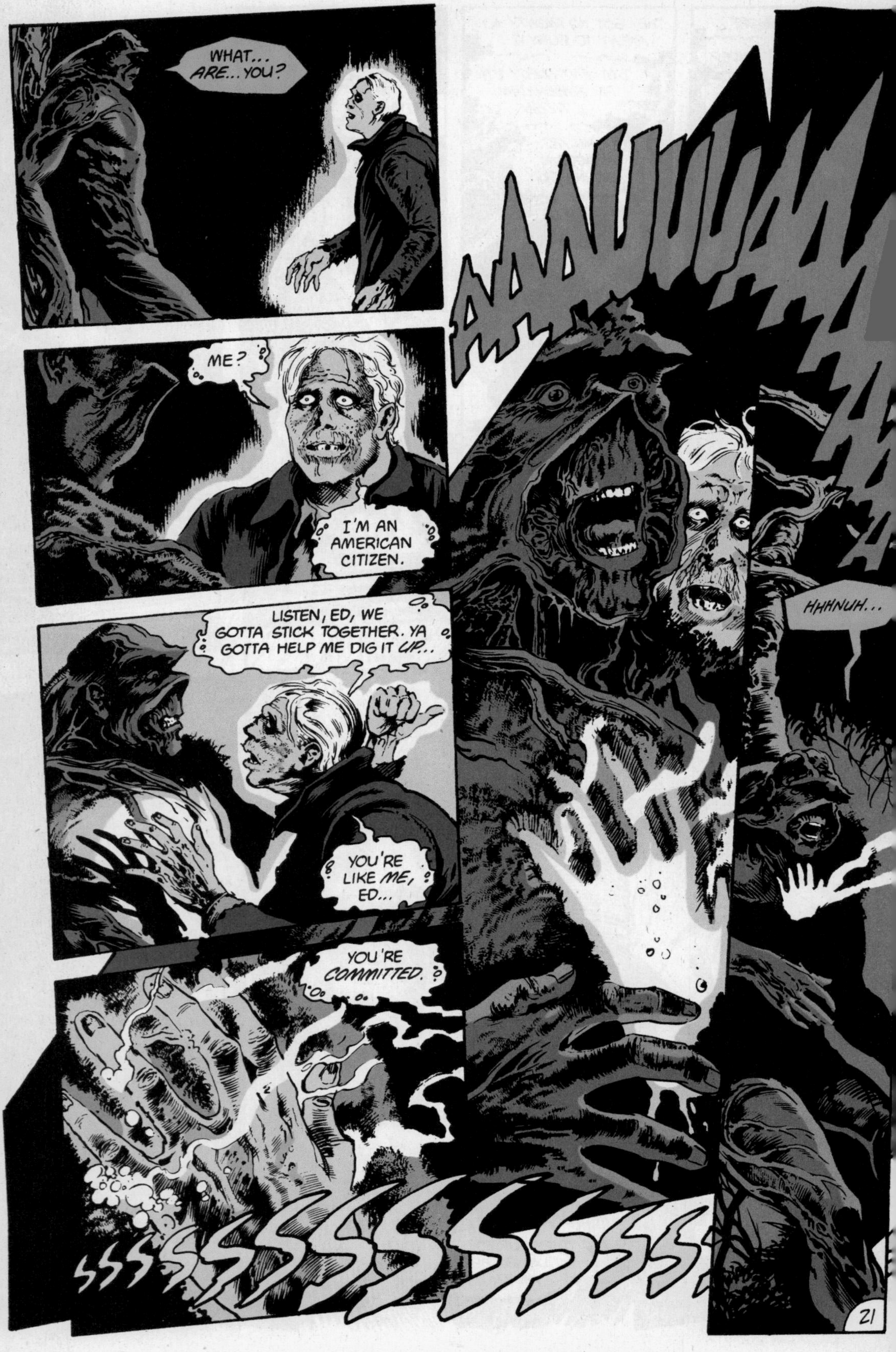
WHAT... ARE... YOU?
ME?
I'M AN AMERICAN CITIZEN.
LISTEN, ED, WE GOTTA STICK TOGETHER. YA GOTTA HELP ME DIG IT UP...
YOU'RE LIKE ME, ED...
YOU'RE COMMITTED.
SSSSSSSSSSSSSS
AAAUUAA
HHHNUH...
21

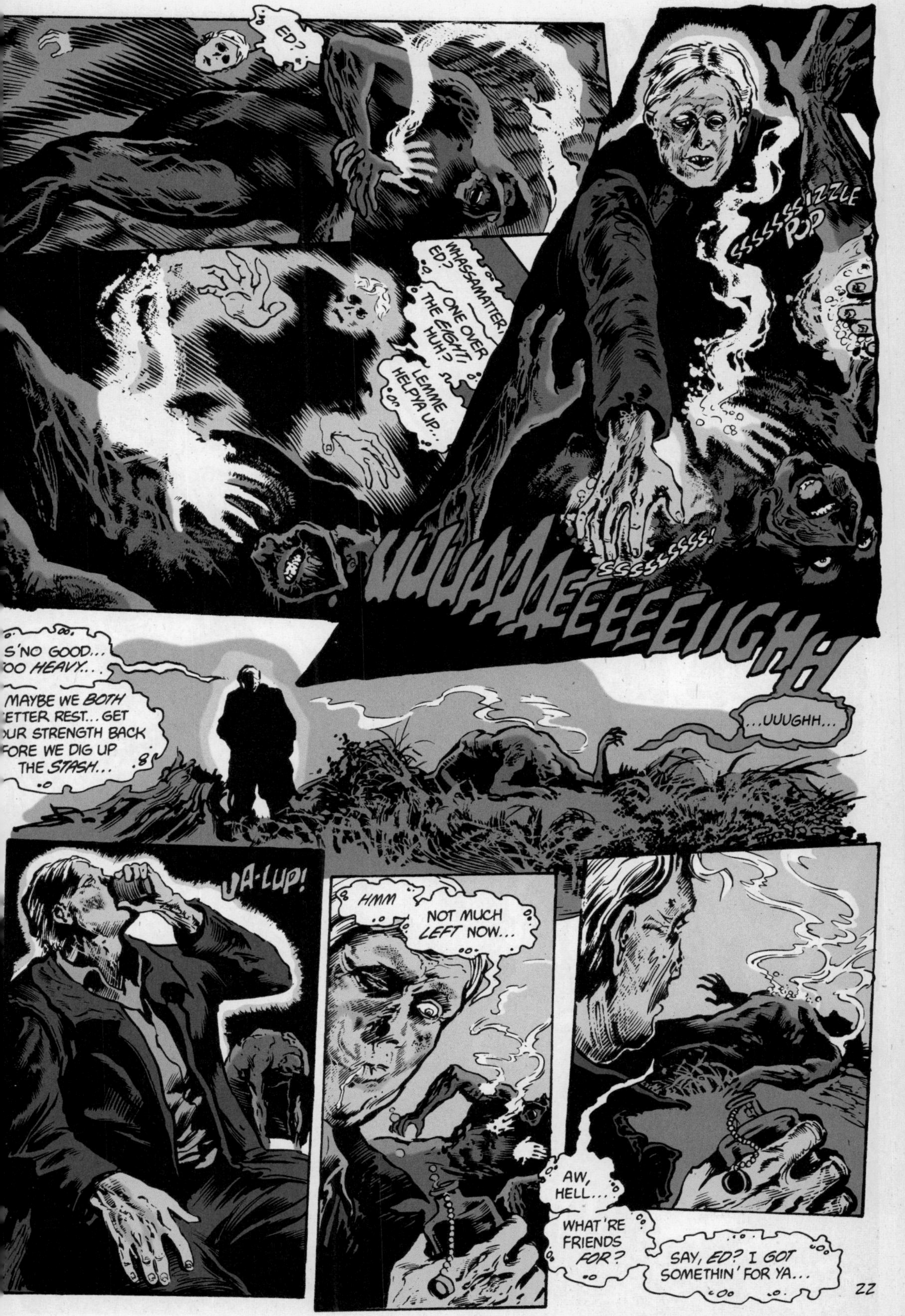
ED?
WHASSAMATTER, ED?
ONE OVER THE EIGHT, HUH?
LEMME HELPYA UP...
SSSSSSSIZZLE POP
SSSSSSSSS!
UUUAAAEEEEEIIGHH
S'NO GOOD... TOO HEAVY...
MAYBE WE BOTH BETTER REST... GET OUR STRENGTH BACK 'FORE WE DIG UP THE STASH...
...UUUGHH...
GA-LUP!
HMM
NOT MUCH LEFT NOW...
AW, HELL...
WHAT'RE FRIENDS FOR?
SAY, ED? I GOT SOMETHIN' FOR YA...
22

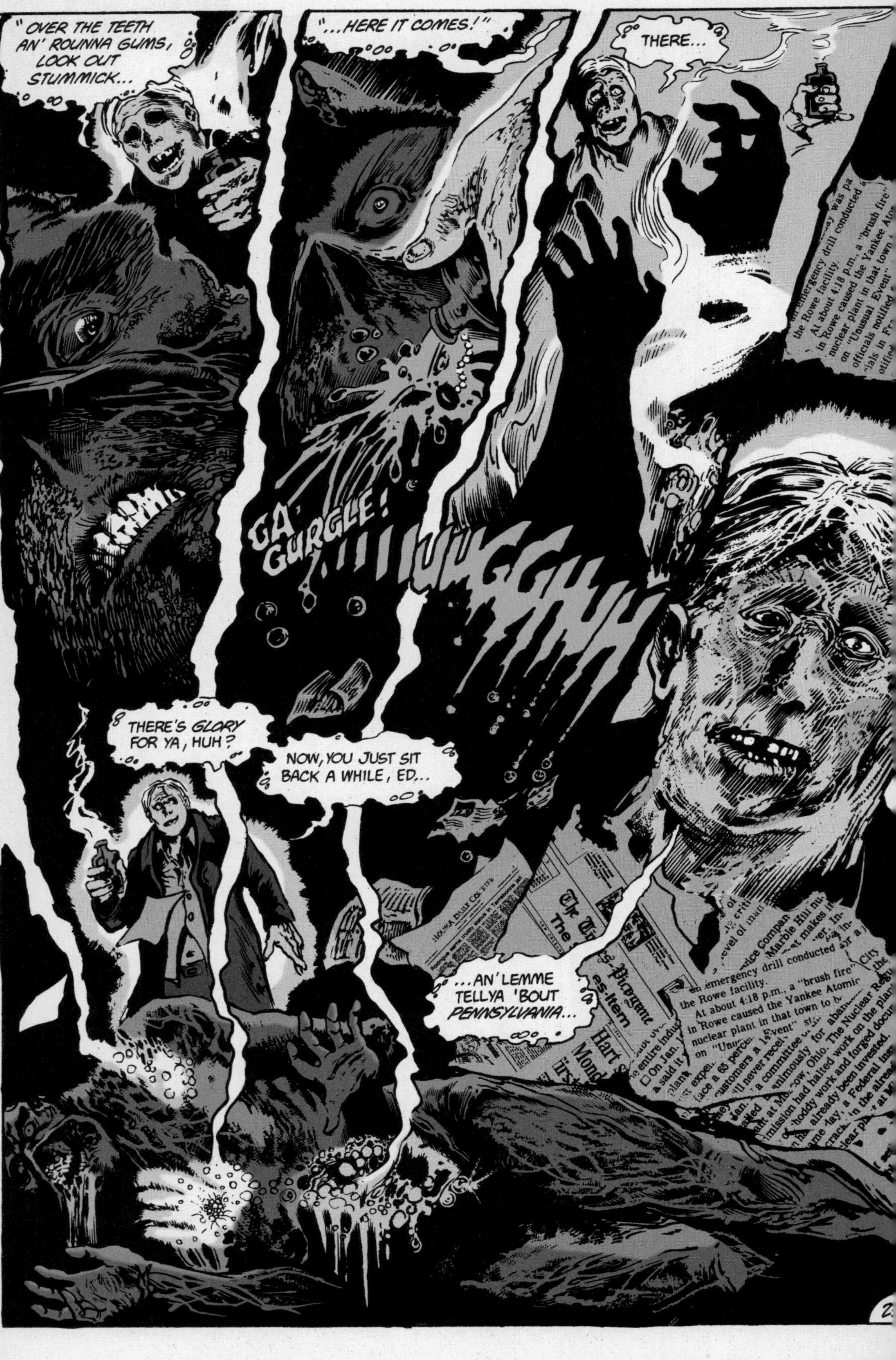
"OVER THE TEETH AN' ROUNNA GUMS, LOOK OUT STUMMICK...
"...HERE IT COMES!"
THERE...
GA-GURGLE!
UUUUGGHHH
THERE'S GLORY FOR YA, HUH?
NOW, YOU JUST SIT BACK A WHILE, ED...
...AN' LEMME TELLYA 'BOUT PENNSYLVANIA...

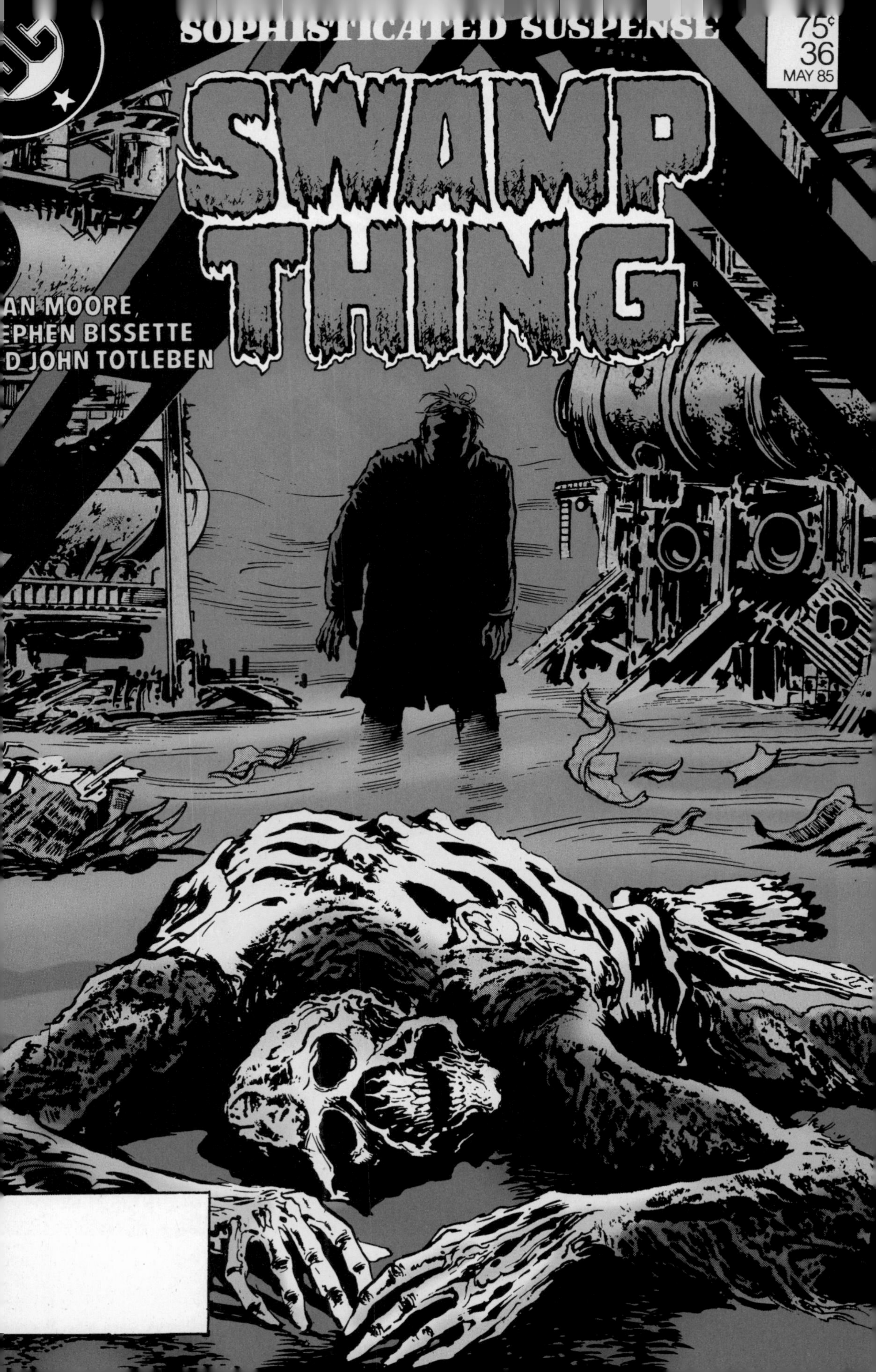
SOPHISTICATED SUSPENSE
75¢
36
MAY 85
SWAMP THING
AN MOORE,
EPHEN BISSETTE
D JOHN TOTLEBEN

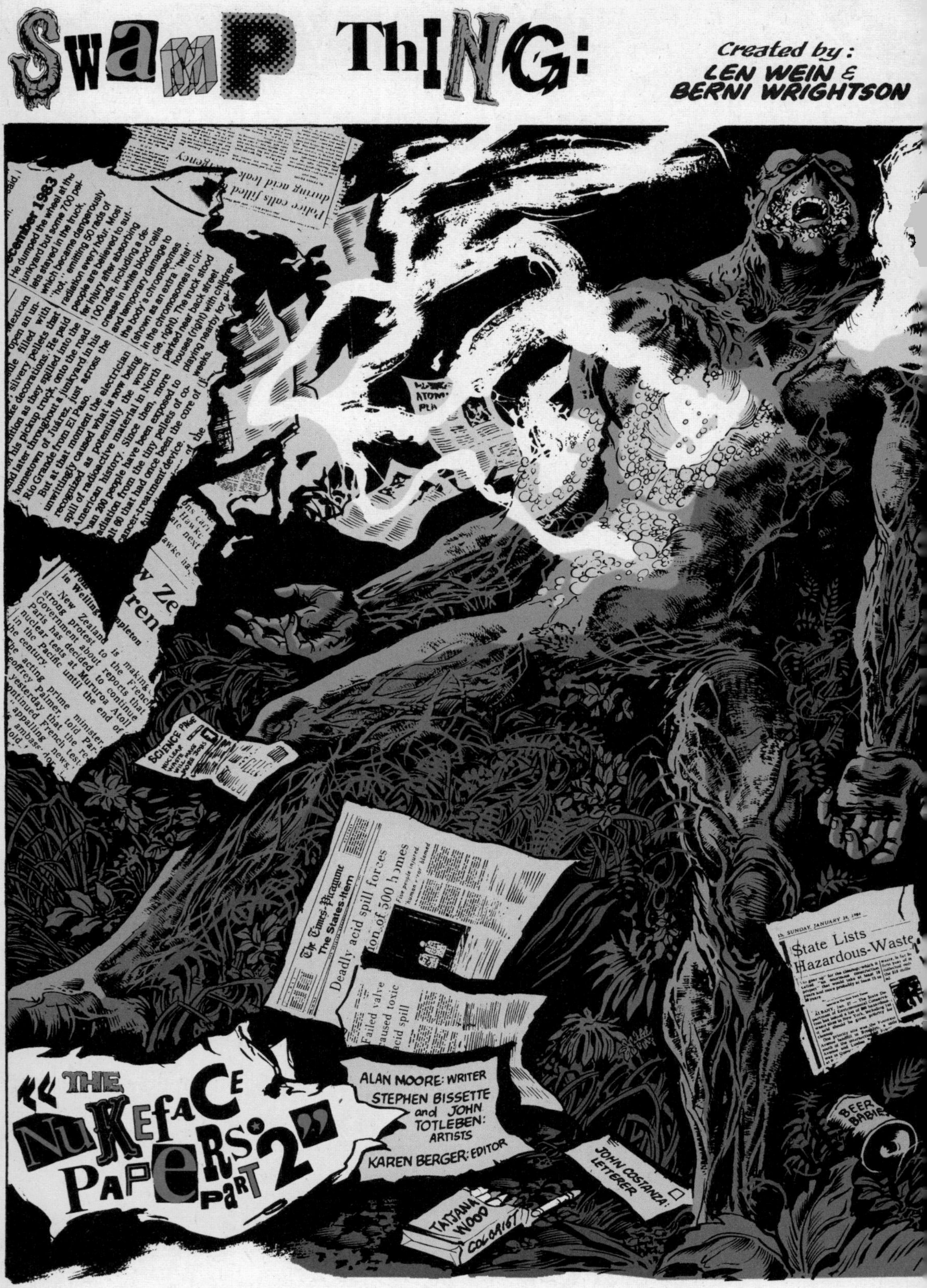
SWAMP THING:
Created by:
LEN WEIN & BERNI WRIGHTSON
"THE NUKEFACE PAPERS: PART 2"
ALAN MOORE: WRITER
STEPHEN BISSETTE and JOHN TOTLEBEN: ARTISTS
KAREN BERGER: EDITOR
JOHN COSTANZA: LETTERER
TATJANA WOOD COLORIST
The Times-Picayune The States-Item
Deadly acid spill forces
Failed valve caused toxic acid spill
SUNDAY, JANUARY 29, 1984
State Lists Hazardous-Waste
SCIENCE PAGE
BEER BABIES

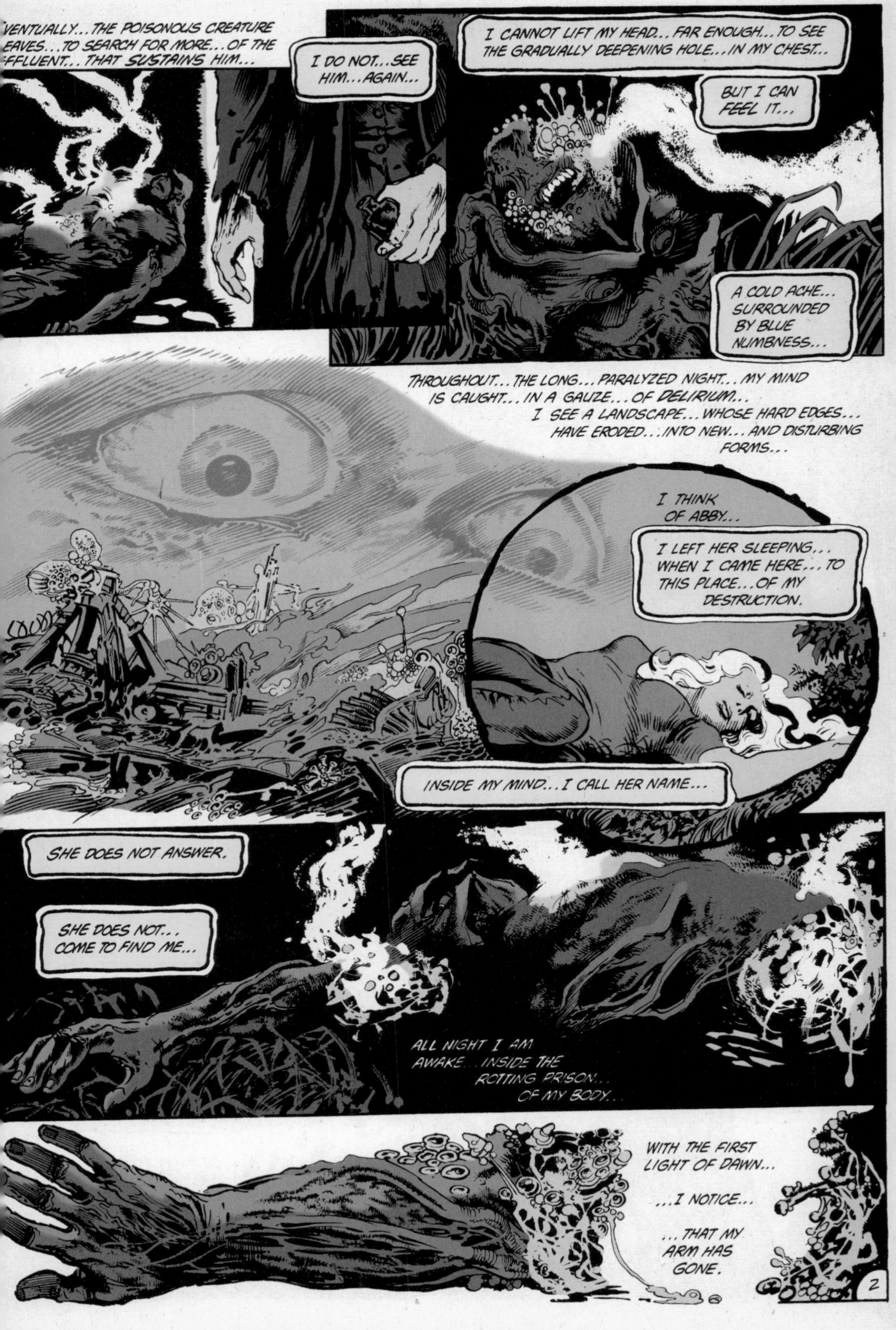
EVENTUALLY...THE POISONOUS CREATURE LEAVES...TO SEARCH FOR MORE...OF THE EFFLUENT...THAT SUSTAINS HIM...
I DO NOT...SEE HIM...AGAIN...
I CANNOT LIFT MY HEAD...FAR ENOUGH...TO SEE THE GRADUALLY DEEPENING HOLE...IN MY CHEST...
BUT I CAN FEEL IT...
A COLD ACHE... SURROUNDED BY BLUE NUMBNESS...
THROUGHOUT...THE LONG...PARALYZED NIGHT...MY MIND IS CAUGHT...IN A GAUZE...OF DELIRIUM...
I SEE A LANDSCAPE...WHOSE HARD EDGES...HAVE ERODED...INTO NEW...AND DISTURBING FORMS...
I THINK OF ABBY...
I LEFT HER SLEEPING...WHEN I CAME HERE...TO THIS PLACE...OF MY DESTRUCTION.
INSIDE MY MIND...I CALL HER NAME...
SHE DOES NOT ANSWER.
SHE DOES NOT...COME TO FIND ME...
ALL NIGHT I AM AWAKE...INSIDE THE ROTTING PRISON...OF MY BODY...
WITH THE FIRST LIGHT OF DAWN...
...I NOTICE...
...THAT MY ARM HAS GONE.
2

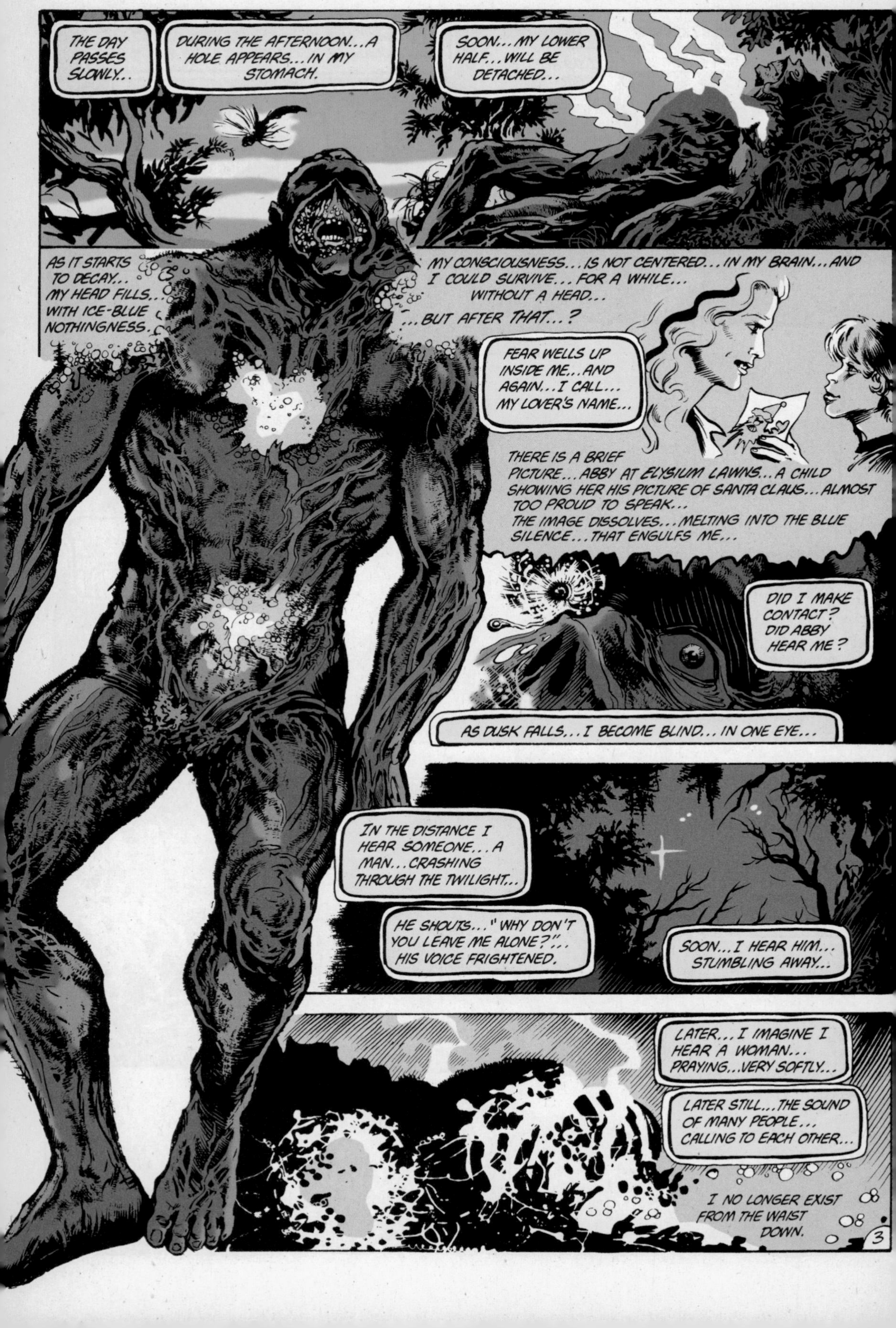
THE DAY PASSES SLOWLY...
DURING THE AFTERNOON...A HOLE APPEARS...IN MY STOMACH.
SOON...MY LOWER HALF...WILL BE DETACHED...
AS IT STARTS TO DECAY... MY HEAD FILLS... WITH ICE-BLUE NOTHINGNESS.
MY CONSCIOUSNESS...IS NOT CENTERED...IN MY BRAIN...AND I COULD SURVIVE... FOR A WHILE... WITHOUT A HEAD...
...BUT AFTER THAT...?
FEAR WELLS UP INSIDE ME...AND AGAIN...I CALL... MY LOVER'S NAME...
THERE IS A BRIEF PICTURE...ABBY AT ELYSIUM LAWNS...A CHILD SHOWING HER HIS PICTURE OF SANTA CLAUS...ALMOST TOO PROUD TO SPEAK...
THE IMAGE DISSOLVES...MELTING INTO THE BLUE SILENCE...THAT ENGULFS ME...
DID I MAKE CONTACT? DID ABBY HEAR ME?
AS DUSK FALLS...I BECOME BLIND...IN ONE EYE...
IN THE DISTANCE I HEAR SOMEONE...A MAN...CRASHING THROUGH THE TWILIGHT...
HE SHOUTS..."WHY DON'T YOU LEAVE ME ALONE?"... HIS VOICE FRIGHTENED.
SOON...I HEAR HIM... STUMBLING AWAY...
LATER...I IMAGINE I HEAR A WOMAN... PRAYING...VERY SOFTLY...
LATER STILL...THE SOUND OF MANY PEOPLE... CALLING TO EACH OTHER...
I NO LONGER EXIST FROM THE WAIST DOWN.
3

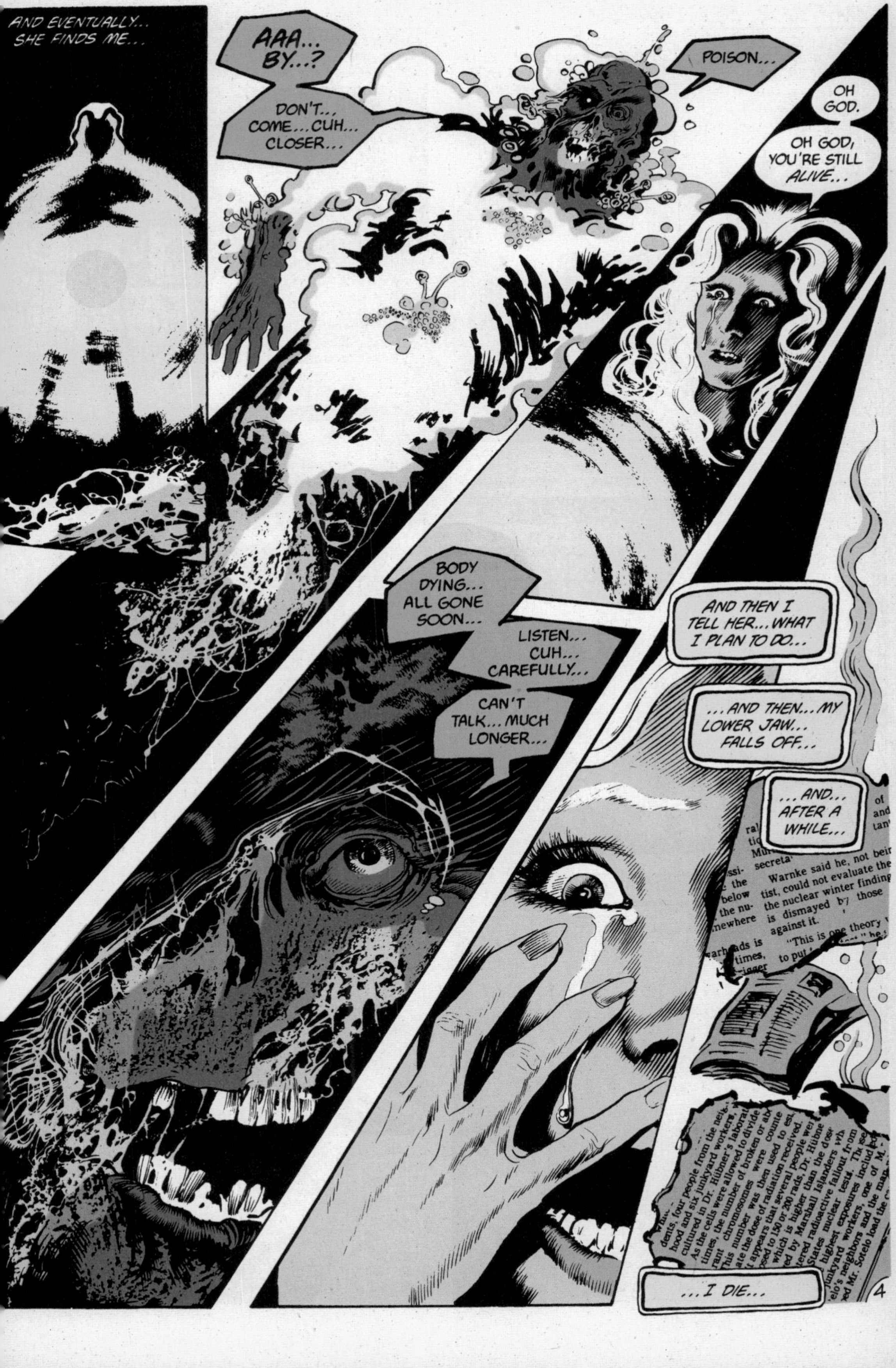
AND EVENTUALLY... SHE FINDS ME...
AAA... BY...?
DON'T... COME...CUH... CLOSER...
POISON...
OH GOD.
OH GOD, YOU'RE STILL ALIVE...
BODY DYING... ALL GONE SOON...
LISTEN... CUH... CAREFULLY...
CAN'T TALK...MUCH LONGER...
AND THEN I TELL HER...WHAT I PLAN TO DO...
...AND THEN...MY LOWER JAW... FALLS OFF...
...AND... AFTER A WHILE...
...I DIE...
4

OFFICER BERNHARDT:

...SO, LIKE, I DUNNO *WHAT* WENT DOWN FOR CERTAIN.

FIRST *I* HEARD OF IT WAS WIDOW *MOREL* TELLIN' ME HOW *DIAGONAL BOB* HAD DISAPPEARED...

"SEEMS THEY'D ARGUED, THE NIGHT BEFORE. SHE SLUNG BOB OUT, NEVER SAW HIM AGAIN...LEAST, NOT TILL SHE IDENTIFIED HIM THIS MORNIN'; BUT THAT WAS *LATER*...

TIME SA

SALE .65 PER QUART

SELF-SERVE GAS FOOD MAGAZINES

FRESH MUD... 69 PER POUND

VITAMIN D MILK MILK

"WHILE SHE'S *BENDIN'* MY EAR, THIS *MONROE* GUY ARRIVES...

"HE'D OVERHEARD WIDOW *MOREL'S* STORY, AN' IT SEEMED TO *UPSET* HIM. I ASKED WHY AN' HE SAID SOMETHIN' ABOUT WINOS GOIN' *MISSIN'* IN *PENNSYLVANIA*, THEN WALKED OFF...

"LATER, I HEARD HE'D *SCARED* SOME NEIGHBOR-HOOD KIDS...

"ANYWAY, HE SEEMED PRETTY *WEIRD*.

TERRE BONNE PARISH

"WHEN HE TURNED UP AT THE *STATION*, LATER ON, WITH THAT STORY...HOW SOME *MONSTER* HAD GOT HIS WIFE AN' WE HADDA *FIND* HER...I THOUGHT, Y'KNOW, 'UH-OH!'

"BUT THEN SHE TURNED UP...AND THEN LATER WE FOUND *BOB*..."

...AND NOW I DUNNO *WHAT* TO THINK.

SAY!

WHO *DEALT* THIS MESS?

Satellite watch o... nuclear cargo

5

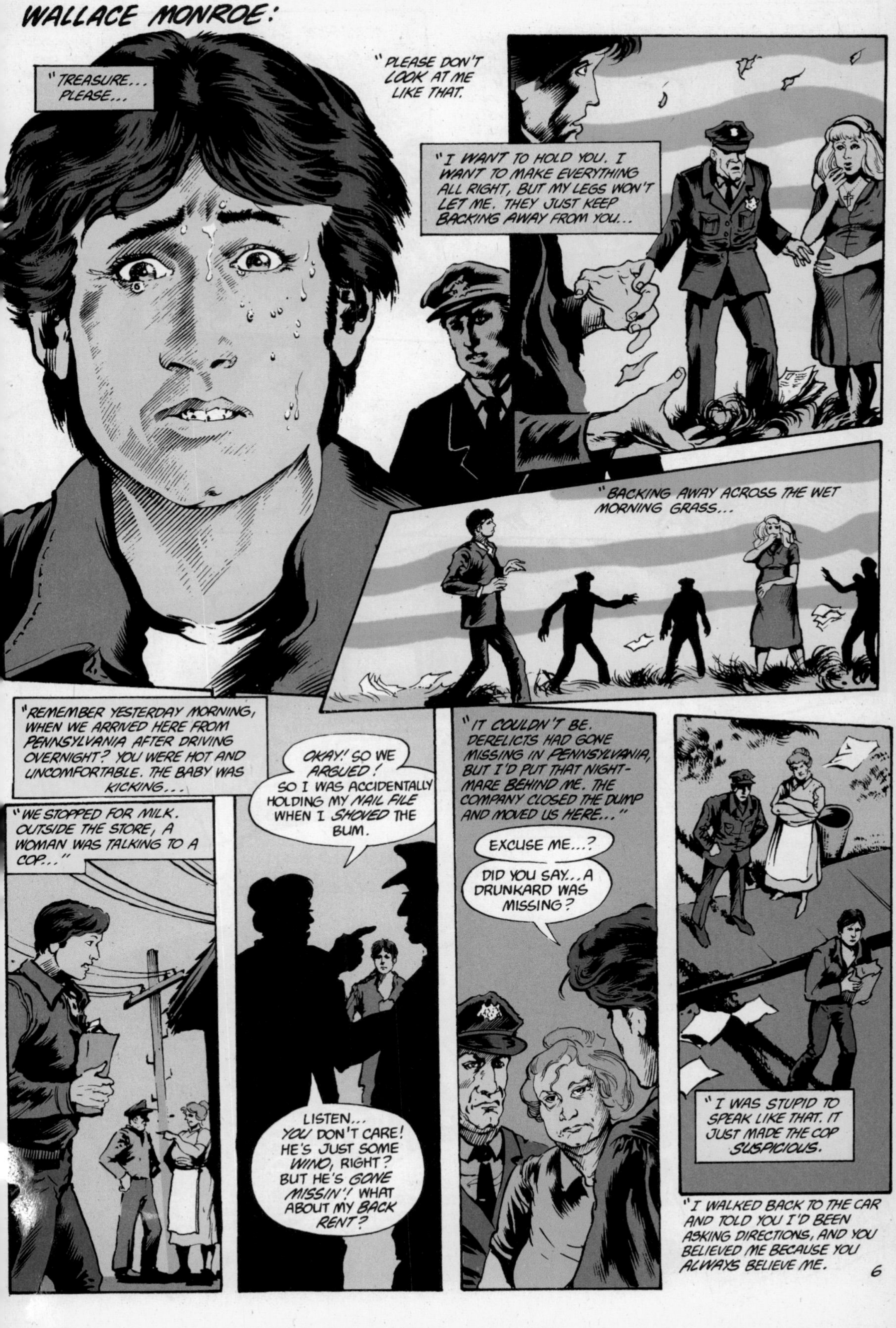
WALLACE MONROE:
"TREASURE... PLEASE...
"PLEASE DON'T LOOK AT ME LIKE THAT.
"I WANT TO HOLD YOU. I WANT TO MAKE EVERYTHING ALL RIGHT, BUT MY LEGS WON'T LET ME. THEY JUST KEEP BACKING AWAY FROM YOU...
"BACKING AWAY ACROSS THE WET MORNING GRASS...
"REMEMBER YESTERDAY MORNING, WHEN WE ARRIVED HERE FROM PENNSYLVANIA AFTER DRIVING OVERNIGHT? YOU WERE HOT AND UNCOMFORTABLE. THE BABY WAS KICKING...
"WE STOPPED FOR MILK. OUTSIDE THE STORE, A WOMAN WAS TALKING TO A COP..."
OKAY! SO WE ARGUED! SO I WAS ACCIDENTALLY HOLDING MY NAIL FILE WHEN I SHOVED THE BUM.
LISTEN... YOU DON'T CARE! HE'S JUST SOME WINO, RIGHT? BUT HE'S GONE MISSIN'! WHAT ABOUT MY BACK RENT?
"IT COULDN'T BE. DERELICTS HAD GONE MISSING IN PENNSYLVANIA, BUT I'D PUT THAT NIGHTMARE BEHIND ME. THE COMPANY CLOSED THE DUMP AND MOVED US HERE..."
EXCUSE ME...?
DID YOU SAY... A DRUNKARD WAS MISSING?
"I WAS STUPID TO SPEAK LIKE THAT. IT JUST MADE THE COP SUSPICIOUS.
"I WALKED BACK TO THE CAR AND TOLD YOU I'D BEEN ASKING DIRECTIONS, AND YOU BELIEVED ME BECAUSE YOU ALWAYS BELIEVE ME.

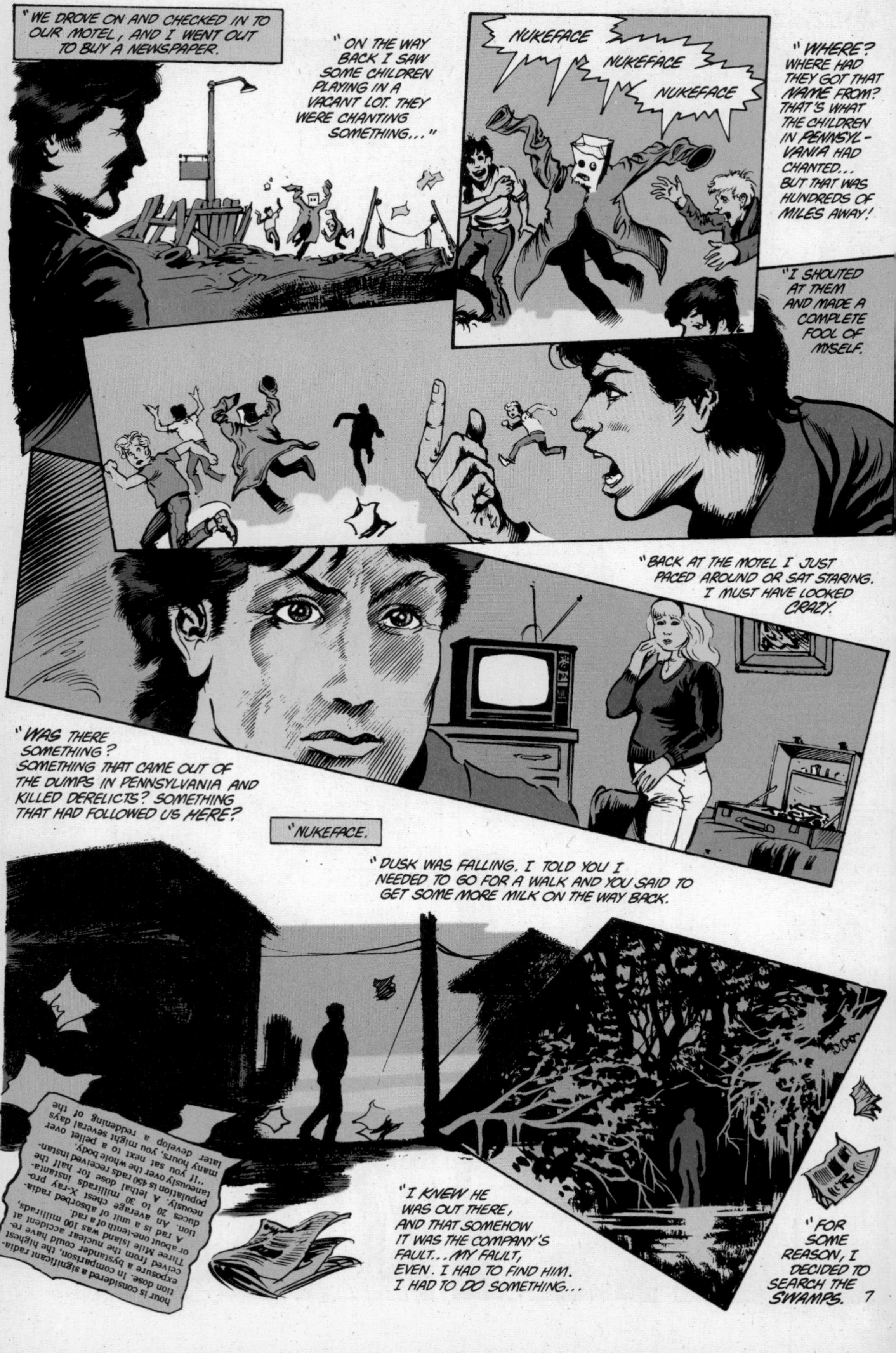
"WE DROVE ON AND CHECKED IN TO OUR MOTEL, AND I WENT OUT TO BUY A NEWSPAPER.
"ON THE WAY BACK I SAW SOME CHILDREN PLAYING IN A VACANT LOT. THEY WERE CHANTING SOMETHING..."
NUKEFACE
NUKEFACE
NUKEFACE
"WHERE? WHERE HAD THEY GOT THAT NAME FROM? THAT'S WHAT THE CHILDREN IN PENNSYL-VANIA HAD CHANTED... BUT THAT WAS HUNDREDS OF MILES AWAY!
"I SHOUTED AT THEM AND MADE A COMPLETE FOOL OF MYSELF.
"BACK AT THE MOTEL I JUST PACED AROUND OR SAT STARING. I MUST HAVE LOOKED CRAZY.
"WAS THERE SOMETHING? SOMETHING THAT CAME OUT OF THE DUMPS IN PENNSYLVANIA AND KILLED DERELICTS? SOMETHING THAT HAD FOLLOWED US HERE?
"NUKEFACE.
"DUSK WAS FALLING. I TOLD YOU I NEEDED TO GO FOR A WALK AND YOU SAID TO GET SOME MORE MILK ON THE WAY BACK.
hour is considered a significant radia-
tion dose. In comparison, the highest
exposure a bystander could have received from the nuclear accident at
Three Mile Island was 100 millirads.
A rad is a unit of absorbed radiation. An average chest X-ray pro-
duces 20 to 30 millirads instanta-
neously. A lethal dose for half the
population is 450 rads received instan-
taneously over the whole body.
"If you sat next to a pellet over
many hours, you might several days
later develop a reddening of the
"I KNEW HE WAS OUT THERE, AND THAT SOMEHOW IT WAS THE COMPANY'S FAULT... MY FAULT, EVEN. I HAD TO FIND HIM. I HAD TO DO SOMETHING...
"FOR SOME REASON, I DECIDED TO SEARCH THE SWAMPS.
7

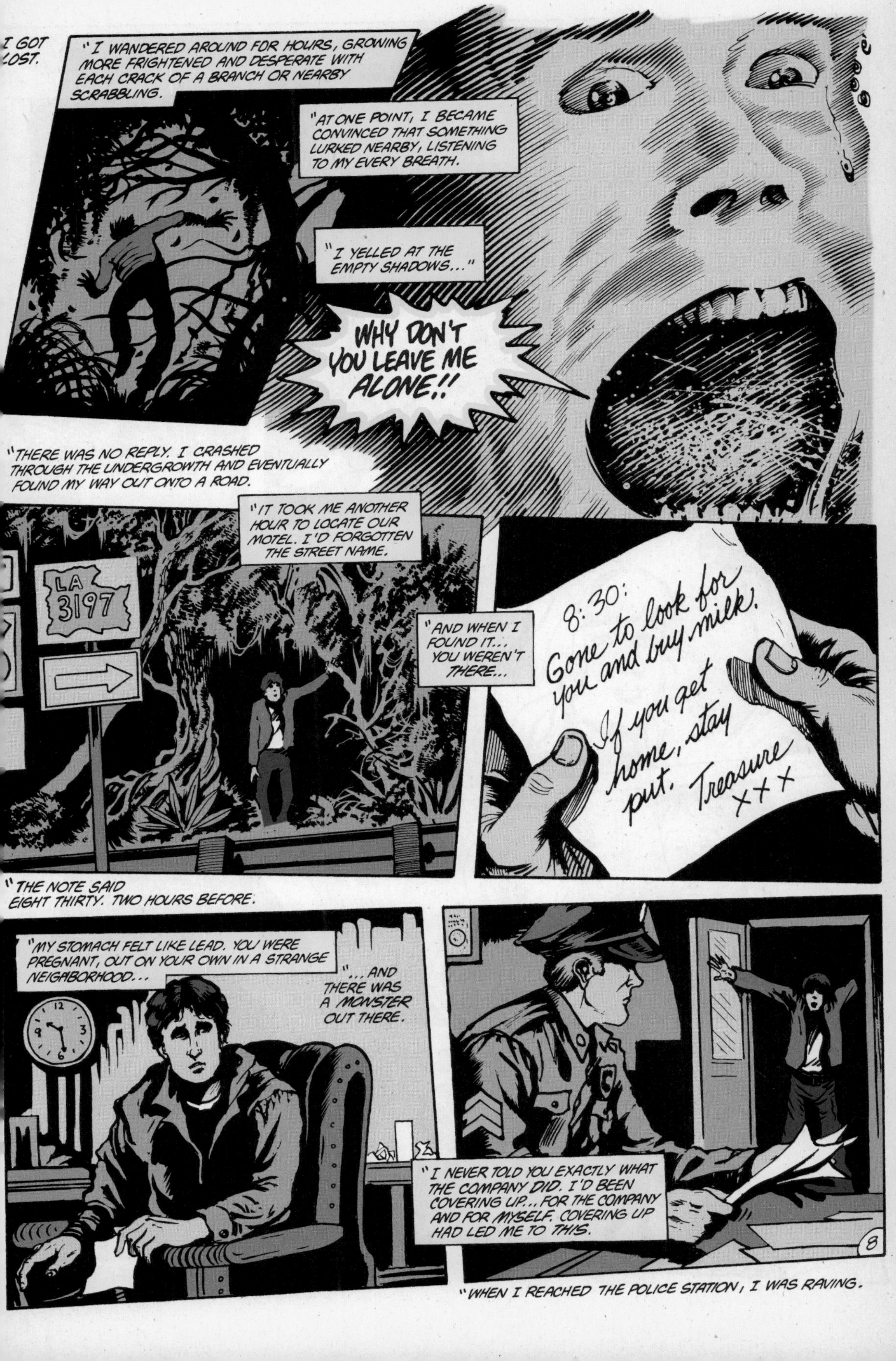
I GOT LOST.
"I WANDERED AROUND FOR HOURS, GROWING MORE FRIGHTENED AND DESPERATE WITH EACH CRACK OF A BRANCH OR NEARBY SCRABBLING.
"AT ONE POINT, I BECAME CONVINCED THAT SOMETHING LURKED NEARBY, LISTENING TO MY EVERY BREATH.
"I YELLED AT THE EMPTY SHADOWS..."
WHY DON'T YOU LEAVE ME ALONE!!
"THERE WAS NO REPLY. I CRASHED THROUGH THE UNDERGROWTH AND EVENTUALLY FOUND MY WAY OUT ONTO A ROAD.
"IT TOOK ME ANOTHER HOUR TO LOCATE OUR MOTEL. I'D FORGOTTEN THE STREET NAME.
LA 3197
"AND WHEN I FOUND IT... YOU WEREN'T THERE...
8:30: Gone to look for you and buy milk. If you get home, stay put. Treasure xxx
"THE NOTE SAID EIGHT THIRTY. TWO HOURS BEFORE.
"MY STOMACH FELT LIKE LEAD. YOU WERE PREGNANT, OUT ON YOUR OWN IN A STRANGE NEIGHBORHOOD...
"...AND THERE WAS A MONSTER OUT THERE.
"I NEVER TOLD YOU EXACTLY WHAT THE COMPANY DID. I'D BEEN COVERING UP... FOR THE COMPANY AND FOR MYSELF. COVERING UP HAD LED ME TO THIS.
8
"WHEN I REACHED THE POLICE STATION, I WAS RAVING.

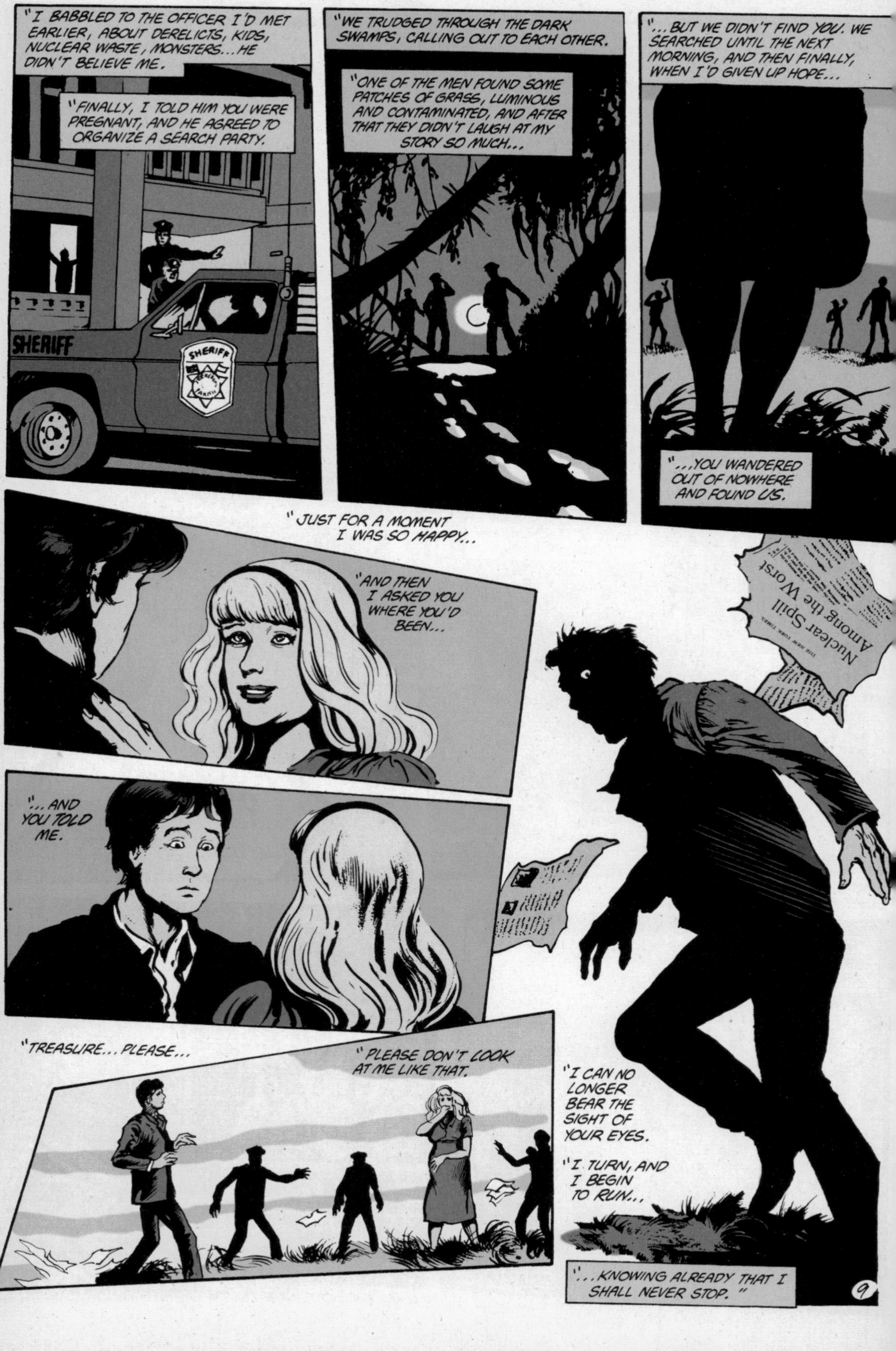
"I BABBLED TO THE OFFICER I'D MET EARLIER, ABOUT DERELICTS, KIDS, NUCLEAR WASTE, MONSTERS... HE DIDN'T BELIEVE ME.
"FINALLY, I TOLD HIM YOU WERE PREGNANT, AND HE AGREED TO ORGANIZE A SEARCH PARTY.
SHERIFF
SHERIFF
"WE TRUDGED THROUGH THE DARK SWAMPS, CALLING OUT TO EACH OTHER.
"ONE OF THE MEN FOUND SOME PATCHES OF GRASS, LUMINOUS AND CONTAMINATED, AND AFTER THAT THEY DIDN'T LAUGH AT MY STORY SO MUCH...
"...BUT WE DIDN'T FIND YOU. WE SEARCHED UNTIL THE NEXT MORNING, AND THEN FINALLY, WHEN I'D GIVEN UP HOPE...
"...YOU WANDERED OUT OF NOWHERE AND FOUND US.
"JUST FOR A MOMENT I WAS SO HAPPY...
"AND THEN I ASKED YOU WHERE YOU'D BEEN...
Nuclear Spill Among the Worst
"...AND YOU TOLD ME.
"TREASURE... PLEASE...
"PLEASE DON'T LOOK AT ME LIKE THAT.
"I CAN NO LONGER BEAR THE SIGHT OF YOUR EYES.
"I TURN, AND I BEGIN TO RUN...
"...KNOWING ALREADY THAT I SHALL NEVER STOP."
9

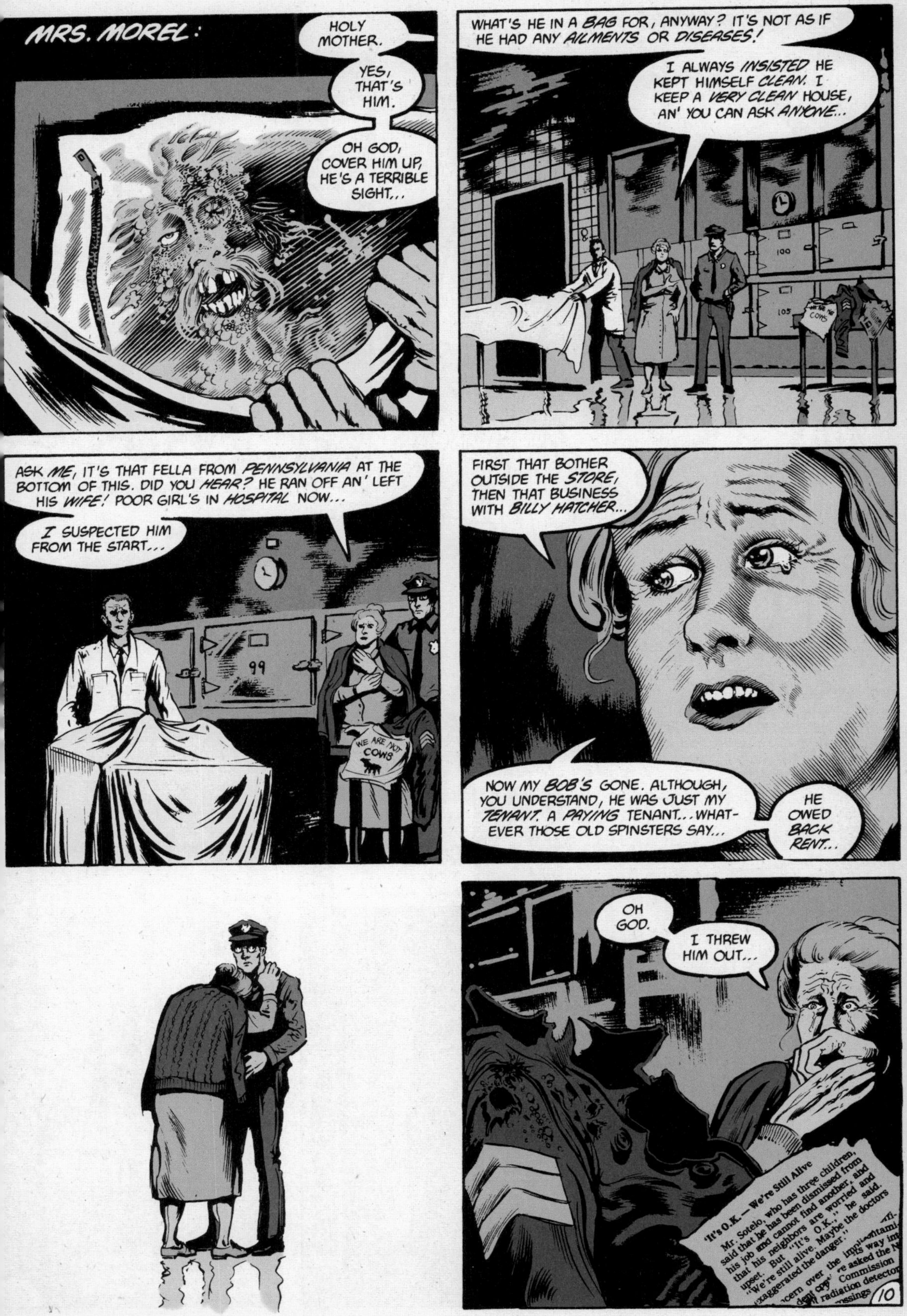
MRS. MOREL:
HOLY MOTHER.
YES, THAT'S HIM.
OH GOD, COVER HIM UP, HE'S A TERRIBLE SIGHT...
WHAT'S HE IN A BAG FOR, ANYWAY? IT'S NOT AS IF HE HAD ANY AILMENTS OR DISEASES!
I ALWAYS INSISTED HE KEPT HIMSELF CLEAN. I KEEP A VERY CLEAN HOUSE, AN' YOU CAN ASK ANYONE...
ASK ME, IT'S THAT FELLA FROM PENNSYLVANIA AT THE BOTTOM OF THIS. DID YOU HEAR? HE RAN OFF AN' LEFT HIS WIFE! POOR GIRL'S IN HOSPITAL NOW...
I SUSPECTED HIM FROM THE START...
99
WE ARE NOT COWS
FIRST THAT BOTHER OUTSIDE THE STORE, THEN THAT BUSINESS WITH BILLY HATCHER...
NOW MY BOB'S GONE. ALTHOUGH, YOU UNDERSTAND, HE WAS JUST MY TENANT. A PAYING TENANT... WHATEVER THOSE OLD SPINSTERS SAY...
HE OWED BACK RENT...
OH GOD.
I THREW HIM OUT...
'It's O.K. — We're Still Alive
10

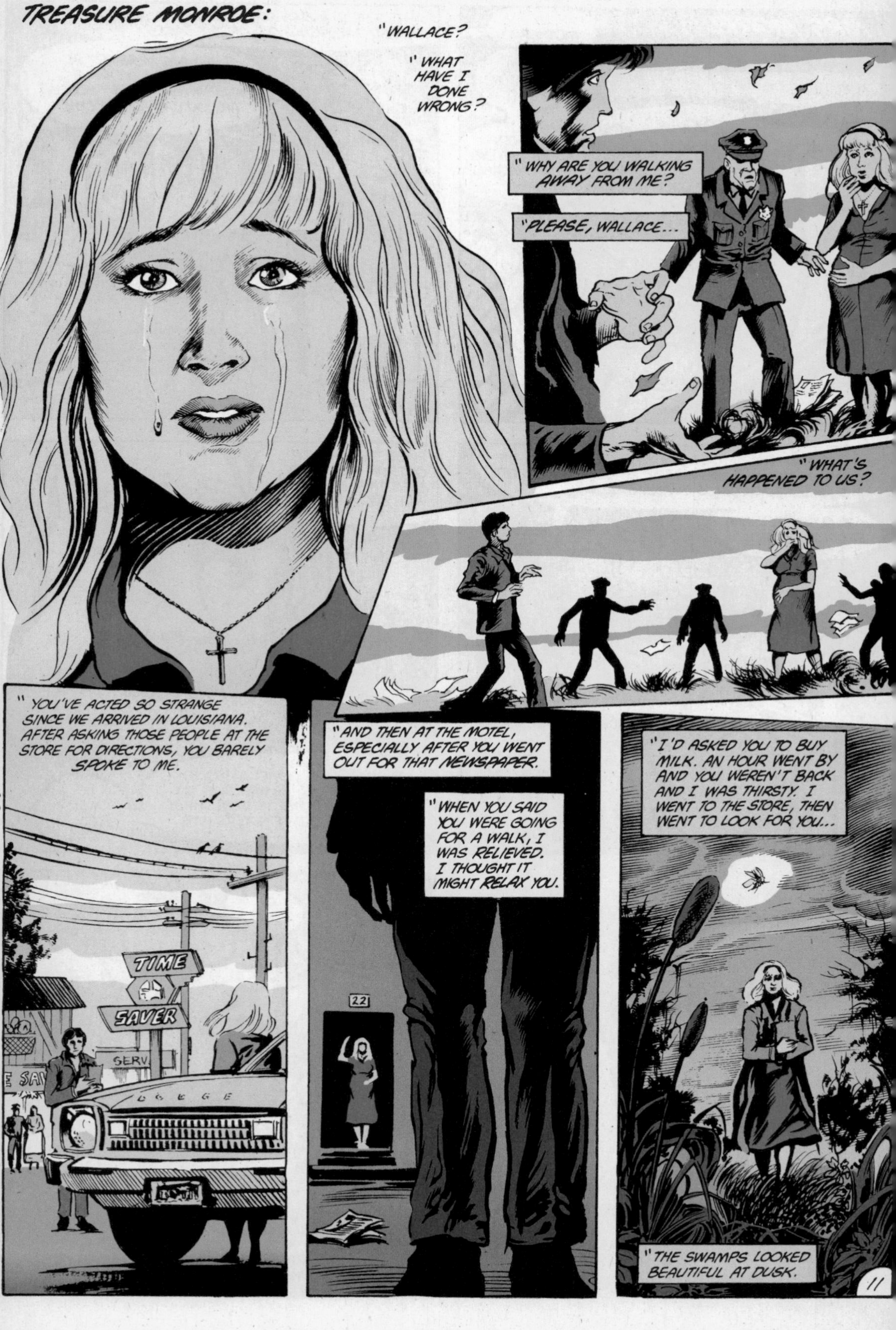
TREASURE MONROE:
"WALLACE?
"WHAT HAVE I DONE WRONG?
"WHY ARE YOU WALKING AWAY FROM ME?
"PLEASE, WALLACE...
"WHAT'S HAPPENED TO US?
"YOU'VE ACTED SO STRANGE SINCE WE ARRIVED IN LOUISIANA. AFTER ASKING THOSE PEOPLE AT THE STORE FOR DIRECTIONS, YOU BARELY SPOKE TO ME.
TIME
SAVER
SERV
"AND THEN AT THE MOTEL, ESPECIALLY AFTER YOU WENT OUT FOR THAT NEWSPAPER.
"WHEN YOU SAID YOU WERE GOING FOR A WALK, I WAS RELIEVED. I THOUGHT IT MIGHT RELAX YOU.
22
"I'D ASKED YOU TO BUY MILK. AN HOUR WENT BY AND YOU WEREN'T BACK AND I WAS THIRSTY. I WENT TO THE STORE, THEN WENT TO LOOK FOR YOU...
"THE SWAMPS LOOKED BEAUTIFUL AT DUSK.
11

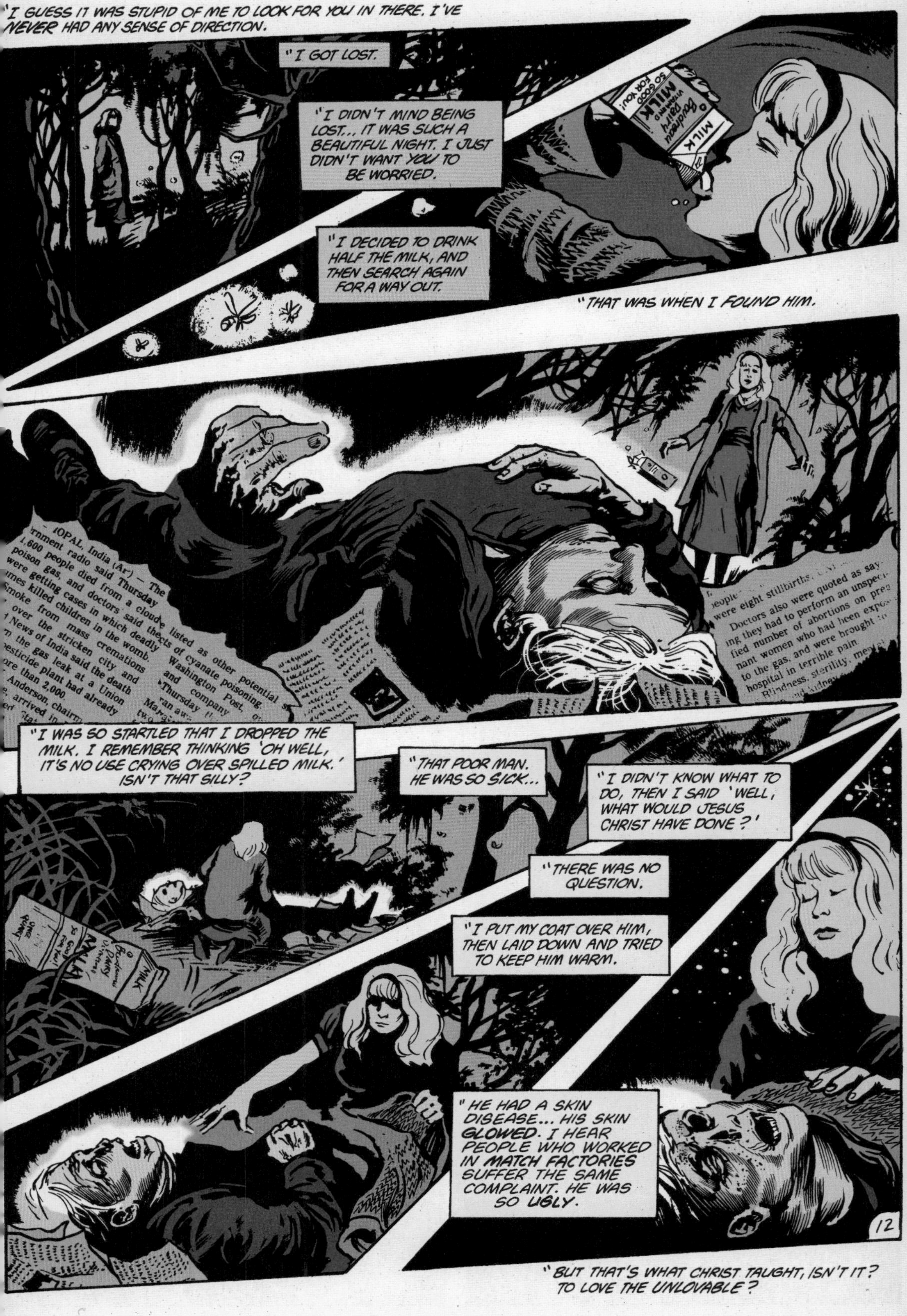
"I GUESS IT WAS STUPID OF ME TO LOOK FOR YOU IN THERE. I'VE NEVER HAD ANY SENSE OF DIRECTION.
"I GOT LOST.
"I DIDN'T MIND BEING LOST... IT WAS SUCH A BEAUTIFUL NIGHT. I JUST DIDN'T WANT YOU TO BE WORRIED.
"I DECIDED TO DRINK HALF THE MILK, AND THEN SEARCH AGAIN FOR A WAY OUT.
"THAT WAS WHEN I FOUND HIM.
"I WAS SO STARTLED THAT I DROPPED THE MILK. I REMEMBER THINKING 'OH WELL, IT'S NO USE CRYING OVER SPILLED MILK.' ISN'T THAT SILLY?
"THAT POOR MAN. HE WAS SO SICK...
"I DIDN'T KNOW WHAT TO DO, THEN I SAID 'WELL, WHAT WOULD JESUS CHRIST HAVE DONE?'
"THERE WAS NO QUESTION.
"I PUT MY COAT OVER HIM, THEN LAID DOWN AND TRIED TO KEEP HIM WARM.
"HE HAD A SKIN DISEASE... HIS SKIN GLOWED. I HEAR PEOPLE WHO WORKED IN MATCH FACTORIES SUFFER THE SAME COMPLAINT. HE WAS SO UGLY.
12
"BUT THAT'S WHAT CHRIST TAUGHT, ISN'T IT? TO LOVE THE UNLOVABLE?

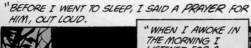

"BEFORE I WENT TO SLEEP, I SAID A *PRAYER* FOR HIM, OUT LOUD.

"WHEN I AWOKE IN THE MORNING I LISTENED FOR A HEARTBEAT, BUT I'M CERTAIN HE WAS DEAD.

" *IN DAYLIGHT, IT WAS EASY TO FIND MY WAY OUT OF THE SWAMP.*

"I RAN STRAIGHT INTO YOU, AND ALL OF THESE *POLICEMEN...*

"YOU LOOKED SO HAPPY TO SEE ME, AND THEN YOU ASKED WHERE I'D BEEN...

"I TOLD YOU ABOUT THE *TRAMP,* AND IT WAS AS IF EVERYTHING TURNED COLD ALL OF A SUDDEN..."

Y-YOU LAY *NEXT* TO HIM? ALL NIGHT? AND HE WAS *GLOWING?*

YES... HE WAS *ILL.* WALLACE, WHAT'S *WRONG?*

OH JEEZ... THOSE *FOOTPRINTS* WE FOUND...

NOTHING. NOTHING'S WRONG.

YOU...YOU JUST STAY THERE, *TREASURE.* EVERYTHING'S OKAY. WE'LL FIND A DOCTOR...

DOCTOR? WALLACE... WALLACE, I DON'T UNDERSTAND...

WUH-WHAT'S WRONG WITH EVERYBODY? I HAVEN'T DONE ANYTHING.

WHY WON'T ANYBODY COME NUH-NEAR ME?

13

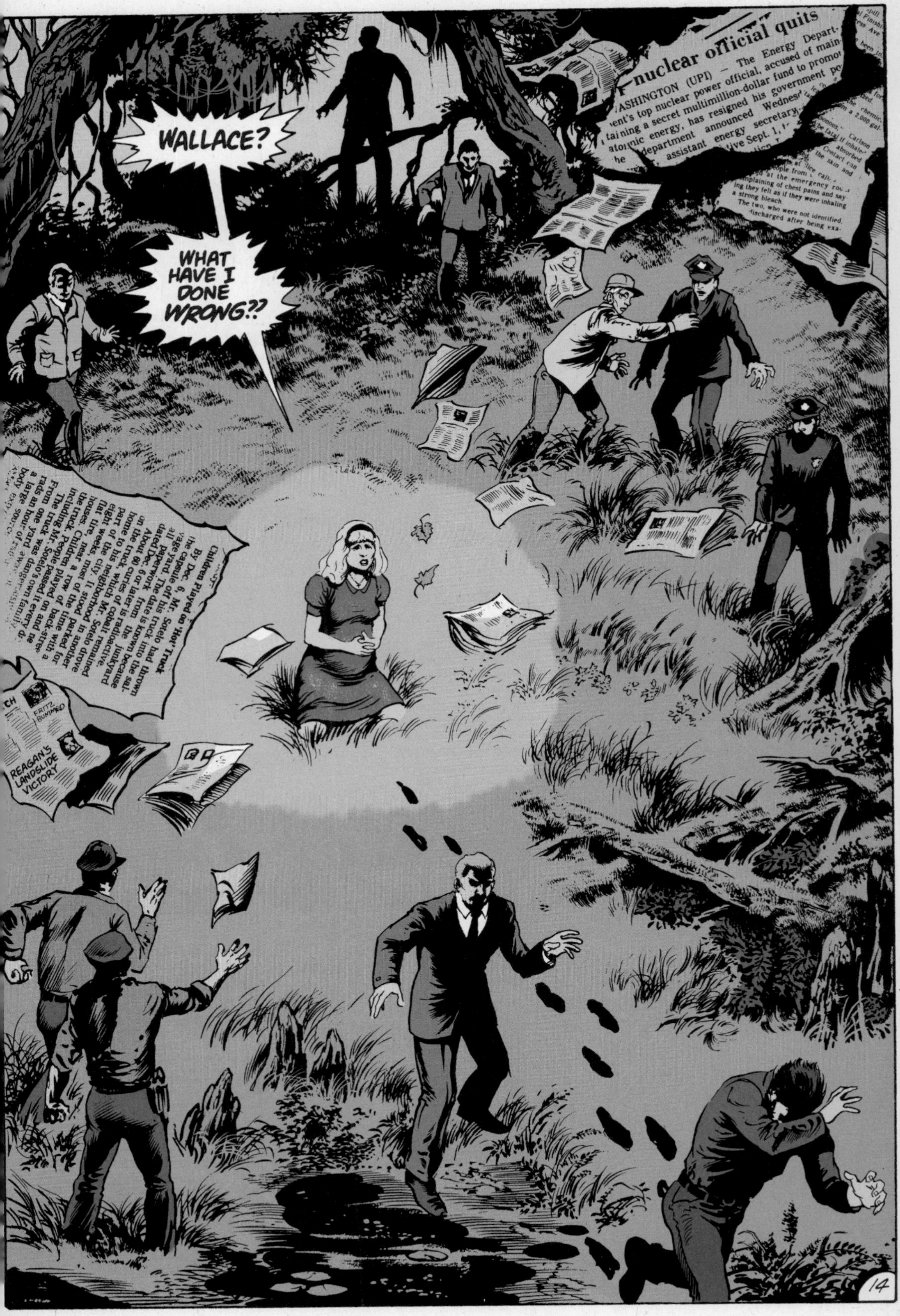
WALLACE?
WHAT HAVE I DONE WRONG??
nuclear official quits
Children Played on 'Hot' Truck
FRITZ BUMMED
REAGAN'S LANDSLIDE VICTORY
14

BILLY HATCHER:

LISTEN, PAY NO ATTENTION TO WHAT *EDDIE* SAID. THAT GUY CAN BE A REAL *HOMO* AT TIMES.

THIS IS WHAT *REALLY* HAPPENED, AN' YOU CAN CUT MY BLEEDIN' HEART OUT IF I TELL A LIE...

"*FIRST THING YESTERDAY MORNING, RIGHT, I'D BEEN FISHIN' OUT IN THE SWAMPS, I SEES THIS GUY.*

"*HE'S A REAL MUTANT, Y'KNOW? ZITS, AND BITS O' STUFF FALLIN' OFF HIS FACE AN' EVERYTHIN'...*

Uranium Shipment

"*I YELL 'NUKEFACE' AT HIM, 'CAUSE, LIKE, THAT WAS THE NAME I THOUGHT UP, AN' THEN I SPLIT.*

"*THAT'S WHAT GAVE ME THE IDEA FOR THIS MASK, SEE?*

"*ANYWAY, LATER, WHEN WE WAS PLAYIN'... YOU WERE THERE, PINTO... THIS CRAZY GUY COMES UP AN' STARTS SHOUTIN' AT US.*

"*'THIS ISN'T PENNSYLVANIA! THOSE DUMPS WERE SAFE!' ALL KINDA CRAZY STUFF...*

"*WE BEAT IT.*"

LATER, *MIKE BERNHARDT'S* BROTHER TOLD ME THE REST...

THIS *MONROE*, THE *CRAZY GUY*, HE LEFT TOWN. IT'S BECAUSE HIS *WIFE* WENT OUT WITH *NUKEFACE*, Y'KNOW, IN THE *WOODS*, AN' NOW SHE'S GONNA HAVE A *SCREWED-UP BABY!*

THIS *WOMAN*, MONROE'S WIFE, WHO'S IN *HOSPITAL* NOW, SHE SAYS THAT WHEN SHE LEFT OL' NUKEFACE, THERE IN THE SWAMPS, HE WAS *DEAD...*

BUT *JOEY* BERNHARDT SAYS HIS BROTHER AIN'T FOUND THE *BODY* YET...

Uranium Shipment We
BERNSTEIN
New York Times
— A French carg...
...he coast of Belgium
...was carrying contain-
...filled with a form of uranium used
...make fuel for nuclear reactors, the
...ip's owner and French Government
...ficials said tonight.
An official in the French Ministry of
...e Environment, Jean-Claude Roure,
...aid an investigation carried out by
French maritime officials near the
wreck revealed "no trace of radioactivity in the area," indicating the containers had not broken during the colli-
sion.
Guy I...
State...

...collected fro...
leakage."
The owner...
Louis, which...
near Ostend...
carrying 450...
ride, a mildly...
is an interm...
duction of r...
used in the m...

OFF AND RUN
Official Spectat...
Marathon is the...
...plement. Run...
...ation, call...

Ron...gan
...resident flie...
...hits R...
...astand...

...SO WHO KNOWS?   15

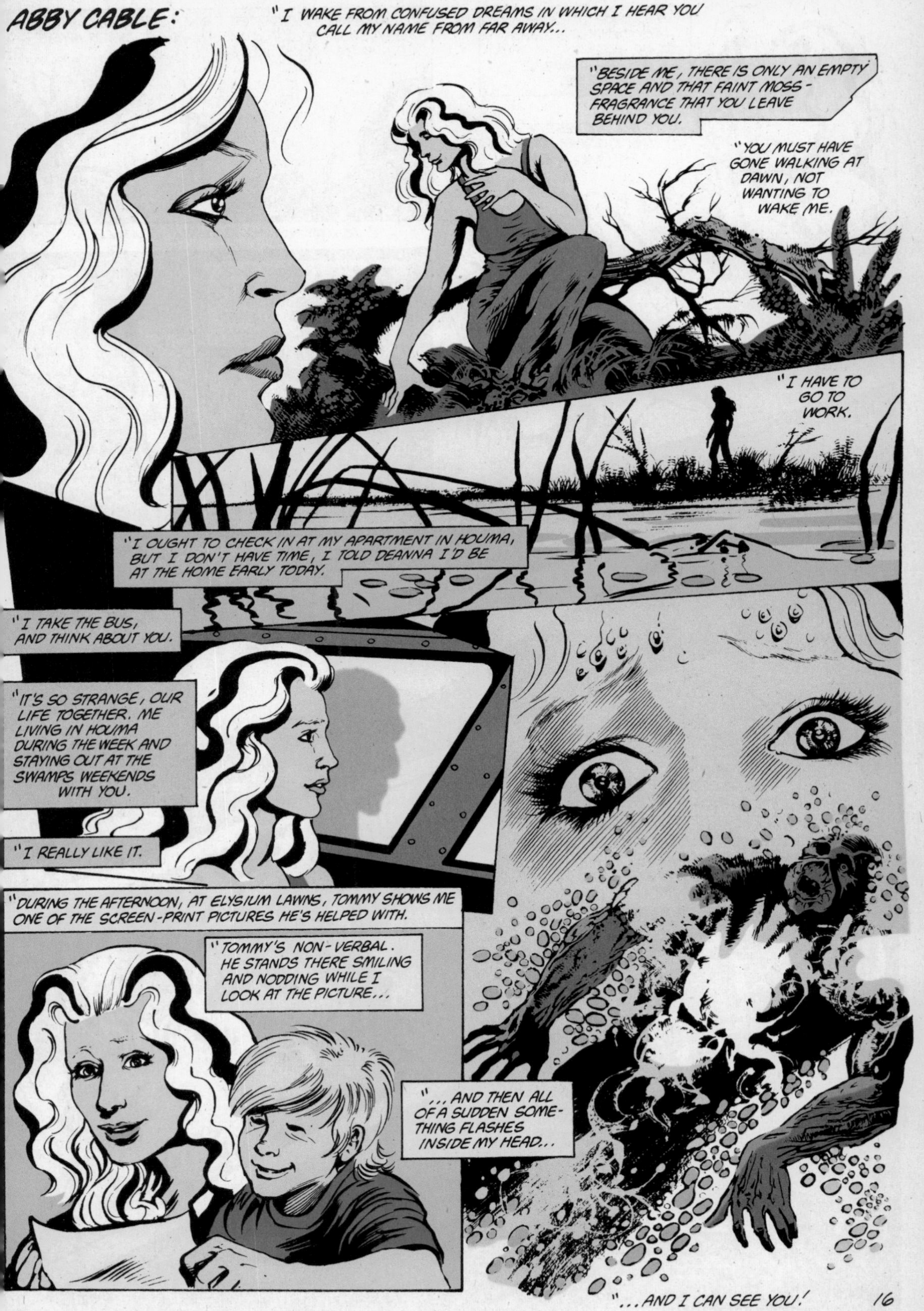
ABBY CABLE:
"I WAKE FROM CONFUSED DREAMS IN WHICH I HEAR YOU CALL MY NAME FROM FAR AWAY...
"BESIDE ME, THERE IS ONLY AN EMPTY SPACE AND THAT FAINT MOSS-FRAGRANCE THAT YOU LEAVE BEHIND YOU.
"YOU MUST HAVE GONE WALKING AT DAWN, NOT WANTING TO WAKE ME.
"I HAVE TO GO TO WORK.
"I OUGHT TO CHECK IN AT MY APARTMENT IN HOUMA, BUT I DON'T HAVE TIME, I TOLD DEANNA I'D BE AT THE HOME EARLY TODAY.
"I TAKE THE BUS, AND THINK ABOUT YOU.
"IT'S SO STRANGE, OUR LIFE TOGETHER. ME LIVING IN HOUMA DURING THE WEEK AND STAYING OUT AT THE SWAMPS WEEKENDS WITH YOU.
"I REALLY LIKE IT.
"DURING THE AFTERNOON, AT ELYSIUM LAWNS, TOMMY SHOWS ME ONE OF THE SCREEN-PRINT PICTURES HE'S HELPED WITH.
"TOMMY'S NON-VERBAL. HE STANDS THERE SMILING AND NODDING WHILE I LOOK AT THE PICTURE...
"...AND THEN ALL OF A SUDDEN SOMETHING FLASHES INSIDE MY HEAD...
"...AND I CAN SEE YOU!
16

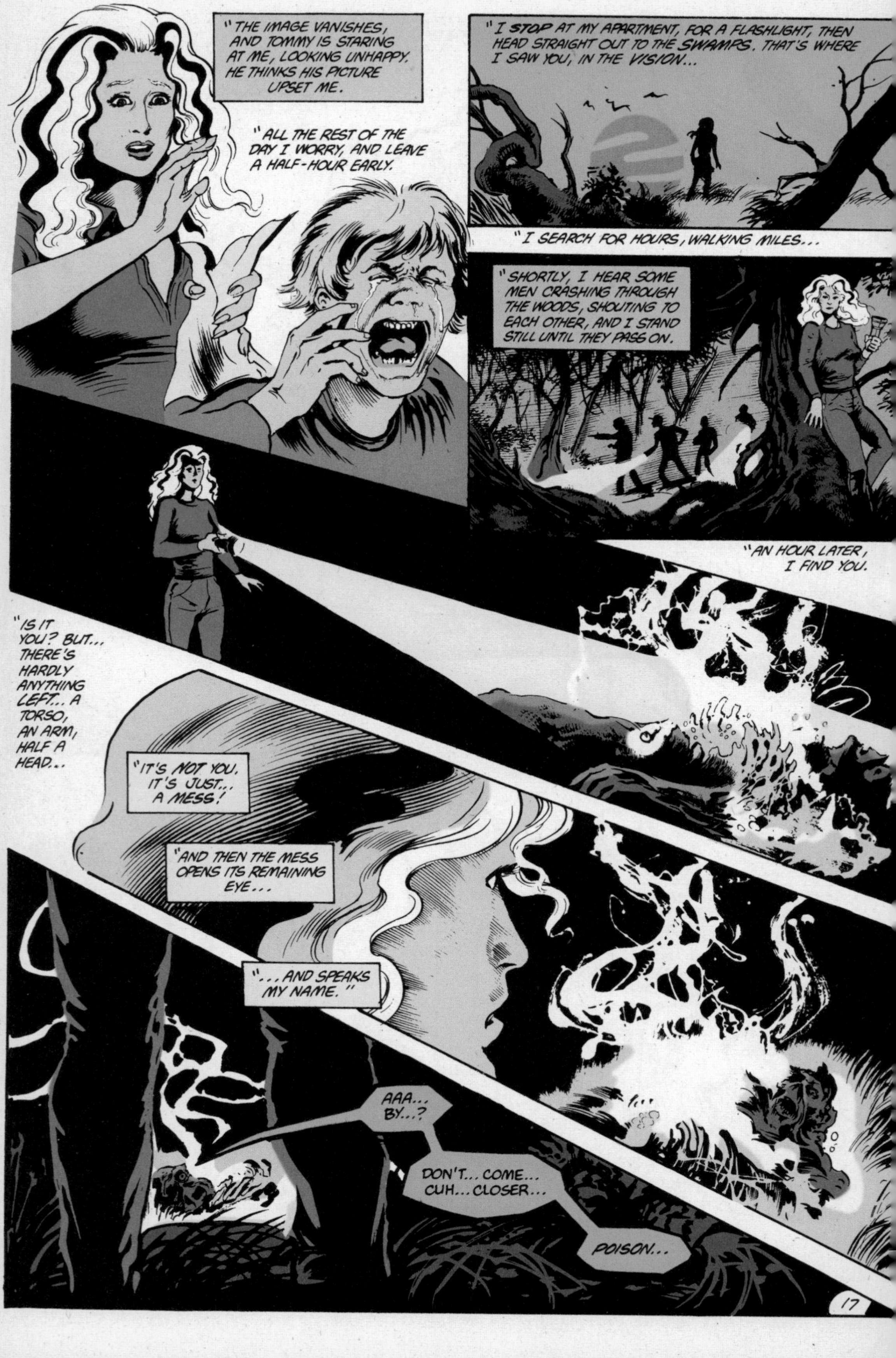
"THE IMAGE VANISHES, AND TOMMY IS STARING AT ME, LOOKING UNHAPPY. HE THINKS HIS PICTURE UPSET ME.
"ALL THE REST OF THE DAY I WORRY, AND LEAVE A HALF-HOUR EARLY.
"I STOP AT MY APARTMENT, FOR A FLASHLIGHT, THEN HEAD STRAIGHT OUT TO THE SWAMPS. THAT'S WHERE I SAW YOU, IN THE VISION...
"I SEARCH FOR HOURS, WALKING MILES...
"SHORTLY, I HEAR SOME MEN CRASHING THROUGH THE WOODS, SHOUTING TO EACH OTHER, AND I STAND STILL UNTIL THEY PASS ON.
"AN HOUR LATER, I FIND YOU.
"IS IT YOU? BUT... THERE'S HARDLY ANYTHING LEFT... A TORSO, AN ARM, HALF A HEAD...
"IT'S NOT YOU. IT'S JUST... A MESS!
"AND THEN THE MESS OPENS ITS REMAINING EYE...
"...AND SPEAKS MY NAME."
AAA... BY...?
DON'T... COME... CUH... CLOSER...
POISON...
17

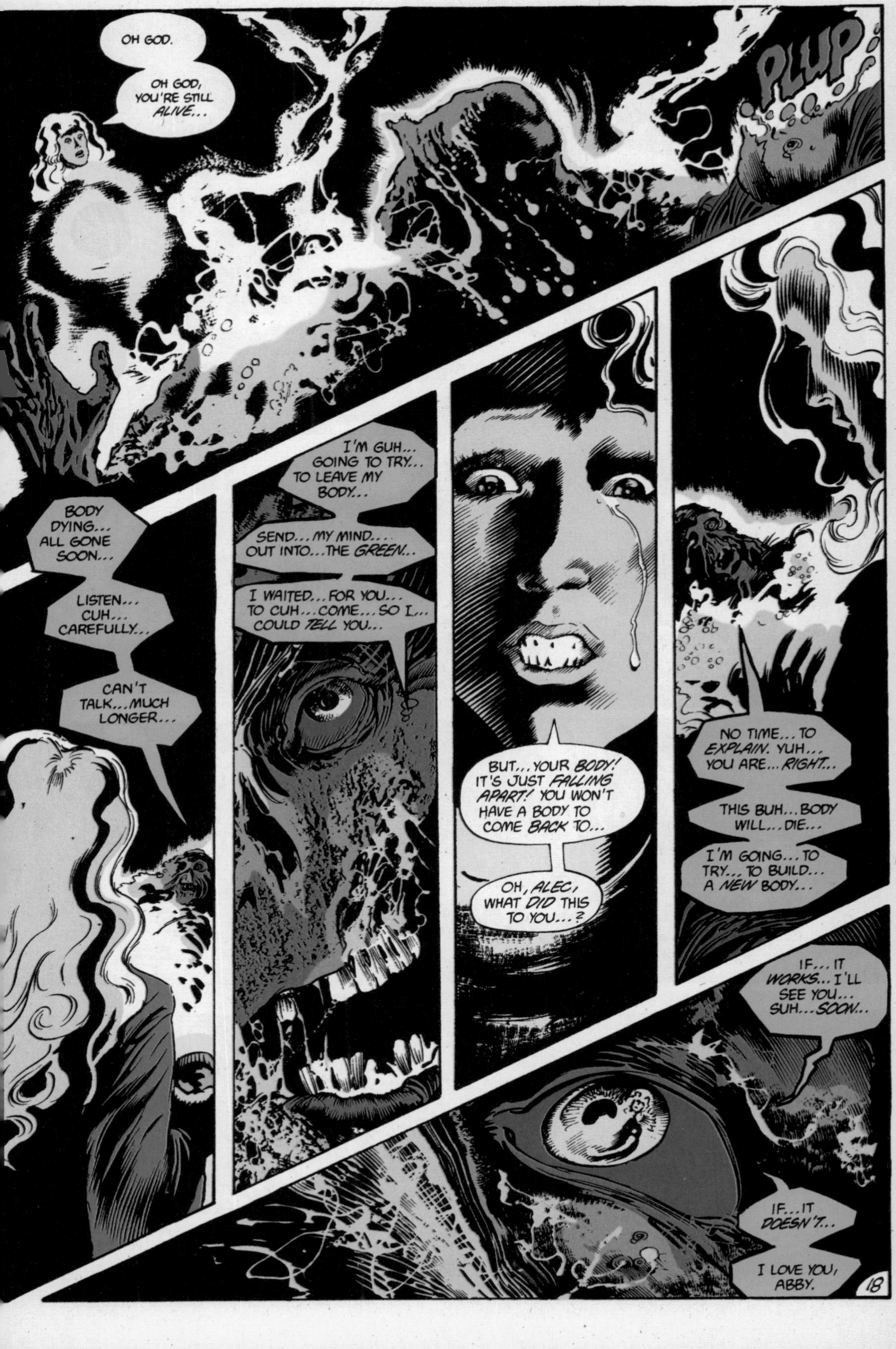
OH GOD.
OH GOD, YOU'RE STILL ALIVE...
PLUP
BODY DYING... ALL GONE SOON...
LISTEN... CUH... CAREFULLY...
CAN'T TALK... MUCH LONGER...
I'M GUH... GOING TO TRY... TO LEAVE MY BODY...
SEND... MY MIND... OUT INTO... THE GREEN...
I WAITED... FOR YOU... TO CUH... COME... SO I... COULD TELL YOU...
BUT... YOUR BODY! IT'S JUST FALLING APART! YOU WON'T HAVE A BODY TO COME BACK TO...
OH, ALEC, WHAT DID THIS TO YOU...?
NO TIME... TO EXPLAIN. YUH... YOU ARE... RIGHT...
THIS BUH... BODY WILL... DIE...
I'M GOING... TO TRY... TO BUILD... A NEW BODY...
IF... IT WORKS... I'LL SEE YOU... SUH... SOON...
IF... IT DOESN'T...
I LOVE YOU, ABBY.
18

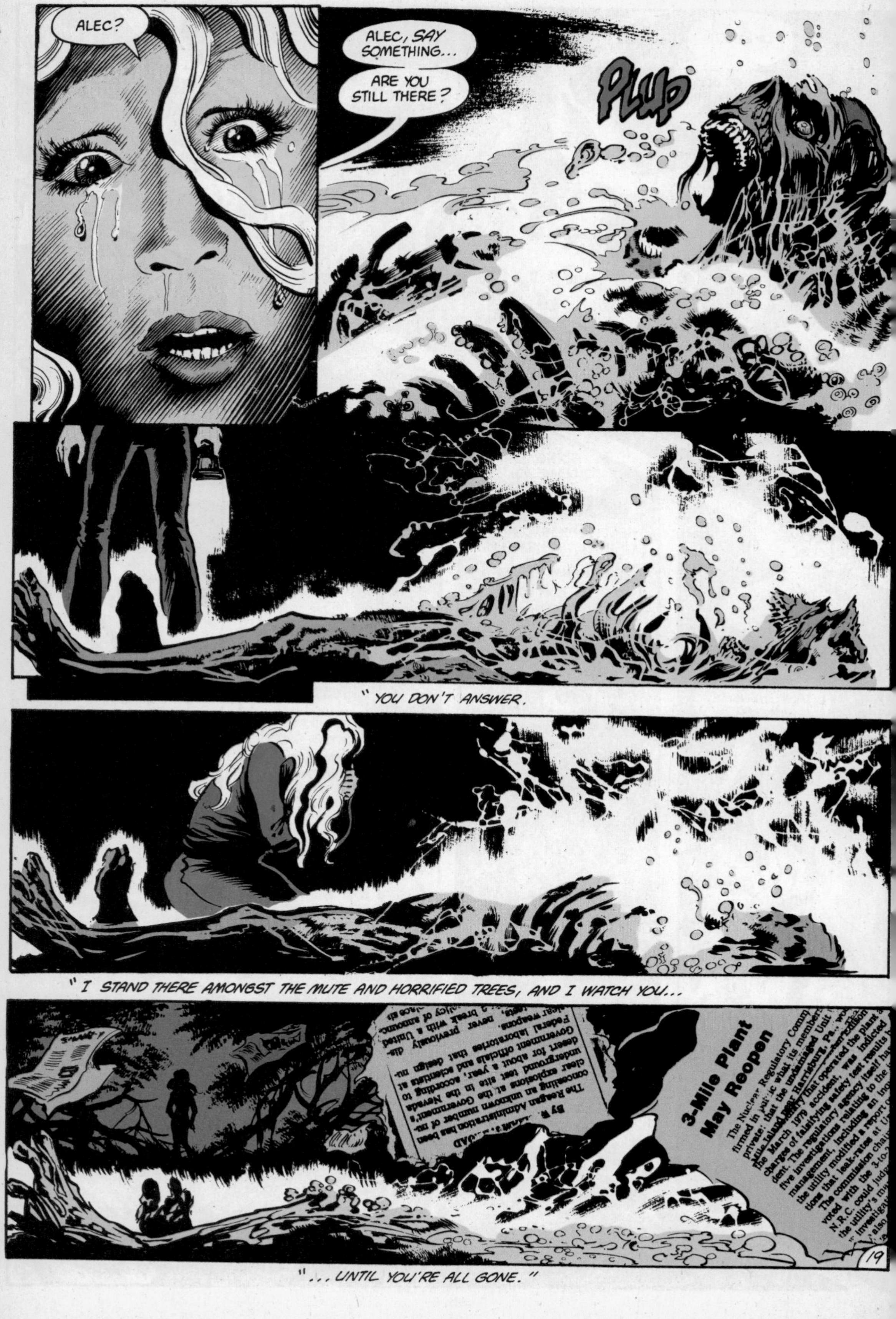
ALEC?
ALEC, SAY SOMETHING...
ARE YOU STILL THERE?
PLUP
"YOU DON'T ANSWER.
"I STAND THERE AMONGST THE MUTE AND HORRIFIED TREES, AND I WATCH YOU...
3-Mile Plant May Reopen
"...UNTIL YOU'RE ALL GONE."

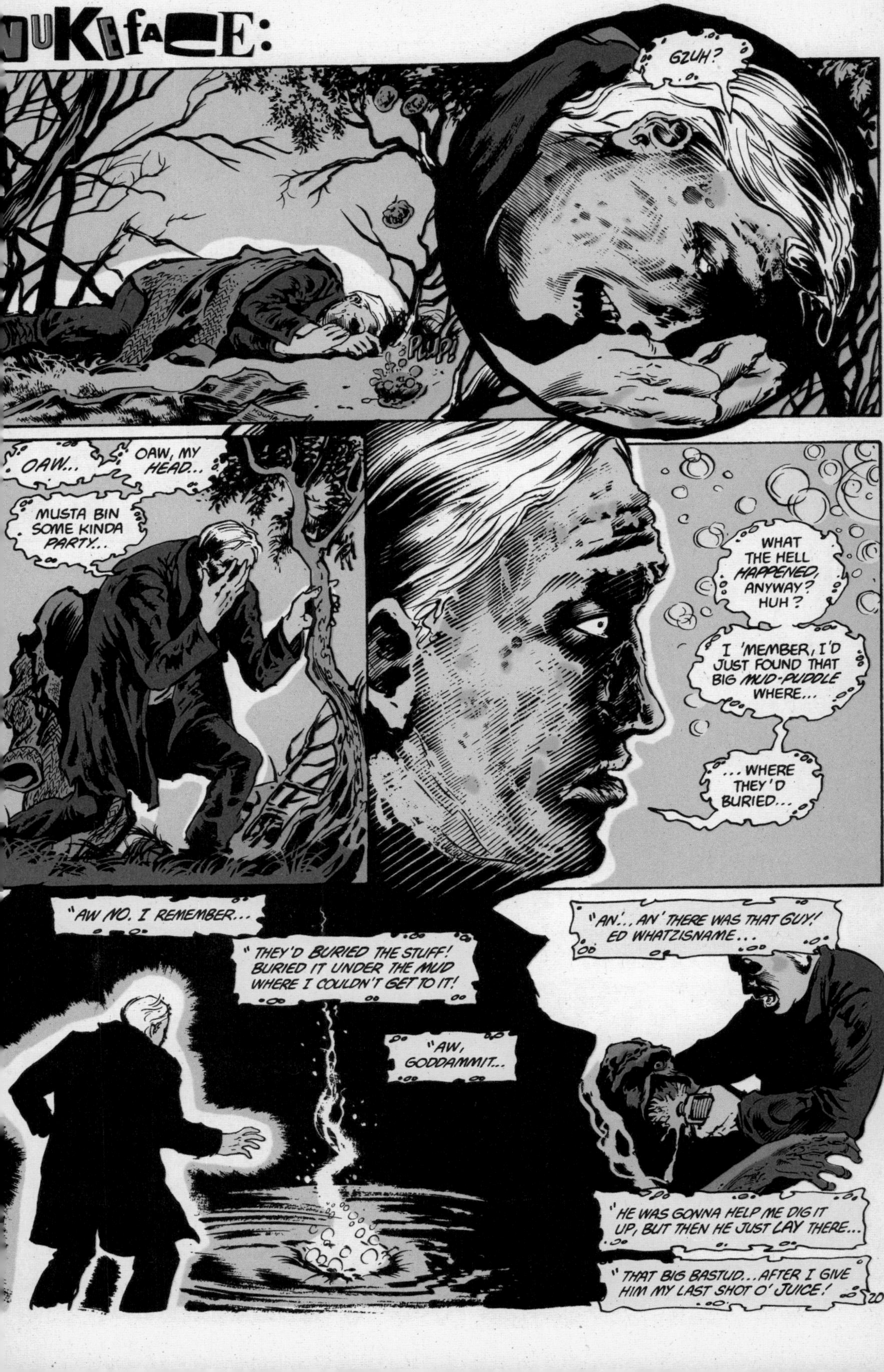
NUKEFACE:
GZUH?
PLUP!
OAW...
OAW, MY HEAD...
MUSTA BIN SOME KINDA PARTY...
WHAT THE HELL HAPPENED, ANYWAY? HUH?
I 'MEMBER, I'D JUST FOUND THAT BIG MUD-PUDDLE WHERE...
...WHERE THEY'D BURIED...
"AW NO. I REMEMBER...
"THEY'D BURIED THE STUFF! BURIED IT UNDER THE MUD WHERE I COULDN'T GET TO IT!
"AW, GODDAMMIT...
"AN'... AN' THERE WAS THAT GUY! ED WHATZISNAME...
"HE WAS GONNA HELP ME DIG IT UP, BUT THEN HE JUST LAY THERE...
"THAT BIG BASTUD... AFTER I GIVE HIM MY LAST SHOT O' JUICE!
20

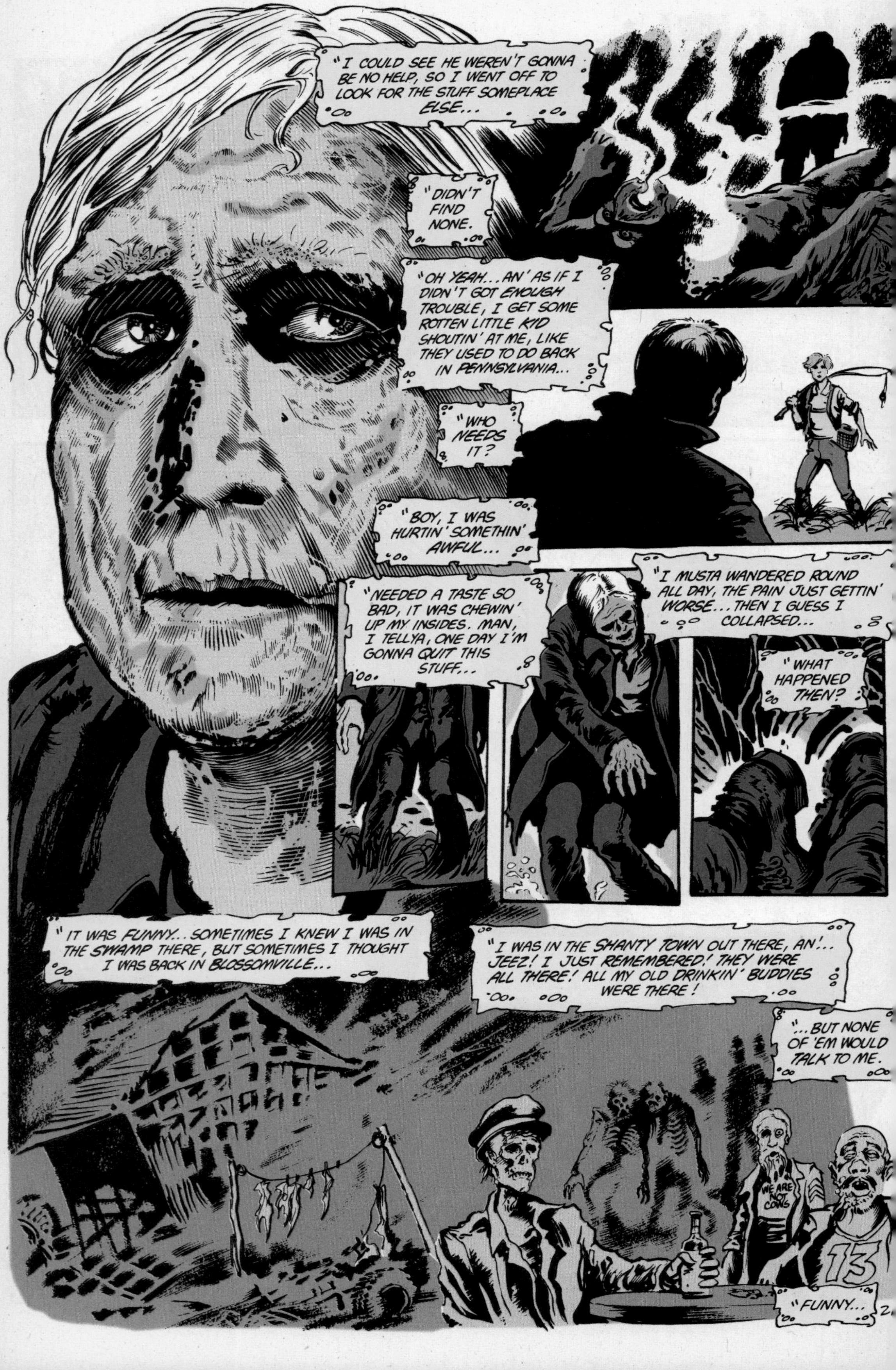
"I COULD SEE HE WEREN'T GONNA BE NO HELP, SO I WENT OFF TO LOOK FOR THE STUFF SOMEPLACE ELSE...
"DIDN'T FIND NONE.
"OH YEAH... AN' AS IF I DIDN'T GOT ENOUGH TROUBLE, I GET SOME ROTTEN LITTLE KID SHOUTIN' AT ME, LIKE THEY USED TO DO BACK IN PENNSYLVANIA...
"WHO NEEDS IT?
"BOY, I WAS HURTIN' SOMETHIN' AWFUL...
"NEEDED A TASTE SO BAD, IT WAS CHEWIN' UP MY INSIDES. MAN, I TELLYA, ONE DAY I'M GONNA QUIT THIS STUFF...
"I MUSTA WANDERED ROUND ALL DAY, THE PAIN JUST GETTIN' WORSE... THEN I GUESS I COLLAPSED...
"WHAT HAPPENED THEN?
"IT WAS FUNNY... SOMETIMES I KNEW I WAS IN THE SWAMP THERE, BUT SOMETIMES I THOUGHT I WAS BACK IN BLOSSOMVILLE...
"I WAS IN THE SHANTY TOWN OUT THERE, AN'... JEEZ! I JUST REMEMBERED! THEY WERE ALL THERE! ALL MY OLD DRINKIN' BUDDIES WERE THERE!
"...BUT NONE OF 'EM WOULD TALK TO ME.
WE ARE NOT COWS
13
"FUNNY...

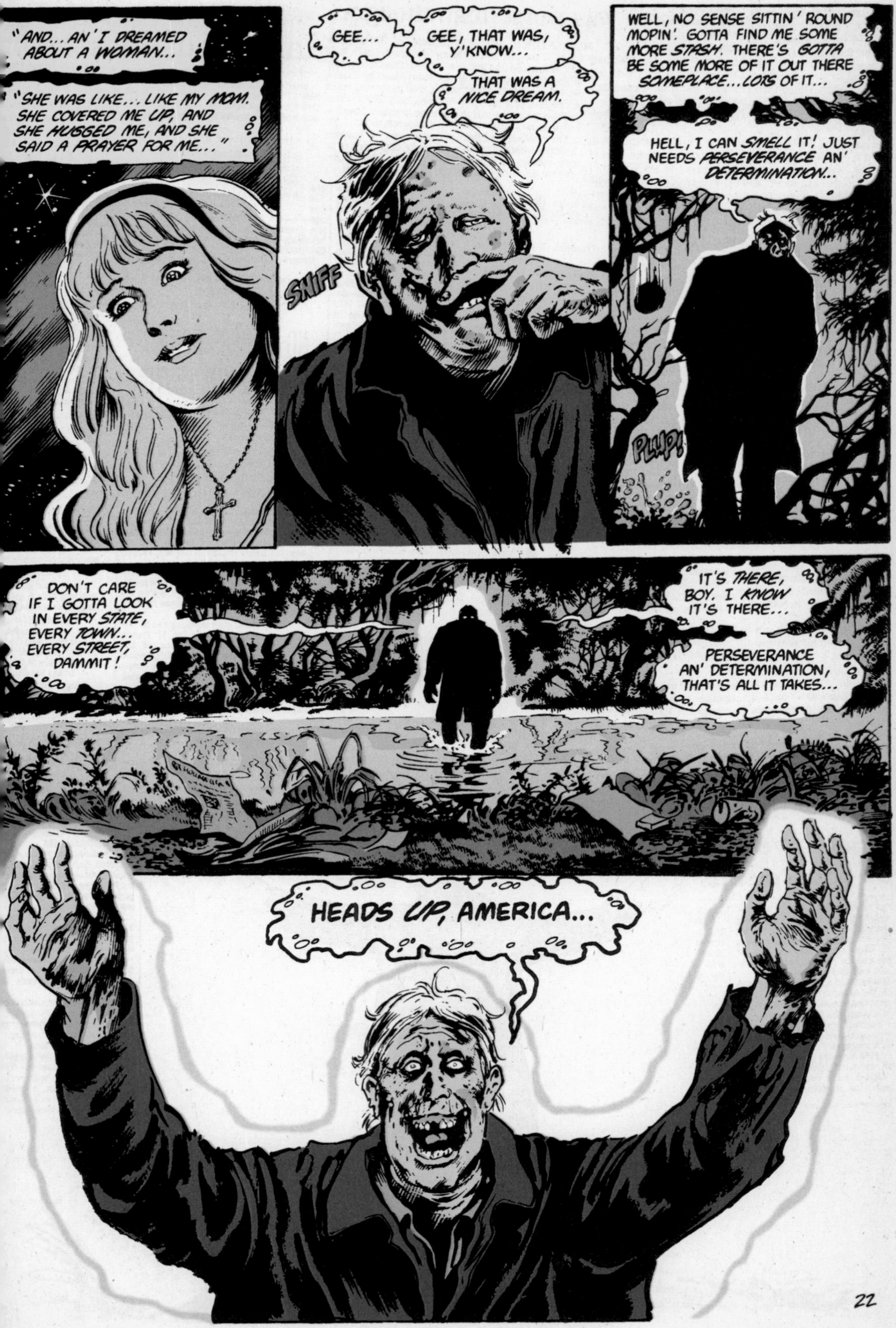
"AND... AN' I DREAMED ABOUT A WOMAN...
"SHE WAS LIKE... LIKE MY MOM. SHE COVERED ME UP, AND SHE HUGGED ME, AND SHE SAID A PRAYER FOR ME..."
GEE...
GEE, THAT WAS, Y'KNOW...
THAT WAS A NICE DREAM.
SNIFF
WELL, NO SENSE SITTIN' ROUND MOPIN'. GOTTA FIND ME SOME MORE STASH. THERE'S GOTTA BE SOME MORE OF IT OUT THERE SOMEPLACE... LOTS OF IT...
HELL, I CAN SMELL IT! JUST NEEDS PERSEVERANCE AN' DETERMINATION...
PLUP!
DON'T CARE IF I GOTTA LOOK IN EVERY STATE, EVERY TOWN... EVERY STREET, DAMMIT!
IT'S THERE, BOY. I KNOW IT'S THERE...
PERSEVERANCE AN' DETERMINATION, THAT'S ALL IT TAKES...
HEADS UP, AMERICA...
22

e unexpected that we're to be ready for. And we — that's all," he said.

Near the schools

son not le away y and is no place.

ing the : monit — I'm — for id.

lf ha ld !," l!" McPherson ve a school ought to be a lot more than it is. Yankee says they'll know if : (radiation) gets out. But ad about them finding a e powder on the ground that they didn't at first re it came from.

ly m in Hinsdale th 24 ho two of my brothers, my father, and my son tion. as fr

it in down there because it grounded plug and Lester e past chief of police, said even use it down there at ."

son also thinks Hinsdale fied fast enough when a y serious situation develops nt Yankee. He said Hin-arenti, after is decl reality. as bor emergency drill a: Yankee, an actual alert two months e Vernon plant, he said. on said Hinsdale is notified ne civil d oth two of my aunts. Three of my uncles. And y zo two of my doctors.

Long ld like ons to the msdale ething happens — instead nt Yankee's notifying state New Hampshire, the message to e ters in Cor relaying th Mutual Aid i id notifying F

Southwestern N and Mutual Aid. "We've got ab plant has 15 two of their hired hands, and they're all buried here in Parowan cemetery. The only one left from those farms is Earl Bunn, and now he's got cancer of the spine and prostate.
Glenna Orton, Parowan, Utah

Well, just within a block of my home there's Wil-ford, he had cancer, and his wife Helen died of stomach cancer. Carl across the street died of throat cancer, and Ernie died of it, and his wife has it now. The boy next to them died of leu-kemia, and my sister across the way there, she

Irma Thomas, St. George, Utah

si Verla's dad, and Paul Stewart, and Dan Potter. Y and my husband Kent ...
Jane Bradshaw, Hiko, Nev.

sirens as a system. They are designed to cover the whole d what isn't covered by red by radios. d shut them off. They don't like the tone alert from when the weather comes on. There's nothing we can do about that. my father, my brother-in-law, my son, and

"Eve my husband ... questio have re It seeks to find out information ch iry, my sister, my niece, my aunt, four uncles, mey my sister-in-law, my mother-in-law, my grand- mother, and my wife ...

Elmer Pickett, St. George, Utah ex-plained the situation from Yankee's viewpoint.

"Our options are limited. What we want to do is get the information out to the appropriate state agencies as that by control cts us three m a prepared message that they're familiar with, and then they relay it through the appropriate channels in state. so that the responsible notified

The flashes would come early in the morning when I was teaching in the old two-room school-house. The children would come in and say, "Mrs. Kelsey! Mrs. Kelsey! Did you see that flash this morning? Did you see it?"
Viola Kelsey, New Harmony, Utah

Cruel Cover-Up' on Job Poisons' ictivate their avar said als y

nd funds are made." ng the questions, she said, were timated cost of notification, the ie emotional damage of notifying rs when no solution might be ble and the possibility that work-uld sue their employers. Crooks cited a 1980 pilot program ch the occupational health insti-tempted to notify chemical plant s in Augusta of increased risk of r cancer from exposure to a po-rcinogen, beta-naphthylamine s it make any difference that 's 1980 Augusta pilot notificat m, more than $300 million in claims have reportedly gainst the companies involv

was worse than thought

MIDDLETOWN, Pa. — The core of Three Mile s Unit 2 reactor came closer to melting down than sly estimated during the 1979 accident, a study d Tuesday reported. The new study, done by EG&G, nc. for the federal government, said temperatures in e reached at least 4,800 degrees, only 280 degrees neltdown and the surface of some uranium began to Previous studies put the temperature at 3,500 s. The Nuclear Regulatory Commission on Tuesday leciding whether to force complete upgrading of ar ncy system at Three Mile Island's undamaged before allowing it to restart, possibly next year.

d — not Avenue and Linden ulevard; one was in Queens, the Edgemere landfill these at Beach nnel Drive and 49th Street way, and 34 were in the w York City. yn landfill, which is on the ica Bay, is owned by the k Service and operated by anitation Department. It s and receives 9,000 tons day. In addition, the de-, between 1974 and 1979 several hund red thousand gallons of hazardous wastes were dumped there illegally.

The Queens landfill covers 173 acres and is owned and operated by the Sani-tation Department. It receives about 500 tons of garbage a day. Hazardous wastes were dumped there illegally as well, the environmental department said. In addition, in March 1983, more ums of organic chemicals ried in the dump. s, the department h the highest pri-orny were so designated because they posed "a significant environmental threat." But, it added, they did not pose an immediate health danger.

"If any sites posing health threat are found, these will automatically sume the highest priority," it said.

The list, which was a compilatic sites previously announced indiv ly, came out this week. The de ment reported last week that the c ould

When our daughter Sybil D. contracted leuke-mia, I asked the doctor up in charge of the he-matology clinic in Salt Lake. wasn't it a little bit more than a coincidence that there should be seven cases of leukemia within a hundred yards of our house?
Blaine Johnson, Cedar City, Utah

Hazardous-Waste

gear up" for the cleanup, which it illed "an enormous construction oject" that would tal at least 10 ars and more probably. least 15 to

First you'd see a flash of light, it'd light this whole house up. Then you'd hear the blast, and then you'd see the mushroom. It was really something. We used to let the kids out in their swimsuits to see it.
Roma Lundberg, St. George, Utah

ate Fed fror staue would bear the the cleanup, including site inspections, bringing the total state contribution to $500 million.

However, the amount of money in the

n. The ones who died got off easy. It's the ones wh roup of 68 vr aslived that have it hard.
Vonda McKinney, Holbrook, Ari

NO ILLNESS FOUND IN DIOXIN TESTING

i was a teacher in Panguitch in '51 when the blasting started. One day after a blast it was my turn to take my phys ed class out on the field, and I didn't want to because I'd read about Hiroshima. But the principal told me I had to Later he died of cancer. So did three of my stu-dents. So did the other phys ed teacher.
St. George, Utah

Doct Exp

KIRKWOOD, ct. 17 (AP) Tests on people exposed to dioxin in eastern Missouri showed no "meaning-ful ill-health effects," health officials say, but many residents are still skepti-cal.

Dr. Henry Falk of the Federal Cen- for Disease Control said at a meet-residents Sunday. "We've not e to find any increase in clini-malities."

ies of such meetings at St. Jo-ospital, he and Dr. H. Denny Jr., the co-director of the ave the results of physical ions of 104 people from nd Stout, both near Imperial, 1 Times Beach. Those exam-ineu w e selected from 800 residents who responded to questionnaires cis l.ted by the state health depart an the Centers for Disease Cont Dr. Donnell said that in the

civil d thinks d for a se cross the

waste, is far be t bothers than Verno collected only led, Hinsdale the $10 milli the nuclear fac ld carr dale fro at Y d in an d come ss a sm . They the gas We have not be meaningful ill-health potential exposure to t ested resider Dr. Falk said there statistical difference groups in the rates of ects, infertility, imi ence of headaches or He also said no chlo that is considered an dioxin exposure, was which 33 in

plant in southwest M dioxin, and the plan with waste oil and s control measure in th

Residents Ne

Lin Sproull of Tim officials that a grou longs was not satisfie

A number of dog died this summer, small birds and thing place," she said. "W health study of our c to see we disar

The preliminary f solved the fficol residents and M which have similar cases pe

Worker at Nuclea ed by Water B

RY, Va., Oct. 17 at the Virginia Company's nuclear p hen he was struck by p that turned into stea from a ruptured expo officials said. radioactivity was rele accident Saturday in the p ondary water system, whic some of the water to the un generators, Rodney Smith, man for the utility, said.

The expansion joint rupt Wayne C. Jones, 23 years ol ton, was performing routi nance on the water system, said. The rupture released pressurized water that turne and knocked Mr. Jones or Smith said.

He said the plant continue because the rupture occurre of the secondary system th fies the steam flow, rather tral part of the system.

In July 1972, two employ Surry plant became the fir the country to die in an accid clear power plant, accordi eral officials, after a stean functioned, spraying them eated steam.

My father and I were both morticians, and when these cancer cases started coming in I had to go into my books to study how to do the em-balming, cancers were so rare. In '56 and '57 all of a sudden they were coming in all the time. By 1960 it was a regular flood.
Elmer Pickett, St. George, Utah

"... HERE I COME!"

"THE END?"

NEXT: "GROWTH PATTERNS"

23

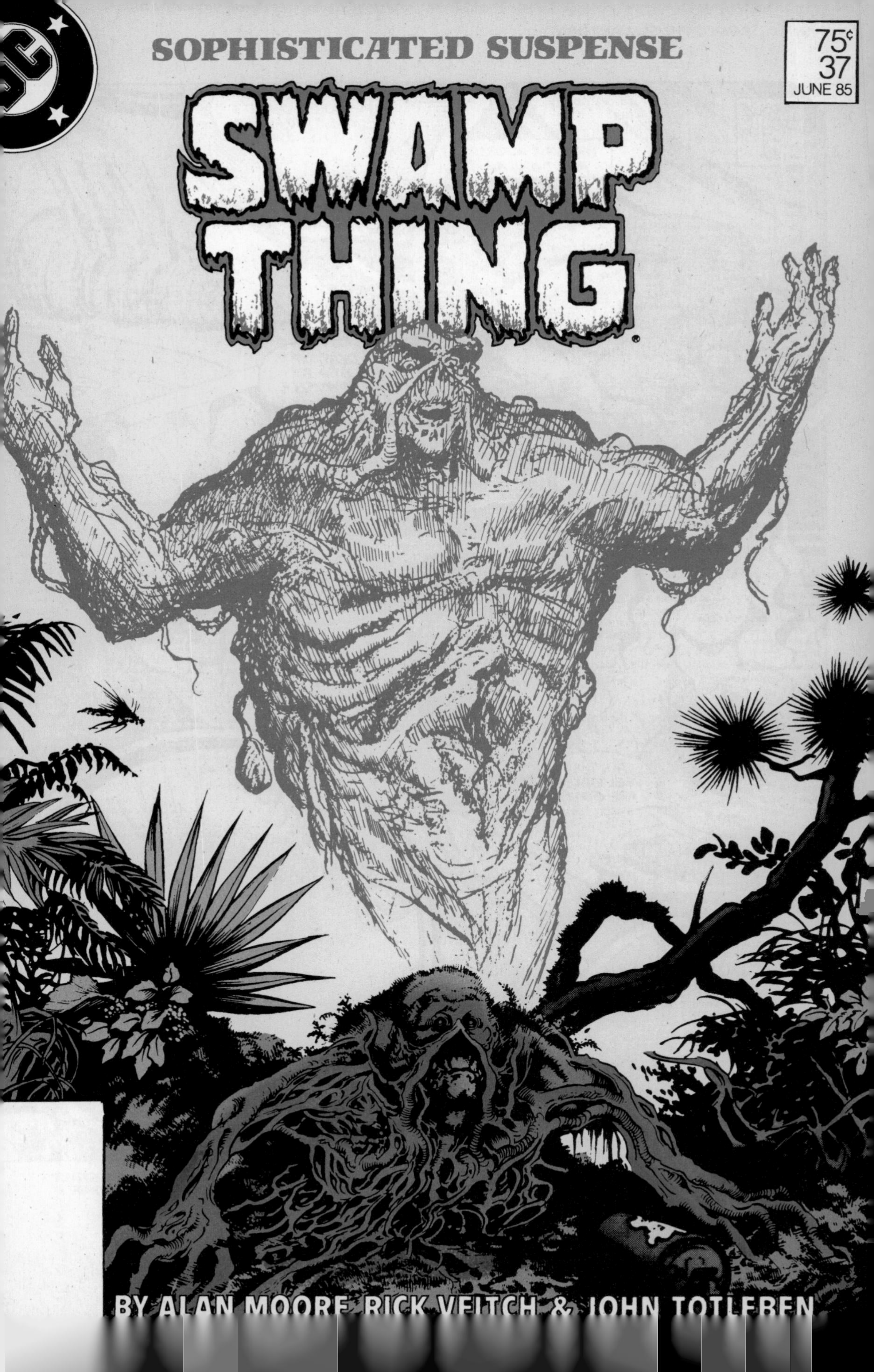
SOPHISTICATED SUSPENSE
75¢
37
JUNE 85
SWAMP THING
BY ALAN MOORE, RICK VEITCH & JOHN TOTLEBEN

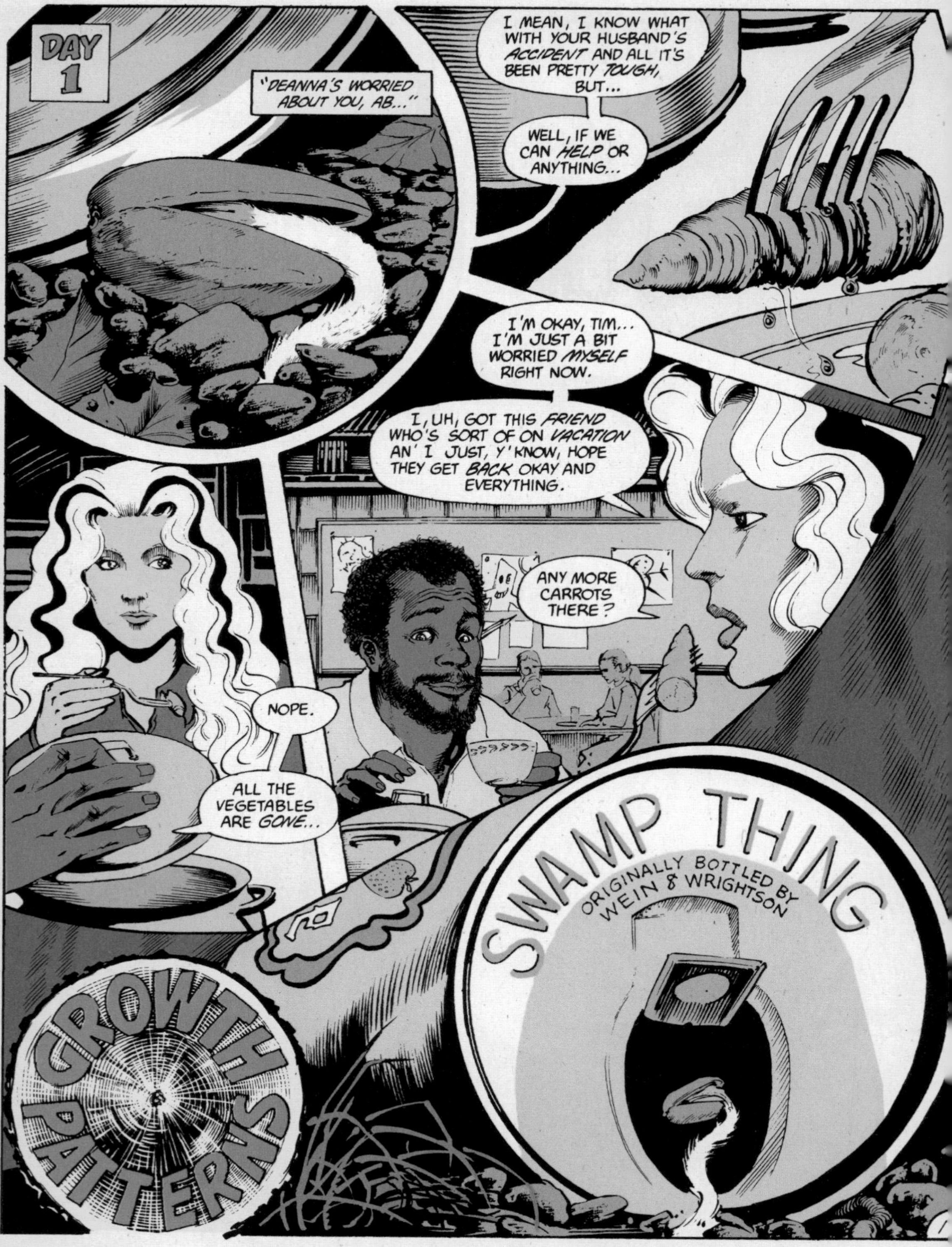
DAY 1
"DEANNA'S WORRIED ABOUT YOU, AB..."
I MEAN, I KNOW WHAT WITH YOUR HUSBAND'S ACCIDENT AND ALL IT'S BEEN PRETTY TOUGH, BUT...
WELL, IF WE CAN HELP OR ANYTHING...
I'M OKAY, TIM... I'M JUST A BIT WORRIED MYSELF RIGHT NOW.
I, UH, GOT THIS FRIEND WHO'S SORT OF ON VACATION AN' I JUST, Y'KNOW, HOPE THEY GET BACK OKAY AND EVERYTHING.
ANY MORE CARROTS THERE?
NOPE.
ALL THE VEGETABLES ARE GONE...
SWAMP THING
ORIGINALLY BOTTLED BY WEIN & WRIGHTSON
GROWTH PATTERNS
1

ALAN MOORE WRITER . RICK VEITCH & JOHN TOTLEBEN ARTISTS . KAREN BERGER EDITOR . TATJANA WOOD COLORIST . JOHN COSTANZA LETTERER

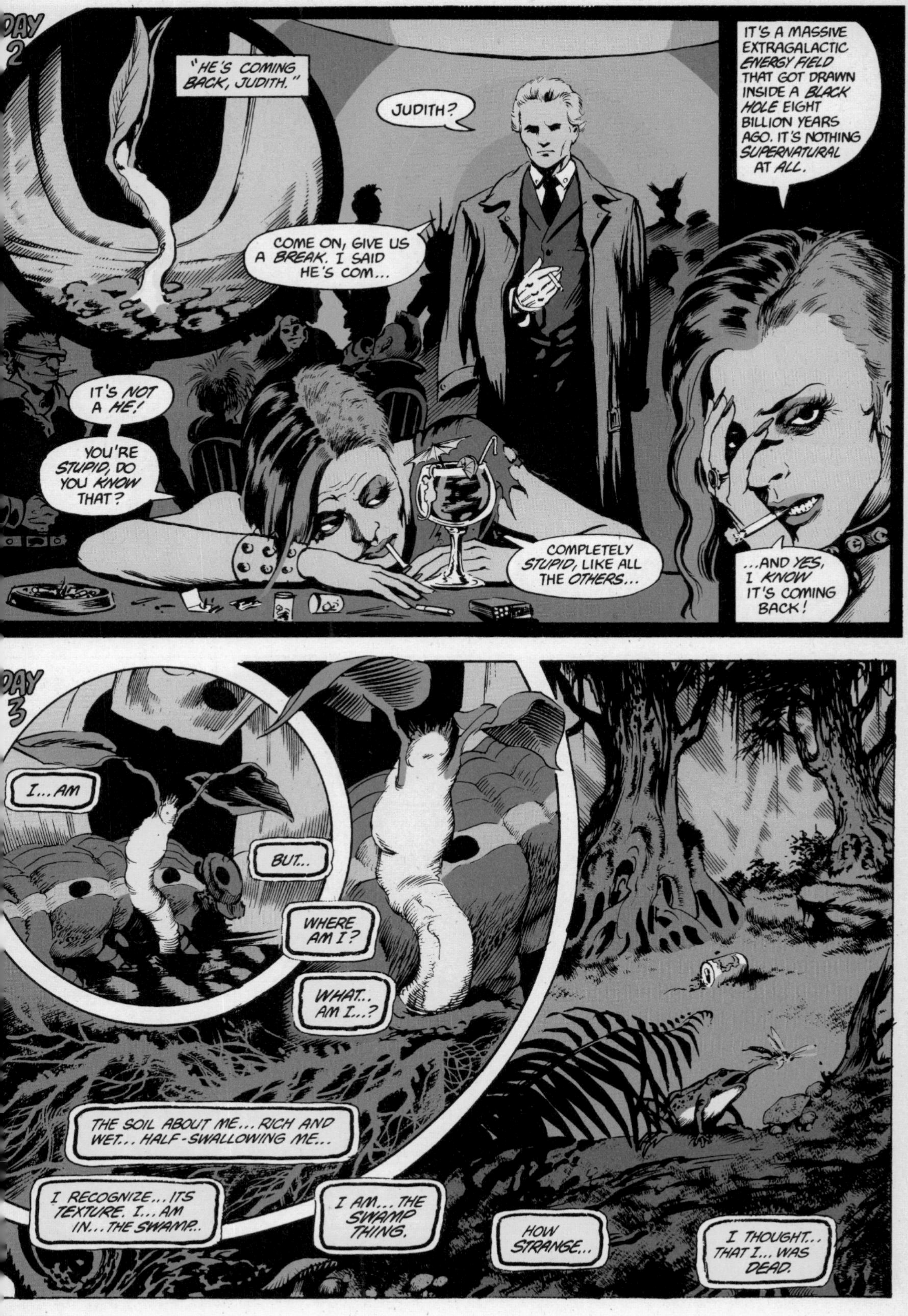
"HE'S COMING BACK, JUDITH."
JUDITH?
COME ON, GIVE US A BREAK. I SAID HE'S COM...
IT'S NOT A HE!
YOU'RE STUPID, DO YOU KNOW THAT?
COMPLETELY STUPID, LIKE ALL THE OTHERS...
IT'S A MASSIVE EXTRAGALACTIC ENERGY FIELD THAT GOT DRAWN INSIDE A BLACK HOLE EIGHT BILLION YEARS AGO. IT'S NOTHING SUPERNATURAL AT ALL.
...AND YES, I KNOW IT'S COMING BACK!
I... AM
BUT...
WHERE AM I?
WHAT... AM I...?
THE SOIL ABOUT ME... RICH AND WET... HALF-SWALLOWING ME...
I RECOGNIZE... ITS TEXTURE. I... AM IN... THE SWAMP...
I AM... THE SWAMP THING.
HOW STRANGE...
I THOUGHT... THAT I... WAS DEAD.

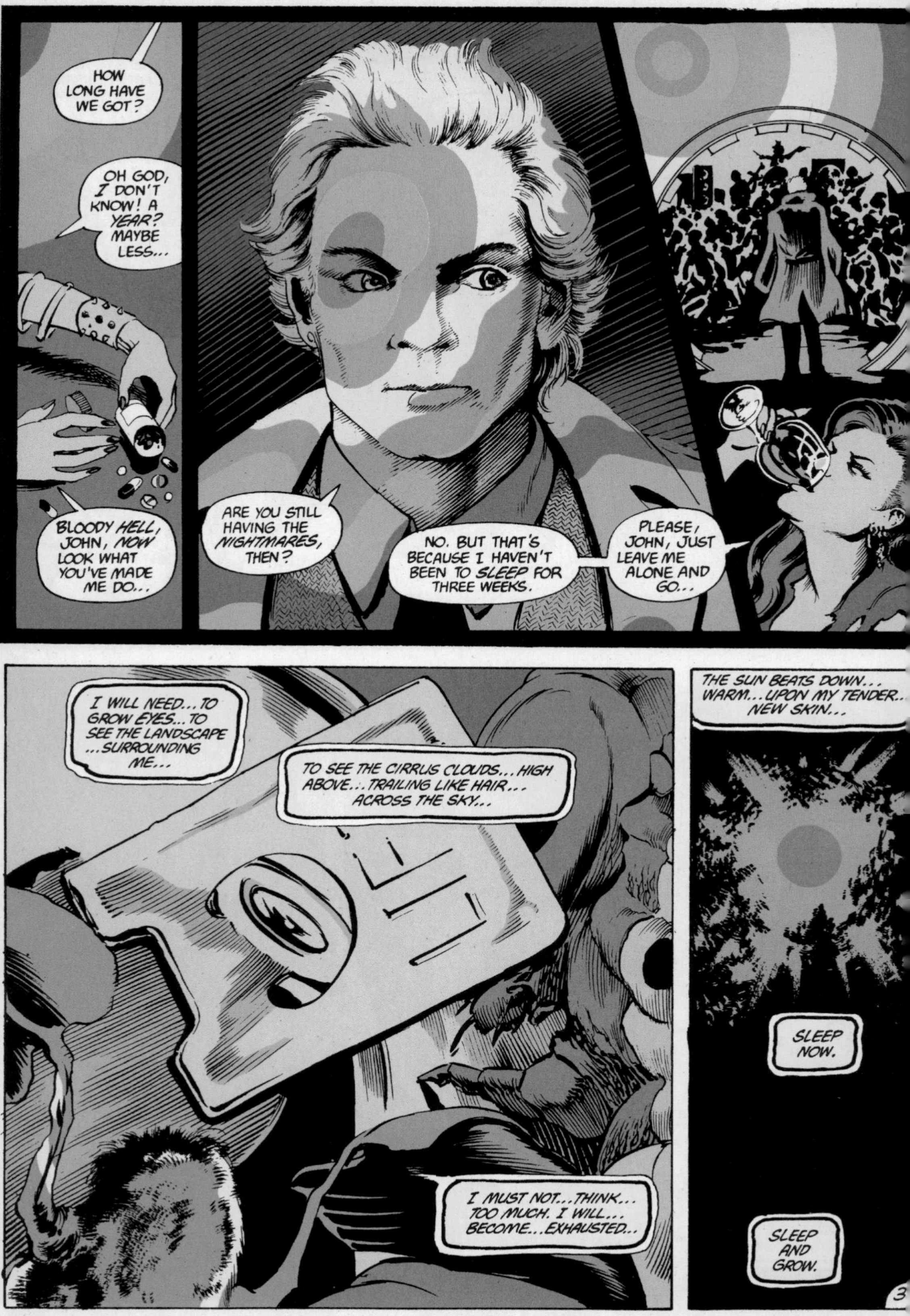
HOW LONG HAVE WE GOT?
OH GOD, I DON'T KNOW! A YEAR? MAYBE LESS...
BLOODY HELL, JOHN, NOW LOOK WHAT YOU'VE MADE ME DO...
ARE YOU STILL HAVING THE NIGHTMARES, THEN?
NO. BUT THAT'S BECAUSE I HAVEN'T BEEN TO SLEEP FOR THREE WEEKS.
PLEASE, JOHN, JUST LEAVE ME ALONE AND GO...
I WILL NEED... TO GROW EYES... TO SEE THE LANDSCAPE ...SURROUNDING ME...
TO SEE THE CIRRUS CLOUDS... HIGH ABOVE... TRAILING LIKE HAIR... ACROSS THE SKY...
I MUST NOT... THINK... TOO MUCH. I WILL... BECOME... EXHAUSTED...
THE SUN BEATS DOWN... WARM... UPON MY TENDER... NEW SKIN...
SLEEP NOW.
SLEEP AND GROW.
3

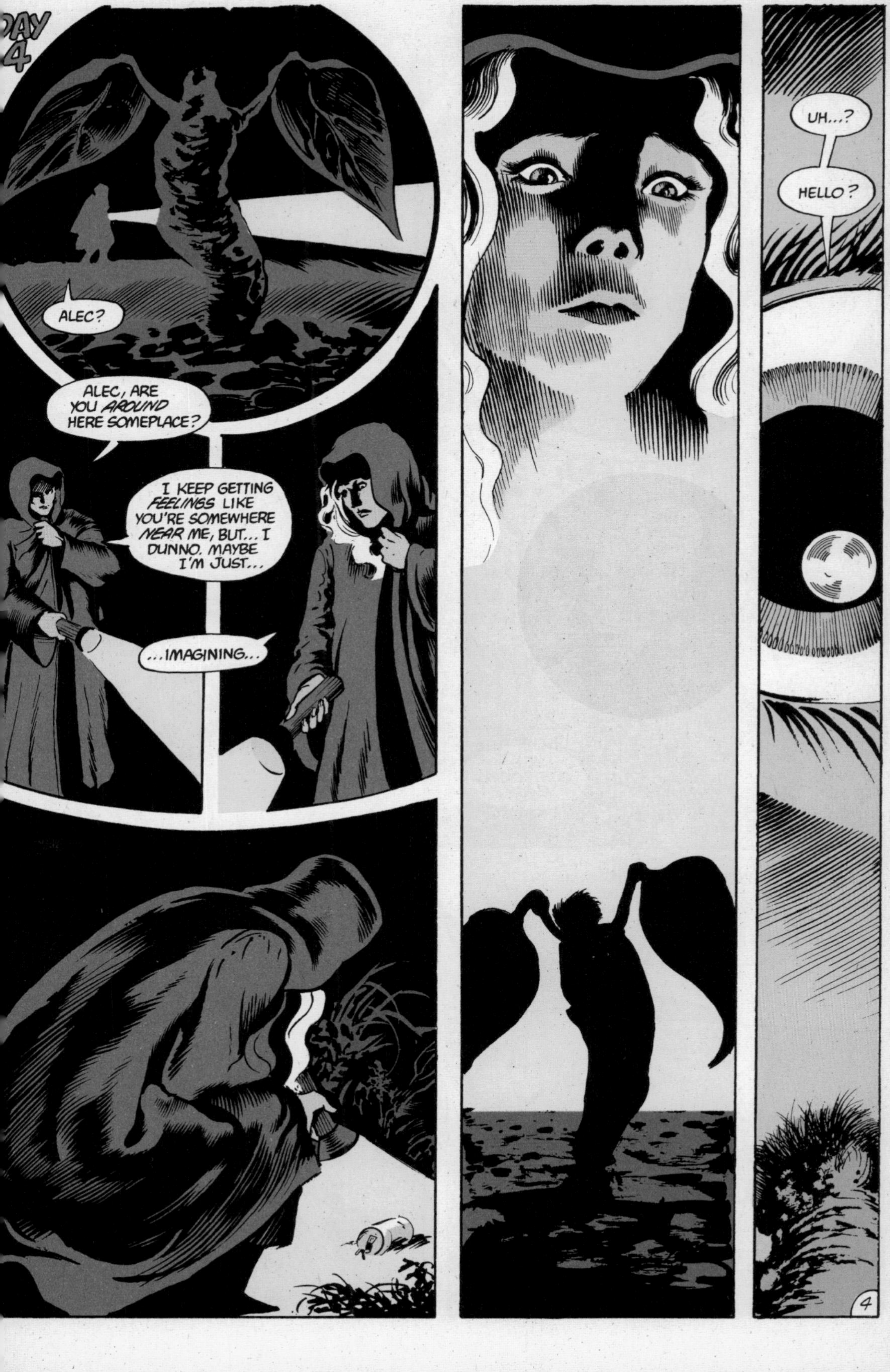
DAY 4
ALEC?
ALEC, ARE YOU AROUND HERE SOMEPLACE?
I KEEP GETTING FEELINGS LIKE YOU'RE SOMEWHERE NEAR ME, BUT... I DUNNO. MAYBE I'M JUST...
...IMAGINING...
UH...?
HELLO?
4

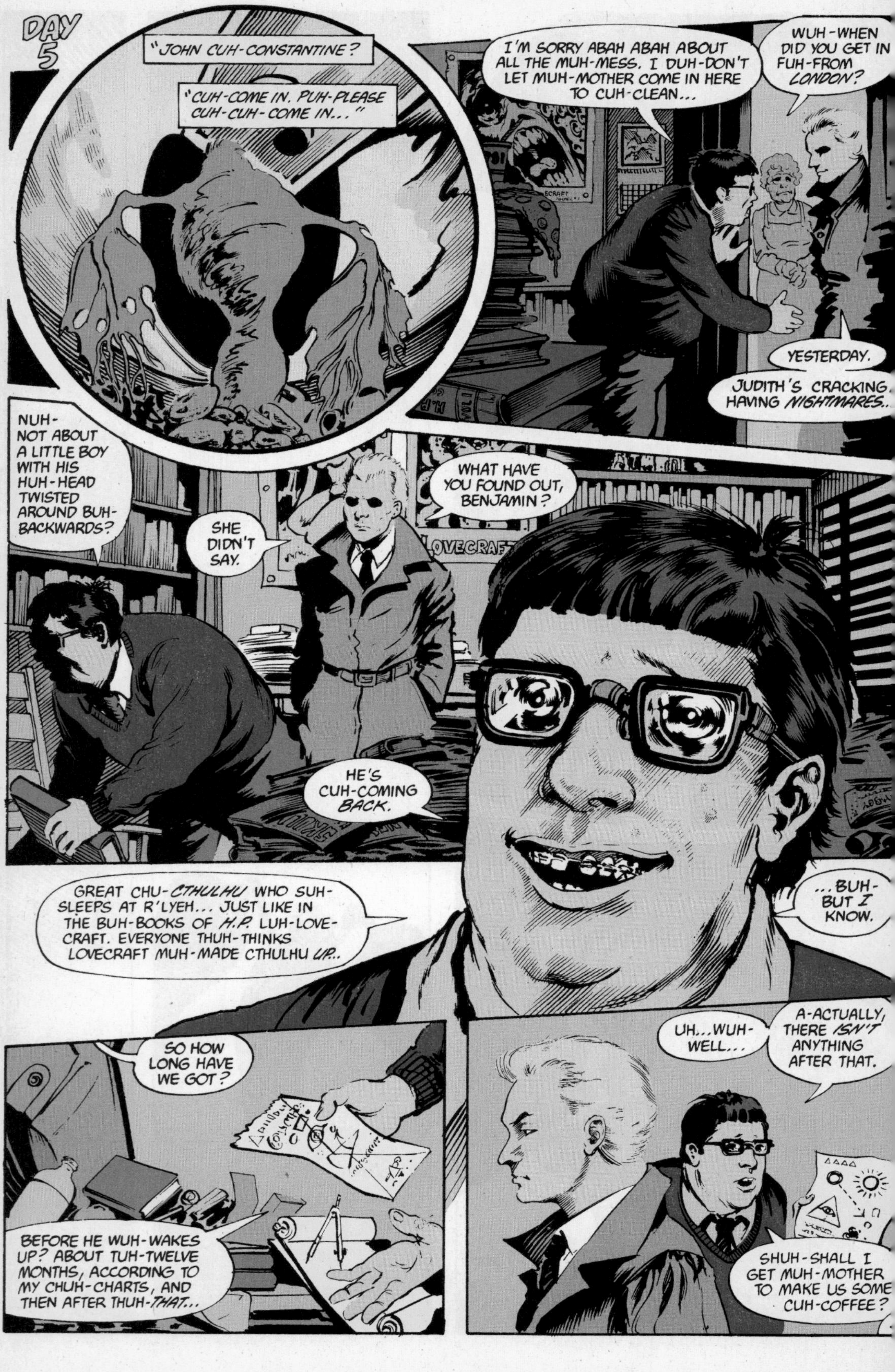
DAY 5
"JOHN CUH-CONSTANTINE?
"CUH-COME IN. PUH-PLEASE CUH-CUH-COME IN..."
I'M SORRY ABAH ABAH ABOUT ALL THE MUH-MESS. I DUH-DON'T LET MUH-MOTHER COME IN HERE TO CUH-CLEAN...
WUH-WHEN DID YOU GET IN FUH-FROM LONDON?
YESTERDAY.
JUDITH'S CRACKING. HAVING NIGHTMARES..
NUH-NOT ABOUT A LITTLE BOY WITH HIS HUH-HEAD TWISTED AROUND BUH-BACKWARDS?
SHE DIDN'T SAY.
WHAT HAVE YOU FOUND OUT, BENJAMIN?
HE'S CUH-COMING BACK.
GREAT CHU-CTHULHU WHO SUH-SLEEPS AT R'LYEH... JUST LIKE IN THE BUH-BOOKS OF H.P. LUH-LOVE-CRAFT. EVERYONE THUH-THINKS LOVECRAFT MUH-MADE CTHULHU UP..
...BUH-BUT I KNOW.
SO HOW LONG HAVE WE GOT?
BEFORE HE WUH-WAKES UP? ABOUT TUH-TWELVE MONTHS, ACCORDING TO MY CHUH-CHARTS, AND THEN AFTER THUH-THAT...
UH...WUH-WELL...
A-ACTUALLY, THERE ISN'T ANYTHING AFTER THAT.
SHUH-SHALL I GET MUH-MOTHER TO MAKE US SOME CUH-COFFEE?

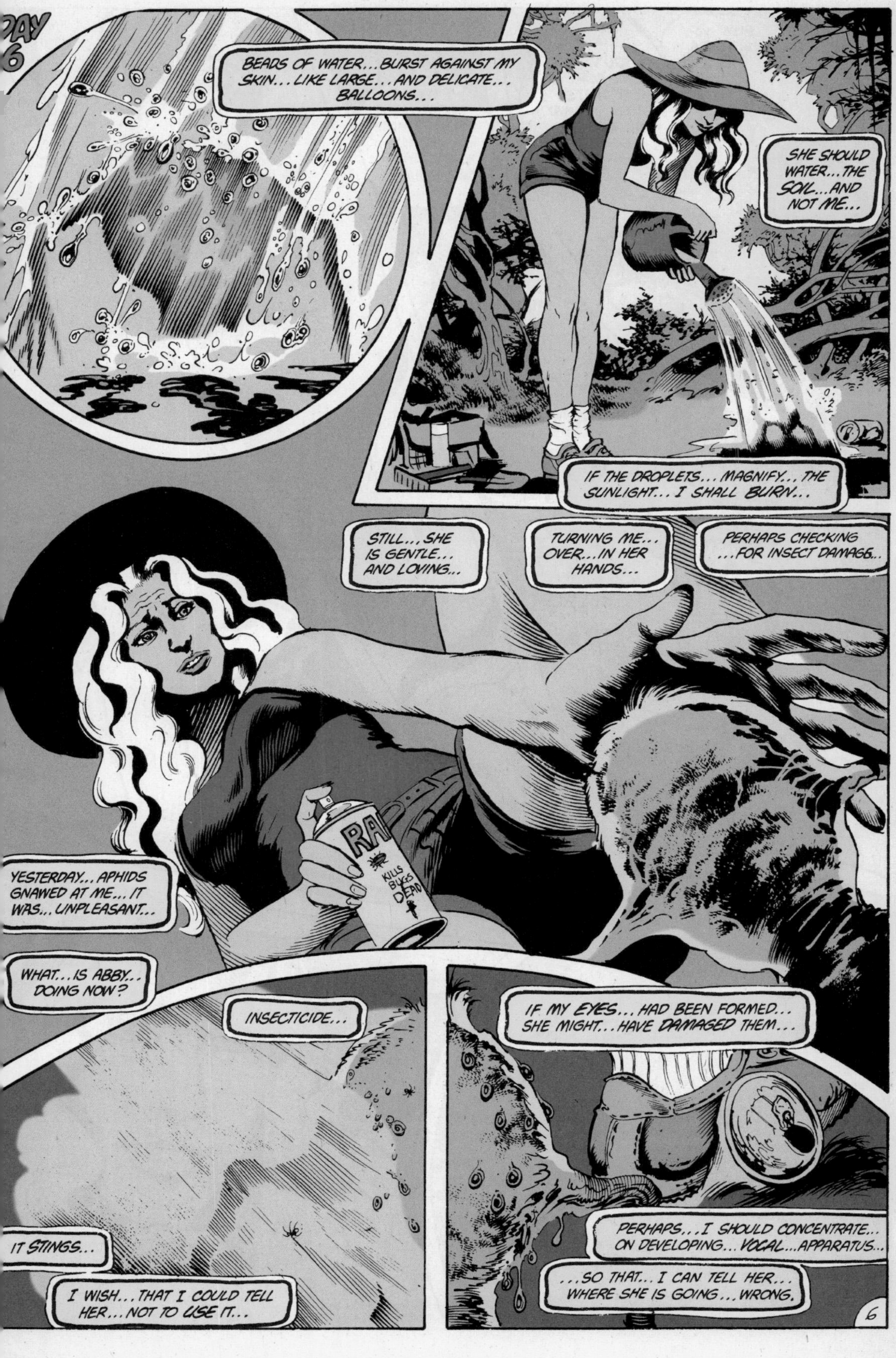
DAY 6
BEADS OF WATER... BURST AGAINST MY SKIN... LIKE LARGE... AND DELICATE... BALLOONS...
SHE SHOULD WATER... THE SOIL... AND NOT ME...
IF THE DROPLETS... MAGNIFY... THE SUNLIGHT... I SHALL BURN...
STILL... SHE IS GENTLE... AND LOVING...
TURNING ME... OVER... IN HER HANDS...
PERHAPS CHECKING ...FOR INSECT DAMAGE...
RAID
KILLS BUGS DEAD
YESTERDAY... APHIDS GNAWED AT ME... IT WAS... UNPLEASANT...
WHAT... IS ABBY... DOING NOW?
INSECTICIDE...
IT STINGS...
I WISH... THAT I COULD TELL HER... NOT TO USE IT...
IF MY EYES... HAD BEEN FORMED... SHE MIGHT... HAVE DAMAGED THEM...
PERHAPS... I SHOULD CONCENTRATE... ON DEVELOPING... VOCAL... APPARATUS...
...SO THAT... I CAN TELL HER... WHERE SHE IS GOING... WRONG.
6

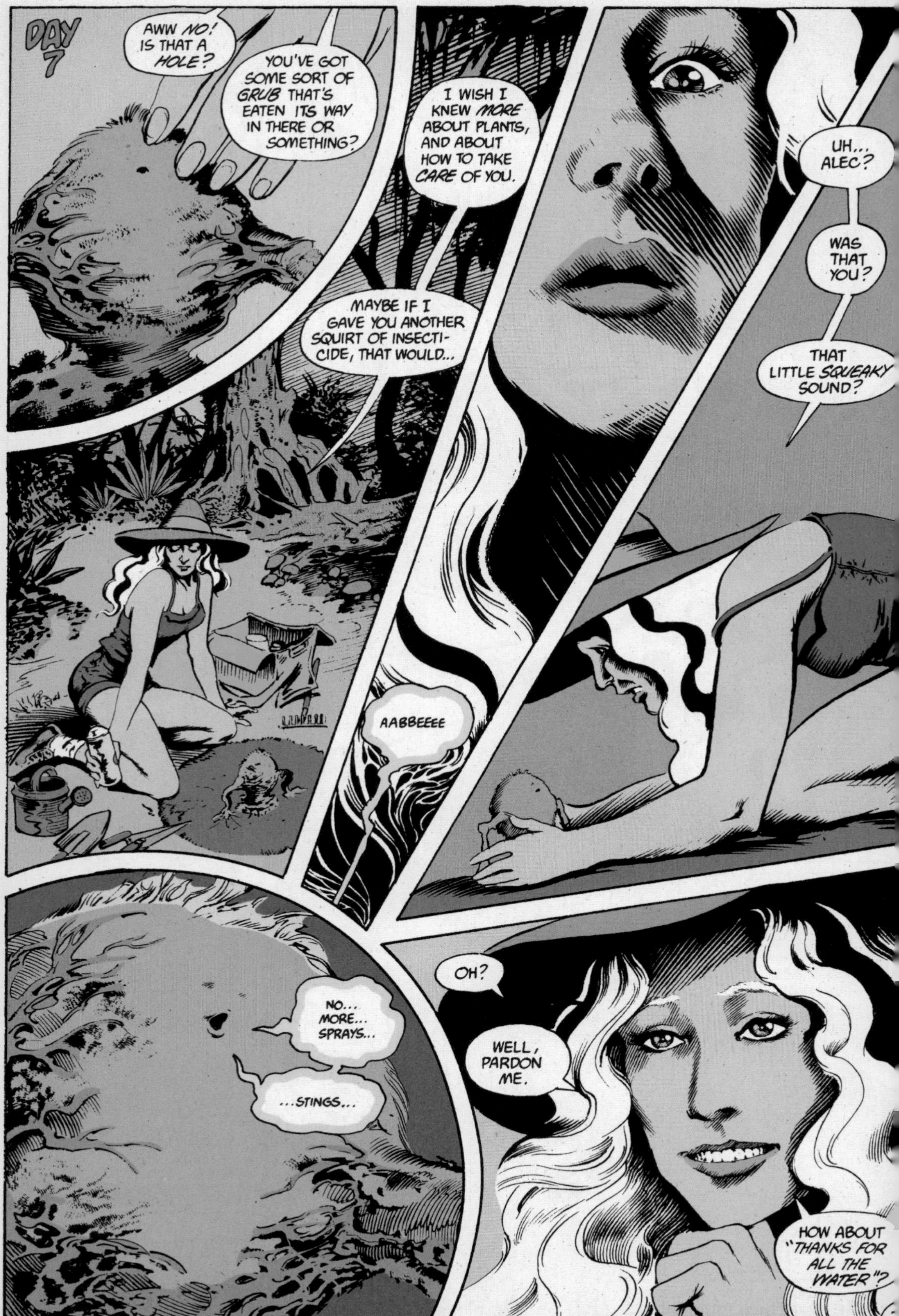
DAY 7
AWW NO! IS THAT A HOLE?
YOU'VE GOT SOME SORT OF GRUB THAT'S EATEN ITS WAY IN THERE OR SOMETHING?
I WISH I KNEW MORE ABOUT PLANTS, AND ABOUT HOW TO TAKE CARE OF YOU.
MAYBE IF I GAVE YOU ANOTHER SQUIRT OF INSECTI- CIDE, THAT WOULD...
AABBEEEE
UH... ALEC?
WAS THAT YOU?
THAT LITTLE SQUEAKY SOUND?
NO... MORE... SPRAYS...
...STINGS...
OH?
WELL, PARDON ME.
HOW ABOUT "THANKS FOR ALL THE WATER"?

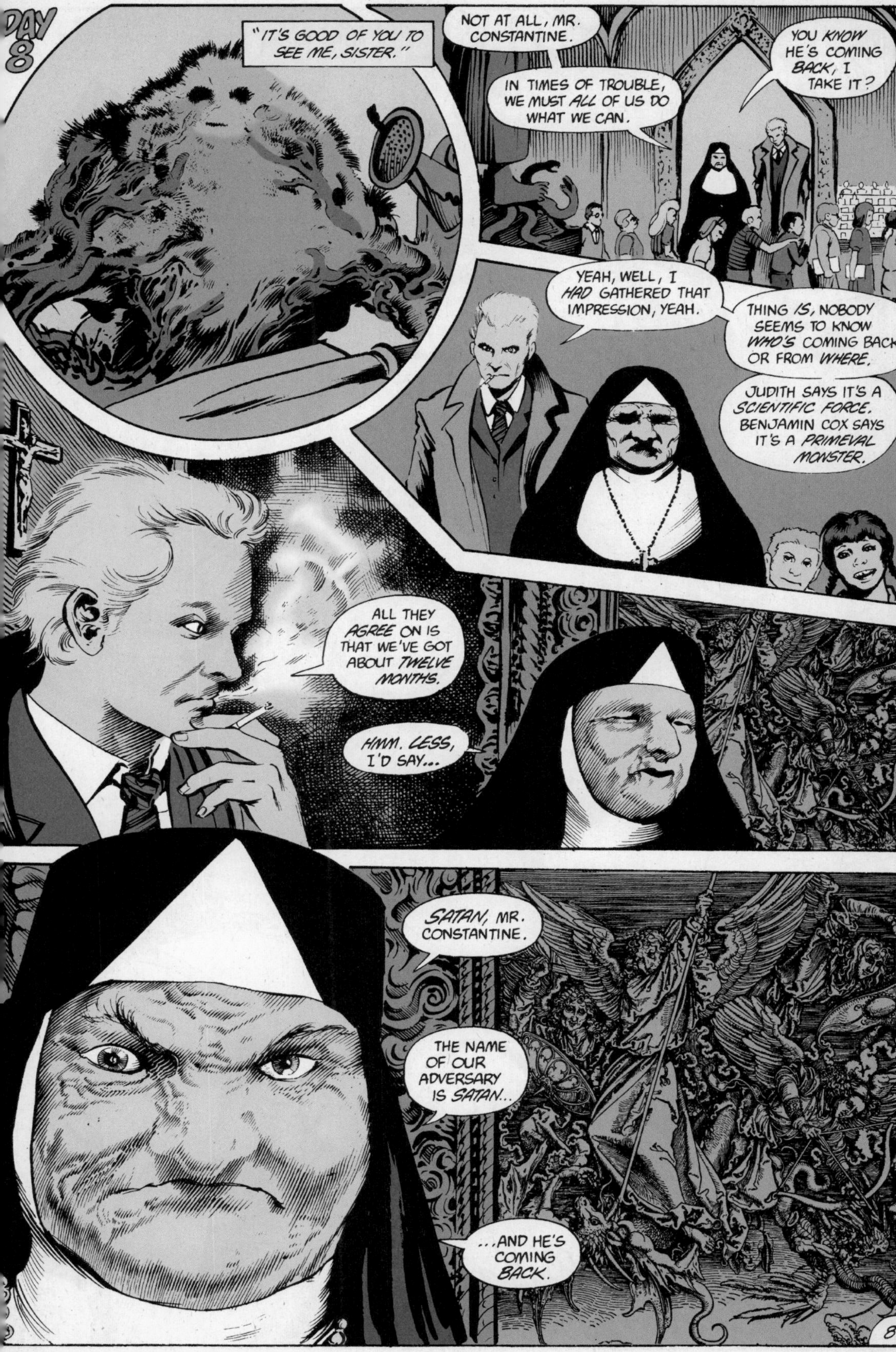
DAY 8
"IT'S GOOD OF YOU TO SEE ME, SISTER."
NOT AT ALL, MR. CONSTANTINE.
IN TIMES OF TROUBLE, WE MUST ALL OF US DO WHAT WE CAN.
YOU KNOW HE'S COMING BACK, I TAKE IT?
YEAH, WELL, I HAD GATHERED THAT IMPRESSION, YEAH.
THING IS, NOBODY SEEMS TO KNOW WHO'S COMING BACK, OR FROM WHERE.
JUDITH SAYS IT'S A SCIENTIFIC FORCE. BENJAMIN COX SAYS IT'S A PRIMEVAL MONSTER.
ALL THEY AGREE ON IS THAT WE'VE GOT ABOUT TWELVE MONTHS.
HMM. LESS, I'D SAY...
SATAN, MR. CONSTANTINE.
THE NAME OF OUR ADVERSARY IS SATAN...
...AND HE'S COMING BACK.
8

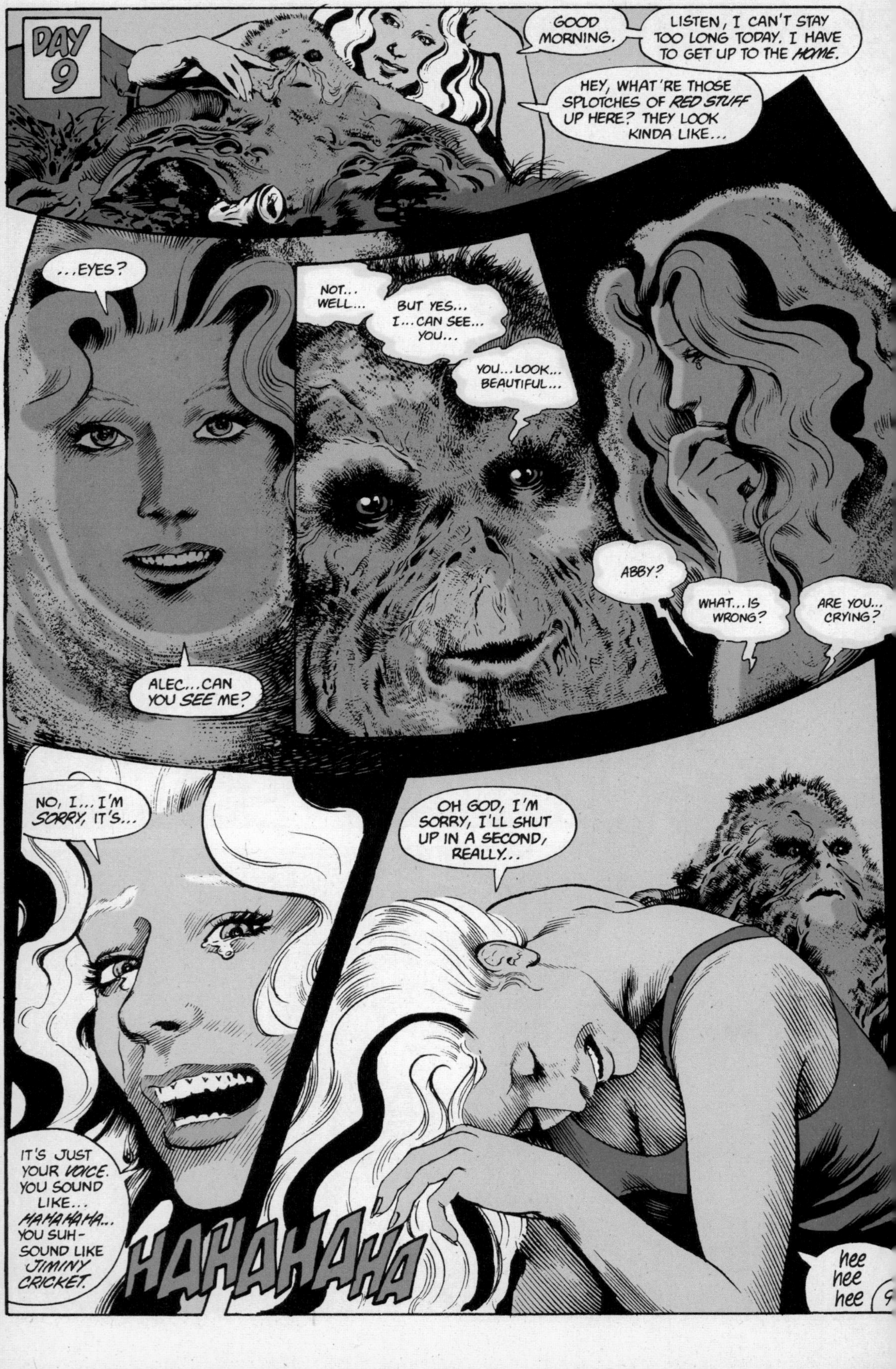
DAY 9
GOOD MORNING.
LISTEN, I CAN'T STAY TOO LONG TODAY. I HAVE TO GET UP TO THE HOME.
HEY, WHAT'RE THOSE SPLOTCHES OF RED STUFF UP HERE? THEY LOOK KINDA LIKE...
...EYES?
ALEC...CAN YOU SEE ME?
NOT... WELL...
BUT YES... I...CAN SEE... YOU...
YOU...LOOK... BEAUTIFUL...
ABBY?
WHAT...IS WRONG?
ARE YOU... CRYING?
NO, I...I'M SORRY, IT'S...
IT'S JUST YOUR VOICE. YOU SOUND LIKE... HAHAHAHA... YOU SUH-SOUND LIKE JIMINY CRICKET.
HAHAHAHA
OH GOD, I'M SORRY, I'LL SHUT UP IN A SECOND, REALLY...
hee hee hee
9

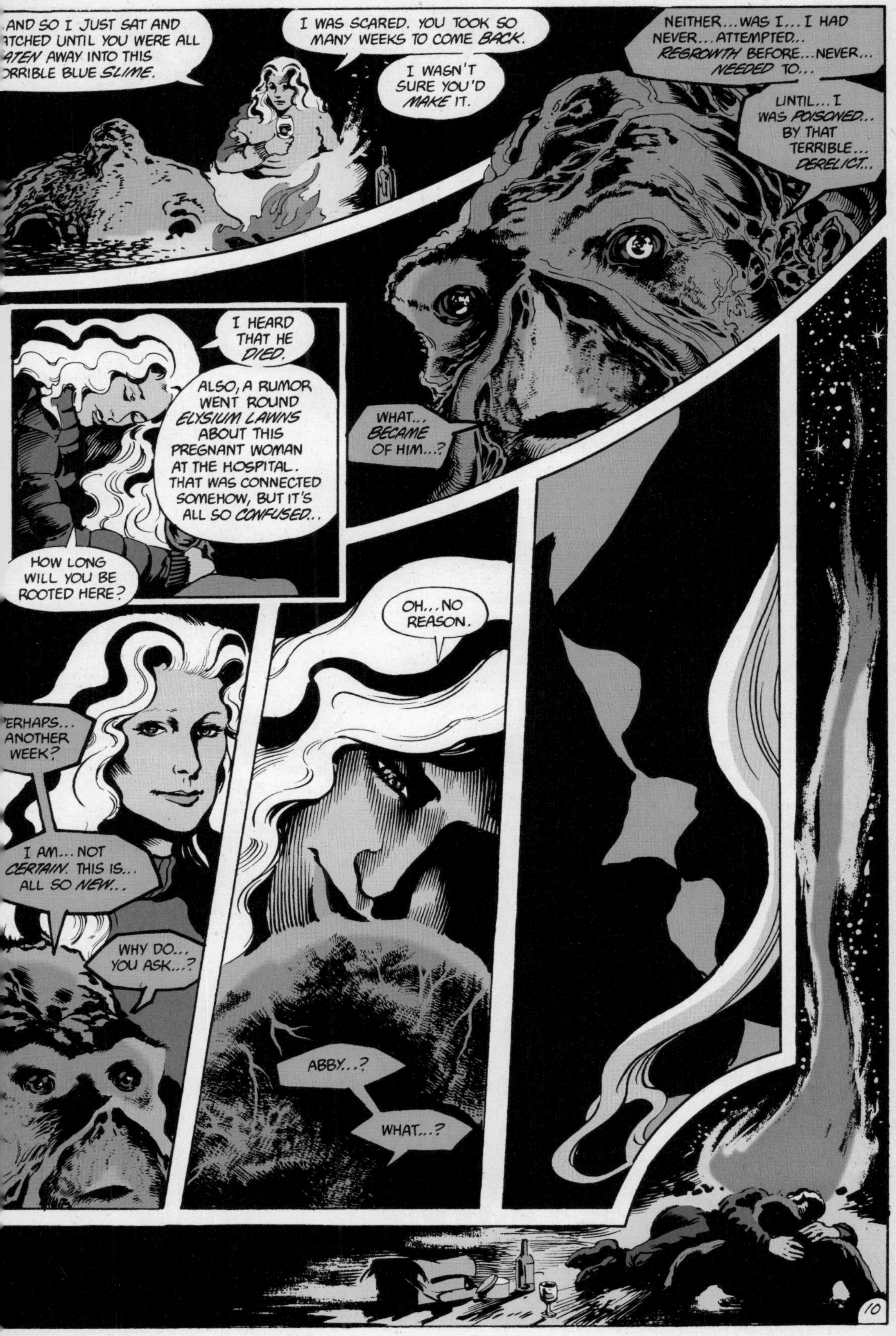
AND SO I JUST SAT AND ATCHED UNTIL YOU WERE ALL ATEN AWAY INTO THIS ORRIBLE BLUE SLIME.
I WAS SCARED. YOU TOOK SO MANY WEEKS TO COME BACK.
I WASN'T SURE YOU'D MAKE IT.
NEITHER... WAS I... I HAD NEVER... ATTEMPTED... REGROWTH BEFORE... NEVER... NEEDED TO...
UNTIL... I WAS POISONED... BY THAT TERRIBLE... DERELICT...
I HEARD THAT HE DIED.
ALSO, A RUMOR WENT ROUND ELYSIUM LAWNS ABOUT THIS PREGNANT WOMAN AT THE HOSPITAL. THAT WAS CONNECTED SOMEHOW, BUT IT'S ALL SO CONFUSED...
WHAT... BECAME OF HIM...?
HOW LONG WILL YOU BE ROOTED HERE?
ERHAPS... ANOTHER WEEK?
I AM... NOT CERTAIN. THIS IS... ALL SO NEW...
WHY DO... YOU ASK...?
OH... NO REASON.
ABBY...?
WHAT...?
10

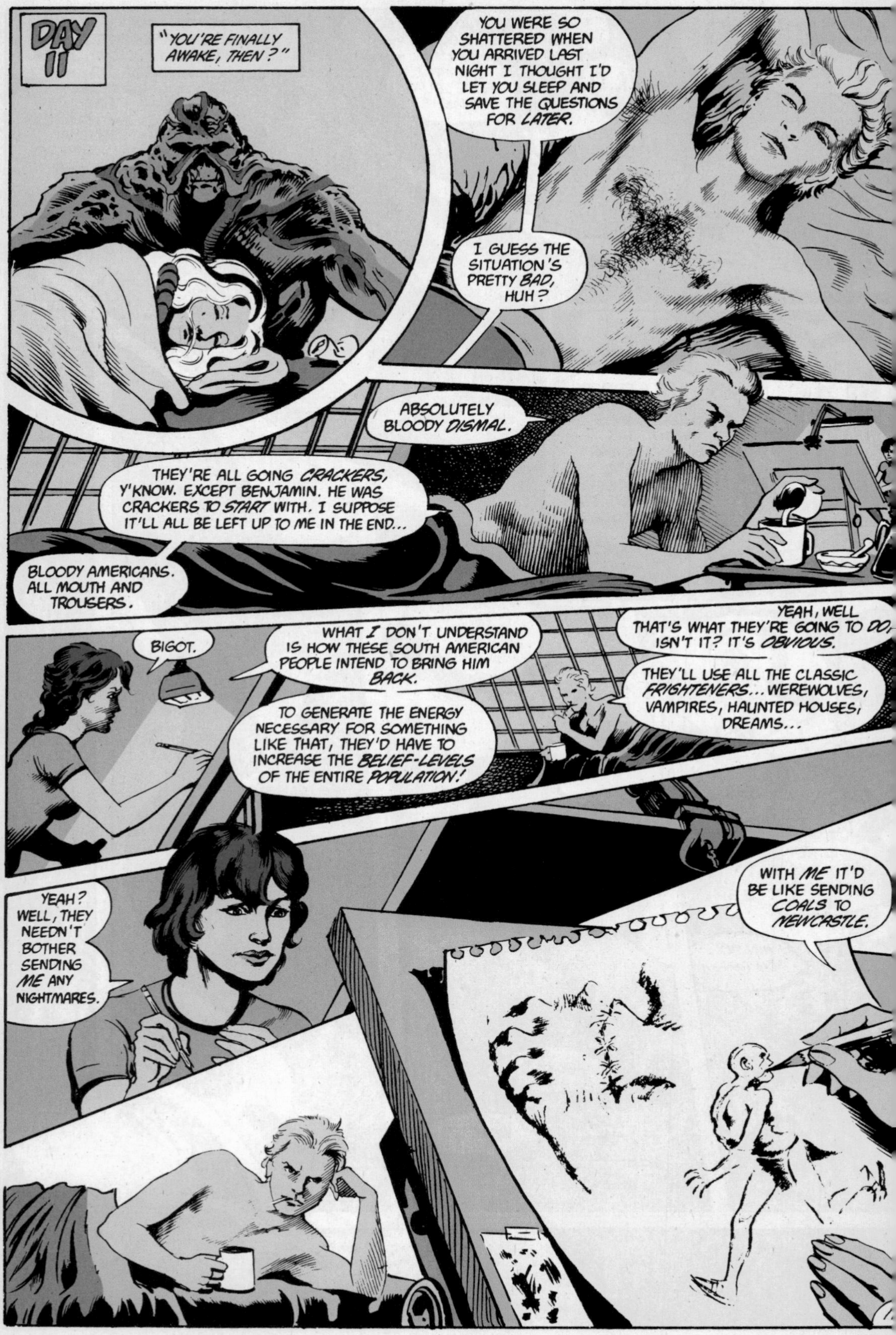
DAY 11
"YOU'RE FINALLY AWAKE, THEN?"
YOU WERE SO SHATTERED WHEN YOU ARRIVED LAST NIGHT I THOUGHT I'D LET YOU SLEEP AND SAVE THE QUESTIONS FOR LATER.
I GUESS THE SITUATION'S PRETTY BAD, HUH?
ABSOLUTELY BLOODY DISMAL.
THEY'RE ALL GOING CRACKERS, Y'KNOW. EXCEPT BENJAMIN. HE WAS CRACKERS TO START WITH. I SUPPOSE IT'LL ALL BE LEFT UP TO ME IN THE END...
BLOODY AMERICANS. ALL MOUTH AND TROUSERS.
BIGOT.
WHAT I DON'T UNDERSTAND IS HOW THESE SOUTH AMERICAN PEOPLE INTEND TO BRING HIM BACK.
TO GENERATE THE ENERGY NECESSARY FOR SOMETHING LIKE THAT, THEY'D HAVE TO INCREASE THE BELIEF-LEVELS OF THE ENTIRE POPULATION!
YEAH, WELL THAT'S WHAT THEY'RE GOING TO DO, ISN'T IT? IT'S OBVIOUS.
THEY'LL USE ALL THE CLASSIC FRIGHTENERS... WEREWOLVES, VAMPIRES, HAUNTED HOUSES, DREAMS...
YEAH? WELL, THEY NEEDN'T BOTHER SENDING ME ANY NIGHTMARES.
WITH ME IT'D BE LIKE SENDING COALS TO NEWCASTLE.

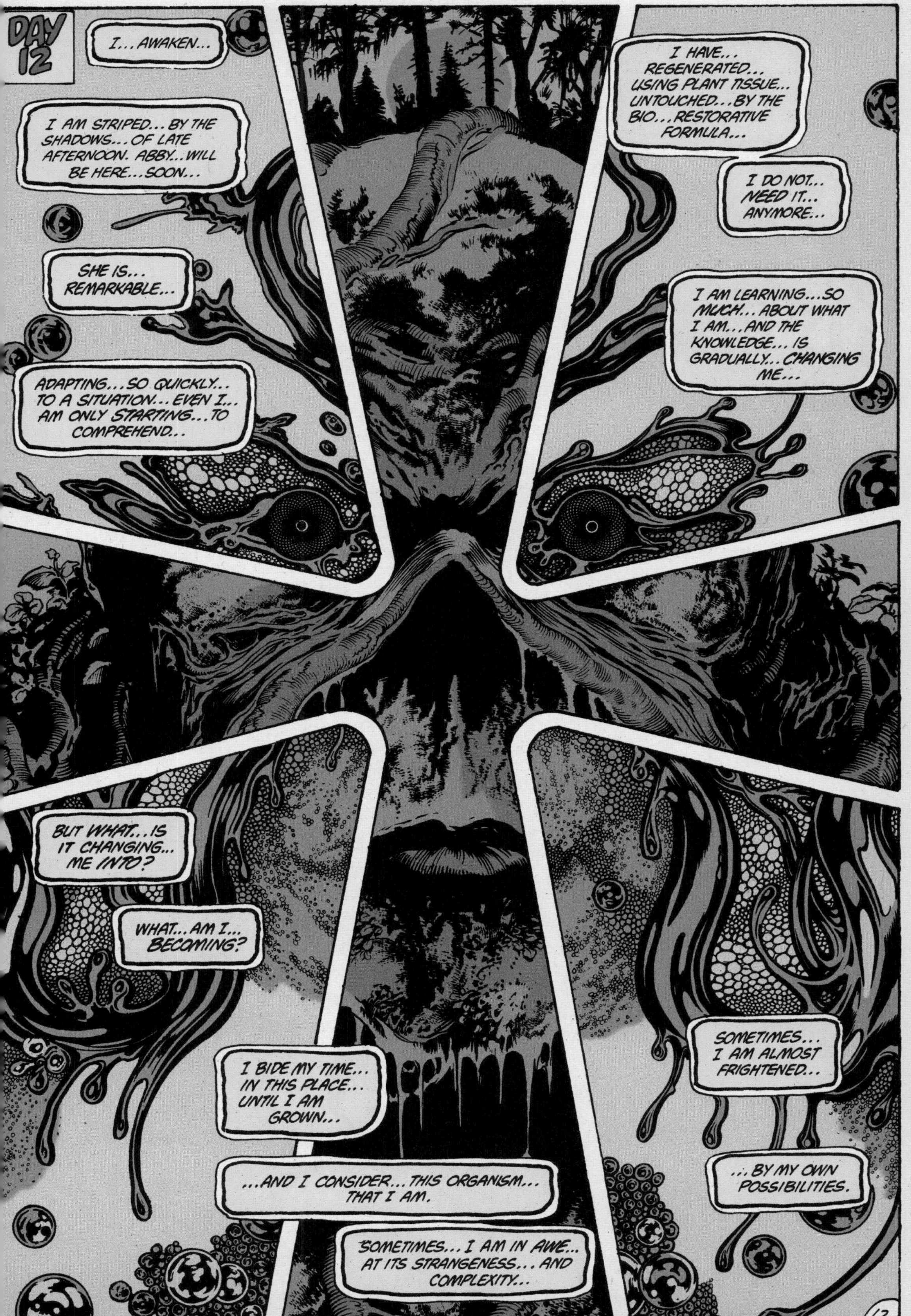
DAY 12
I... AWAKEN...
I AM STRIPED... BY THE SHADOWS... OF LATE AFTERNOON. ABBY... WILL BE HERE... SOON...
SHE IS... REMARKABLE...
ADAPTING... SO QUICKLY... TO A SITUATION... EVEN I... AM ONLY STARTING... TO COMPREHEND...
I HAVE... REGENERATED... USING PLANT TISSUE... UNTOUCHED... BY THE BIO... RESTORATIVE FORMULA...
I DO NOT... NEED IT... ANYMORE...
I AM LEARNING... SO MUCH... ABOUT WHAT I AM... AND THE KNOWLEDGE... IS GRADUALLY... CHANGING ME...
BUT WHAT... IS IT CHANGING... ME INTO?
WHAT... AM I... BECOMING?
I BIDE MY TIME... IN THIS PLACE... UNTIL I AM GROWN...
...AND I CONSIDER... THIS ORGANISM... THAT I AM.
SOMETIMES... I AM IN AWE... AT ITS STRANGENESS... AND COMPLEXITY...
SOMETIMES... I AM ALMOST FRIGHTENED...
...BY MY OWN POSSIBILITIES.
12

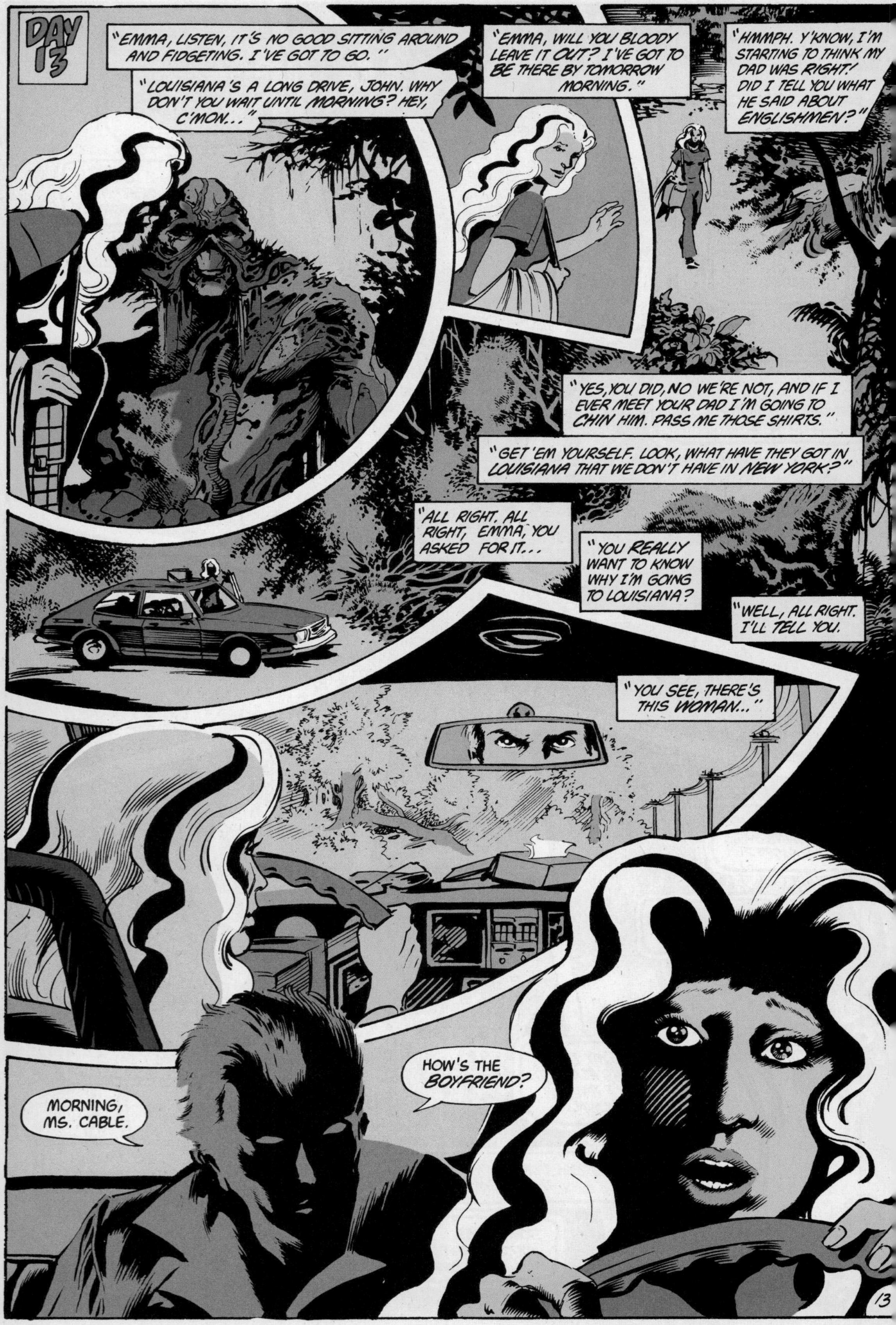
DAY 13
"EMMA, LISTEN, IT'S NO GOOD SITTING AROUND AND FIDGETING. I'VE GOT TO GO."
"LOUISIANA'S A LONG DRIVE, JOHN. WHY DON'T YOU WAIT UNTIL MORNING? HEY, C'MON..."
"EMMA, WILL YOU BLOODY LEAVE IT OUT? I'VE GOT TO BE THERE BY TOMORROW MORNING."
"HMMPH. Y'KNOW, I'M STARTING TO THINK MY DAD WAS RIGHT! DID I TELL YOU WHAT HE SAID ABOUT ENGLISHMEN?"
"YES, YOU DID, NO WE'RE NOT, AND IF I EVER MEET YOUR DAD I'M GOING TO CHIN HIM. PASS ME THOSE SHIRTS."
"GET 'EM YOURSELF. LOOK, WHAT HAVE THEY GOT IN LOUISIANA THAT WE DON'T HAVE IN NEW YORK?"
"ALL RIGHT. ALL RIGHT, EMMA, YOU ASKED FOR IT...
"YOU REALLY WANT TO KNOW WHY I'M GOING TO LOUISIANA?
"WELL, ALL RIGHT. I'LL TELL YOU.
"YOU SEE, THERE'S THIS WOMAN..."
MORNING, MS. CABLE.
HOW'S THE BOYFRIEND?
13

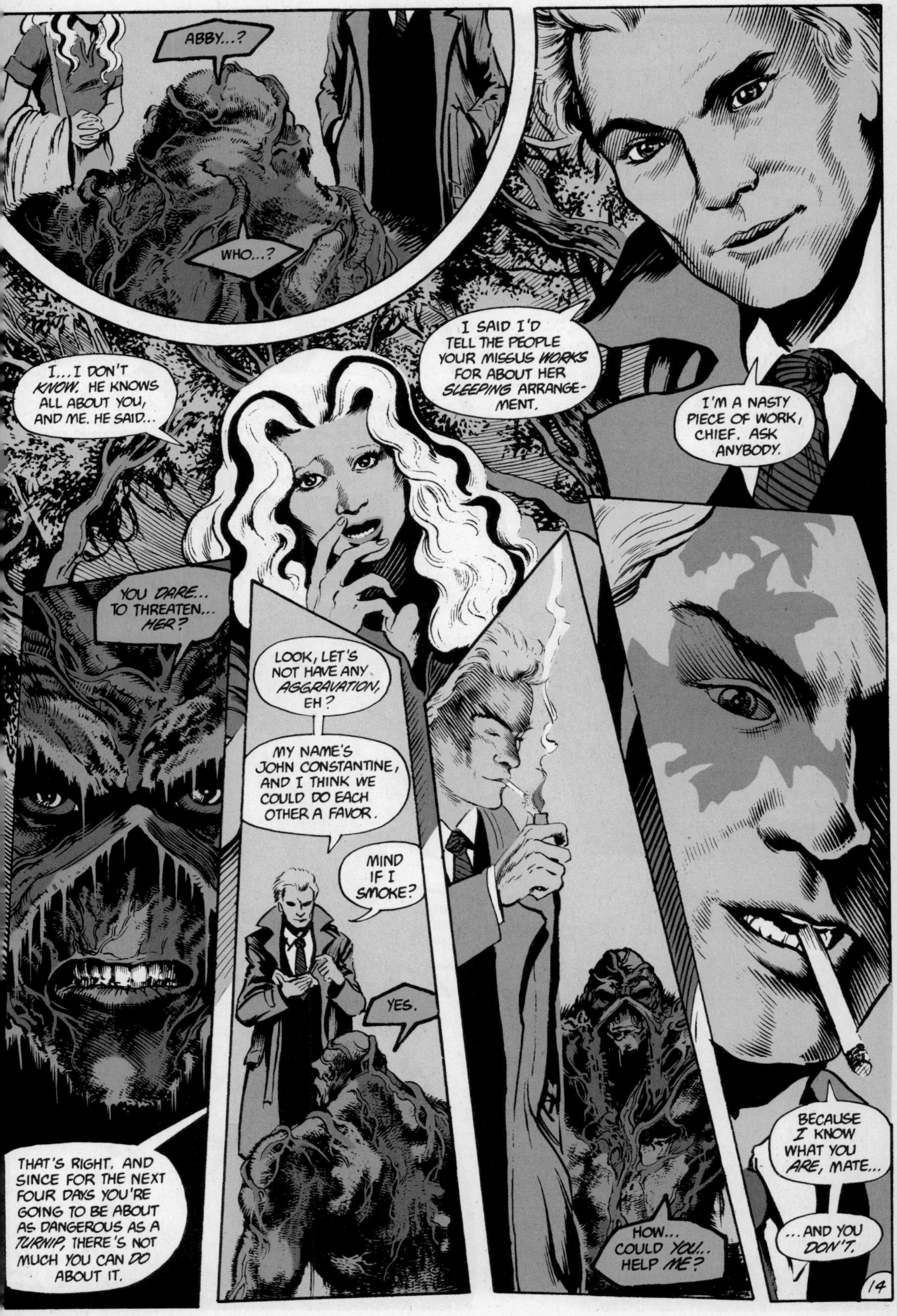
ABBY...?
WHO...?
I SAID I'D TELL THE PEOPLE YOUR MISSUS WORKS FOR ABOUT HER SLEEPING ARRANGE-MENT.
I'M A NASTY PIECE OF WORK, CHIEF. ASK ANYBODY.
I... I DON'T KNOW. HE KNOWS ALL ABOUT YOU, AND ME. HE SAID...
YOU DARE... TO THREATEN... HER?
LOOK, LET'S NOT HAVE ANY AGGRAVATION, EH?
MY NAME'S JOHN CONSTANTINE, AND I THINK WE COULD DO EACH OTHER A FAVOR.
MIND IF I SMOKE?
YES.
THAT'S RIGHT. AND SINCE FOR THE NEXT FOUR DAYS YOU'RE GOING TO BE ABOUT AS DANGEROUS AS A TURNIP, THERE'S NOT MUCH YOU CAN DO ABOUT IT.
HOW... COULD YOU... HELP ME?
BECAUSE I KNOW WHAT YOU ARE, MATE...
...AND YOU DON'T.
14

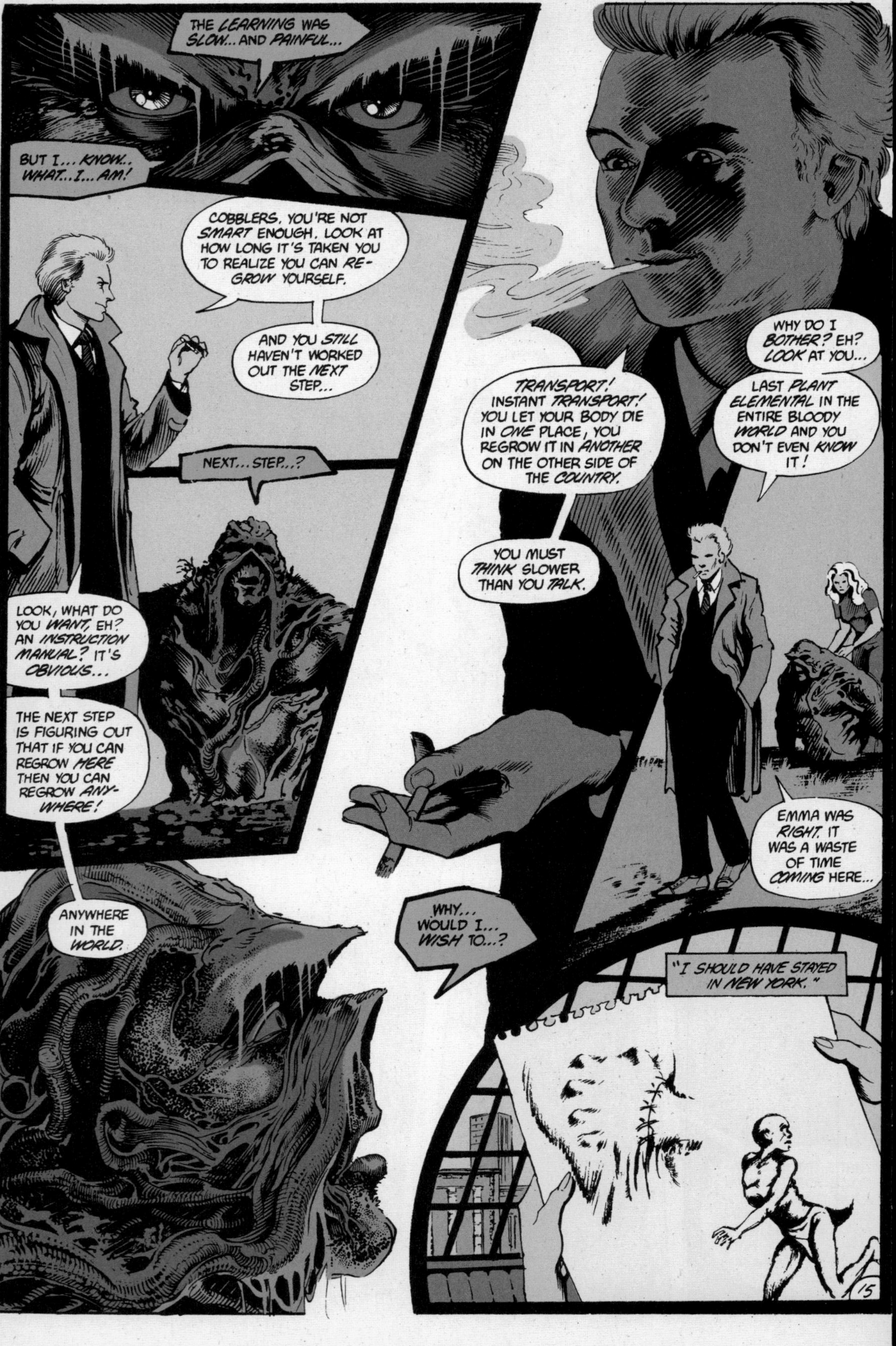
THE LEARNING WAS SLOW... AND PAINFUL...
BUT I... KNOW.. WHAT...I...AM!
COBBLERS, YOU'RE NOT SMART ENOUGH. LOOK AT HOW LONG IT'S TAKEN YOU TO REALIZE YOU CAN RE-GROW YOURSELF.
AND YOU STILL HAVEN'T WORKED OUT THE NEXT STEP...
NEXT... STEP...?
LOOK, WHAT DO YOU WANT, EH? AN INSTRUCTION MANUAL? IT'S OBVIOUS...
THE NEXT STEP IS FIGURING OUT THAT IF YOU CAN REGROW HERE THEN YOU CAN REGROW ANY-WHERE!
ANYWHERE IN THE WORLD.
TRANSPORT! INSTANT TRANSPORT! YOU LET YOUR BODY DIE IN ONE PLACE, YOU REGROW IT IN ANOTHER ON THE OTHER SIDE OF THE COUNTRY.
YOU MUST THINK SLOWER THAN YOU TALK.
WHY... WOULD I... WISH TO...?
WHY DO I BOTHER? EH? LOOK AT YOU...
LAST PLANT ELEMENTAL IN THE ENTIRE BLOODY WORLD AND YOU DON'T EVEN KNOW IT!
EMMA WAS RIGHT. IT WAS A WASTE OF TIME COMING HERE...
"I SHOULD HAVE STAYED IN NEW YORK."
15

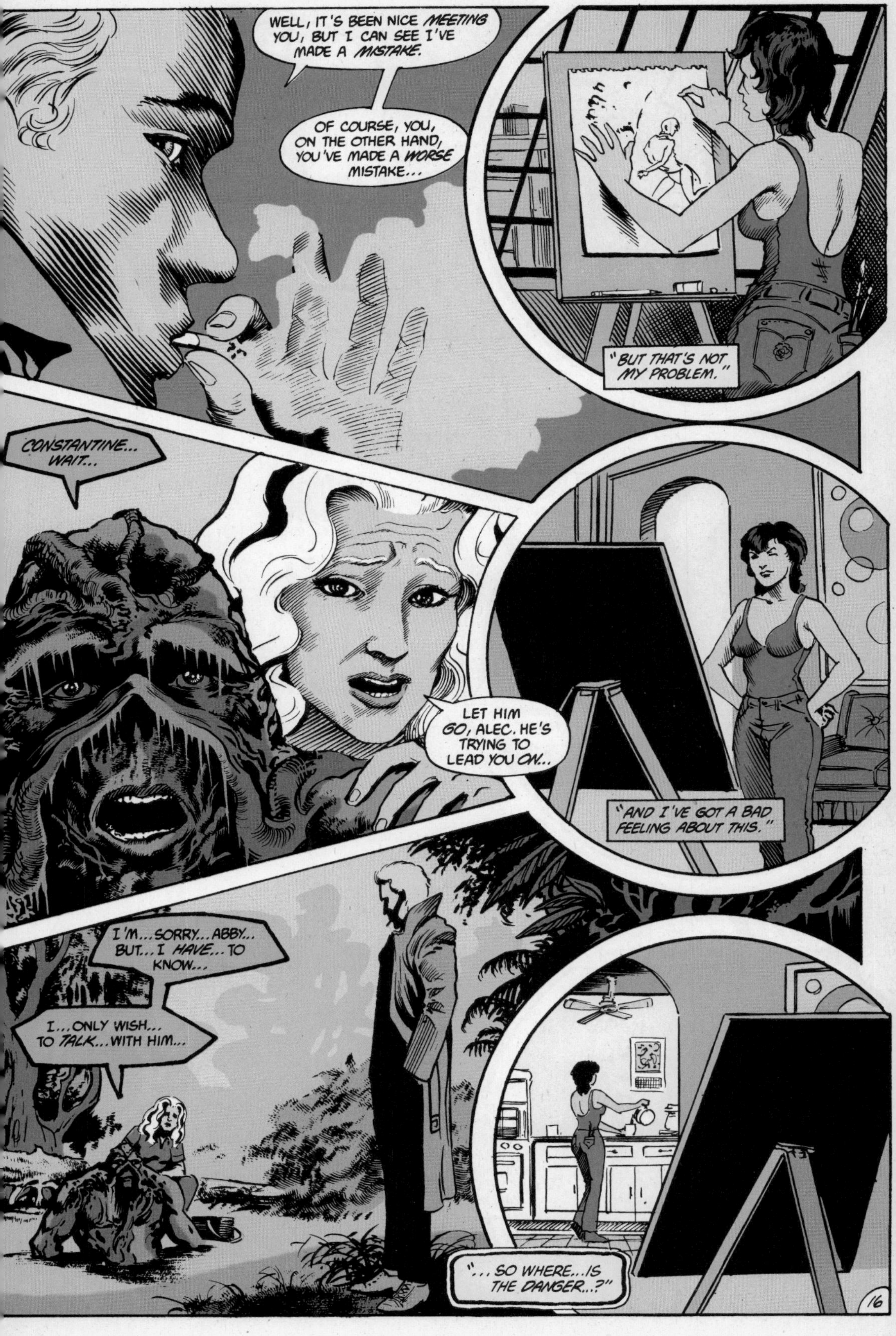
WELL, IT'S BEEN NICE MEETING YOU, BUT I CAN SEE I'VE MADE A MISTAKE.
OF COURSE, YOU, ON THE OTHER HAND, YOU'VE MADE A WORSE MISTAKE...
"BUT THAT'S NOT MY PROBLEM."
CONSTANTINE... WAIT...
LET HIM GO, ALEC. HE'S TRYING TO LEAD YOU ON...
"AND I'VE GOT A BAD FEELING ABOUT THIS."
I'M... SORRY... ABBY... BUT... I HAVE... TO KNOW...
I... ONLY WISH... TO TALK... WITH HIM...
"... SO WHERE... IS THE DANGER...?"
16

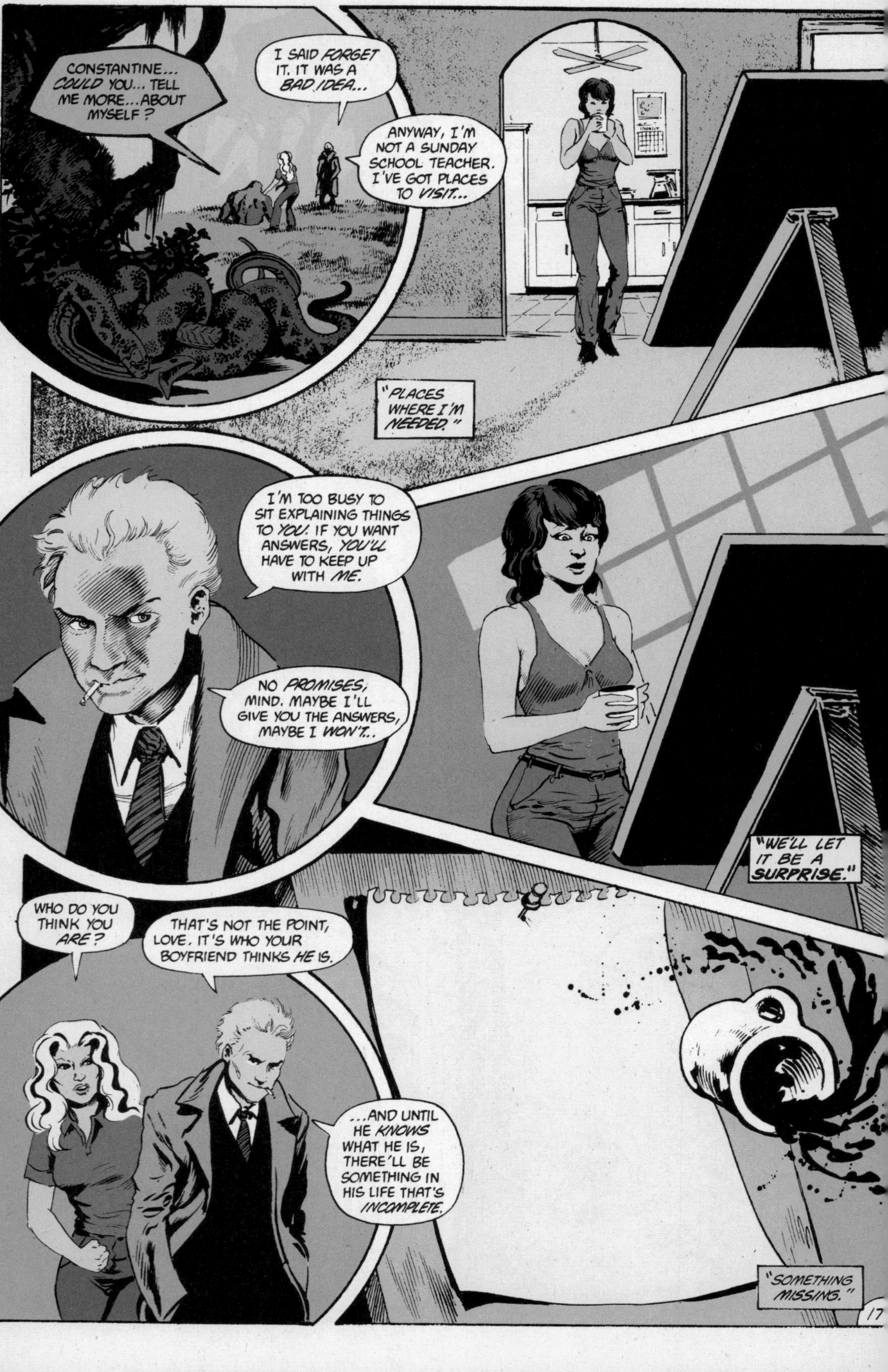
CONSTANTINE... COULD YOU... TELL ME MORE... ABOUT MYSELF?
I SAID FORGET IT. IT WAS A BAD IDEA...
ANYWAY, I'M NOT A SUNDAY SCHOOL TEACHER. I'VE GOT PLACES TO VISIT...
"PLACES WHERE I'M NEEDED."
I'M TOO BUSY TO SIT EXPLAINING THINGS TO YOU. IF YOU WANT ANSWERS, YOU'LL HAVE TO KEEP UP WITH ME.
NO PROMISES, MIND. MAYBE I'LL GIVE YOU THE ANSWERS, MAYBE I WON'T...
"WE'LL LET IT BE A SURPRISE."
WHO DO YOU THINK YOU ARE?
THAT'S NOT THE POINT, LOVE. IT'S WHO YOUR BOYFRIEND THINKS HE IS.
...AND UNTIL HE KNOWS WHAT HE IS, THERE'LL BE SOMETHING IN HIS LIFE THAT'S INCOMPLETE.
"SOMETHING MISSING."
17

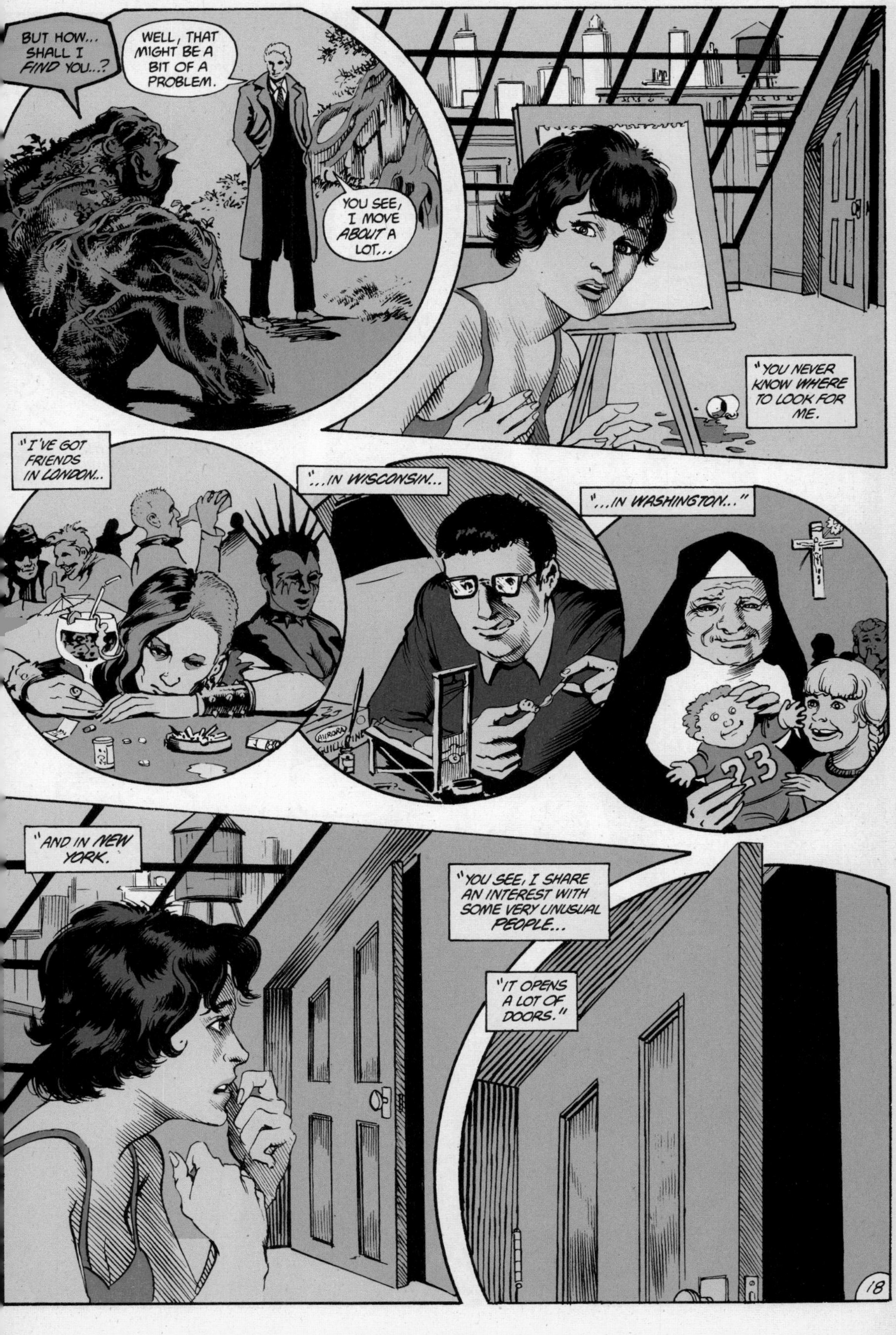
BUT HOW... SHALL I FIND YOU...?
WELL, THAT MIGHT BE A BIT OF A PROBLEM.
YOU SEE, I MOVE ABOUT A LOT...
"YOU NEVER KNOW WHERE TO LOOK FOR ME.
"I'VE GOT FRIENDS IN LONDON...
"...IN WISCONSIN...
"...IN WASHINGTON..."
"AND IN NEW YORK.
"YOU SEE, I SHARE AN INTEREST WITH SOME VERY UNUSUAL PEOPLE...
"IT OPENS A LOT OF DOORS."
18

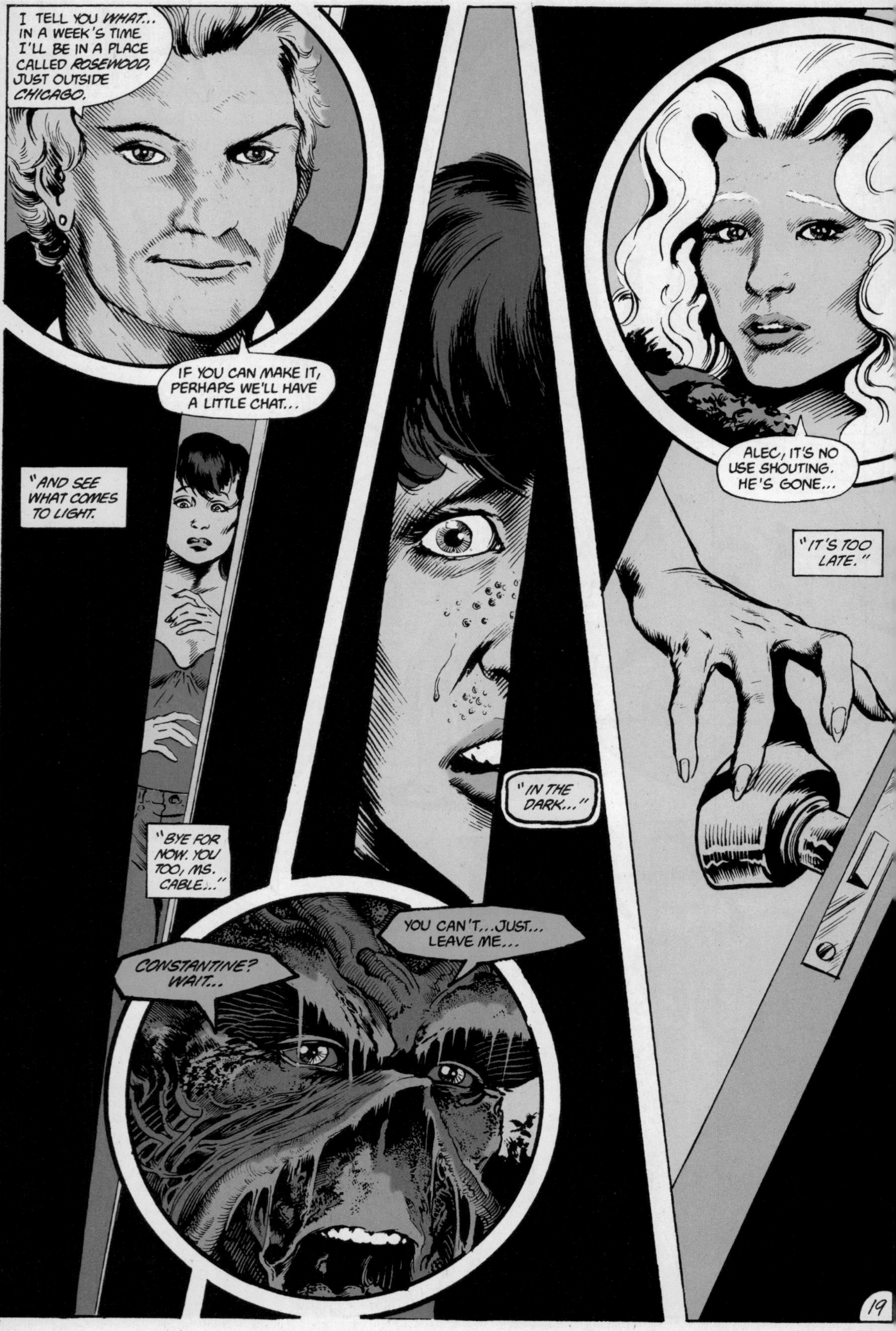
I TELL YOU WHAT... IN A WEEK'S TIME I'LL BE IN A PLACE CALLED ROSEWOOD, JUST OUTSIDE CHICAGO.
IF YOU CAN MAKE IT, PERHAPS WE'LL HAVE A LITTLE CHAT...
"AND SEE WHAT COMES TO LIGHT.
"IN THE DARK..."
"BYE FOR NOW. YOU TOO, MS. CABLE..."
ALEC, IT'S NO USE SHOUTING. HE'S GONE...
"IT'S TOO LATE."
CONSTANTINE? WAIT...
YOU CAN'T...JUST... LEAVE ME...
19

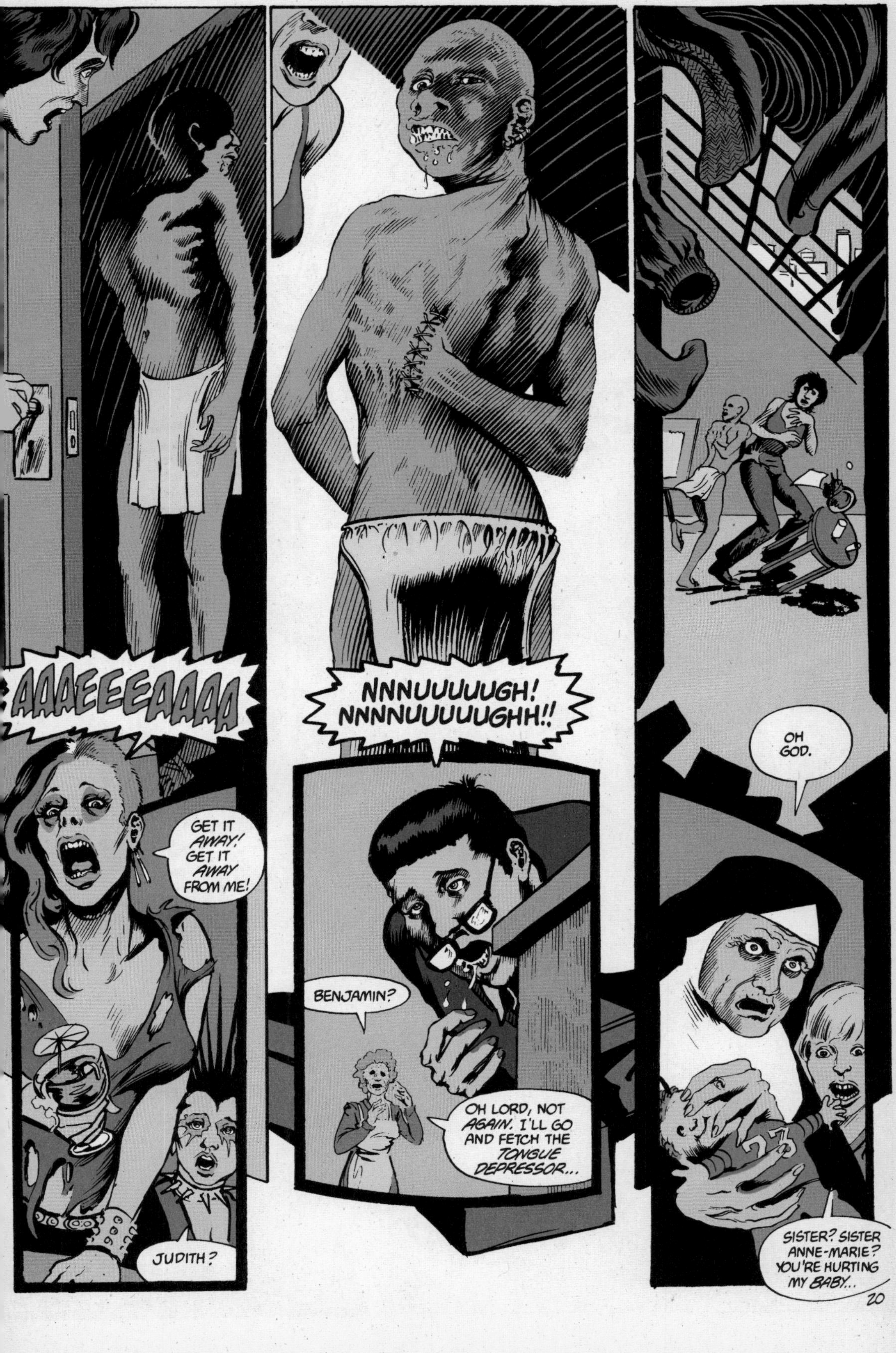
AAAEEEAAAA
NNNUUUUUGH! NNNNUUUUUGHH!!
OH GOD.
GET IT AWAY! GET IT AWAY FROM ME!
JUDITH?
BENJAMIN?
OH LORD, NOT AGAIN. I'LL GO AND FETCH THE TONGUE DEPRESSOR...
SISTER? SISTER ANNE-MARIE? YOU'RE HURTING MY BABY...
20

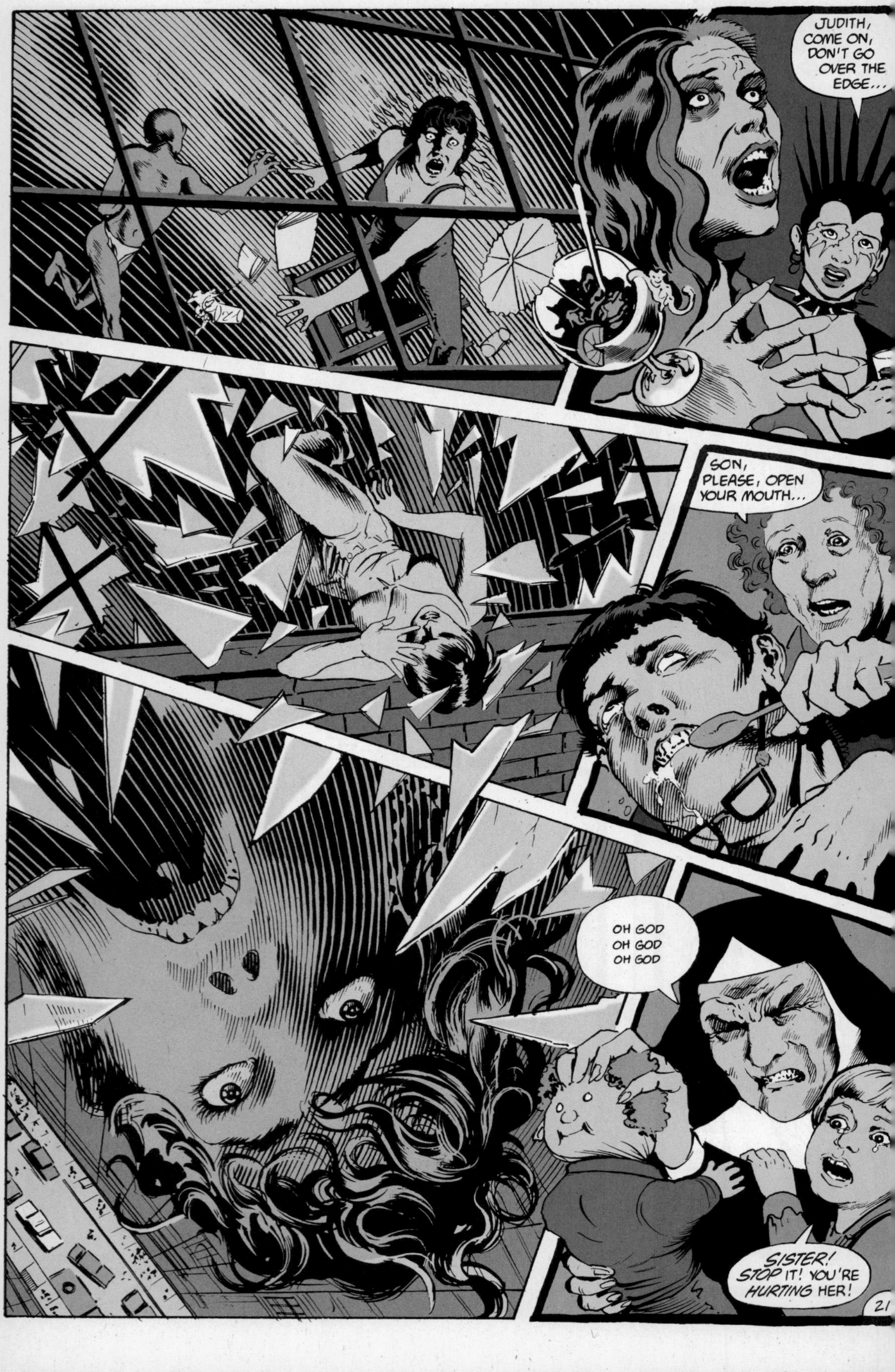
JUDITH, COME ON, DON'T GO OVER THE EDGE...
SON, PLEASE, OPEN YOUR MOUTH...
OH GOD OH GOD OH GOD
SISTER! STOP IT! YOU'RE HURTING HER!
21

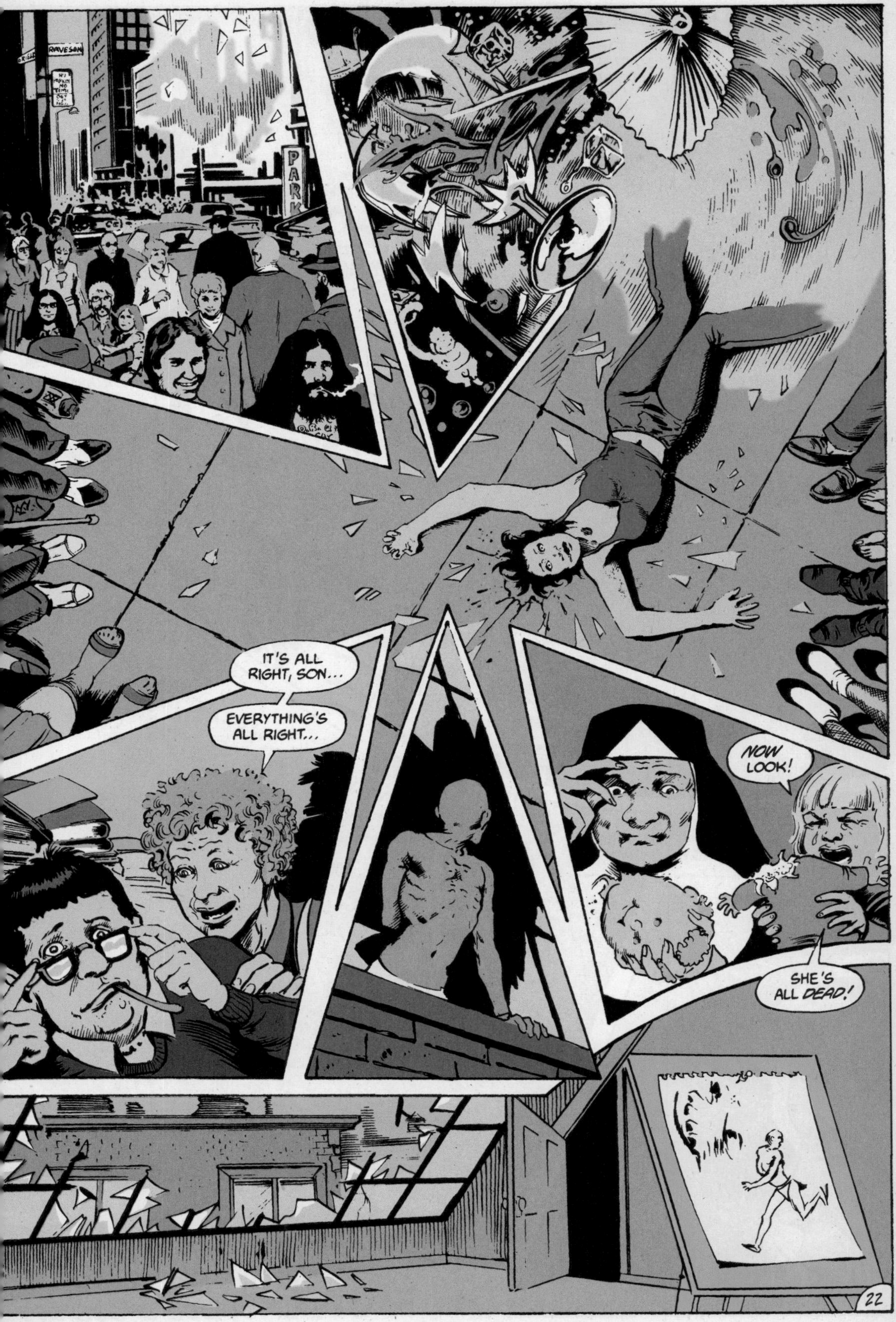
RAVESON
PARK
IT'S ALL RIGHT, SON...
EVERYTHING'S ALL RIGHT...
NOW LOOK!
SHE'S ALL DEAD!
22

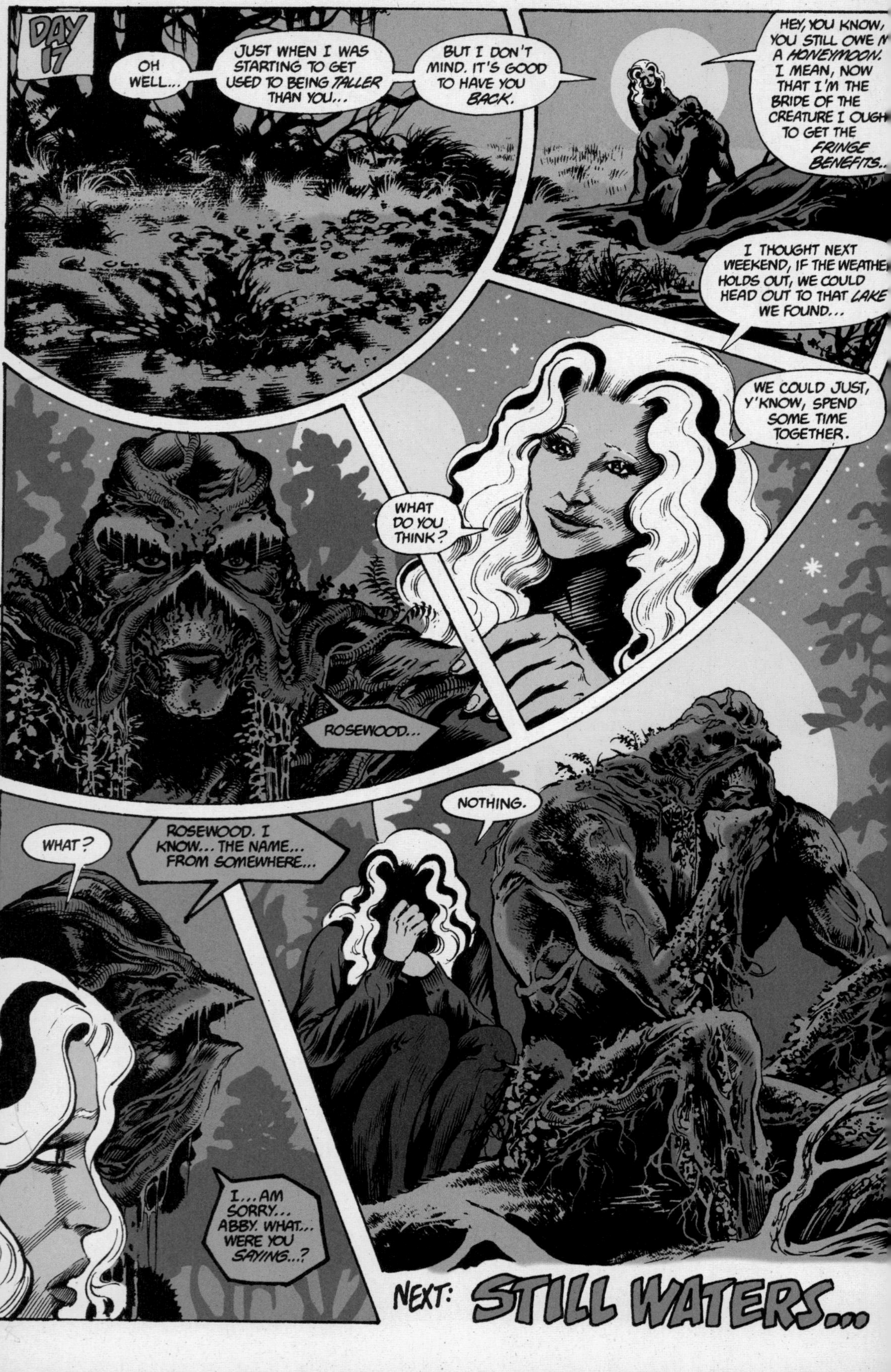
DAY 17
OH WELL...
JUST WHEN I WAS STARTING TO GET USED TO BEING TALLER THAN YOU...
BUT I DON'T MIND. IT'S GOOD TO HAVE YOU BACK.
HEY, YOU KNOW, YOU STILL OWE M A HONEYMOON. I MEAN, NOW THAT I'M THE BRIDE OF THE CREATURE I OUGH TO GET THE FRINGE BENEFITS...
I THOUGHT NEXT WEEKEND, IF THE WEATHE HOLDS OUT, WE COULD HEAD OUT TO THAT LAKE WE FOUND...
WE COULD JUST, Y'KNOW, SPEND SOME TIME TOGETHER.
WHAT DO YOU THINK?
ROSEWOOD...
WHAT?
ROSEWOOD. I KNOW... THE NAME... FROM SOMEWHERE...
NOTHING.
I... AM SORRY... ABBY. WHAT... WERE YOU SAYING...?
NEXT: STILL WATERS...

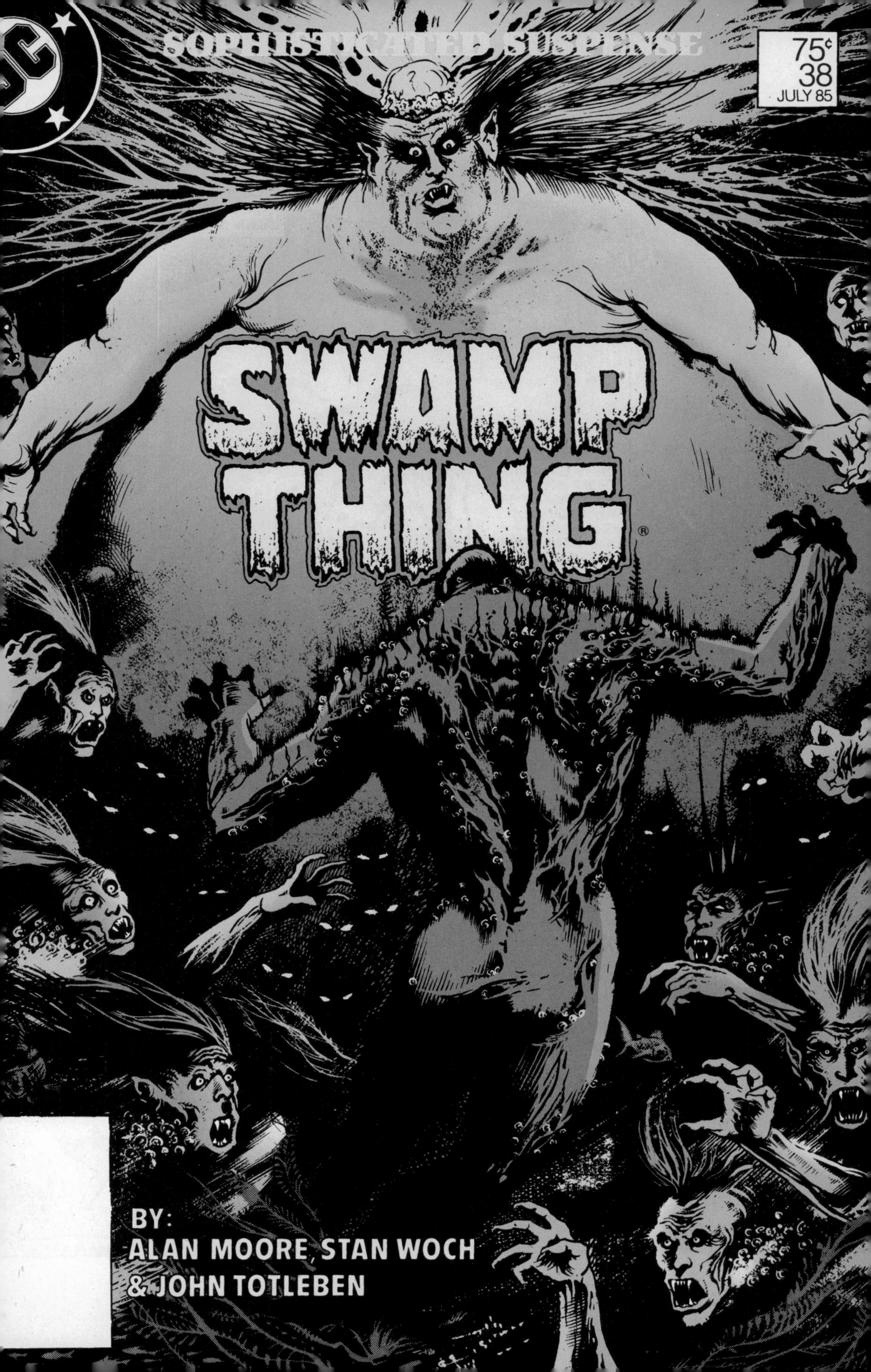
SOPHISTICATED SUSPENSE
75¢
38
JULY 85
SWAMP THING
BY:
ALAN MOORE, STAN WOCH
& JOHN TOTLEBEN

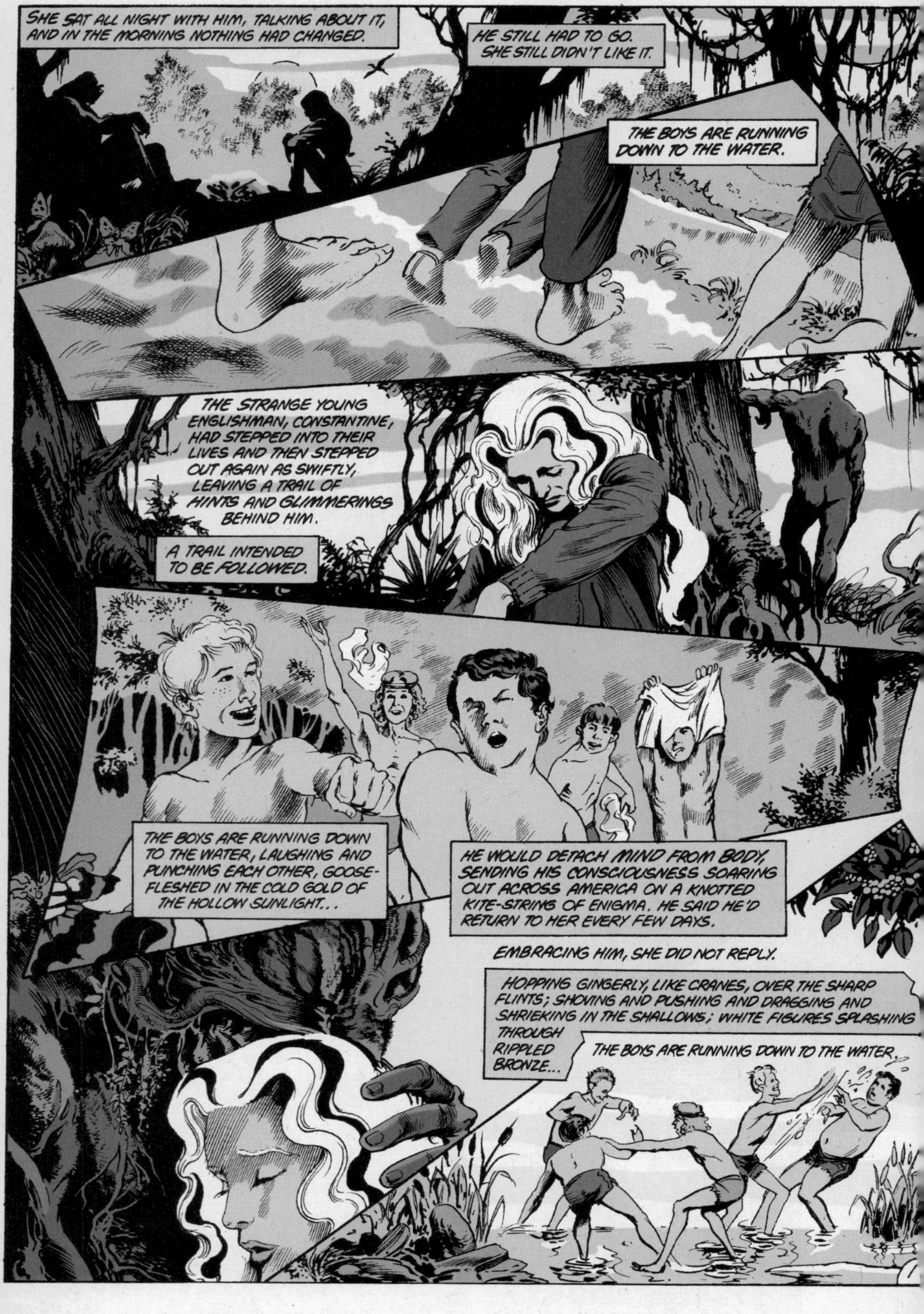
SHE SAT ALL NIGHT WITH HIM, TALKING ABOUT IT, AND IN THE MORNING NOTHING HAD CHANGED.
HE STILL HAD TO GO. SHE STILL DIDN'T LIKE IT.
THE BOYS ARE RUNNING DOWN TO THE WATER.
THE STRANGE YOUNG ENGLISHMAN, CONSTANTINE, HAD STEPPED INTO THEIR LIVES AND THEN STEPPED OUT AGAIN AS SWIFTLY, LEAVING A TRAIL OF HINTS AND GLIMMERINGS BEHIND HIM.
A TRAIL INTENDED TO BE FOLLOWED.
THE BOYS ARE RUNNING DOWN TO THE WATER, LAUGHING AND PUNCHING EACH OTHER, GOOSE-FLESHED IN THE COLD GOLD OF THE HOLLOW SUNLIGHT...
HE WOULD DETACH MIND FROM BODY, SENDING HIS CONSCIOUSNESS SOARING OUT ACROSS AMERICA ON A KNOTTED KITE-STRING OF ENIGMA. HE SAID HE'D RETURN TO HER EVERY FEW DAYS.
EMBRACING HIM, SHE DID NOT REPLY.
HOPPING GINGERLY, LIKE CRANES, OVER THE SHARP FLINTS; SHOVING AND PUSHING AND DRAGGING AND SHRIEKING IN THE SHALLOWS; WHITE FIGURES SPLASHING THROUGH RIPPLED BRONZE...
THE BOYS ARE RUNNING DOWN TO THE WATER...

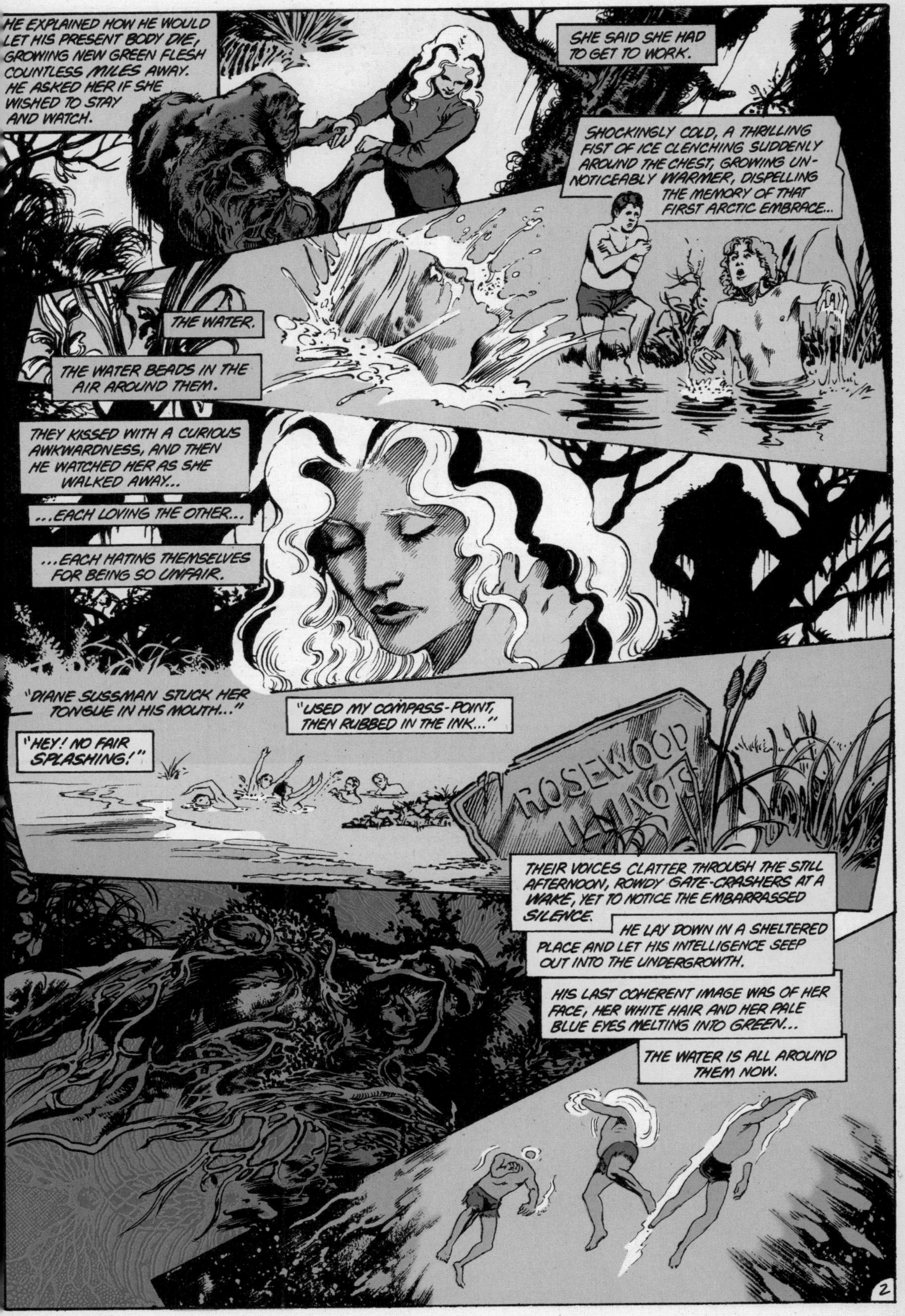
HE EXPLAINED HOW HE WOULD LET HIS PRESENT BODY DIE, GROWING NEW GREEN FLESH COUNTLESS MILES AWAY. HE ASKED HER IF SHE WISHED TO STAY AND WATCH.
SHE SAID SHE HAD TO GET TO WORK.
SHOCKINGLY COLD, A THRILLING FIST OF ICE CLENCHING SUDDENLY AROUND THE CHEST, GROWING UNNOTICEABLY WARMER, DISPELLING THE MEMORY OF THAT FIRST ARCTIC EMBRACE...
THE WATER.
THE WATER BEADS IN THE AIR AROUND THEM.
THEY KISSED WITH A CURIOUS AWKWARDNESS, AND THEN HE WATCHED HER AS SHE WALKED AWAY...
...EACH LOVING THE OTHER...
...EACH HATING THEMSELVES FOR BEING SO UNFAIR.
"DIANE SUSSMAN STUCK HER TONGUE IN HIS MOUTH..."
"USED MY COMPASS-POINT, THEN RUBBED IN THE INK..."
"HEY! NO FAIR SPLASHING!"
ROSEWOOD ILLINOIS
THEIR VOICES CLATTER THROUGH THE STILL AFTERNOON, ROWDY GATE-CRASHERS AT A WAKE, YET TO NOTICE THE EMBARRASSED SILENCE.
HE LAY DOWN IN A SHELTERED PLACE AND LET HIS INTELLIGENCE SEEP OUT INTO THE UNDERGROWTH.
HIS LAST COHERENT IMAGE WAS OF HER FACE, HER WHITE HAIR AND HER PALE BLUE EYES MELTING INTO GREEN...
THE WATER IS ALL AROUND THEM NOW.
2

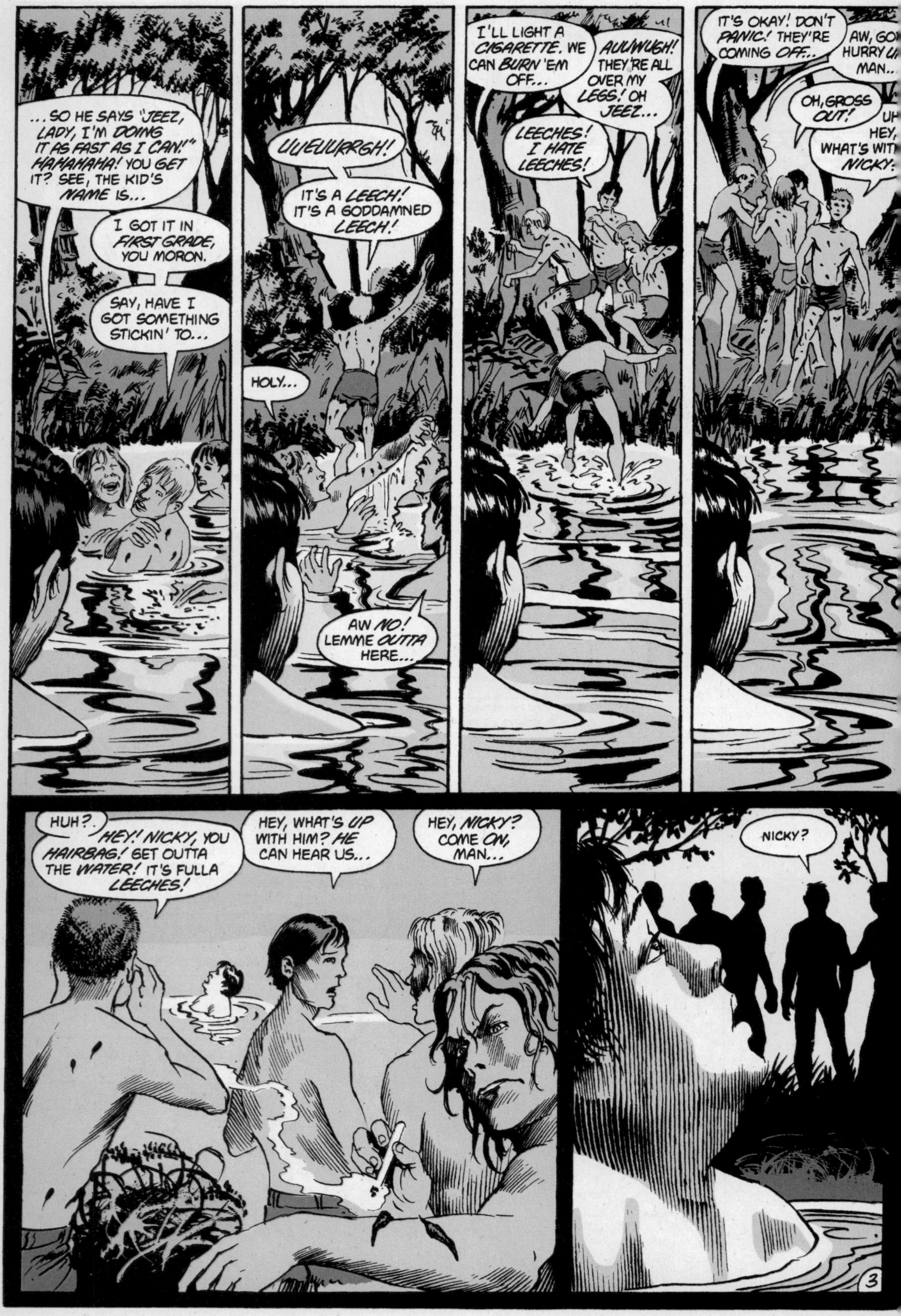
...SO HE SAYS "JEEZ, LADY, I'M DOING IT AS FAST AS I CAN!" HAHAHAHA! YOU GET IT? SEE, THE KID'S NAME IS...
I GOT IT IN FIRST GRADE, YOU MORON.
SAY, HAVE I GOT SOMETHING STICKIN' TO...
UUEUURRGH!
IT'S A LEECH! IT'S A GODDAMNED LEECH!
HOLY...
AW NO! LEMME OUTTA HERE...
I'LL LIGHT A CIGARETTE. WE CAN BURN 'EM OFF...
AUUWUGH! THEY'RE ALL OVER MY LEGS! OH JEEZ...
LEECHES! I HATE LEECHES!
IT'S OKAY! DON'T PANIC! THEY'RE COMING OFF...
OH, GROSS OUT!
HUH?
HEY! NICKY, YOU HAIRBAG! GET OUTTA THE WATER! IT'S FULLA LEECHES!
HEY, WHAT'S UP WITH HIM? HE CAN HEAR US...
HEY, NICKY? COME ON, MAN...
NICKY?
3

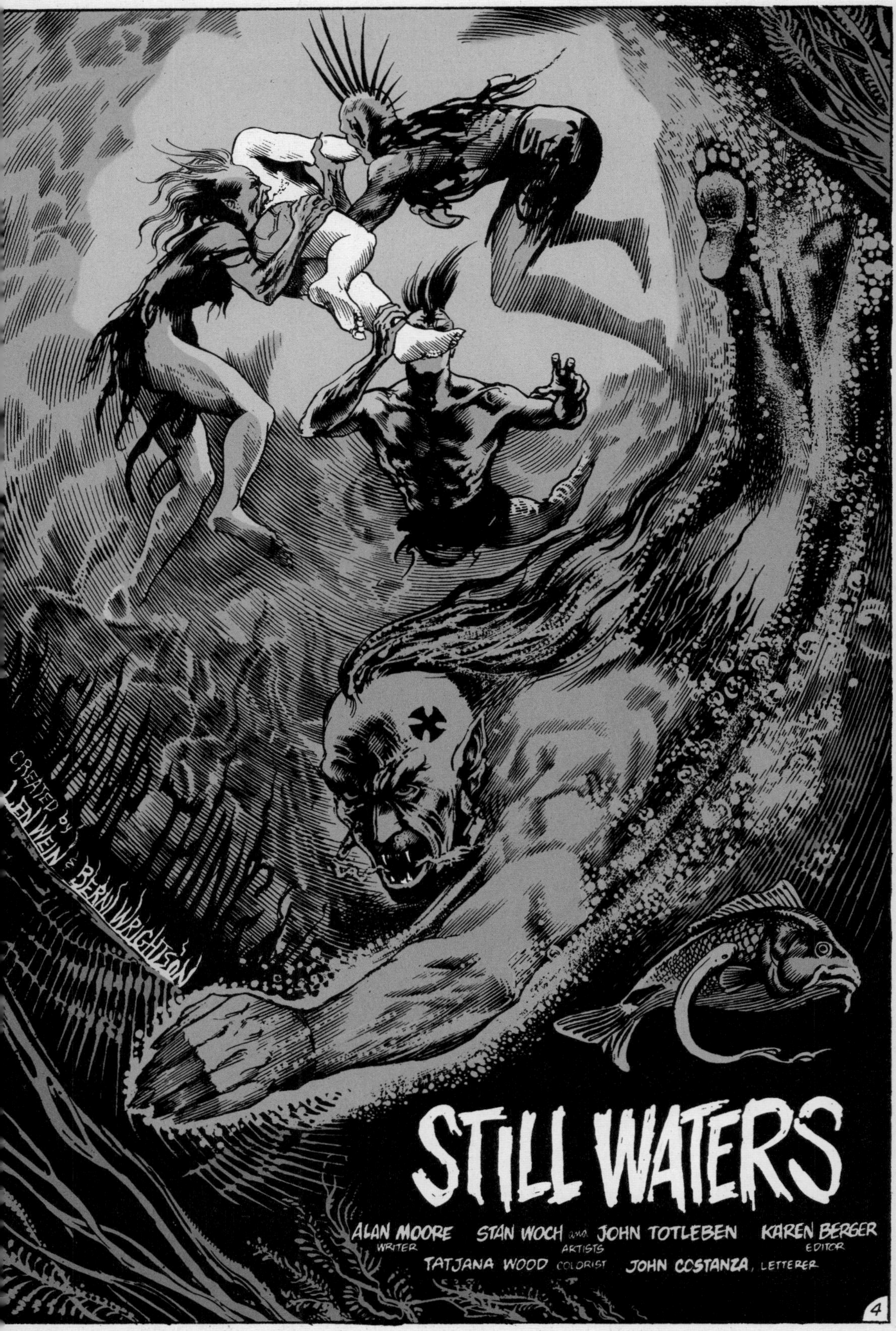
CREATED by LEN WEIN & BERNI WRIGHTSON
STILL WATERS
ALAN MOORE WRITER
STAN WOCH and JOHN TOTLEBEN ARTISTS
KAREN BERGER EDITOR
TATJANA WOOD COLORIST
JOHN COSTANZA, LETTERER
4

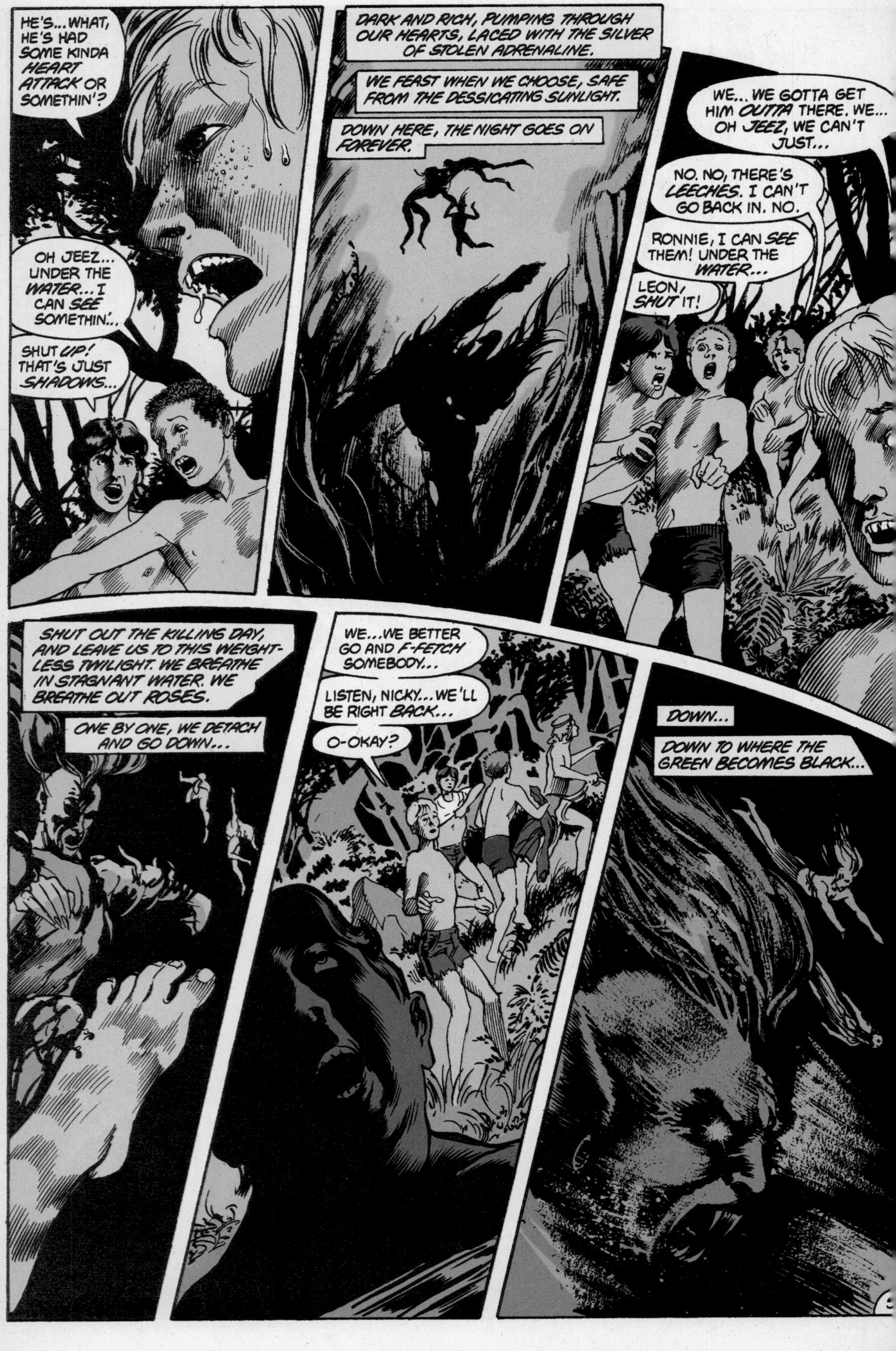
HE'S... WHAT, HE'S HAD SOME KINDA HEART ATTACK OR SOMETHIN'?
OH JEEZ... UNDER THE WATER... I CAN SEE SOMETHIN'...
SHUT UP! THAT'S JUST SHADOWS...
DARK AND RICH, PUMPING THROUGH OUR HEARTS, LACED WITH THE SILVER OF STOLEN ADRENALINE.
WE FEAST WHEN WE CHOOSE, SAFE FROM THE DESSICATING SUNLIGHT.
DOWN HERE, THE NIGHT GOES ON FOREVER.
WE... WE GOTTA GET HIM OUTTA THERE. WE... OH JEEZ, WE CAN'T JUST...
NO. NO, THERE'S LEECHES. I CAN'T GO BACK IN. NO.
RONNIE, I CAN SEE THEM! UNDER THE WATER...
LEON, SHUT IT!
SHUT OUT THE KILLING DAY, AND LEAVE US TO THIS WEIGHTLESS TWILIGHT. WE BREATHE IN STAGNANT WATER. WE BREATHE OUT ROSES.
ONE BY ONE, WE DETACH AND GO DOWN...
WE... WE BETTER GO AND F-FETCH SOMEBODY...
LISTEN, NICKY... WE'LL BE RIGHT BACK...
O-OKAY?
DOWN...
DOWN TO WHERE THE GREEN BECOMES BLACK...

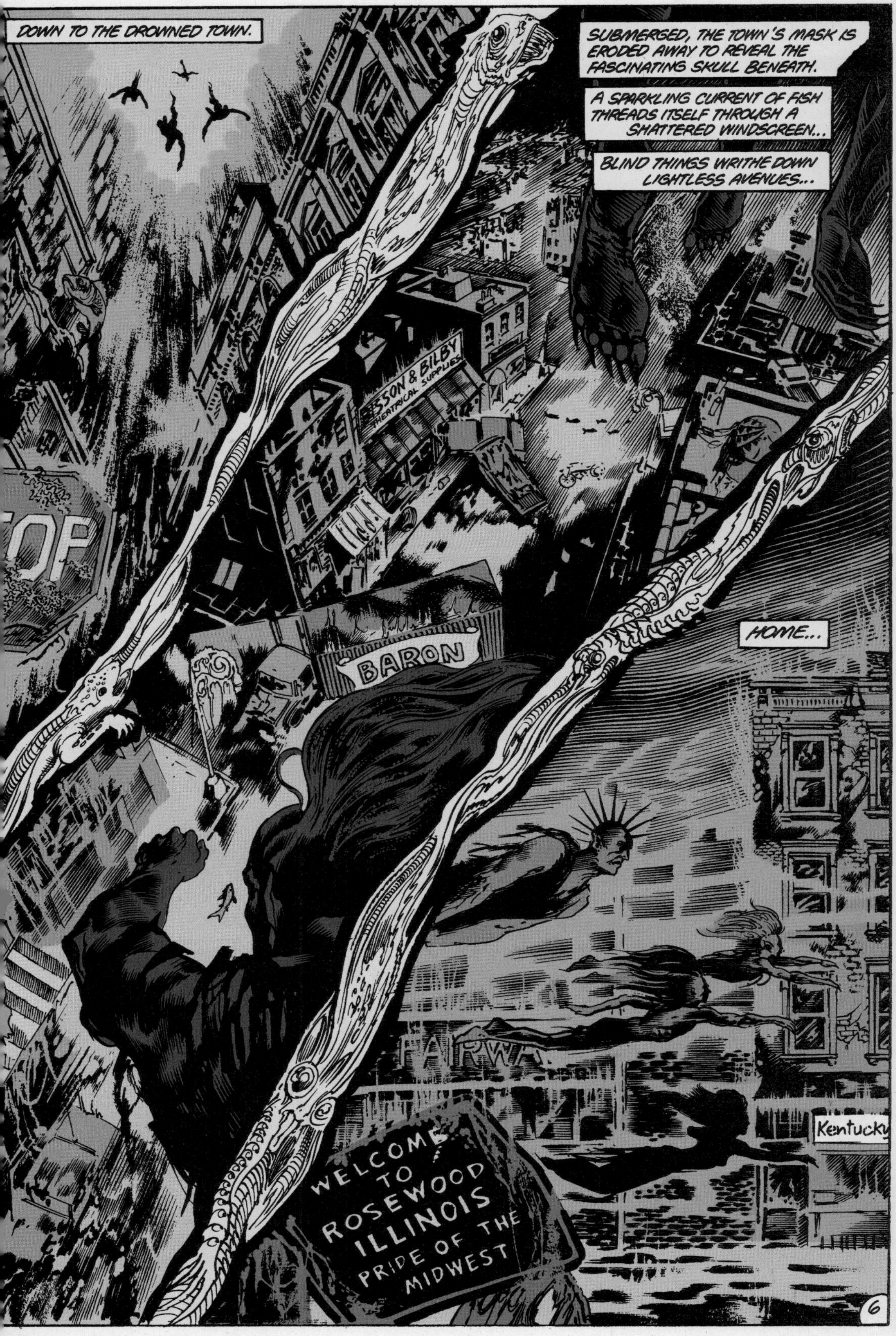
DOWN TO THE DROWNED TOWN.
SUBMERGED, THE TOWN'S MASK IS ERODED AWAY TO REVEAL THE FASCINATING SKULL BENEATH.
A SPARKLING CURRENT OF FISH THREADS ITSELF THROUGH A SHATTERED WINDSCREEN...
BLIND THINGS WRITHE DOWN LIGHTLESS AVENUES...
BISSON & BILBY THEATRICAL SUPPLIES
OP
BARON
HOME...
Kentucky
WELCOME TO ROSEWOOD ILLINOIS PRIDE OF THE MIDWEST
6

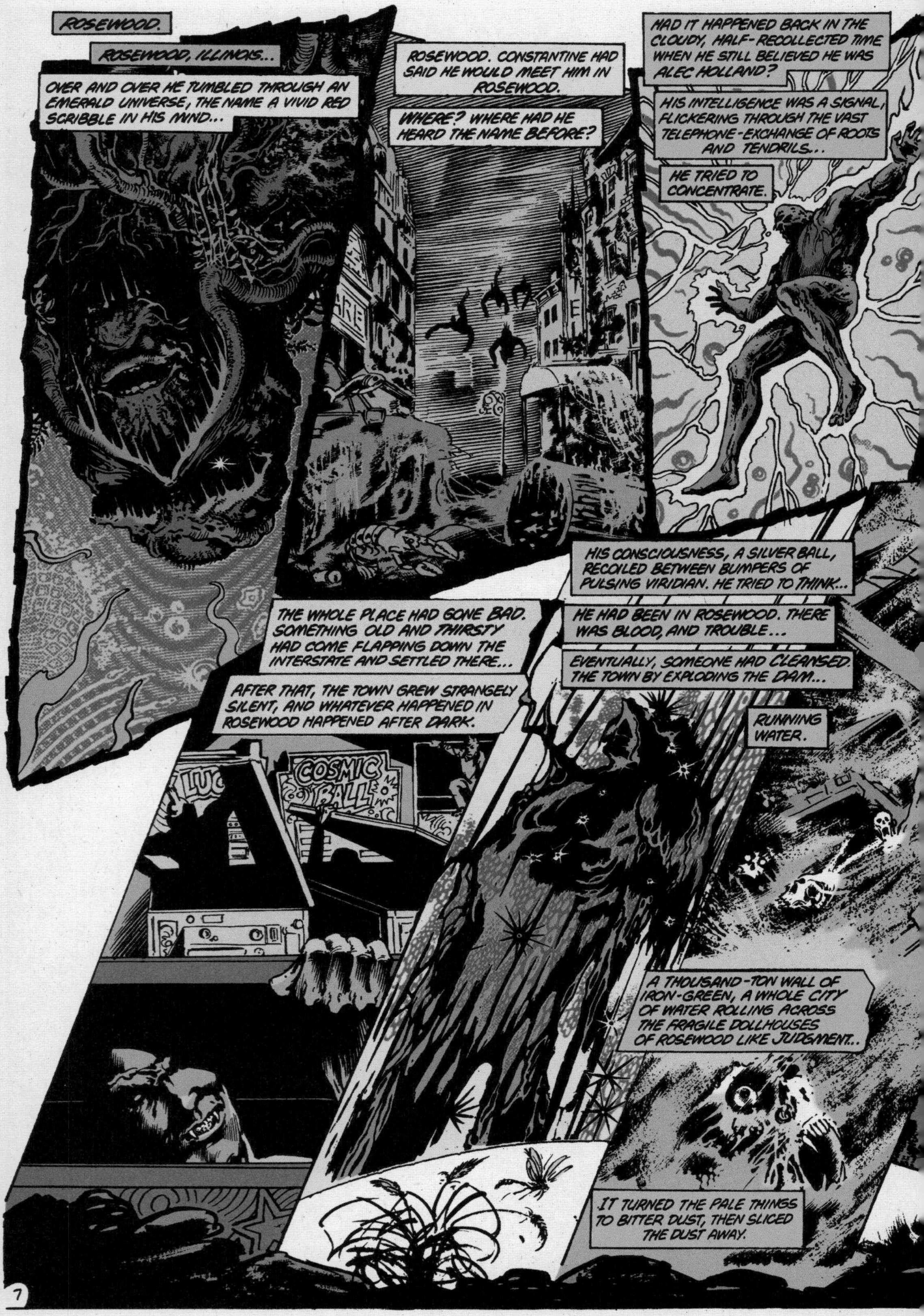
ROSEWOOD.
ROSEWOOD, ILLINOIS...
OVER AND OVER HE TUMBLED THROUGH AN EMERALD UNIVERSE, THE NAME A VIVID RED SCRIBBLE IN HIS MIND...
ROSEWOOD. CONSTANTINE HAD SAID HE WOULD MEET HIM IN ROSEWOOD.
WHERE? WHERE HAD HE HEARD THE NAME BEFORE?
HAD IT HAPPENED BACK IN THE CLOUDY, HALF-RECOLLECTED TIME WHEN HE STILL BELIEVED HE WAS ALEC HOLLAND?
HIS INTELLIGENCE WAS A SIGNAL, FLICKERING THROUGH THE VAST TELEPHONE-EXCHANGE OF ROOTS AND TENDRILS...
HE TRIED TO CONCENTRATE.
HIS CONSCIOUSNESS, A SILVER BALL, RECOILED BETWEEN BUMPERS OF PULSING VIRIDIAN. HE TRIED TO THINK...
THE WHOLE PLACE HAD GONE BAD. SOMETHING OLD AND THIRSTY HAD COME FLAPPING DOWN THE INTERSTATE AND SETTLED THERE...
AFTER THAT, THE TOWN GREW STRANGELY SILENT, AND WHATEVER HAPPENED IN ROSEWOOD HAPPENED AFTER DARK.
HE HAD BEEN IN ROSEWOOD. THERE WAS BLOOD, AND TROUBLE...
EVENTUALLY, SOMEONE HAD CLEANSED THE TOWN BY EXPLODING THE DAM...
RUNNING WATER.
COSMIC BALL
A THOUSAND-TON WALL OF IRON-GREEN, A WHOLE CITY OF WATER ROLLING ACROSS THE FRAGILE DOLLHOUSES OF ROSEWOOD LIKE JUDGMENT...
IT TURNED THE PALE THINGS TO BITTER DUST, THEN SLICED THE DUST AWAY.
7

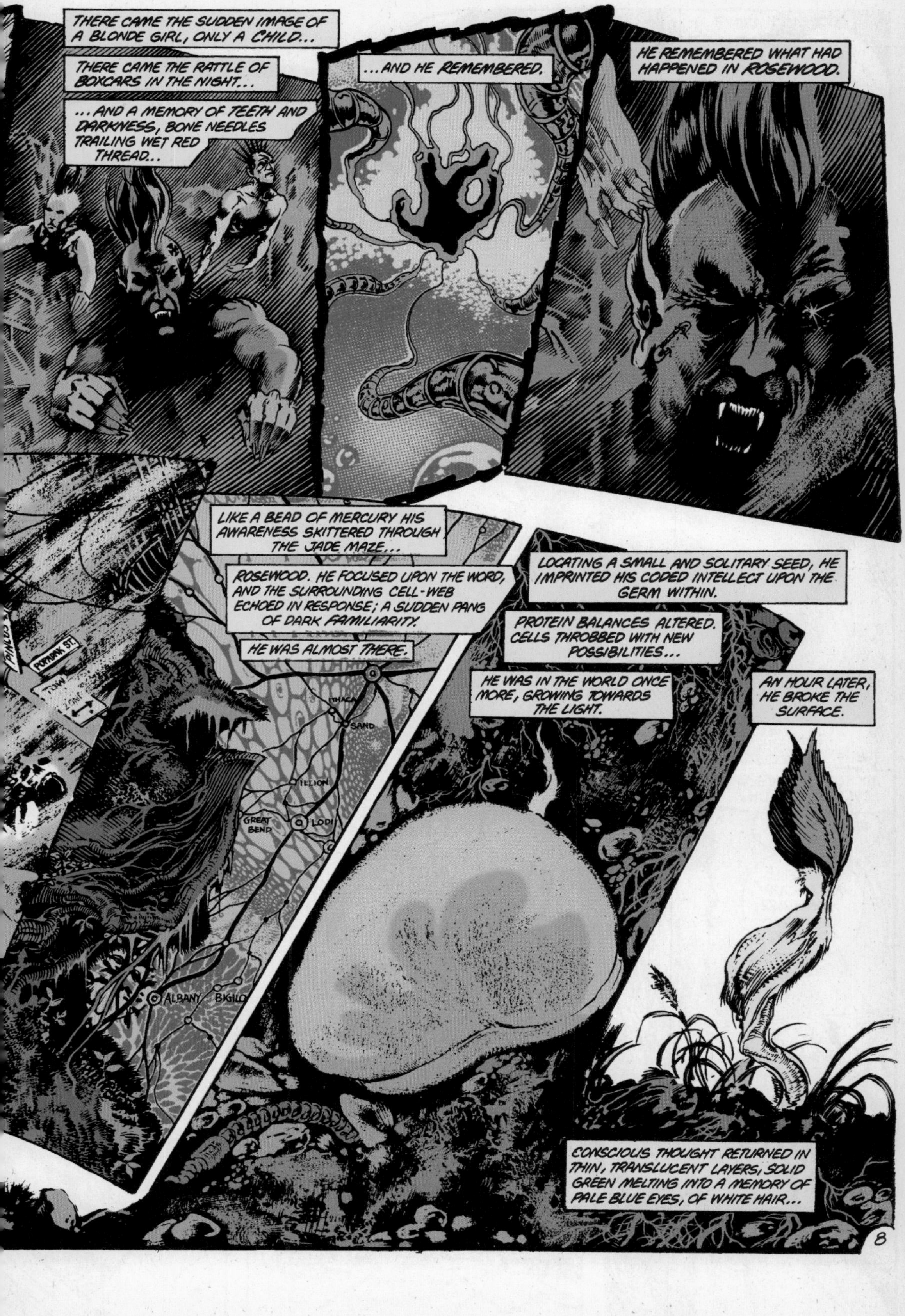
THERE CAME THE SUDDEN IMAGE OF A BLONDE GIRL, ONLY A CHILD...
THERE CAME THE RATTLE OF BOXCARS IN THE NIGHT...
...AND A MEMORY OF TEETH AND DARKNESS, BONE NEEDLES TRAILING WET RED THREAD...
...AND HE REMEMBERED.
HE REMEMBERED WHAT HAD HAPPENED IN ROSEWOOD.
LIKE A BEAD OF MERCURY HIS AWARENESS SKITTERED THROUGH THE JADE MAZE...
ROSEWOOD. HE FOCUSED UPON THE WORD, AND THE SURROUNDING CELL-WEB ECHOED IN RESPONSE; A SUDDEN PANG OF DARK FAMILIARITY.
HE WAS ALMOST THERE.
ITHACA
SAND
ILLION
GREAT BEND
LODI
ALBANY
LOCATING A SMALL AND SOLITARY SEED, HE IMPRINTED HIS CODED INTELLECT UPON THE GERM WITHIN.
PROTEIN BALANCES ALTERED. CELLS THROBBED WITH NEW POSSIBILITIES...
HE WAS IN THE WORLD ONCE MORE, GROWING TOWARDS THE LIGHT.
AN HOUR LATER, HE BROKE THE SURFACE.
CONSCIOUS THOUGHT RETURNED IN THIN, TRANSLUCENT LAYERS; SOLID GREEN MELTING INTO A MEMORY OF PALE BLUE EYES, OF WHITE HAIR...
8

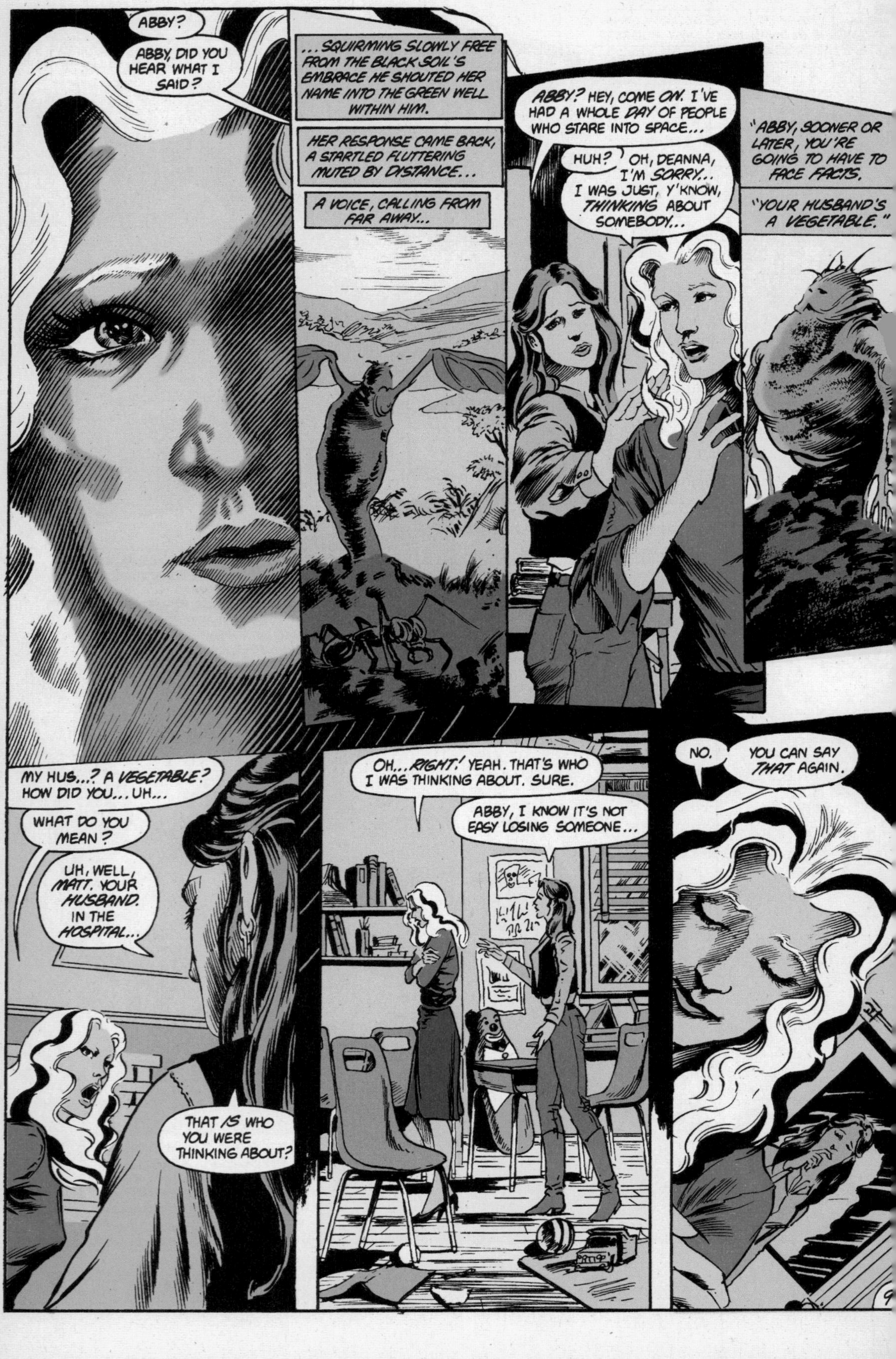
ABBY?
ABBY, DID YOU HEAR WHAT I SAID?
...SQUIRMING SLOWLY FREE FROM THE BLACK SOIL'S EMBRACE HE SHOUTED HER NAME INTO THE GREEN WELL WITHIN HIM.
HER RESPONSE CAME BACK, A STARTLED FLUTTERING MUTED BY DISTANCE...
A VOICE, CALLING FROM FAR AWAY...
ABBY? HEY, COME ON. I'VE HAD A WHOLE DAY OF PEOPLE WHO STARE INTO SPACE...
HUH?
OH, DEANNA, I'M SORRY... I WAS JUST, Y'KNOW, THINKING ABOUT SOMEBODY...
"ABBY, SOONER OR LATER, YOU'RE GOING TO HAVE TO FACE FACTS.
"YOUR HUSBAND'S A VEGETABLE."
MY HUS...? A VEGETABLE? HOW DID YOU... UH...
WHAT DO YOU MEAN?
UH, WELL, MATT. YOUR HUSBAND. IN THE HOSPITAL...
THAT IS WHO YOU WERE THINKING ABOUT?
OH... RIGHT! YEAH. THAT'S WHO I WAS THINKING ABOUT. SURE.
ABBY, I KNOW IT'S NOT EASY LOSING SOMEONE...
NO.
YOU CAN SAY THAT AGAIN.
9

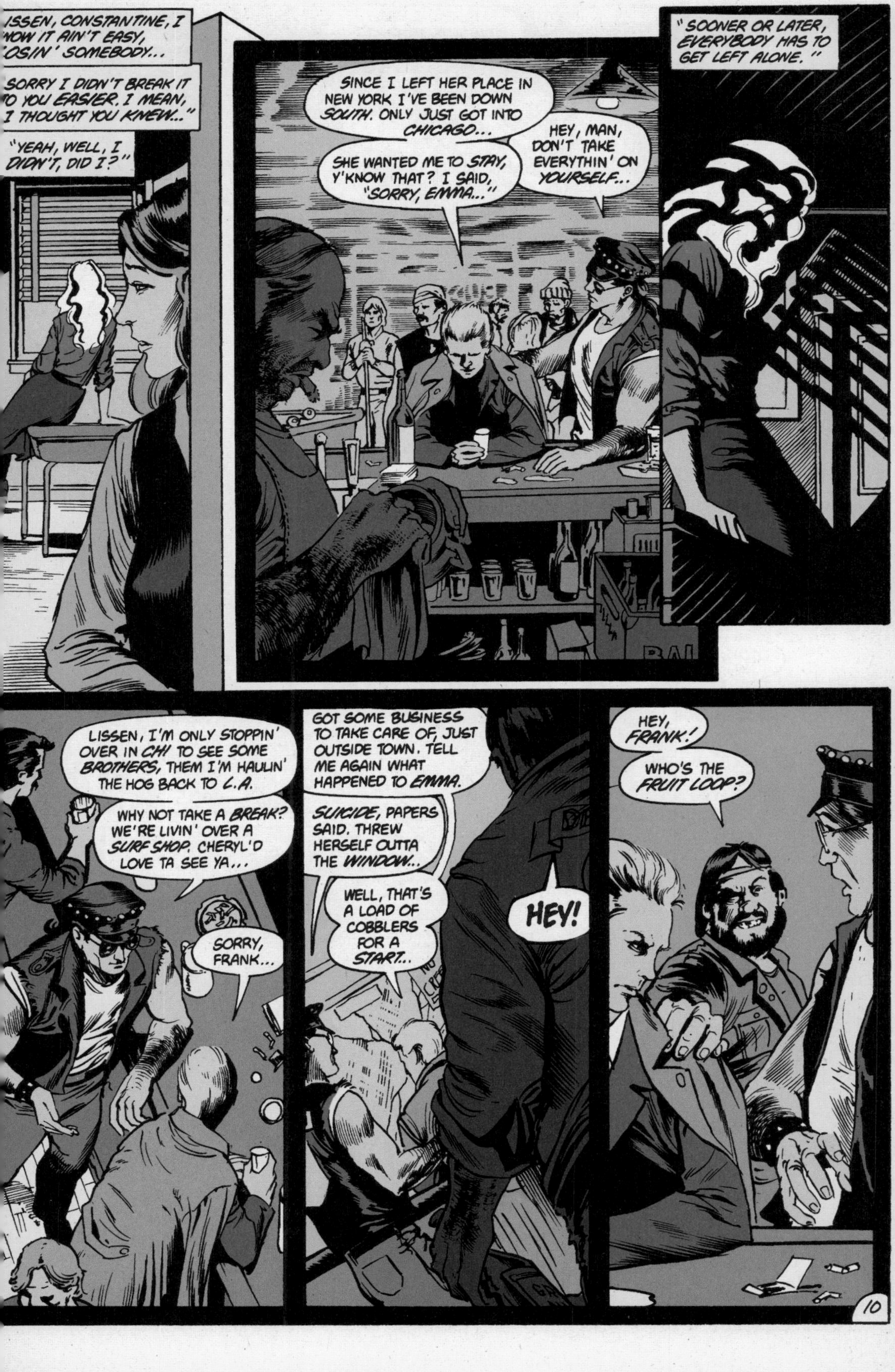
LISSEN, CONSTANTINE, I KNOW IT AIN'T EASY, LOSIN' SOMEBODY...
SORRY I DIDN'T BREAK IT TO YOU EASIER. I MEAN, I THOUGHT YOU KNEW..."
"YEAH, WELL, I DIDN'T, DID I?"
SINCE I LEFT HER PLACE IN NEW YORK I'VE BEEN DOWN SOUTH. ONLY JUST GOT INTO CHICAGO...
SHE WANTED ME TO STAY, Y'KNOW THAT? I SAID, "SORRY, EMMA..."
HEY, MAN, DON'T TAKE EVERYTHIN' ON YOURSELF...
"SOONER OR LATER, EVERYBODY HAS TO GET LEFT ALONE."
LISSEN, I'M ONLY STOPPIN' OVER IN CHI TO SEE SOME BROTHERS, THEM I'M HAULIN' THE HOG BACK TO L.A.
WHY NOT TAKE A BREAK? WE'RE LIVIN' OVER A SURF SHOP. CHERYL'D LOVE TA SEE YA...
SORRY, FRANK...
GOT SOME BUSINESS TO TAKE CARE OF, JUST OUTSIDE TOWN. TELL ME AGAIN WHAT HAPPENED TO EMMA.
SUICIDE, PAPERS SAID. THREW HERSELF OUTTA THE WINDOW...
WELL, THAT'S A LOAD OF COBBLERS FOR A START...
HEY!
HEY, FRANK!
WHO'S THE FRUIT LOOP?
10

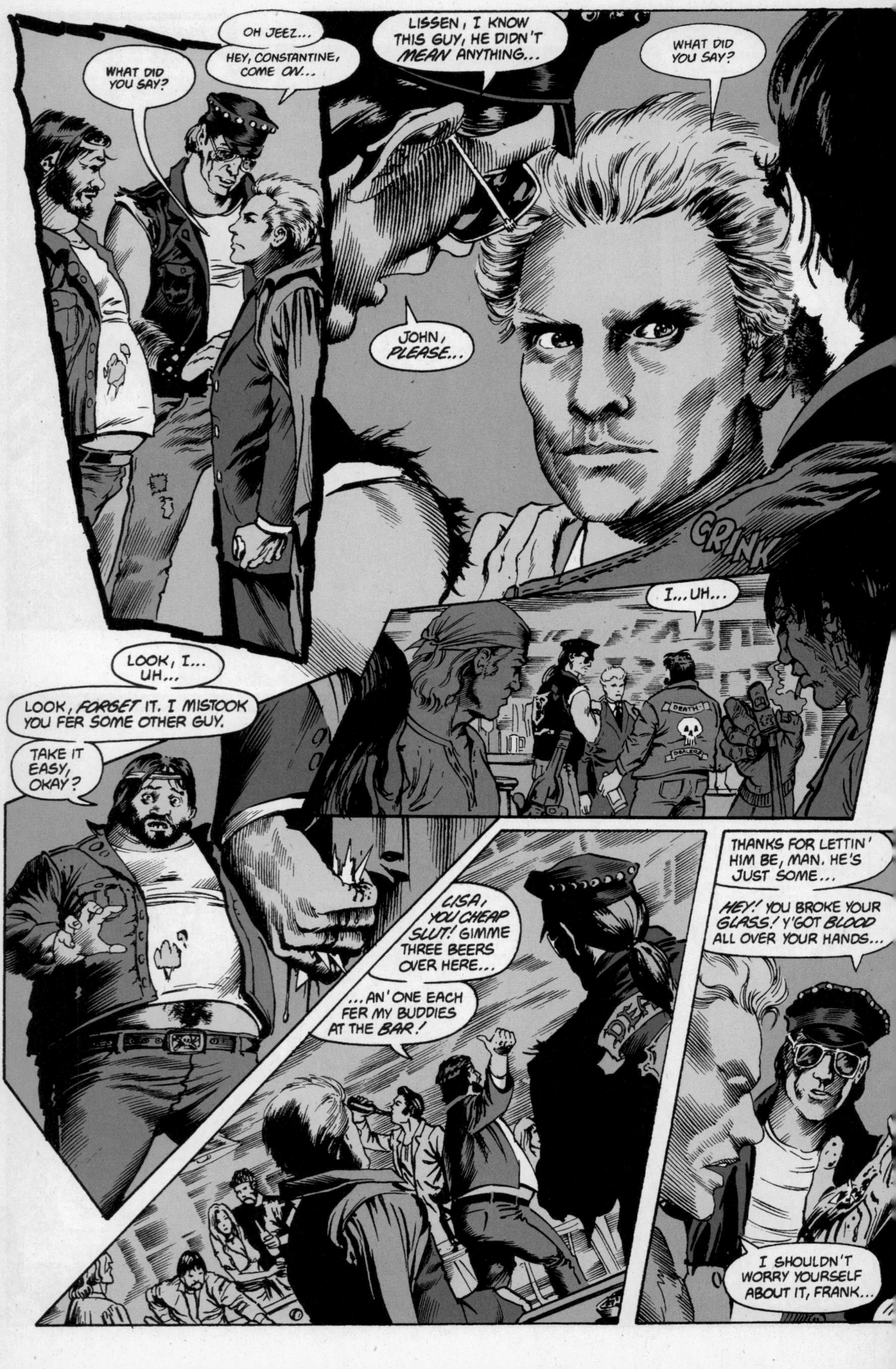

WHAT DID YOU SAY?
OH JEEZ...
HEY, CONSTANTINE, COME ON...
LISSEN, I KNOW THIS GUY, HE DIDN'T MEAN ANYTHING...
WHAT DID YOU SAY?
JOHN, PLEASE...
CRINK
I... UH...
LOOK, I... UH...
LOOK, FORGET IT. I MISTOOK YOU FER SOME OTHER GUY.
TAKE IT EASY, OKAY?
LISA, YOU CHEAP SLUT! GIMME THREE BEERS OVER HERE...
...AN' ONE EACH FER MY BUDDIES AT THE BAR!
THANKS FOR LETTIN' HIM BE, MAN. HE'S JUST SOME...
HEY! YOU BROKE YOUR GLASS! Y'GOT BLOOD ALL OVER YOUR HANDS...
I SHOULDN'T WORRY YOURSELF ABOUT IT, FRANK...

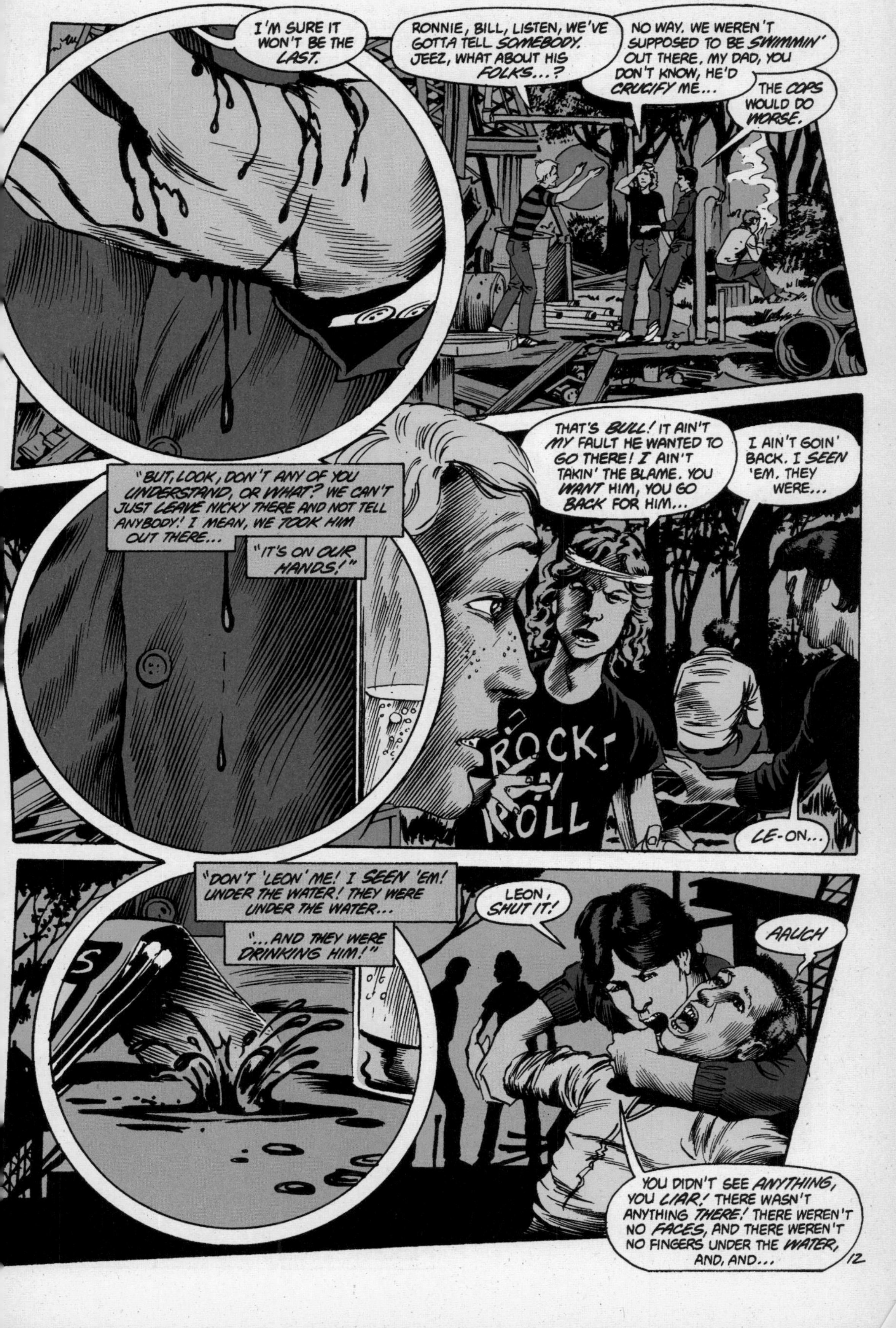
I'M SURE IT WON'T BE THE LAST.
RONNIE, BILL, LISTEN, WE'VE GOTTA TELL SOMEBODY. JEEZ, WHAT ABOUT HIS FOLKS...?
NO WAY. WE WEREN'T SUPPOSED TO BE SWIMMIN' OUT THERE. MY DAD, YOU DON'T KNOW, HE'D CRUCIFY ME...
THE COPS WOULD DO WORSE.
"BUT, LOOK, DON'T ANY OF YOU UNDERSTAND, OR WHAT? WE CAN'T JUST LEAVE NICKY THERE AND NOT TELL ANYBODY! I MEAN, WE TOOK HIM OUT THERE...
"IT'S ON OUR HANDS!"
THAT'S BULL! IT AIN'T MY FAULT HE WANTED TO GO THERE! I AIN'T TAKIN' THE BLAME. YOU WANT HIM, YOU GO BACK FOR HIM...
I AIN'T GOIN' BACK. I SEEN 'EM. THEY WERE...
ROCK N ROLL
LE-ON...
"DON'T 'LEON' ME! I SEEN 'EM! UNDER THE WATER! THEY WERE UNDER THE WATER...
"...AND THEY WERE DRINKING HIM!"
LEON, SHUT IT!
AAUCH
YOU DIDN'T SEE ANYTHING, YOU LIAR! THERE WASN'T ANYTHING THERE! THERE WEREN'T NO FACES, AND THERE WEREN'T NO FINGERS UNDER THE WATER, AND, AND...
12

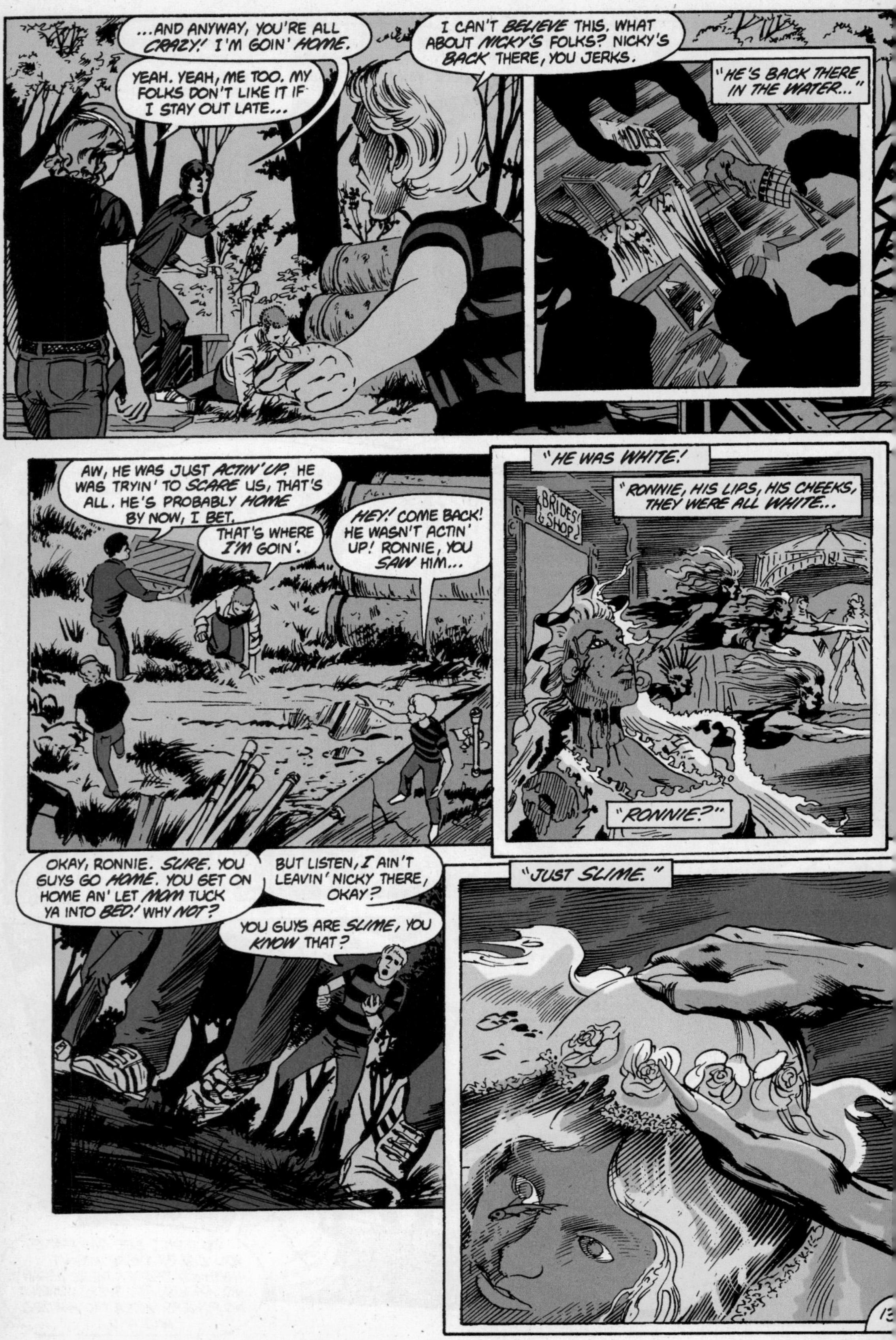
...AND ANYWAY, YOU'RE ALL CRAZY! I'M GOIN' HOME.
YEAH. YEAH, ME TOO. MY FOLKS DON'T LIKE IT IF I STAY OUT LATE...
I CAN'T BELIEVE THIS. WHAT ABOUT NICKY'S FOLKS? NICKY'S BACK THERE, YOU JERKS.
"HE'S BACK THERE IN THE WATER..."
AW, HE WAS JUST ACTIN' UP. HE WAS TRYIN' TO SCARE US, THAT'S ALL. HE'S PROBABLY HOME BY NOW, I BET.
THAT'S WHERE I'M GOIN'.
HEY! COME BACK! HE WASN'T ACTIN' UP! RONNIE, YOU SAW HIM...
"HE WAS WHITE!
"RONNIE, HIS LIPS, HIS CHEEKS, THEY WERE ALL WHITE...
BRIDES SHOP
"RONNIE?"
OKAY, RONNIE. SURE. YOU GUYS GO HOME. YOU GET ON HOME AN' LET MOM TUCK YA INTO BED! WHY NOT?
BUT LISTEN, I AIN'T LEAVIN' NICKY THERE, OKAY?
YOU GUYS ARE SLIME, YOU KNOW THAT?
"JUST SLIME."
13

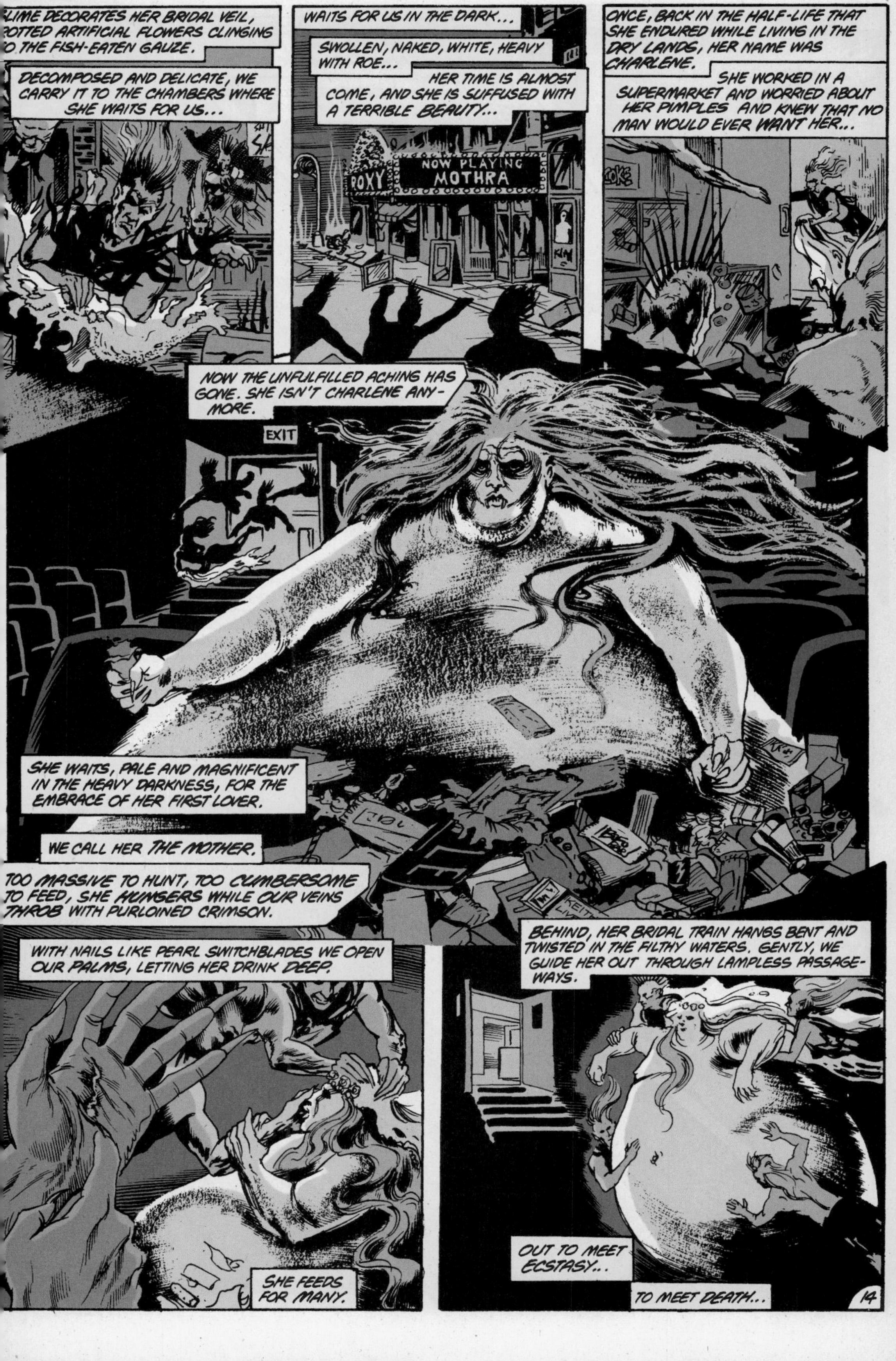
SLIME DECORATES HER BRIDAL VEIL, ROTTED ARTIFICIAL FLOWERS CLINGING TO THE FISH-EATEN GAUZE.
DECOMPOSED AND DELICATE, WE CARRY IT TO THE CHAMBERS WHERE SHE WAITS FOR US...
WAITS FOR US IN THE DARK...
SWOLLEN, NAKED, WHITE, HEAVY WITH ROE...
HER TIME IS ALMOST COME, AND SHE IS SUFFUSED WITH A TERRIBLE BEAUTY...
NOW PLAYING MOTHRA
ROXY
ONCE, BACK IN THE HALF-LIFE THAT SHE ENDURED WHILE LIVING IN THE DRY LANDS, HER NAME WAS CHARLENE.
SHE WORKED IN A SUPERMARKET AND WORRIED ABOUT HER PIMPLES AND KNEW THAT NO MAN WOULD EVER WANT HER...
NOW THE UNFULFILLED ACHING HAS GONE. SHE ISN'T CHARLENE ANY-MORE.
EXIT
SHE WAITS, PALE AND MAGNIFICENT IN THE HEAVY DARKNESS, FOR THE EMBRACE OF HER FIRST LOVER.
WE CALL HER THE MOTHER.
TOO MASSIVE TO HUNT, TOO CUMBERSOME TO FEED, SHE HUNGERS WHILE OUR VEINS THROB WITH PURLOINED CRIMSON.
WITH NAILS LIKE PEARL SWITCHBLADES WE OPEN OUR PALMS, LETTING HER DRINK DEEP.
SHE FEEDS FOR MANY.
BEHIND, HER BRIDAL TRAIN HANGS BENT AND TWISTED IN THE FILTHY WATERS. GENTLY, WE GUIDE HER OUT THROUGH LAMPLESS PASSAGE-WAYS.
OUT TO MEET ECSTASY...
TO MEET DEATH...
14

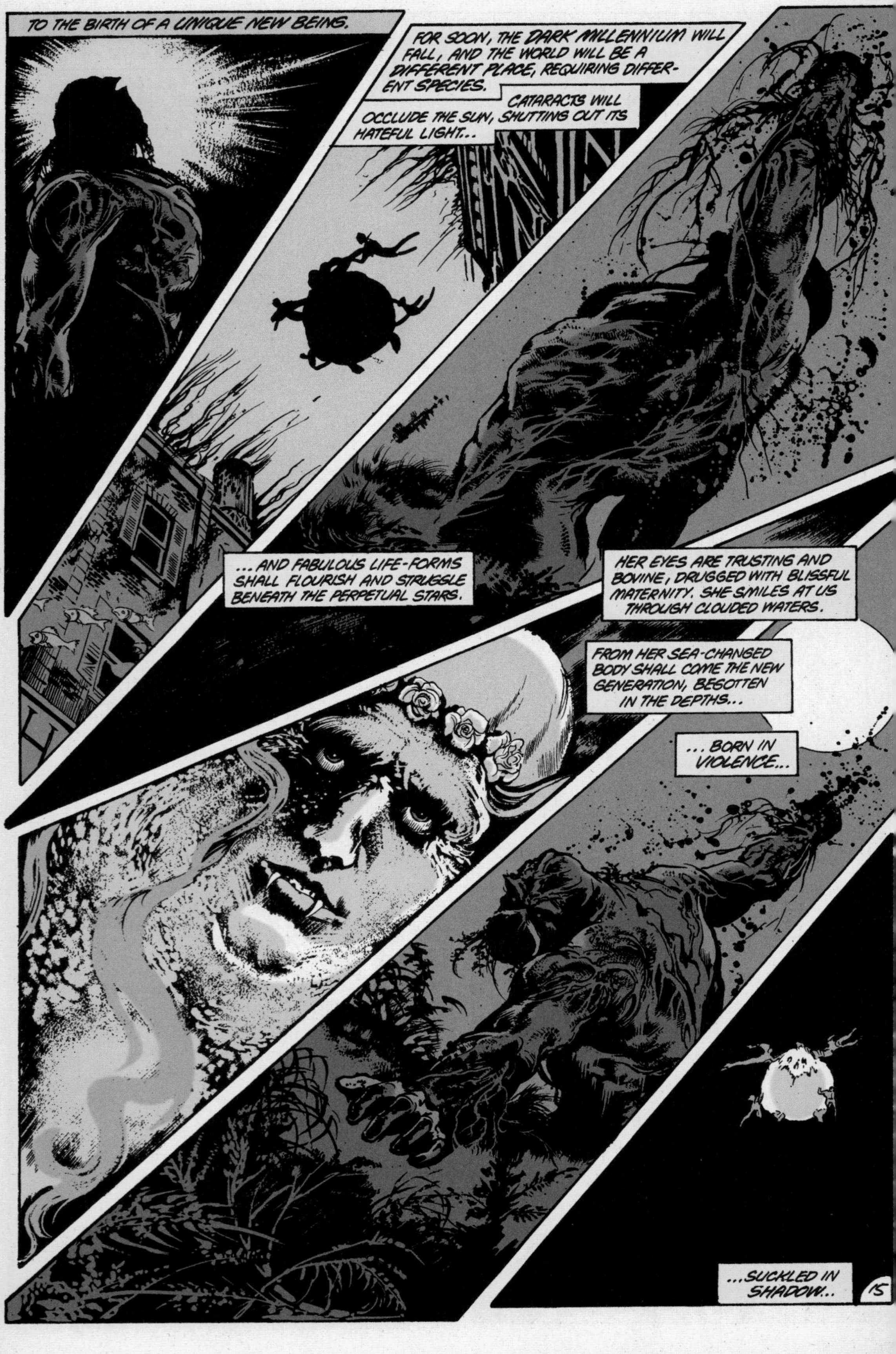
TO THE BIRTH OF A UNIQUE NEW BEING.
FOR SOON, THE DARK MILLENNIUM WILL FALL, AND THE WORLD WILL BE A DIFFERENT PLACE, REQUIRING DIFFERENT SPECIES.
CATARACTS WILL OCCLUDE THE SUN, SHUTTING OUT ITS HATEFUL LIGHT...
...AND FABULOUS LIFE-FORMS SHALL FLOURISH AND STRUGGLE BENEATH THE PERPETUAL STARS.
HER EYES ARE TRUSTING AND BOVINE, DRUGGED WITH BLISSFUL MATERNITY. SHE SMILES AT US THROUGH CLOUDED WATERS.
FROM HER SEA-CHANGED BODY SHALL COME THE NEW GENERATION, BEGOTTEN IN THE DEPTHS...
...BORN IN VIOLENCE...
...SUCKLED IN SHADOW...
15

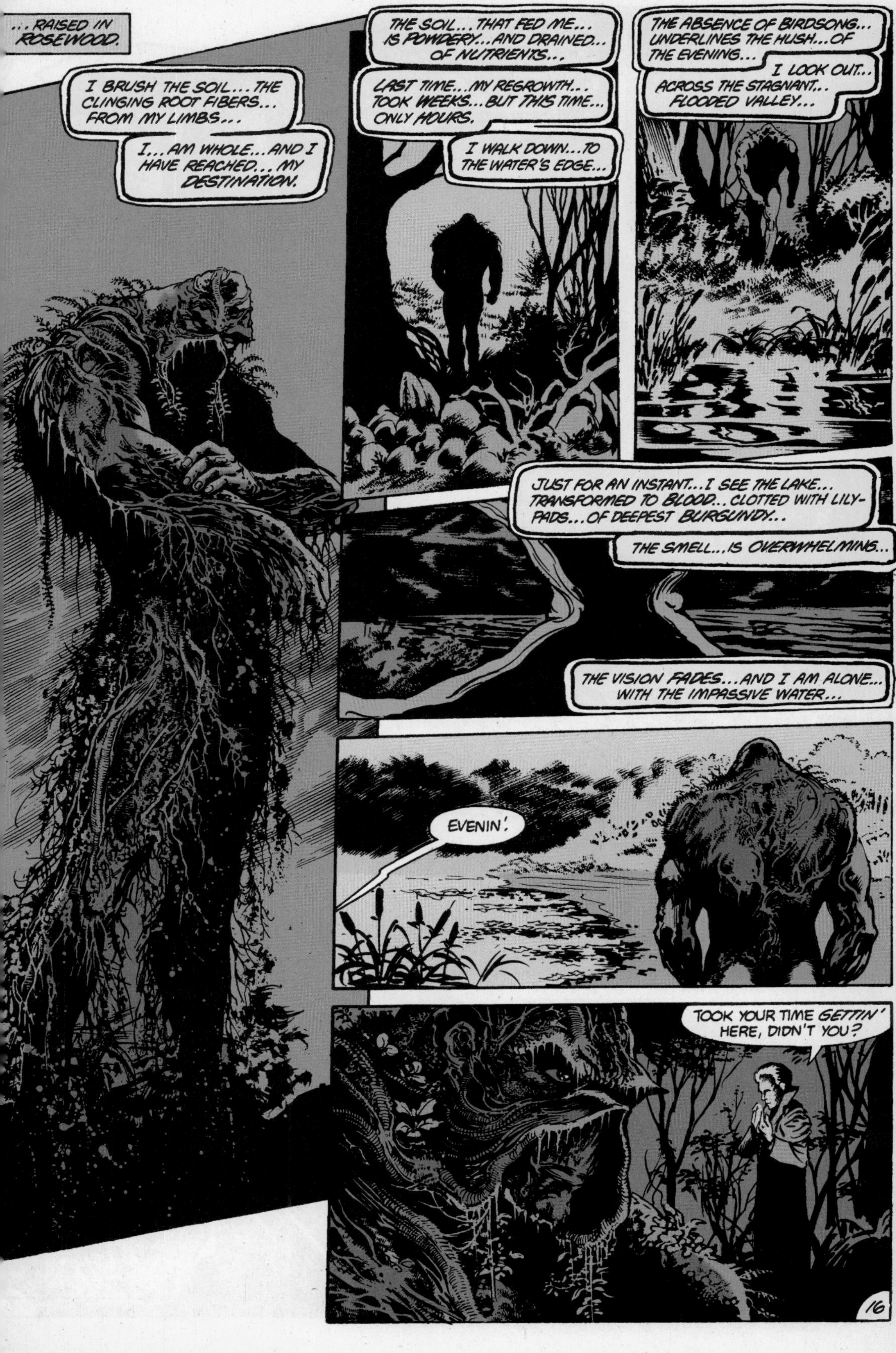
...RAISED IN ROSEWOOD.
I BRUSH THE SOIL... THE CLINGING ROOT FIBERS... FROM MY LIMBS...
I... AM WHOLE... AND I HAVE REACHED... MY DESTINATION.
THE SOIL... THAT FED ME... IS POWDERY... AND DRAINED... OF NUTRIENTS...
LAST TIME... MY REGROWTH... TOOK WEEKS... BUT THIS TIME... ONLY HOURS.
I WALK DOWN... TO THE WATER'S EDGE...
THE ABSENCE OF BIRDSONG... UNDERLINES THE HUSH... OF THE EVENING...
I LOOK OUT... ACROSS THE STAGNANT... FLOODED VALLEY...
JUST FOR AN INSTANT... I SEE THE LAKE... TRANSFORMED TO BLOOD... CLOTTED WITH LILY-PADS... OF DEEPEST BURGUNDY...
THE SMELL... IS OVERWHELMING...
THE VISION FADES... AND I AM ALONE... WITH THE IMPASSIVE WATER...
EVENIN'.
TOOK YOUR TIME GETTIN' HERE, DIDN'T YOU?
16

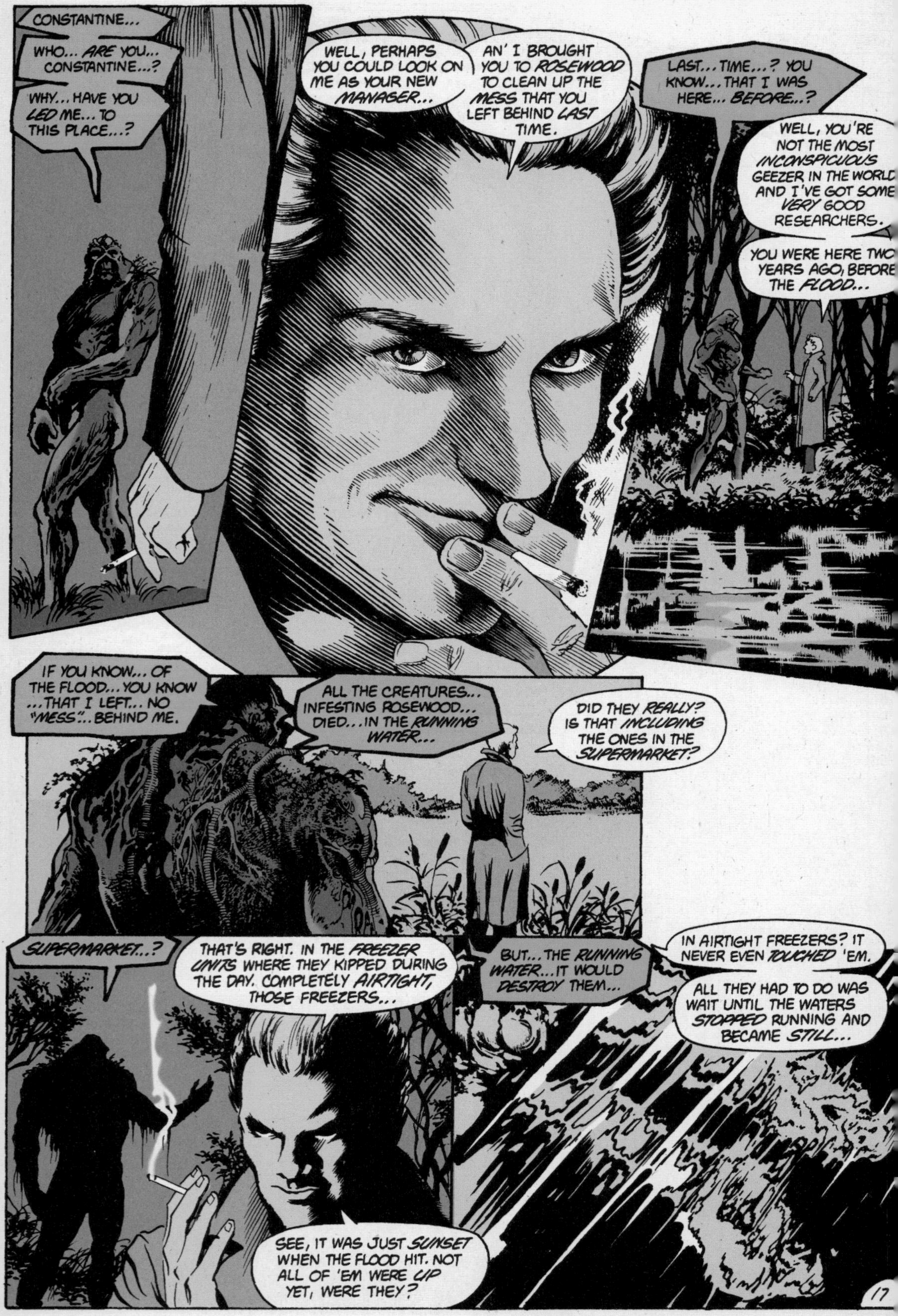
CONSTANTINE...
WHO... ARE YOU... CONSTANTINE...?
WHY... HAVE YOU LED ME... TO THIS PLACE...?
WELL, PERHAPS YOU COULD LOOK ON ME AS YOUR NEW MANAGER...
AN' I BROUGHT YOU TO ROSEWOOD TO CLEAN UP THE MESS THAT YOU LEFT BEHIND LAST TIME.
LAST... TIME...? YOU KNOW... THAT I WAS HERE... BEFORE...?
WELL, YOU'RE NOT THE MOST INCONSPICUOUS GEEZER IN THE WORLD AND I'VE GOT SOME VERY GOOD RESEARCHERS.
YOU WERE HERE TWO YEARS AGO, BEFORE THE FLOOD...
IF YOU KNOW... OF THE FLOOD... YOU KNOW ...THAT I LEFT... NO "MESS"... BEHIND ME.
ALL THE CREATURES... INFESTING ROSEWOOD... DIED... IN THE RUNNING WATER...
DID THEY REALLY? IS THAT INCLUDING THE ONES IN THE SUPERMARKET?
SUPERMARKET...?
THAT'S RIGHT. IN THE FREEZER UNITS WHERE THEY KIPPED DURING THE DAY. COMPLETELY AIRTIGHT, THOSE FREEZERS...
SEE, IT WAS JUST SUNSET WHEN THE FLOOD HIT. NOT ALL OF 'EM WERE UP YET, WERE THEY?
BUT... THE RUNNING WATER... IT WOULD DESTROY THEM...
IN AIRTIGHT FREEZERS? IT NEVER EVEN TOUCHED 'EM.
ALL THEY HAD TO DO WAS WAIT UNTIL THE WATERS STOPPED RUNNING AND BECAME STILL...
17

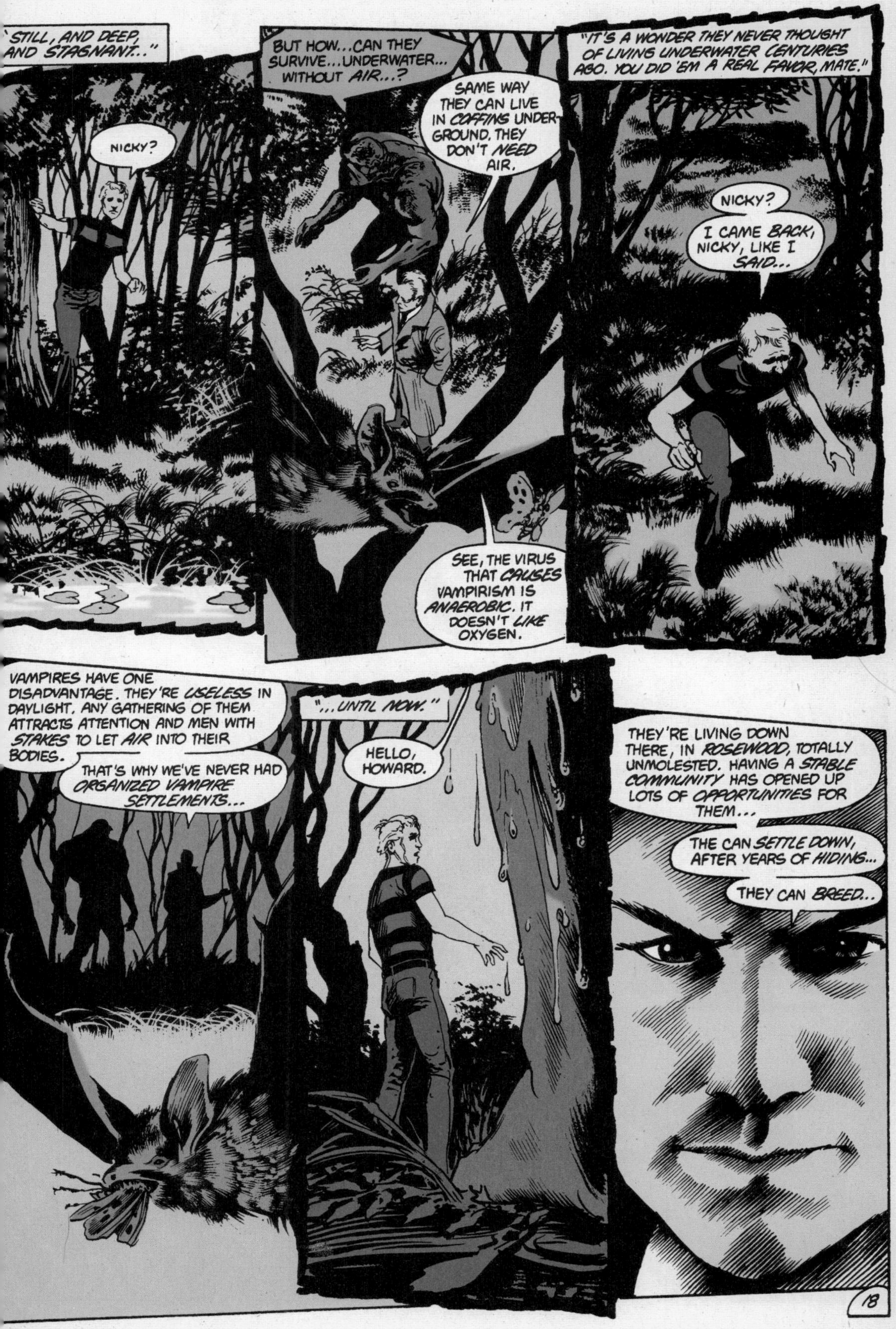
"STILL, AND DEEP, AND STAGNANT..."
NICKY?
BUT HOW...CAN THEY SURVIVE...UNDERWATER... WITHOUT AIR...?
SAME WAY THEY CAN LIVE IN COFFINS UNDERGROUND. THEY DON'T NEED AIR.
SEE, THE VIRUS THAT CAUSES VAMPIRISM IS ANAEROBIC. IT DOESN'T LIKE OXYGEN.
"IT'S A WONDER THEY NEVER THOUGHT OF LIVING UNDERWATER CENTURIES AGO. YOU DID 'EM A REAL FAVOR, MATE."
NICKY?
I CAME BACK, NICKY, LIKE I SAID...
VAMPIRES HAVE ONE DISADVANTAGE. THEY'RE USELESS IN DAYLIGHT. ANY GATHERING OF THEM ATTRACTS ATTENTION AND MEN WITH STAKES TO LET AIR INTO THEIR BODIES.
THAT'S WHY WE'VE NEVER HAD ORGANIZED VAMPIRE SETTLEMENTS...
"...UNTIL NOW."
HELLO, HOWARD.
THEY'RE LIVING DOWN THERE, IN ROSEWOOD, TOTALLY UNMOLESTED. HAVING A STABLE COMMUNITY HAS OPENED UP LOTS OF OPPORTUNITIES FOR THEM...
THE CAN SETTLE DOWN, AFTER YEARS OF HIDING...
THEY CAN BREED...
18

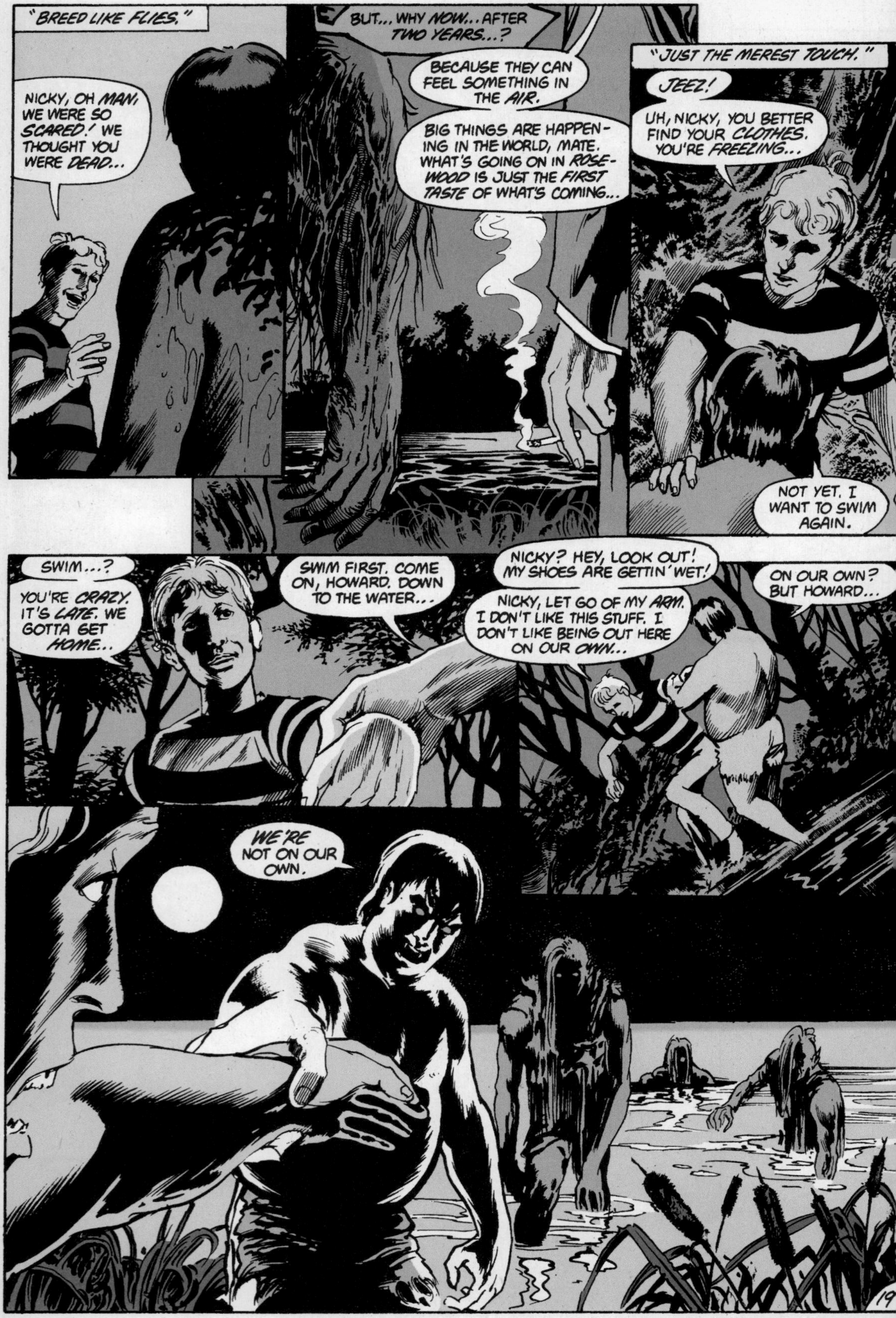
"BREED LIKE FLIES."
NICKY, OH MAN, WE WERE SO SCARED! WE THOUGHT YOU WERE DEAD...
BUT... WHY NOW... AFTER TWO YEARS...?
BECAUSE THEY CAN FEEL SOMETHING IN THE AIR.
BIG THINGS ARE HAPPENING IN THE WORLD, MATE. WHAT'S GOING ON IN ROSEWOOD IS JUST THE FIRST TASTE OF WHAT'S COMING...
"JUST THE MEREST TOUCH."
JEEZ!
UH, NICKY, YOU BETTER FIND YOUR CLOTHES. YOU'RE FREEZING...
NOT YET. I WANT TO SWIM AGAIN.
SWIM...?
YOU'RE CRAZY. IT'S LATE. WE GOTTA GET HOME...
SWIM FIRST. COME ON, HOWARD. DOWN TO THE WATER...
NICKY? HEY, LOOK OUT! MY SHOES ARE GETTIN' WET!
NICKY, LET GO OF MY ARM. I DON'T LIKE THIS STUFF. I DON'T LIKE BEING OUT HERE ON OUR OWN...
ON OUR OWN? BUT HOWARD...
WE'RE NOT ON OUR OWN.
19

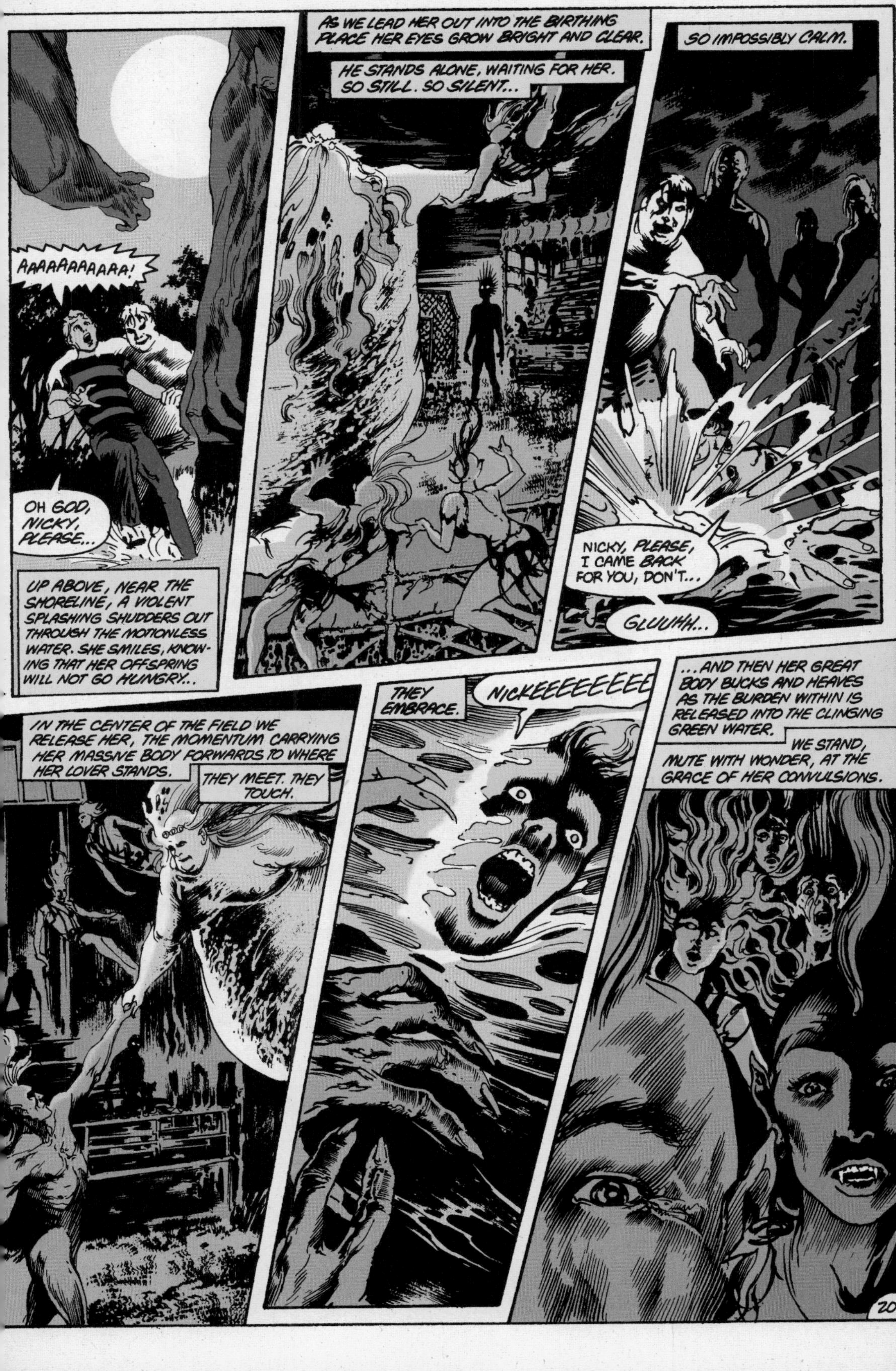
AAAAAAAAAAA!
OH GOD, NICKY, PLEASE...
UP ABOVE, NEAR THE SHORELINE, A VIOLENT SPLASHING SHUDDERS OUT THROUGH THE MOTIONLESS WATER. SHE SMILES, KNOWING THAT HER OFFSPRING WILL NOT GO HUNGRY...
AS WE LEAD HER OUT INTO THE BIRTHING PLACE HER EYES GROW BRIGHT AND CLEAR.
HE STANDS ALONE, WAITING FOR HER. SO STILL. SO SILENT...
SO IMPOSSIBLY CALM.
NICKY, PLEASE, I CAME BACK FOR YOU, DON'T...
GLUUHH...
IN THE CENTER OF THE FIELD WE RELEASE HER, THE MOMENTUM CARRYING HER MASSIVE BODY FORWARDS TO WHERE HER LOVER STANDS.
THEY MEET. THEY TOUCH.
THEY EMBRACE.
NICKEEEEEEEEE
...AND THEN HER GREAT BODY BUCKS AND HEAVES AS THE BURDEN WITHIN IS RELEASED INTO THE CLINGING GREEN WATER.
WE STAND, MUTE WITH WONDER, AT THE GRACE OF HER CONVULSIONS.
20

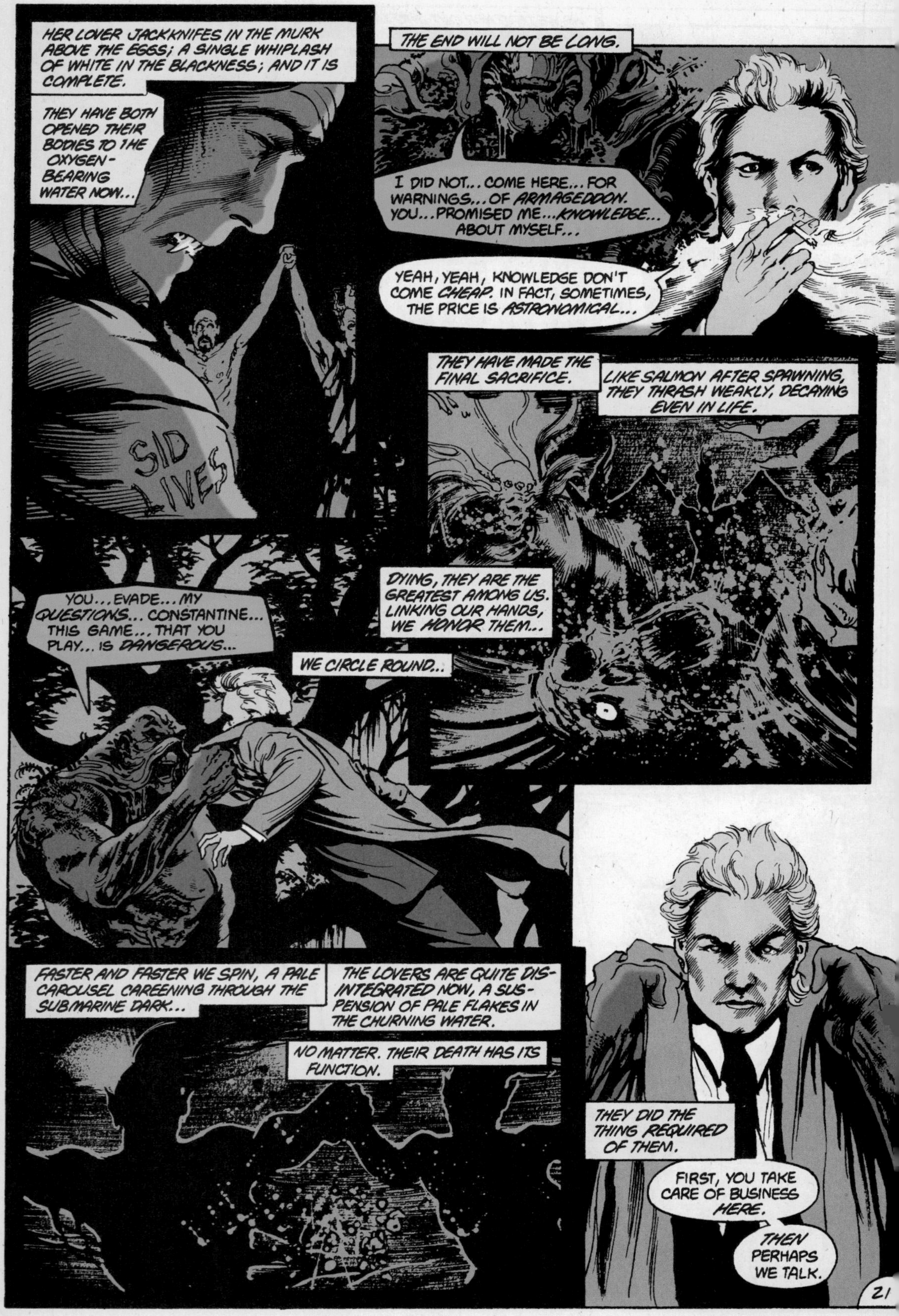
HER LOVER JACKKNIFES IN THE MURK ABOVE THE EGGS; A SINGLE WHIPLASH OF WHITE IN THE BLACKNESS; AND IT IS COMPLETE.
THEY HAVE BOTH OPENED THEIR BODIES TO THE OXYGEN-BEARING WATER NOW...
SID LIVES
THE END WILL NOT BE LONG.
I DID NOT... COME HERE... FOR WARNINGS... OF ARMAGEDDON. YOU... PROMISED ME... KNOWLEDGE... ABOUT MYSELF...
YEAH, YEAH, KNOWLEDGE DON'T COME CHEAP. IN FACT, SOMETIMES, THE PRICE IS ASTRONOMICAL...
THEY HAVE MADE THE FINAL SACRIFICE.
LIKE SALMON AFTER SPAWNING, THEY THRASH WEAKLY, DECAYING EVEN IN LIFE.
DYING, THEY ARE THE GREATEST AMONG US. LINKING OUR HANDS, WE HONOR THEM...
YOU... EVADE... MY QUESTIONS... CONSTANTINE... THIS GAME... THAT YOU PLAY... IS DANGEROUS...
WE CIRCLE ROUND...
FASTER AND FASTER WE SPIN, A PALE CAROUSEL CAREENING THROUGH THE SUBMARINE DARK...
THE LOVERS ARE QUITE DIS-INTEGRATED NOW, A SUS-PENSION OF PALE FLAKES IN THE CHURNING WATER.
NO MATTER. THEIR DEATH HAS ITS FUNCTION.
THEY DID THE THING REQUIRED OF THEM.
FIRST, YOU TAKE CARE OF BUSINESS HERE.
THEN PERHAPS WE TALK.
21

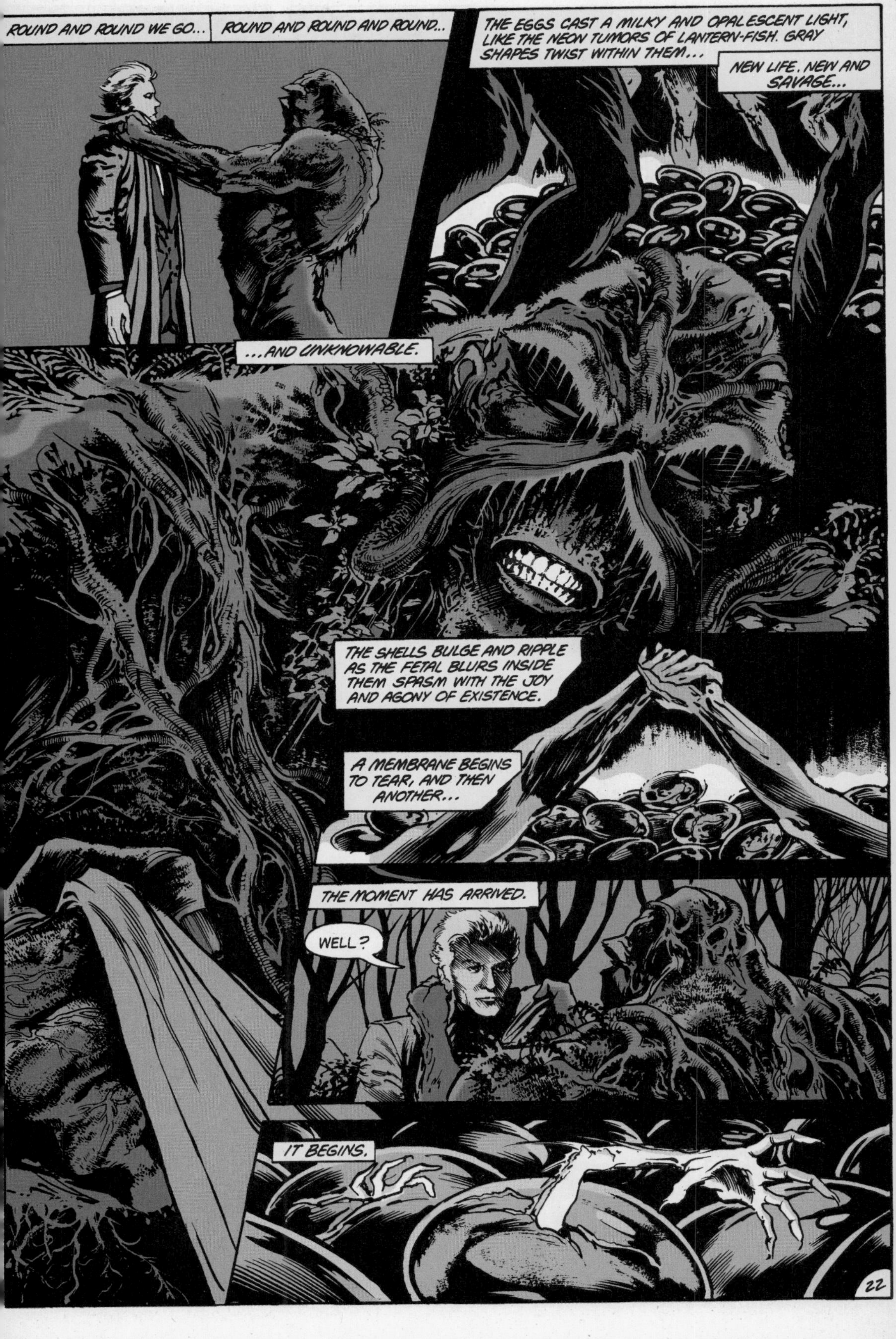
ROUND AND ROUND WE GO...
ROUND AND ROUND AND ROUND...
THE EGGS CAST A MILKY AND OPALESCENT LIGHT, LIKE THE NEON TUMORS OF LANTERN-FISH. GRAY SHAPES TWIST WITHIN THEM...
NEW LIFE. NEW AND SAVAGE...
...AND UNKNOWABLE.
THE SHELLS BULGE AND RIPPLE AS THE FETAL BLURS INSIDE THEM SPASM WITH THE JOY AND AGONY OF EXISTENCE.
A MEMBRANE BEGINS TO TEAR, AND THEN ANOTHER...
THE MOMENT HAS ARRIVED.
WELL?
IT BEGINS.
22

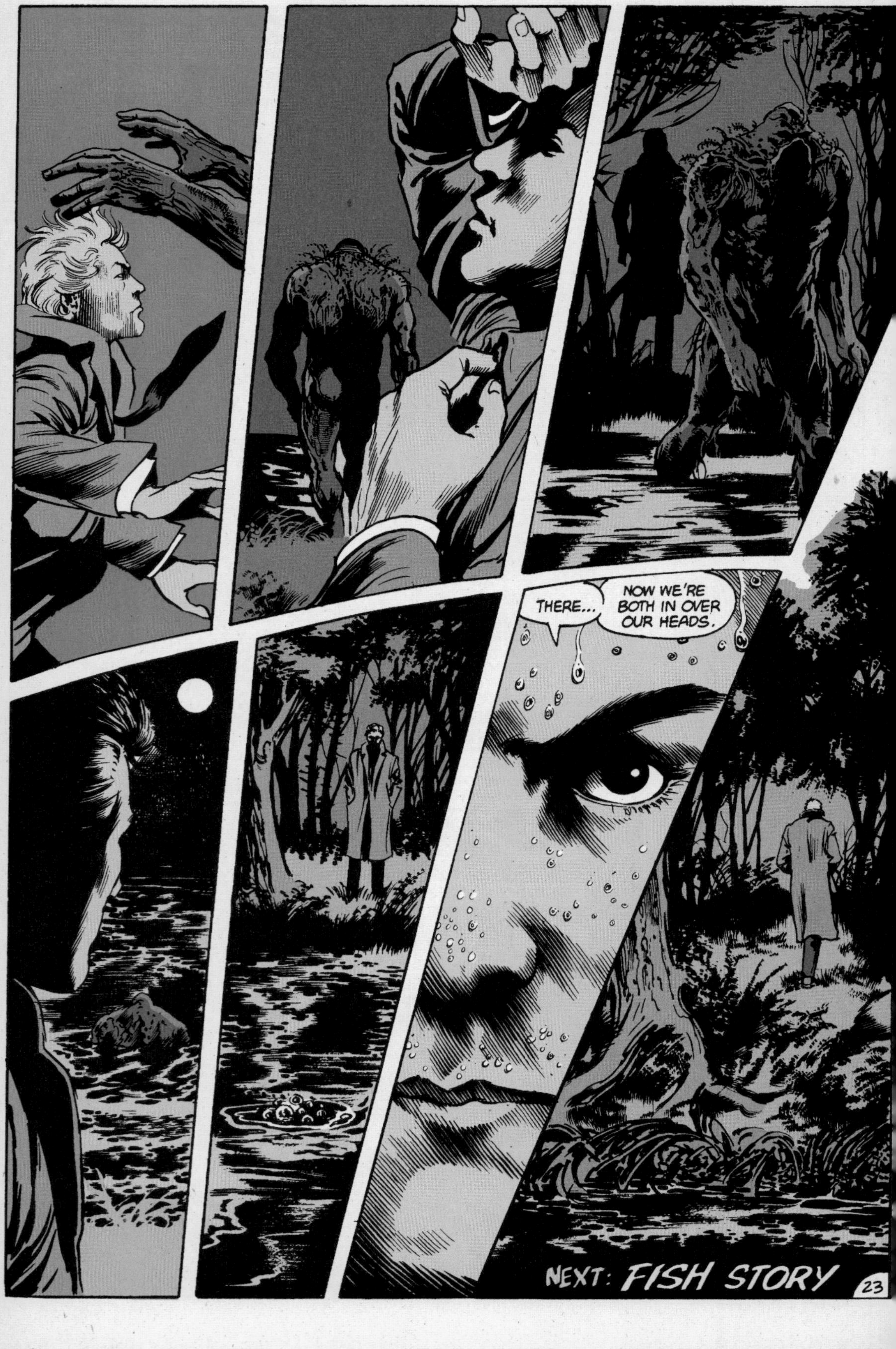
THERE...
NOW WE'RE BOTH IN OVER OUR HEADS.
NEXT: FISH STORY
23

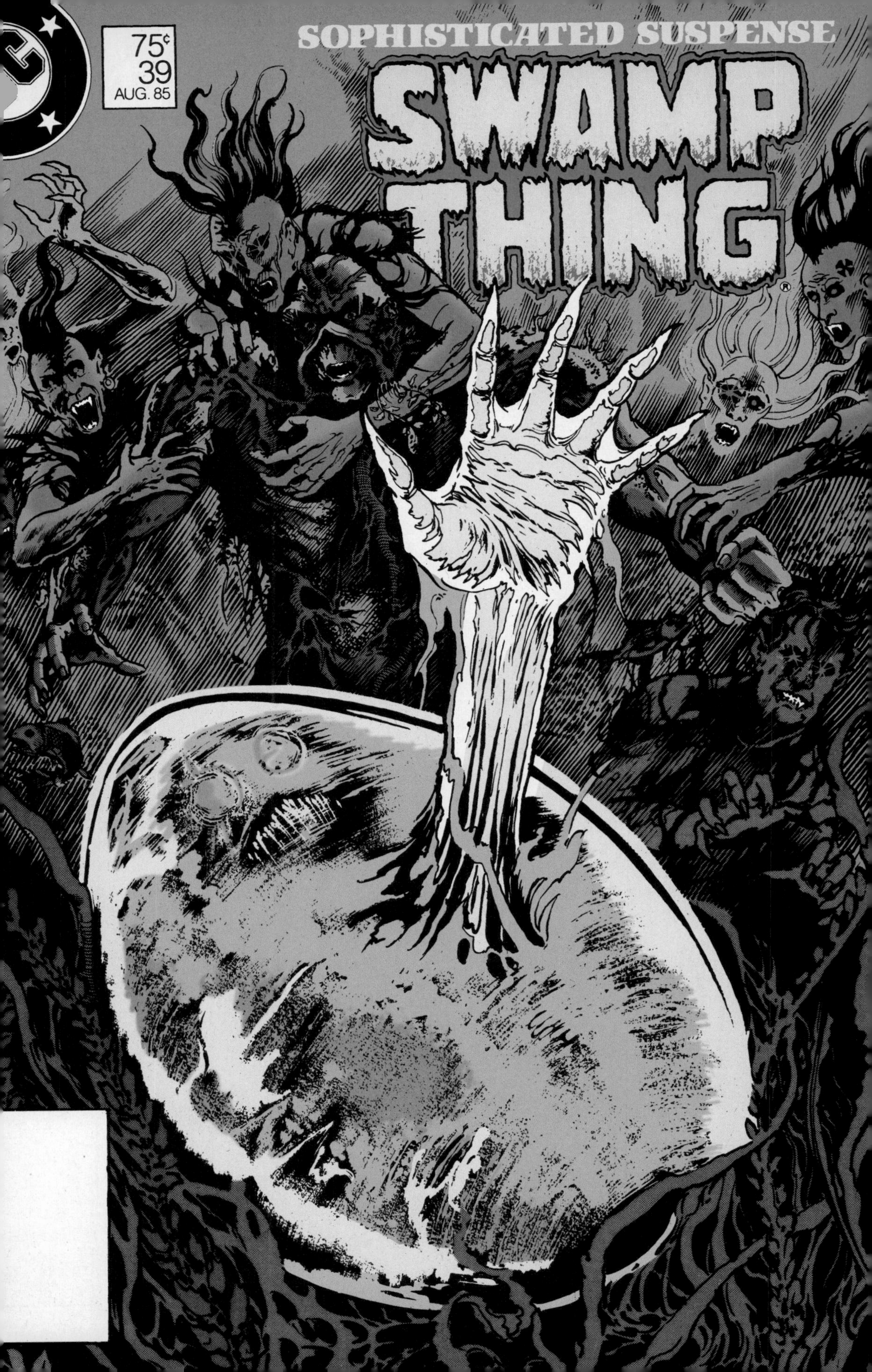
75¢
39
AUG. 85
SOPHISTICATED SUSPENSE
SWAMP THING

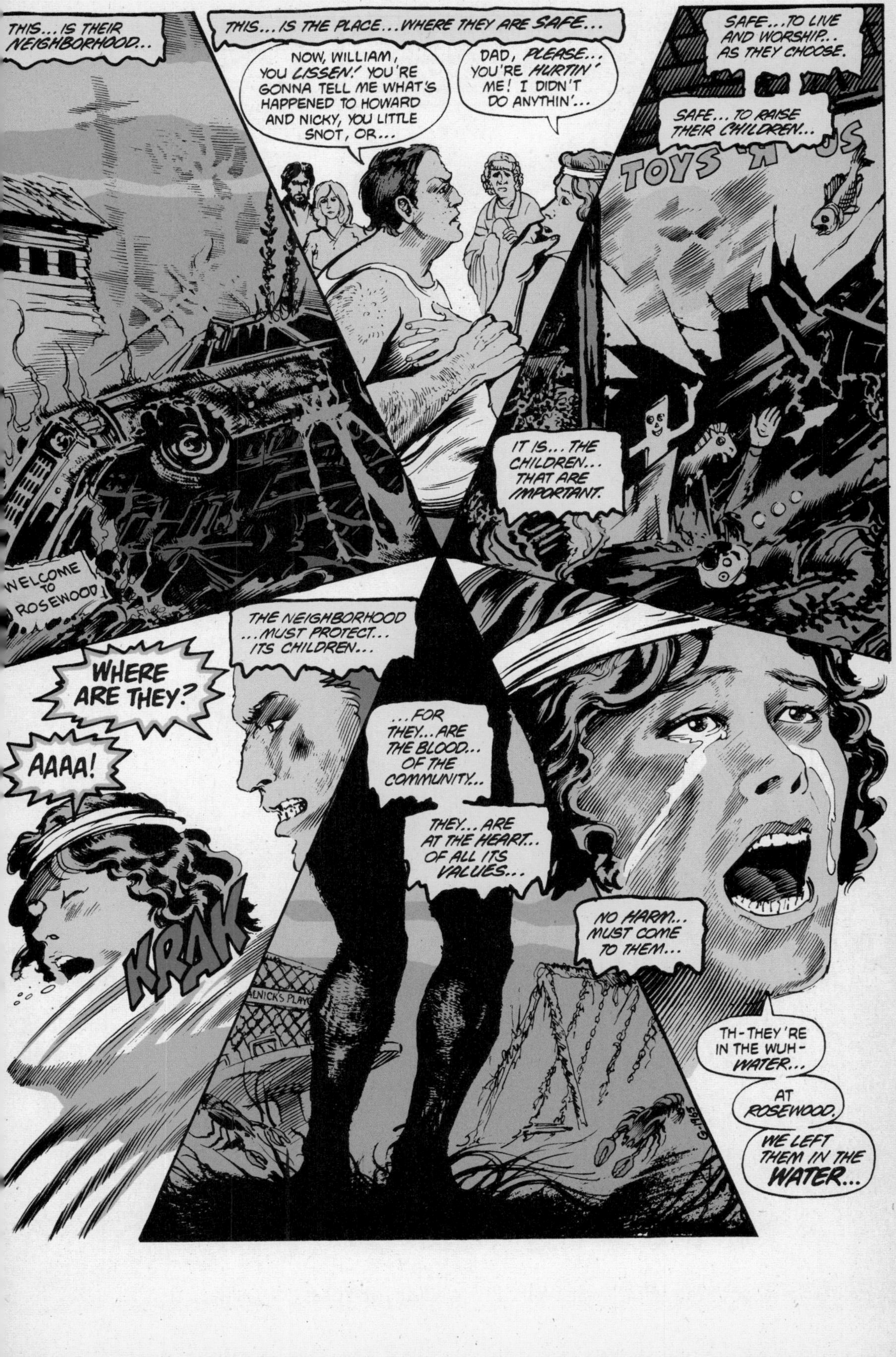
THIS... IS THEIR NEIGHBORHOOD...
WELCOME TO ROSEWOOD
THIS... IS THE PLACE... WHERE THEY ARE SAFE...
NOW, WILLIAM, YOU LISSEN! YOU'RE GONNA TELL ME WHAT'S HAPPENED TO HOWARD AND NICKY, YOU LITTLE SNOT, OR...
DAD, PLEASE... YOU'RE HURTIN' ME! I DIDN'T DO ANYTHIN'...
SAFE... TO LIVE AND WORSHIP... AS THEY CHOOSE.
SAFE... TO RAISE THEIR CHILDREN...
TOYS 'R' US
IT IS... THE CHILDREN... THAT ARE IMPORTANT.
THE NEIGHBORHOOD ...MUST PROTECT... ITS CHILDREN...
WHERE ARE THEY?
AAAA!
KRAK
...FOR THEY... ARE THE BLOOD... OF THE COMMUNITY...
THEY... ARE AT THE HEART... OF ALL ITS VALUES...
NO HARM... MUST COME TO THEM...
TH-THEY'RE IN THE WUH-WATER...
AT ROSEWOOD.
WE LEFT THEM IN THE WATER...

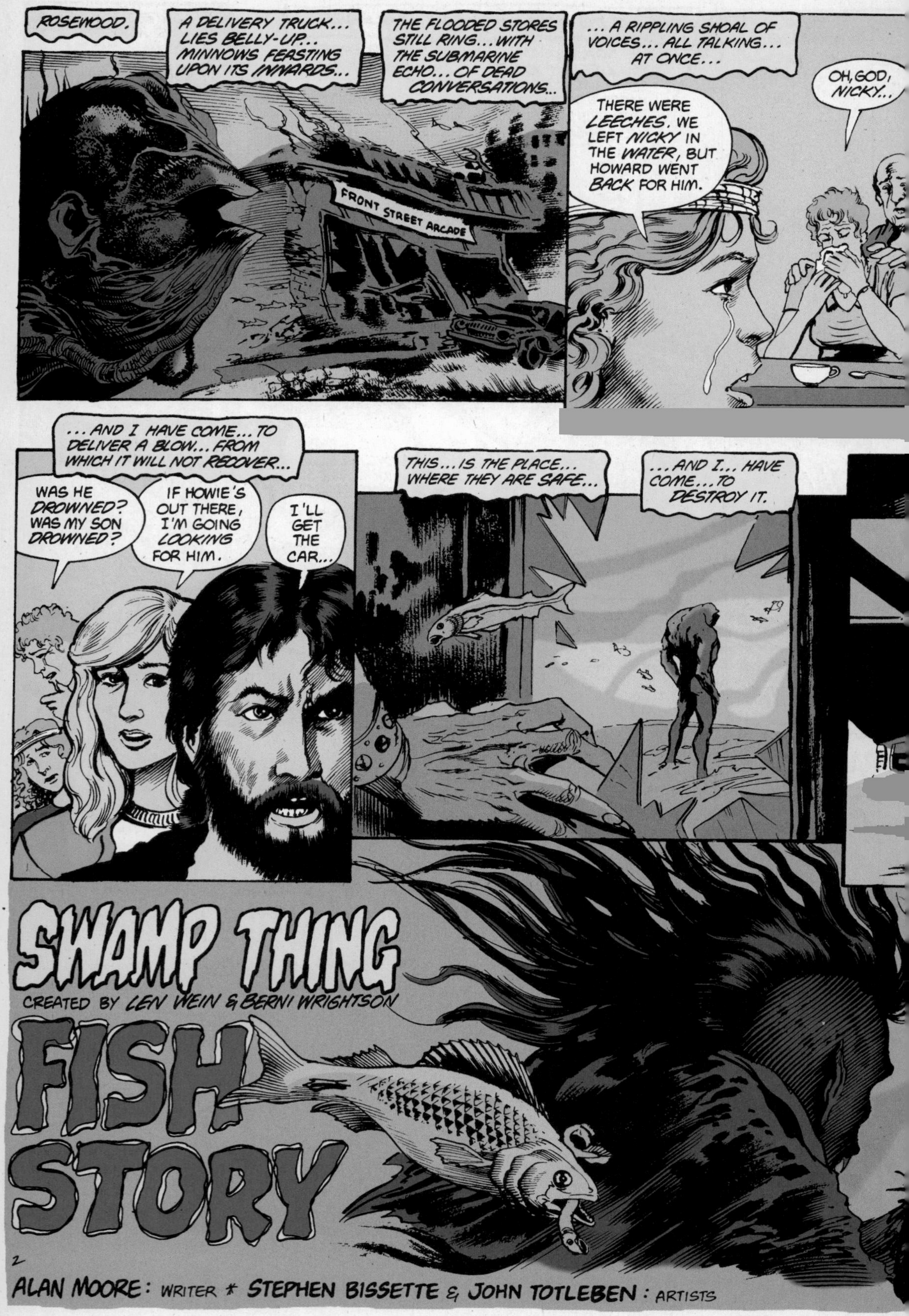
ROSEWOOD.
A DELIVERY TRUCK... LIES BELLY-UP... MINNOWS FEASTING UPON ITS INNARDS...
THE FLOODED STORES STILL RING... WITH THE SUBMARINE ECHO... OF DEAD CONVERSATIONS...
FRONT STREET ARCADE
... A RIPPLING SHOAL OF VOICES... ALL TALKING... AT ONCE...
THERE WERE LEECHES. WE LEFT NICKY IN THE WATER, BUT HOWARD WENT BACK FOR HIM.
OH, GOD, NICKY...
... AND I HAVE COME... TO DELIVER A BLOW... FROM WHICH IT WILL NOT RECOVER...
WAS HE DROWNED? WAS MY SON DROWNED?
IF HOWIE'S OUT THERE, I'M GOING LOOKING FOR HIM.
I'LL GET THE CAR...
THIS... IS THE PLACE... WHERE THEY ARE SAFE...
... AND I... HAVE COME... TO DESTROY IT.
SWAMP THING
CREATED BY LEN WEIN & BERNI WRIGHTSON
FISH STORY
2
ALAN MOORE: WRITER * STEPHEN BISSETTE & JOHN TOTLEBEN: ARTISTS

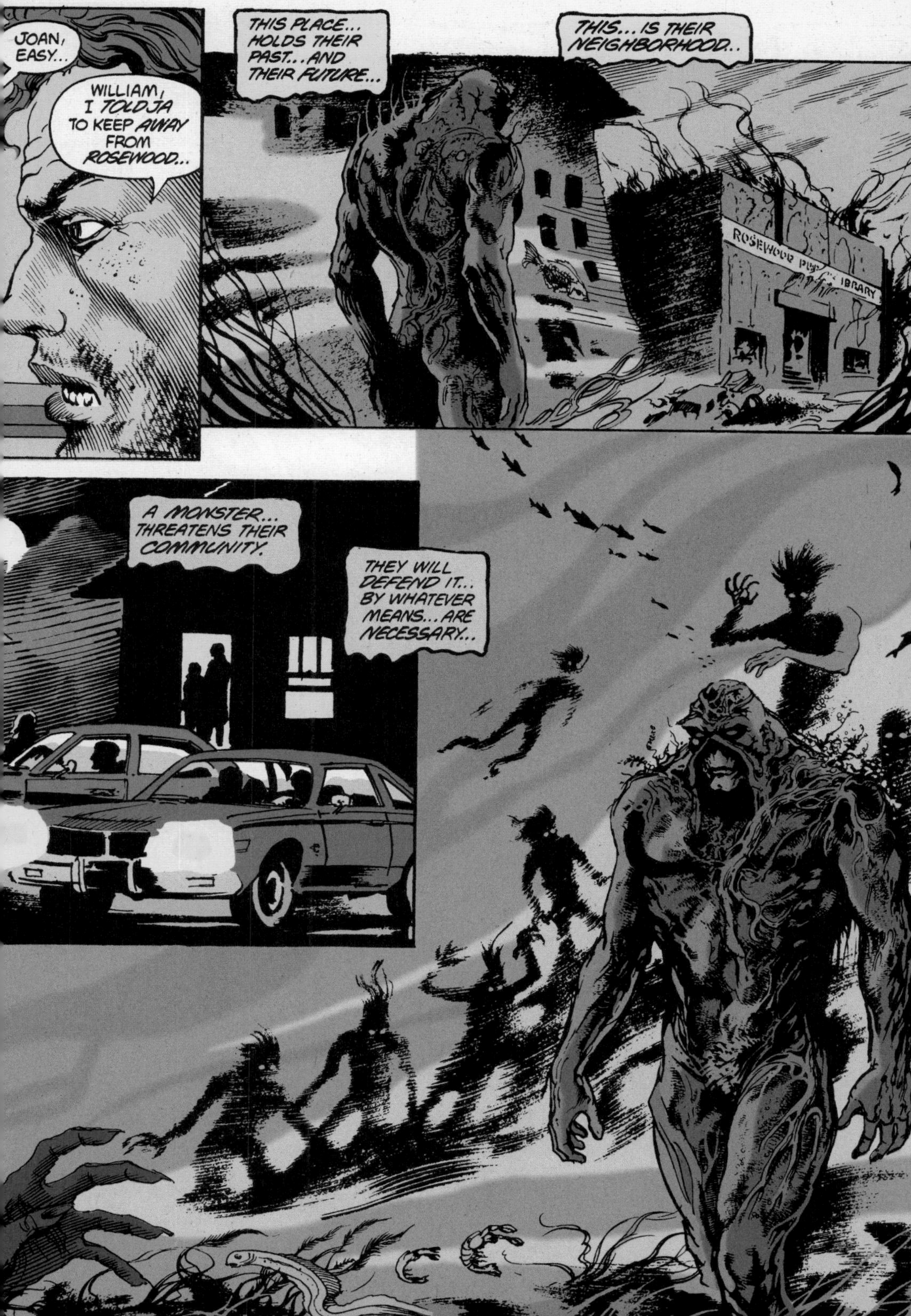
JOAN, EASY...
WILLIAM, I TOLDJA TO KEEP AWAY FROM ROSEWOOD...
THIS PLACE... HOLDS THEIR PAST... AND THEIR FUTURE...
THIS... IS THEIR NEIGHBORHOOD...
ROSEWOOD
LIBRARY
A MONSTER... THREATENS THEIR COMMUNITY.
THEY WILL DEFEND IT... BY WHATEVER MEANS... ARE NECESSARY...
3
KAREN BERGER: EDITOR * TATJANA WOOD: COLORIST * JOHN COSTANZA: LETTERER

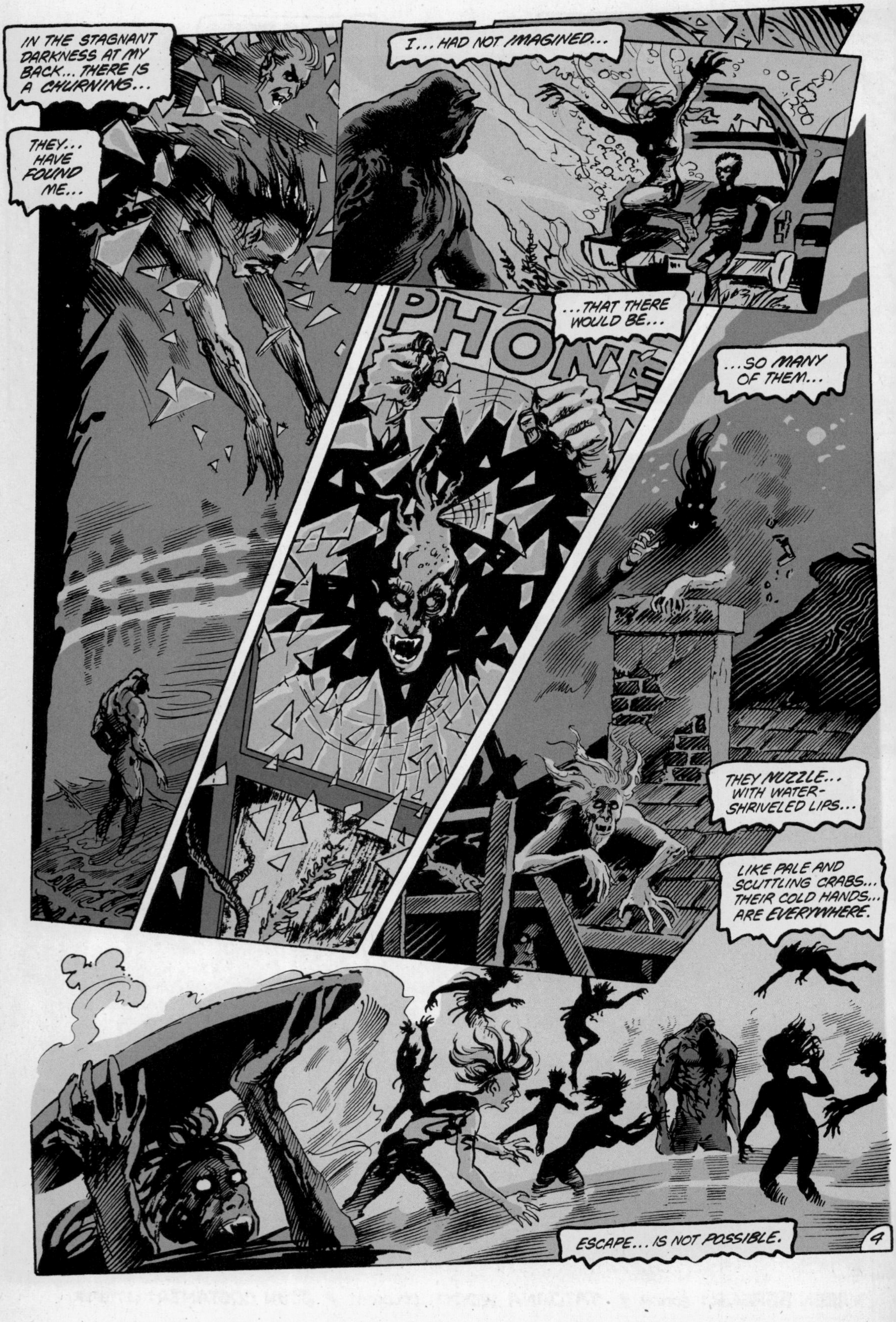
IN THE STAGNANT DARKNESS AT MY BACK... THERE IS A CHURNING...
THEY... HAVE FOUND ME...
I... HAD NOT IMAGINED...
PHONE
...THAT THERE WOULD BE...
...SO MANY OF THEM...
THEY NUZZLE... WITH WATER-SHRIVELED LIPS...
LIKE PALE AND SCUTTLING CRABS... THEIR COLD HANDS... ARE EVERYWHERE.
ESCAPE... IS NOT POSSIBLE.
4

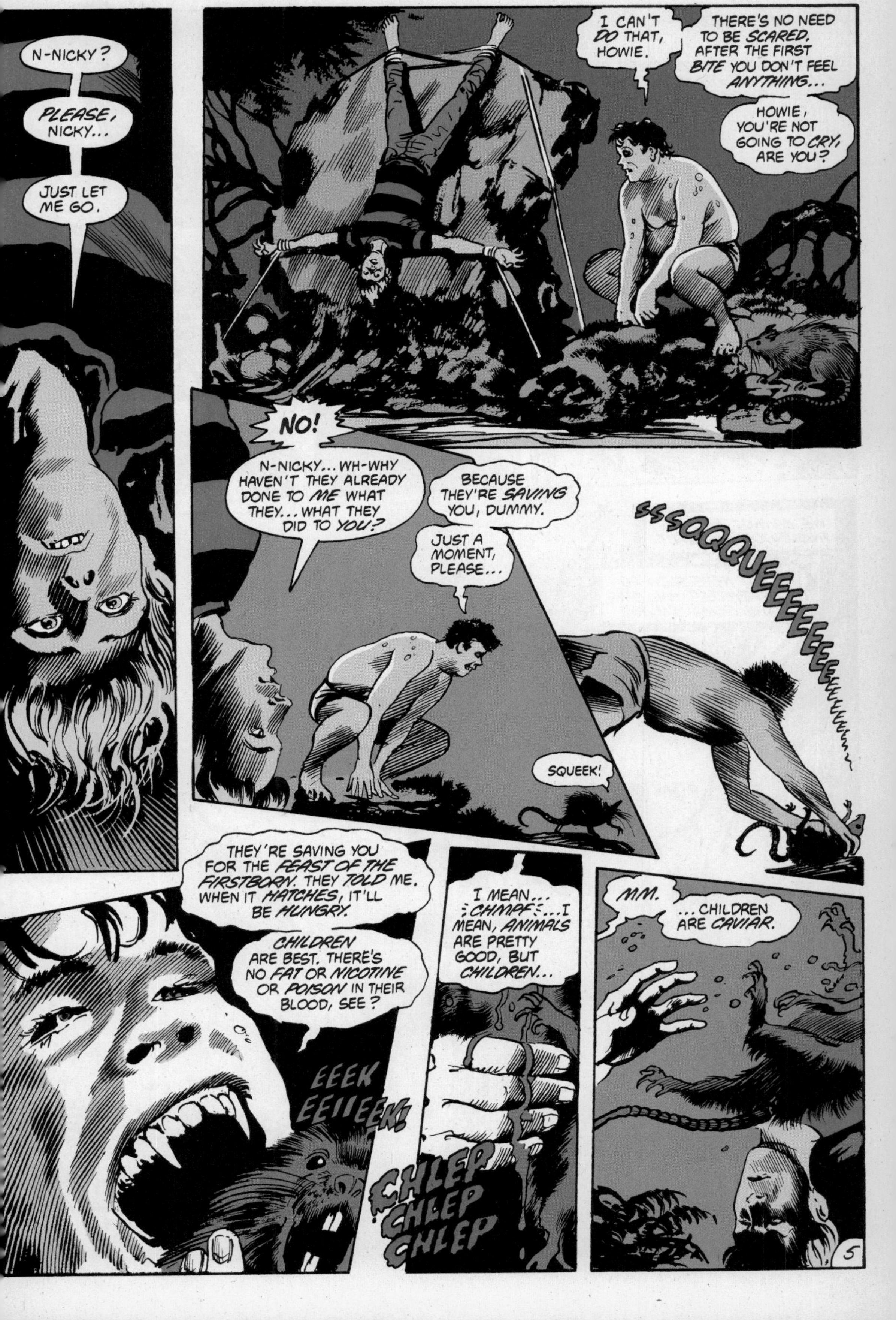
N-NICKY?
PLEASE, NICKY...
JUST LET ME GO.
I CAN'T DO THAT, HOWIE.
THERE'S NO NEED TO BE SCARED. AFTER THE FIRST BITE YOU DON'T FEEL ANYTHING...
HOWIE, YOU'RE NOT GOING TO CRY, ARE YOU?
NO!
N-NICKY... WH-WHY HAVEN'T THEY ALREADY DONE TO ME WHAT THEY... WHAT THEY DID TO YOU?
BECAUSE THEY'RE SAVING YOU, DUMMY.
JUST A MOMENT, PLEASE...
SSSQQQUEEEEEEEEEEEEEEEE
SQUEEK!
THEY'RE SAVING YOU FOR THE FEAST OF THE FIRSTBORN. THEY TOLD ME. WHEN IT HATCHES, IT'LL BE HUNGRY.
CHILDREN ARE BEST. THERE'S NO FAT OR NICOTINE OR POISON IN THEIR BLOOD, SEE?
EEEK EEIIEEK!
I MEAN... CHMPF... I MEAN, ANIMALS ARE PRETTY GOOD, BUT CHILDREN...
CHLEP CHLEP CHLEP
MM.
...CHILDREN ARE CAVIAR.
5

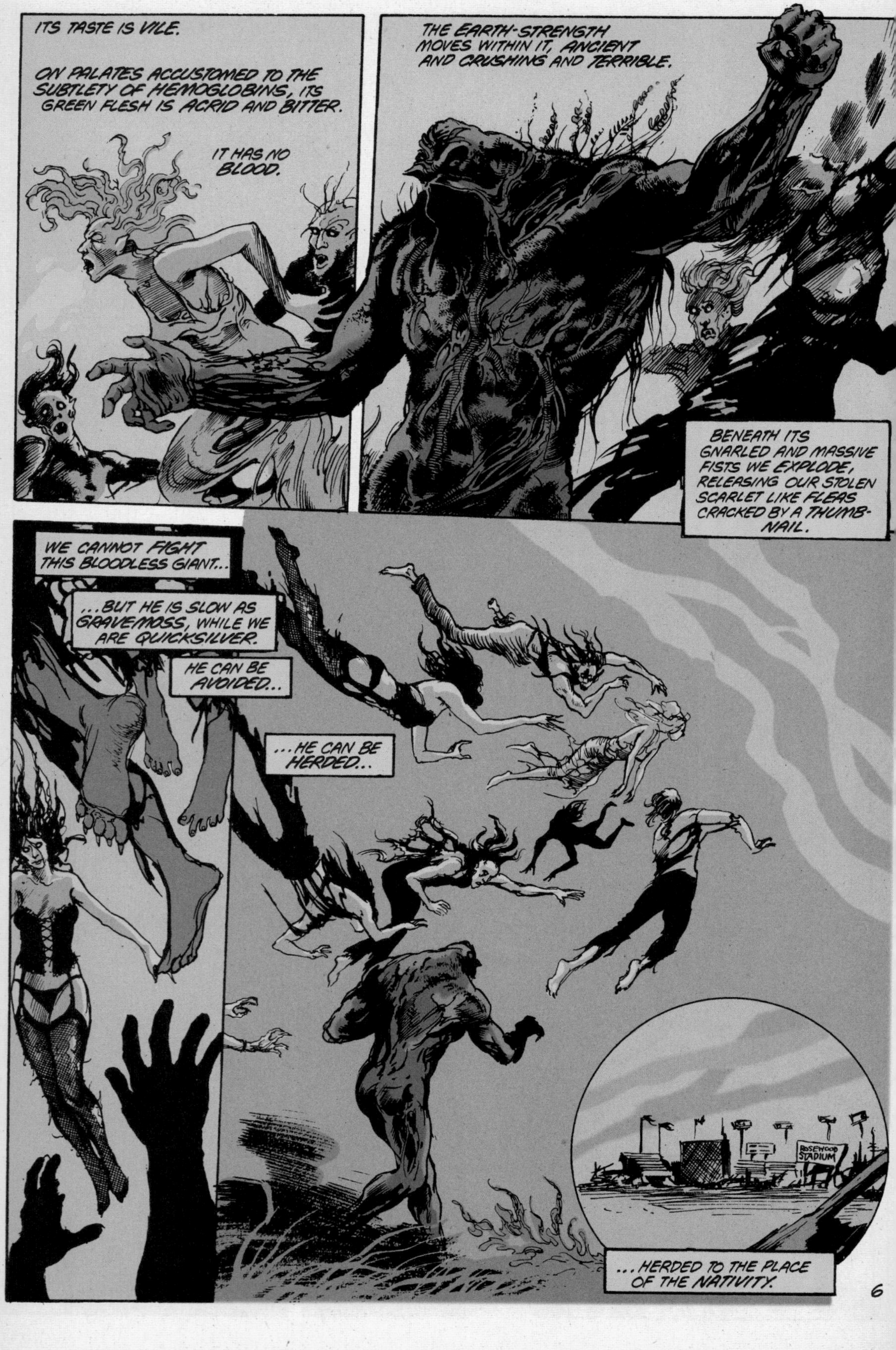
ITS TASTE IS VILE.
ON PALATES ACCUSTOMED TO THE SUBTLETY OF HEMOGLOBINS, ITS GREEN FLESH IS ACRID AND BITTER.
IT HAS NO BLOOD.
THE EARTH-STRENGTH MOVES WITHIN IT, ANCIENT AND CRUSHING AND TERRIBLE.
BENEATH ITS GNARLED AND MASSIVE FISTS WE EXPLODE, RELEASING OUR STOLEN SCARLET LIKE FLEAS CRACKED BY A THUMB-NAIL.
WE CANNOT FIGHT THIS BLOODLESS GIANT...
...BUT HE IS SLOW AS GRAVEMOSS, WHILE WE ARE QUICKSILVER.
HE CAN BE AVOIDED...
...HE CAN BE HERDED...
ROSEWOOD STADIUM
...HERDED TO THE PLACE OF THE NATIVITY.
6

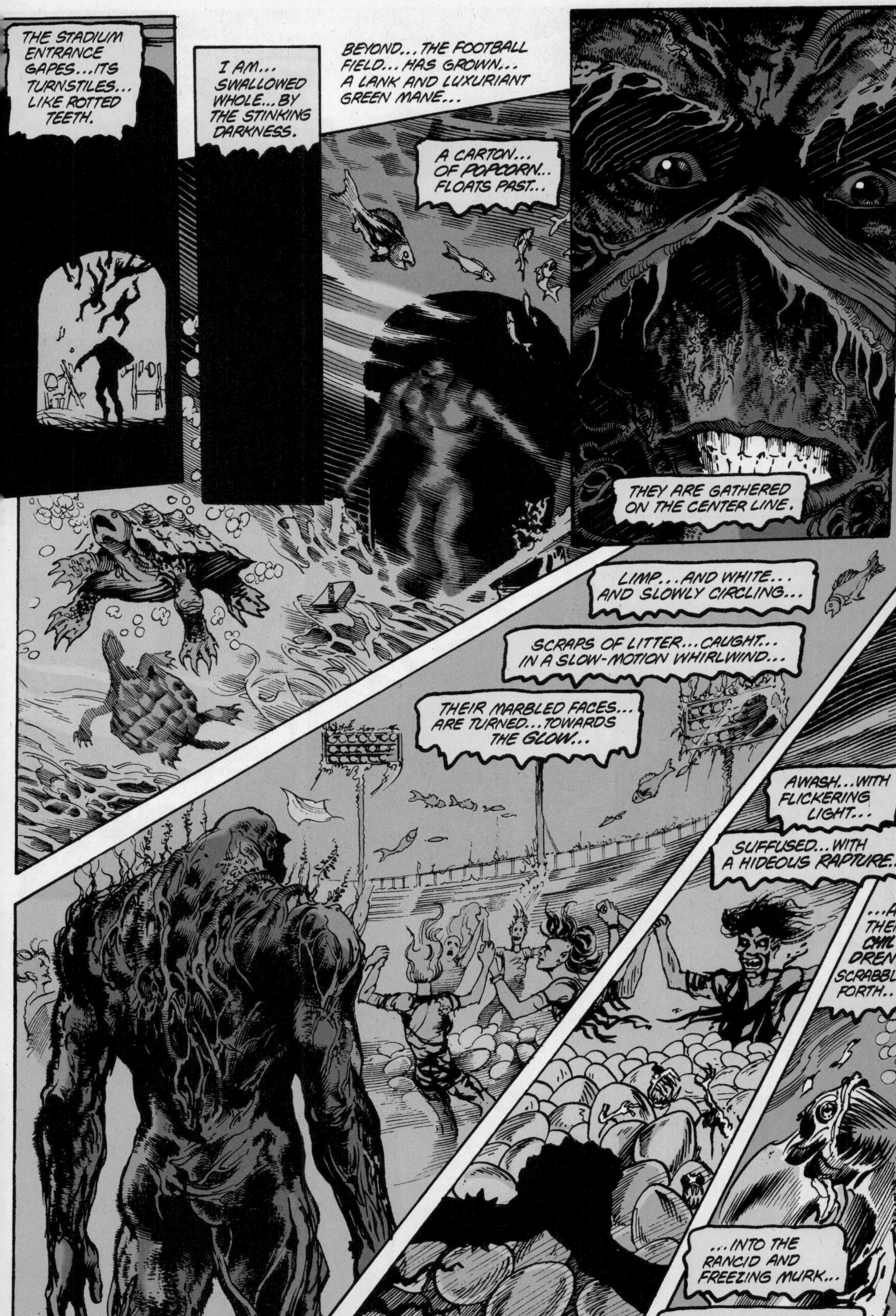
THE STADIUM ENTRANCE GAPES...ITS TURNSTILES... LIKE ROTTED TEETH.
I AM... SWALLOWED WHOLE... BY THE STINKING DARKNESS.
BEYOND... THE FOOTBALL FIELD... HAS GROWN... A LANK AND LUXURIANT GREEN MANE...
A CARTON... OF POPCORN... FLOATS PAST...
THEY ARE GATHERED ON THE CENTER LINE.
LIMP... AND WHITE... AND SLOWLY CIRCLING...
SCRAPS OF LITTER... CAUGHT... IN A SLOW-MOTION WHIRLWIND...
THEIR MARBLED FACES... ARE TURNED... TOWARDS THE GLOW...
AWASH... WITH FLICKERING LIGHT...
SUFFUSED... WITH A HIDEOUS RAPTURE...
...AS THEIR CHIL-DREN SCRABBLE FORTH...
...INTO THE RANCID AND FREEZING MURK...
...OF THEIR FIRST DAY.
7

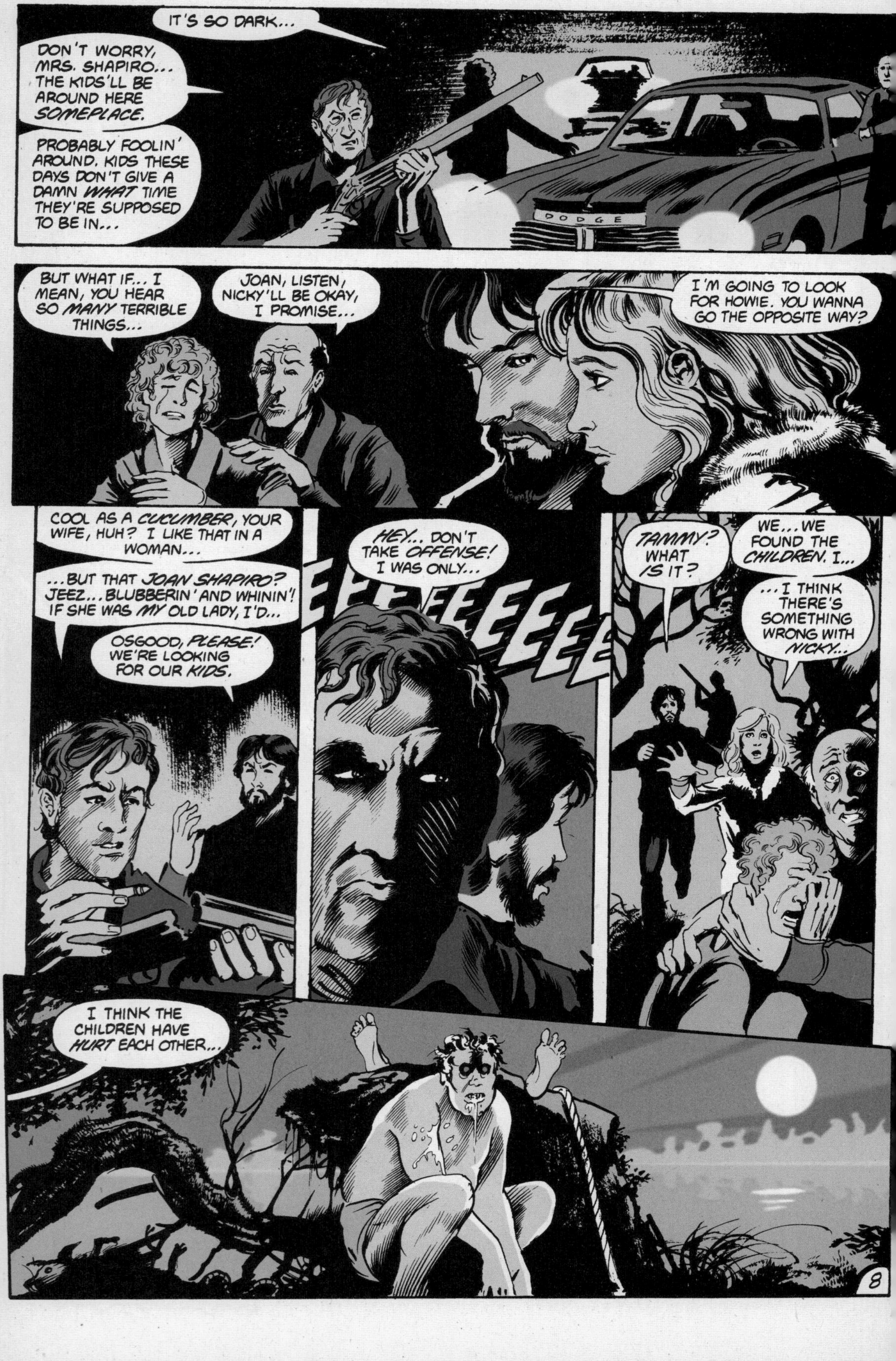
IT'S SO DARK...
DON'T WORRY, MRS. SHAPIRO... THE KIDS'LL BE AROUND HERE SOMEPLACE.
PROBABLY FOOLIN' AROUND. KIDS THESE DAYS DON'T GIVE A DAMN WHAT TIME THEY'RE SUPPOSED TO BE IN...
DODGE
BUT WHAT IF... I MEAN, YOU HEAR SO MANY TERRIBLE THINGS...
JOAN, LISTEN, NICKY'LL BE OKAY, I PROMISE...
I'M GOING TO LOOK FOR HOWIE. YOU WANNA GO THE OPPOSITE WAY?
COOL AS A CUCUMBER, YOUR WIFE, HUH? I LIKE THAT IN A WOMAN...
...BUT THAT JOAN SHAPIRO? JEEZ...BLUBBERIN' AND WHININ'! IF SHE WAS MY OLD LADY, I'D...
OSGOOD, PLEASE! WE'RE LOOKING FOR OUR KIDS.
HEY... DON'T TAKE OFFENSE! I WAS ONLY...
EEEEEEEEEE
TAMMY? WHAT IS IT?
WE... WE FOUND THE CHILDREN. I...
...I THINK THERE'S SOMETHING WRONG WITH NICKY...
I THINK THE CHILDREN HAVE HURT EACH OTHER...
8

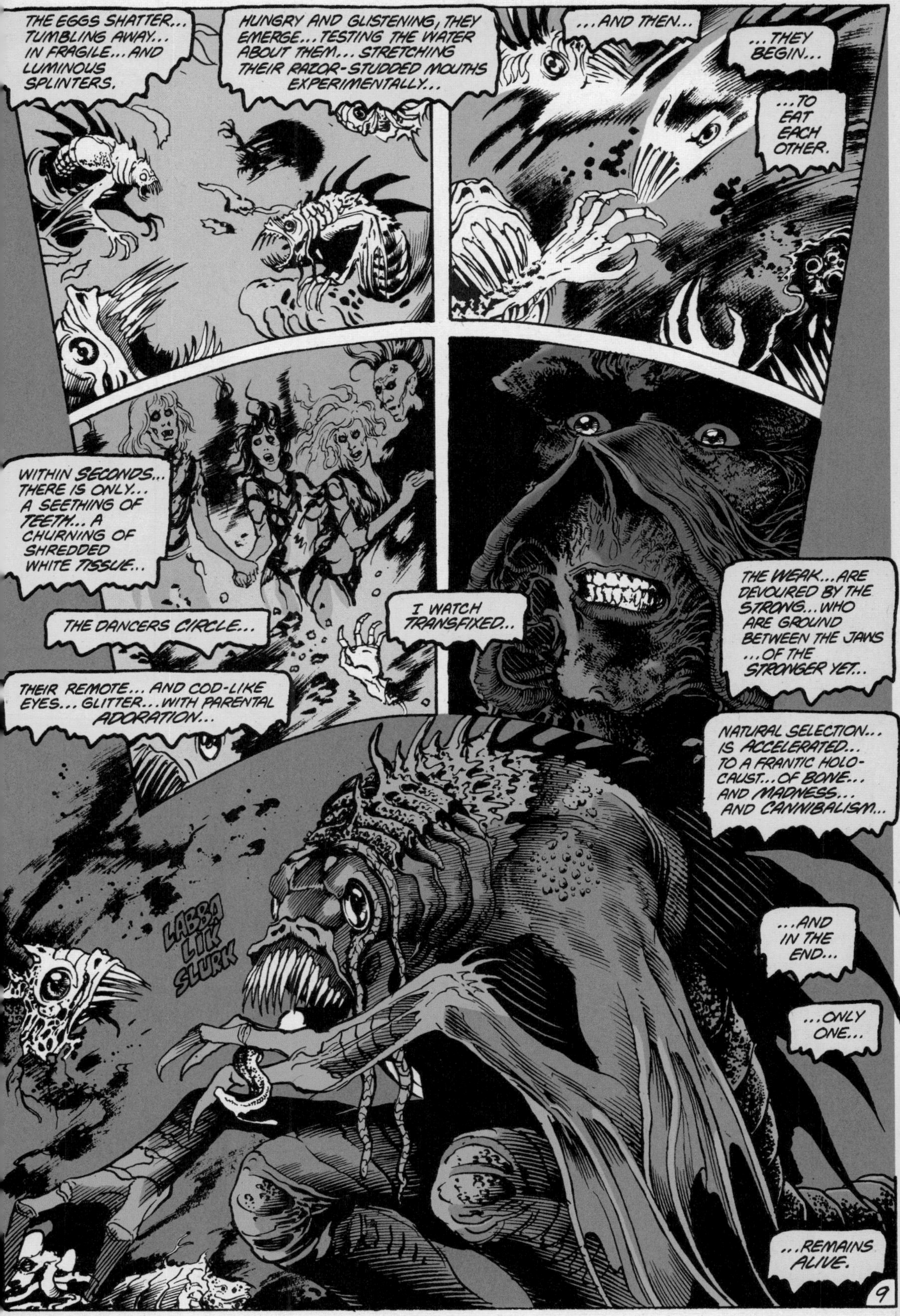
THE EGGS SHATTER... TUMBLING AWAY... IN FRAGILE... AND LUMINOUS SPLINTERS.
HUNGRY AND GLISTENING, THEY EMERGE... TESTING THE WATER ABOUT THEM... STRETCHING THEIR RAZOR-STUDDED MOUTHS EXPERIMENTALLY...
...AND THEN...
...THEY BEGIN...
...TO EAT EACH OTHER.
WITHIN SECONDS... THERE IS ONLY... A SEETHING OF TEETH... A CHURNING OF SHREDDED WHITE TISSUE...
THE DANCERS CIRCLE...
THEIR REMOTE... AND COD-LIKE EYES... GLITTER... WITH PARENTAL ADORATION...
I WATCH TRANSFIXED...
THE WEAK... ARE DEVOURED BY THE STRONG... WHO ARE GROUND BETWEEN THE JAWS ...OF THE STRONGER YET...
NATURAL SELECTION... IS ACCELERATED... TO A FRANTIC HOLO-CAUST... OF BONE... AND MADNESS... AND CANNIBALISM...
LABBA LIK SLURK
...AND IN THE END...
...ONLY ONE...
...REMAINS ALIVE.
9

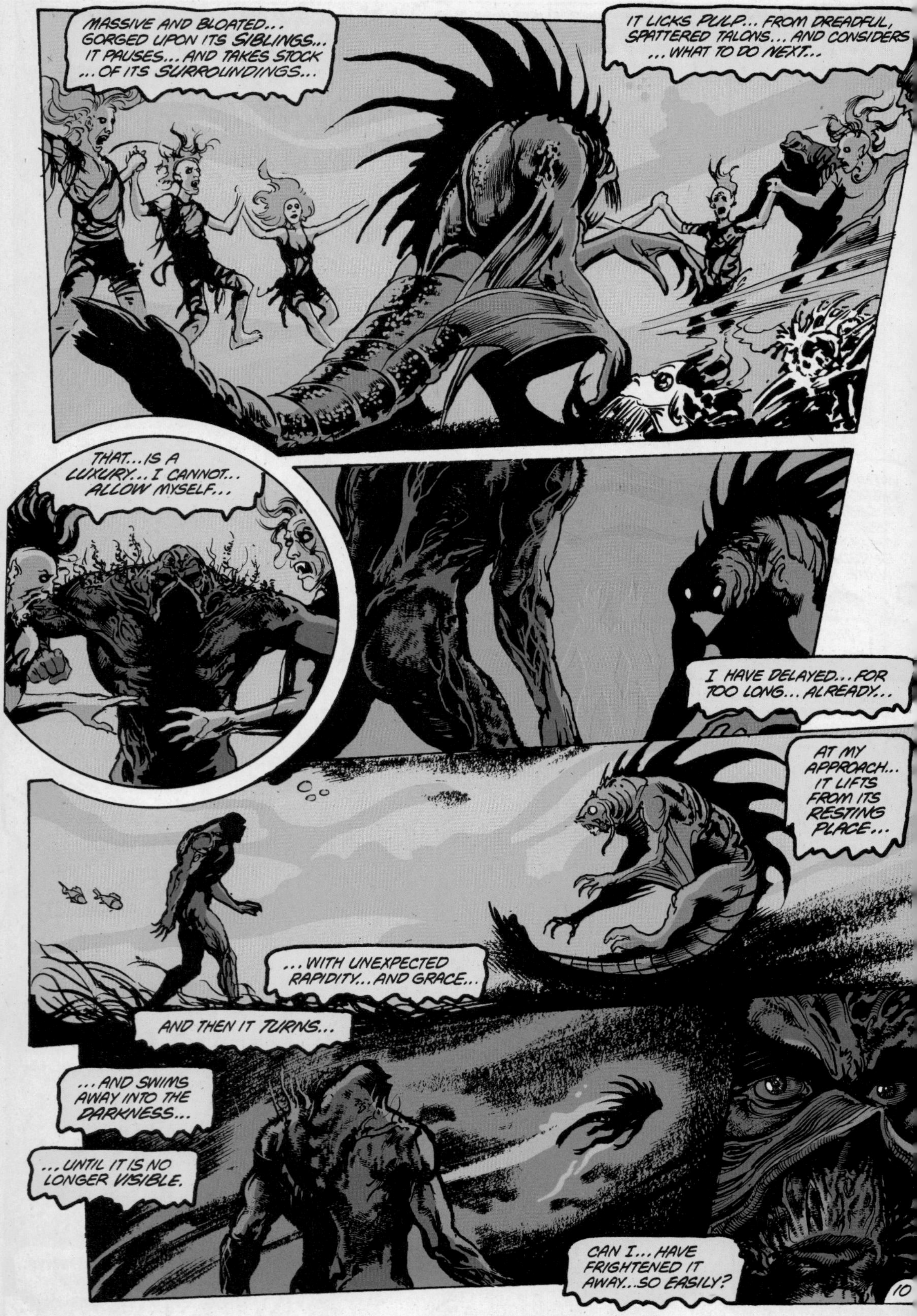
MASSIVE AND BLOATED... GORGED UPON ITS SIBLINGS... IT PAUSES... AND TAKES STOCK ...OF ITS SURROUNDINGS...
IT LICKS PULP... FROM DREADFUL, SPATTERED TALONS... AND CONSIDERS ...WHAT TO DO NEXT...
THAT...IS A LUXURY... I CANNOT... ALLOW MYSELF...
I HAVE DELAYED... FOR TOO LONG... ALREADY...
AT MY APPROACH... IT LIFTS FROM ITS RESTING PLACE...
...WITH UNEXPECTED RAPIDITY... AND GRACE...
AND THEN IT TURNS...
...AND SWIMS AWAY INTO THE DARKNESS...
...UNTIL IT IS NO LONGER VISIBLE.
CAN I... HAVE FRIGHTENED IT AWAY... SO EASILY?
10

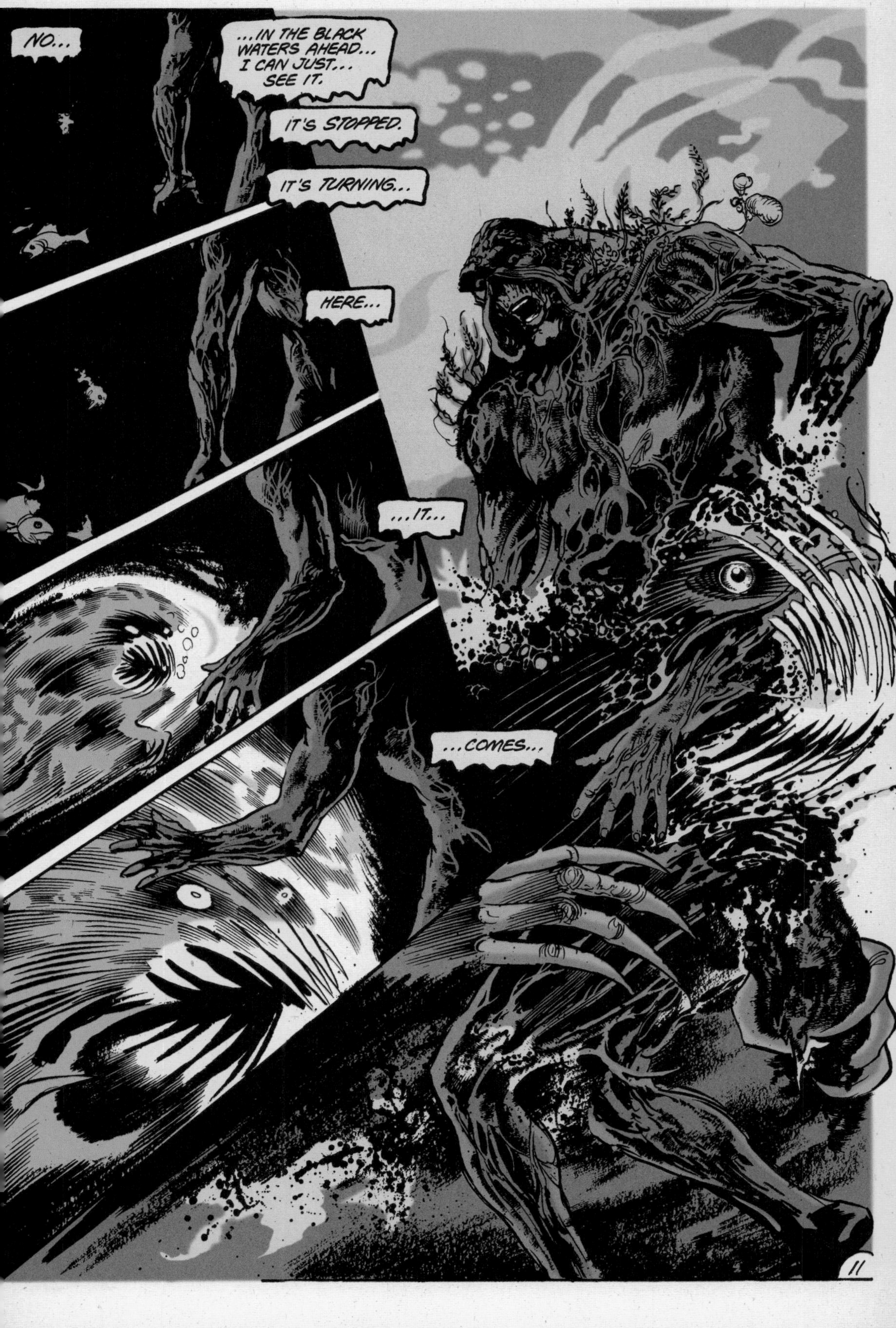
NO...
...IN THE BLACK WATERS AHEAD... I CAN JUST... SEE IT.
IT'S STOPPED.
IT'S TURNING...
HERE...
...IT...
...COMES...
11

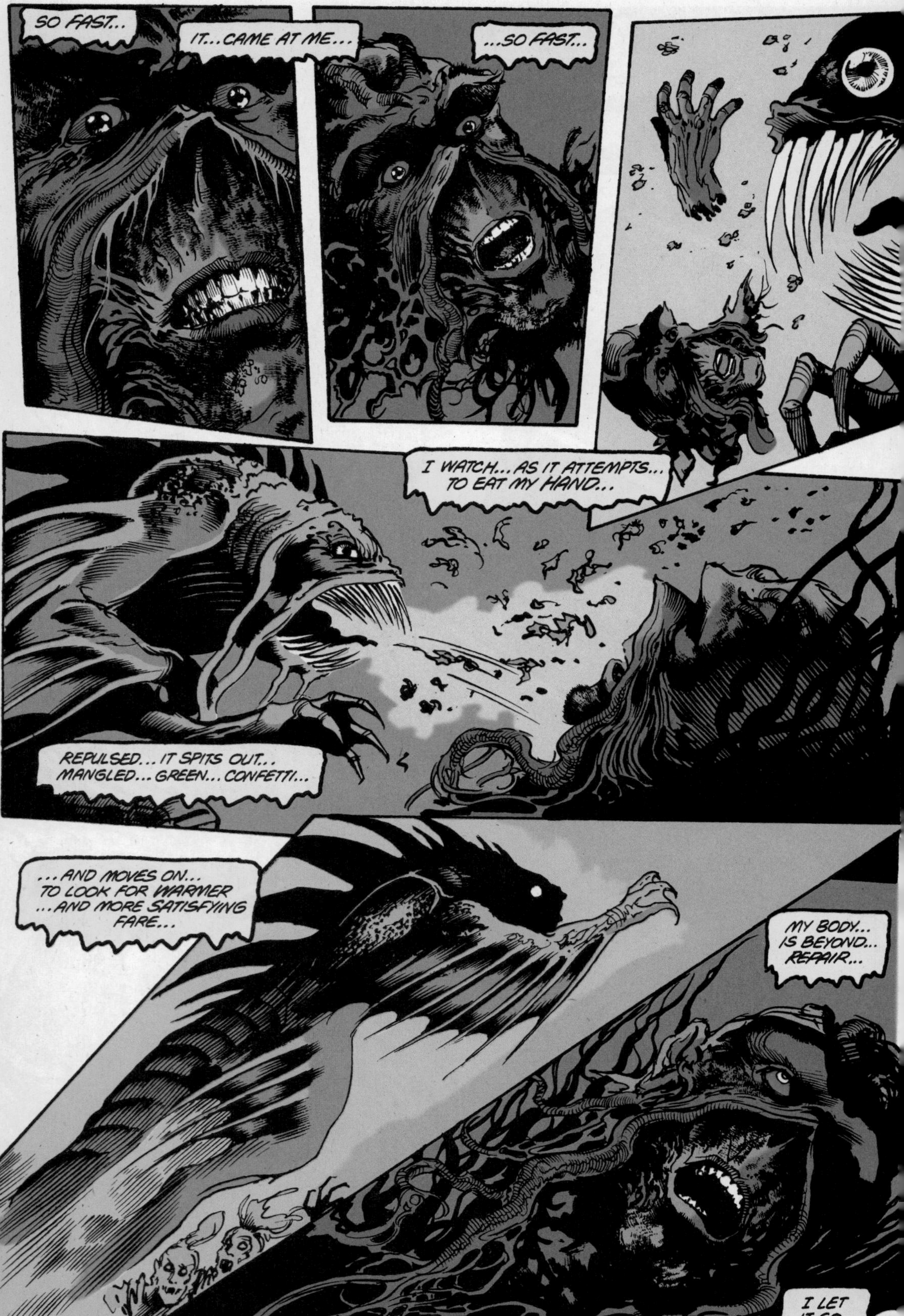
SO FAST...
IT...CAME AT ME...
...SO FAST...
I WATCH... AS IT ATTEMPTS... TO EAT MY HAND...
REPULSED... IT SPITS OUT... MANGLED... GREEN... CONFETTI...
...AND MOVES ON... TO LOOK FOR WARMER ...AND MORE SATISFYING FARE...
MY BODY... IS BEYOND... REPAIR...
I LET IT GO...
12

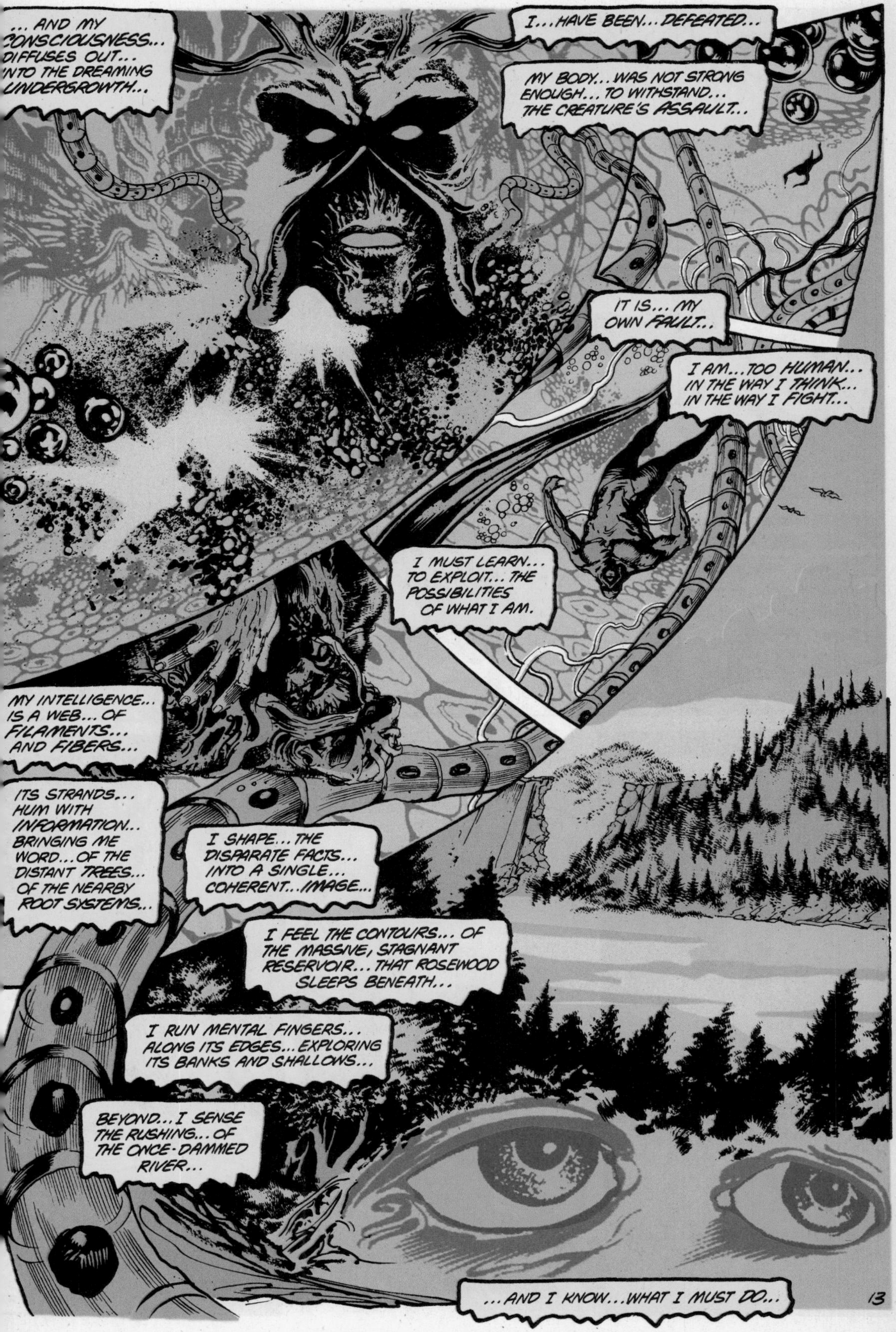
... AND MY CONSCIOUSNESS... DIFFUSES OUT... INTO THE DREAMING UNDERGROWTH...
I... HAVE BEEN... DEFEATED...
MY BODY... WAS NOT STRONG ENOUGH... TO WITHSTAND... THE CREATURE'S ASSAULT...
IT IS... MY OWN FAULT...
I AM... TOO HUMAN... IN THE WAY I THINK... IN THE WAY I FIGHT...
I MUST LEARN... TO EXPLOIT... THE POSSIBILITIES OF WHAT I AM.
MY INTELLIGENCE... IS A WEB... OF FILAMENTS... AND FIBERS...
ITS STRANDS... HUM WITH INFORMATION... BRINGING ME WORD... OF THE DISTANT TREES... OF THE NEARBY ROOT SYSTEMS...
I SHAPE... THE DISPARATE FACTS... INTO A SINGLE... COHERENT... IMAGE...
I FEEL THE CONTOURS... OF THE MASSIVE, STAGNANT RESERVOIR... THAT ROSEWOOD SLEEPS BENEATH...
I RUN MENTAL FINGERS... ALONG ITS EDGES... EXPLORING ITS BANKS AND SHALLOWS...
BEYOND... I SENSE THE RUSHING... OF THE ONCE-DAMMED RIVER...
... AND I KNOW... WHAT I MUST DO...
13

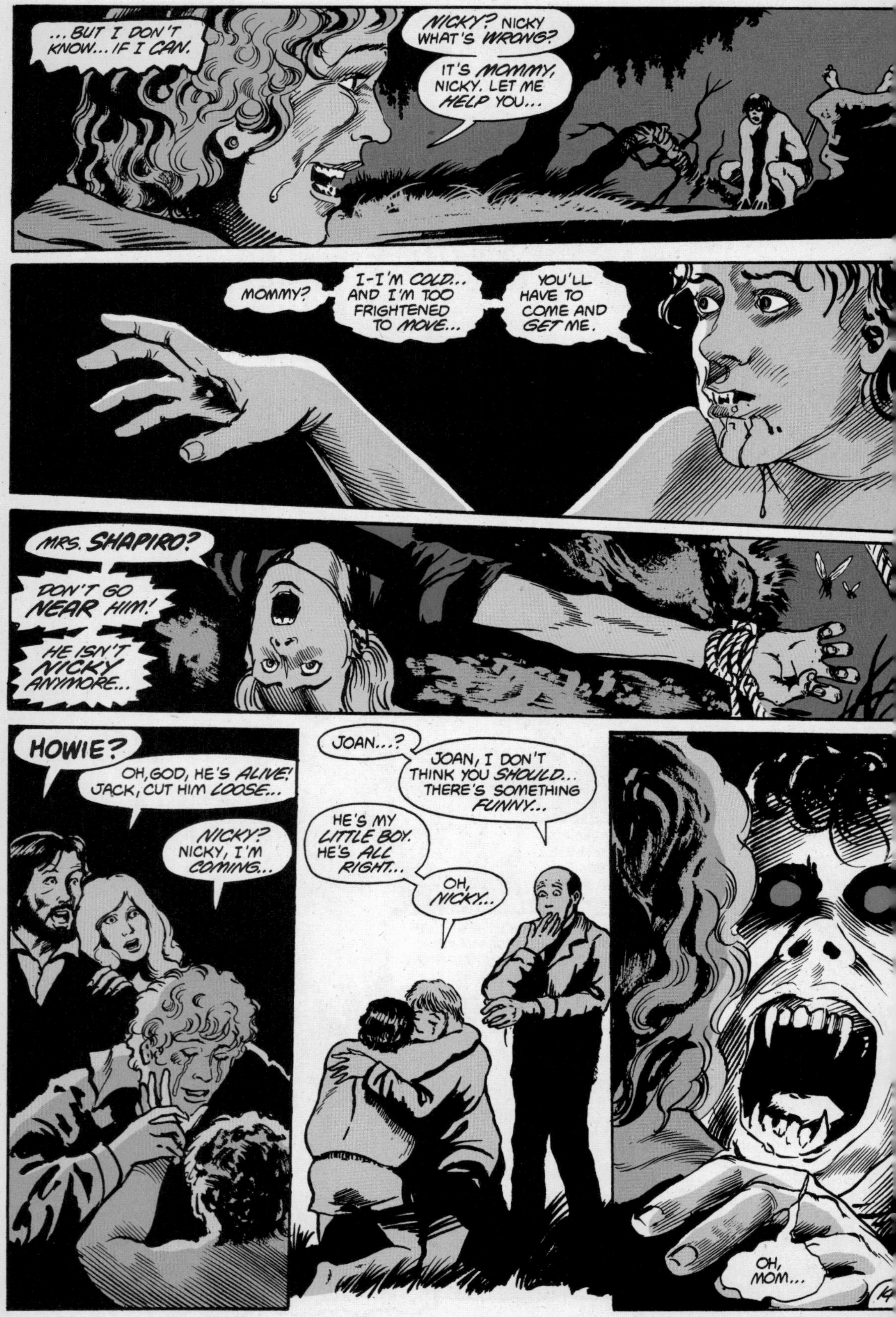
...BUT I DON'T KNOW... IF I CAN.
NICKY? NICKY WHAT'S WRONG?
IT'S MOMMY, NICKY. LET ME HELP YOU...
MOMMY?
I-I'M COLD... AND I'M TOO FRIGHTENED TO MOVE...
YOU'LL HAVE TO COME AND GET ME.
MRS. SHAPIRO?
DON'T GO NEAR HIM!
HE ISN'T NICKY ANYMORE...
HOWIE?
OH, GOD, HE'S ALIVE! JACK, CUT HIM LOOSE...
NICKY? NICKY, I'M COMING...
JOAN...?
JOAN, I DON'T THINK YOU SHOULD... THERE'S SOMETHING FUNNY...
HE'S MY LITTLE BOY. HE'S ALL RIGHT...
OH, NICKY...
OH, MOM...

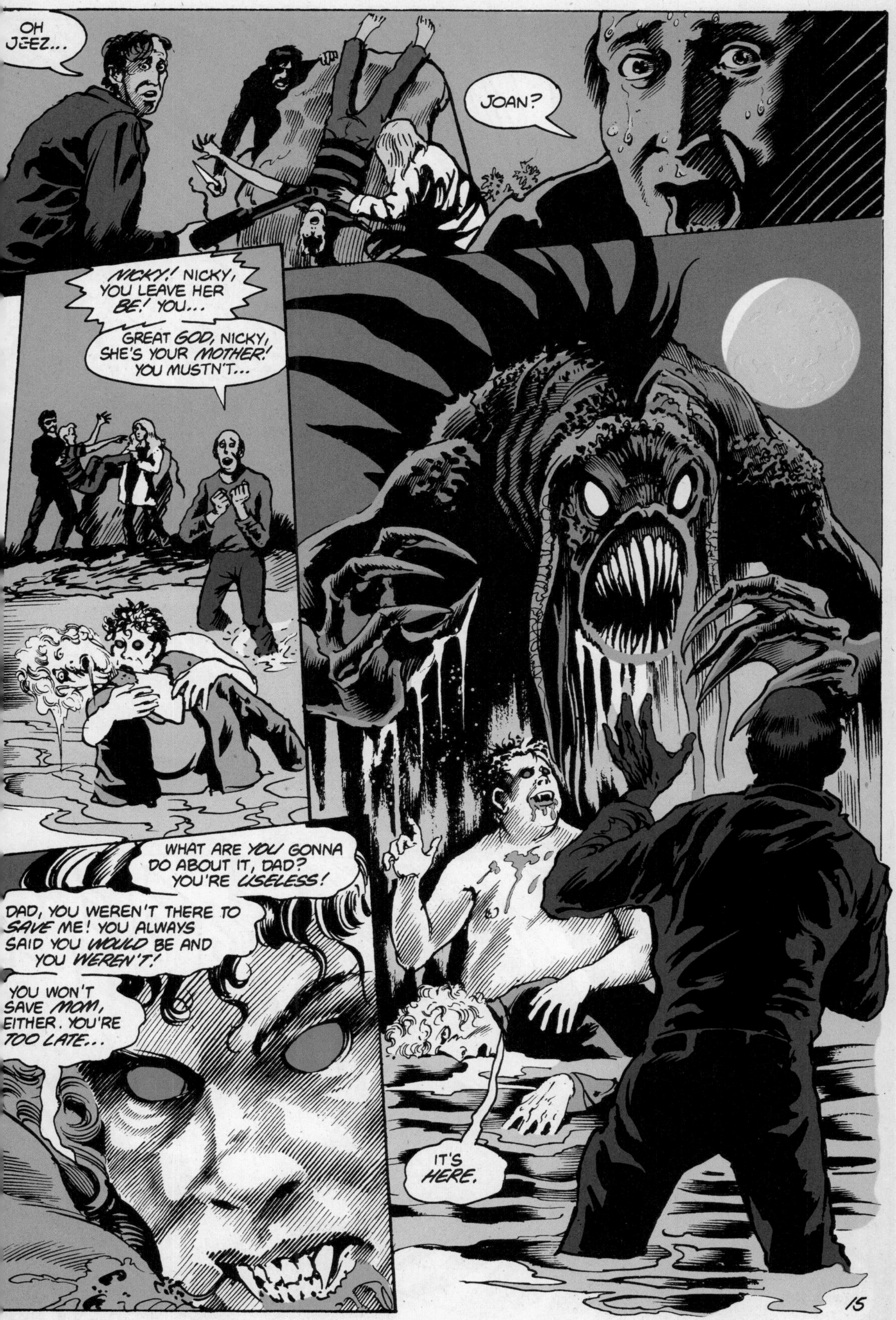
OH JEEZ...
JOAN?
NICKY! NICKY, YOU LEAVE HER BE! YOU...
GREAT GOD, NICKY, SHE'S YOUR MOTHER! YOU MUSTN'T...
WHAT ARE YOU GONNA DO ABOUT IT, DAD? YOU'RE USELESS!
DAD, YOU WEREN'T THERE TO SAVE ME! YOU ALWAYS SAID YOU WOULD BE AND YOU WEREN'T!
YOU WON'T SAVE MOM, EITHER. YOU'RE TOO LATE...
IT'S HERE.
15

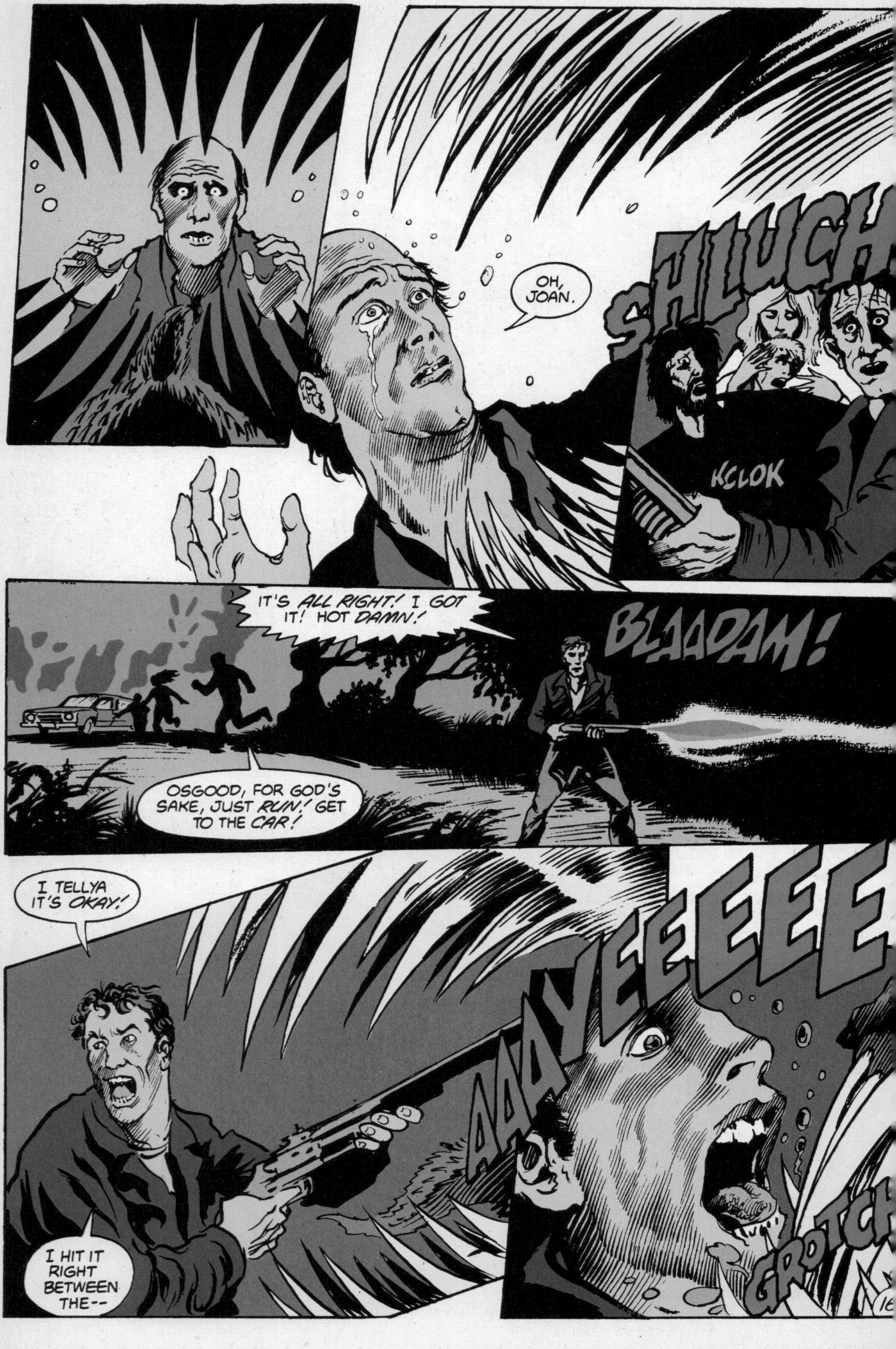
OH, JOAN.
SHLUCH
KCLOK
IT'S ALL RIGHT! I GOT IT! HOT DAMN!
BLAADAM!
OSGOOD, FOR GOD'S SAKE, JUST RUN! GET TO THE CAR!
I TELLYA IT'S OKAY!
I HIT IT RIGHT BETWEEN THE--
AAAYEEEEEE
GROTCH

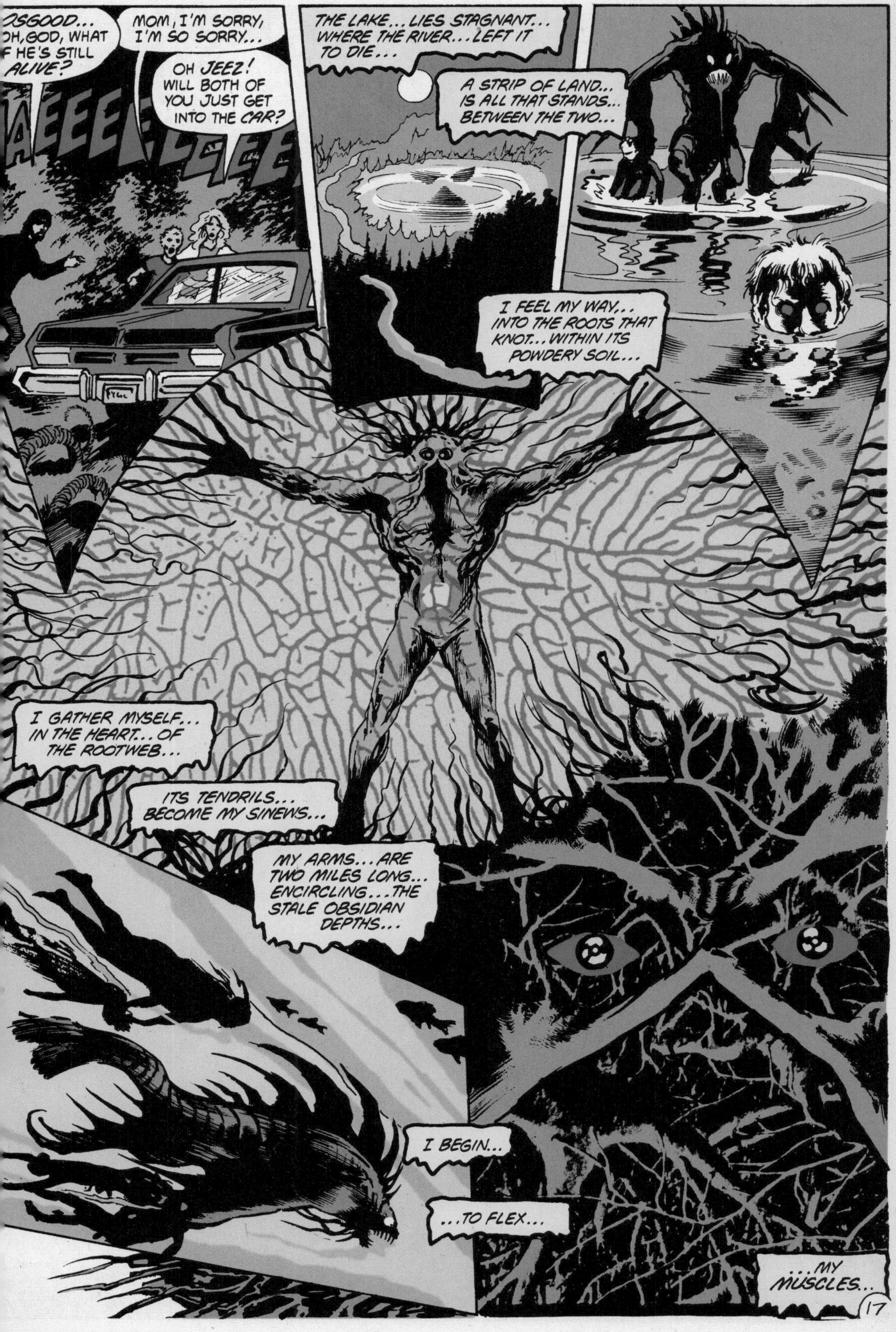
OSGOOD... OH, GOD, WHAT IF HE'S STILL ALIVE?
MOM, I'M SORRY, I'M SO SORRY...
OH JEEZ! WILL BOTH OF YOU JUST GET INTO THE CAR?
AEEEEEEEEE
THE LAKE... LIES STAGNANT... WHERE THE RIVER... LEFT IT TO DIE...
A STRIP OF LAND... IS ALL THAT STANDS... BETWEEN THE TWO...
I FEEL MY WAY... INTO THE ROOTS THAT KNOT... WITHIN ITS POWDERY SOIL...
I GATHER MYSELF... IN THE HEART... OF THE ROOTWEB...
ITS TENDRILS... BECOME MY SINEWS...
MY ARMS... ARE TWO MILES LONG... ENCIRCLING... THE STALE OBSIDIAN DEPTHS...
I BEGIN...
...TO FLEX...
...MY MUSCLES...
17

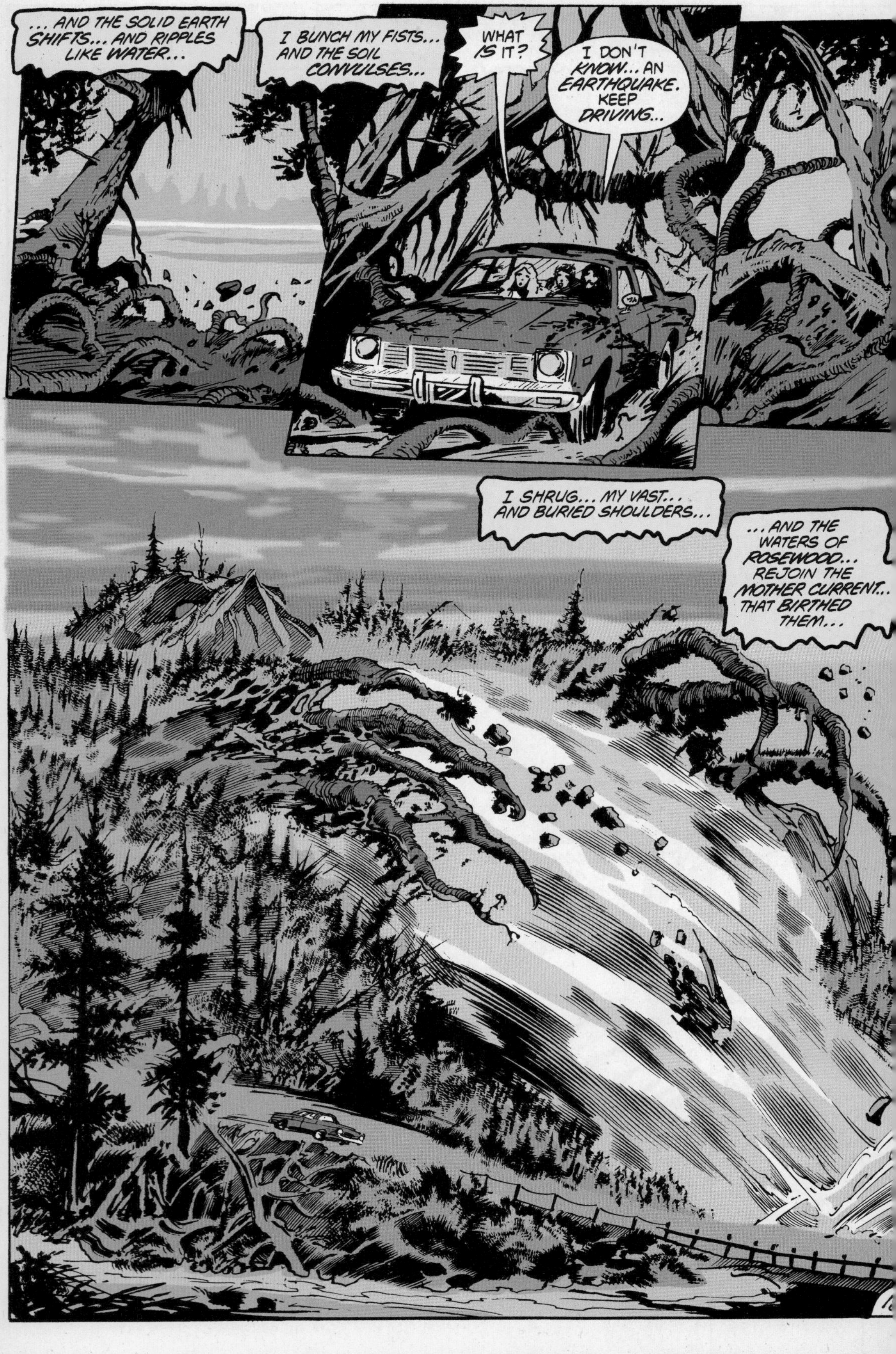

... AND THE SOLID EARTH SHIFTS... AND RIPPLES LIKE WATER...
I BUNCH MY FISTS... AND THE SOIL CONVULSES...
WHAT IS IT?
I DON'T KNOW... AN EARTHQUAKE. KEEP DRIVING...
I SHRUG... MY VAST... AND BURIED SHOULDERS...
... AND THE WATERS OF ROSEWOOD... REJOIN THE MOTHER CURRENT... THAT BIRTHED THEM...

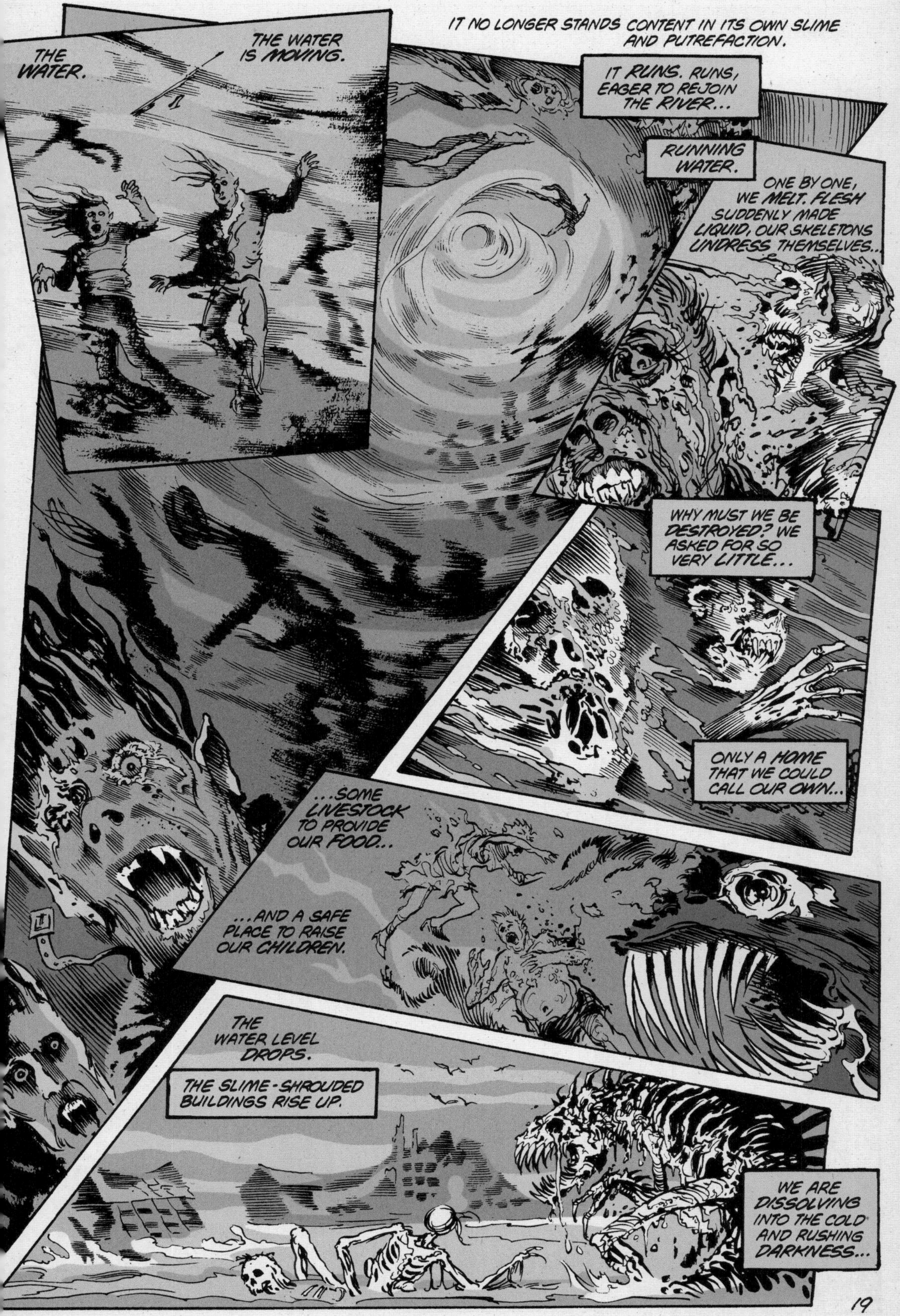
THE WATER.
THE WATER IS MOVING.
IT NO LONGER STANDS CONTENT IN ITS OWN SLIME AND PUTREFACTION.
IT RUNS. RUNS, EAGER TO REJOIN THE RIVER...
RUNNING WATER.
ONE BY ONE, WE MELT. FLESH SUDDENLY MADE LIQUID, OUR SKELETONS UNDRESS THEMSELVES...
WHY MUST WE BE DESTROYED? WE ASKED FOR SO VERY LITTLE...
ONLY A HOME THAT WE COULD CALL OUR OWN...
...SOME LIVESTOCK TO PROVIDE OUR FOOD...
...AND A SAFE PLACE TO RAISE OUR CHILDREN.
THE WATER LEVEL DROPS.
THE SLIME-SHROUDED BUILDINGS RISE UP.
WE ARE DISSOLVING INTO THE COLD AND RUSHING DARKNESS...

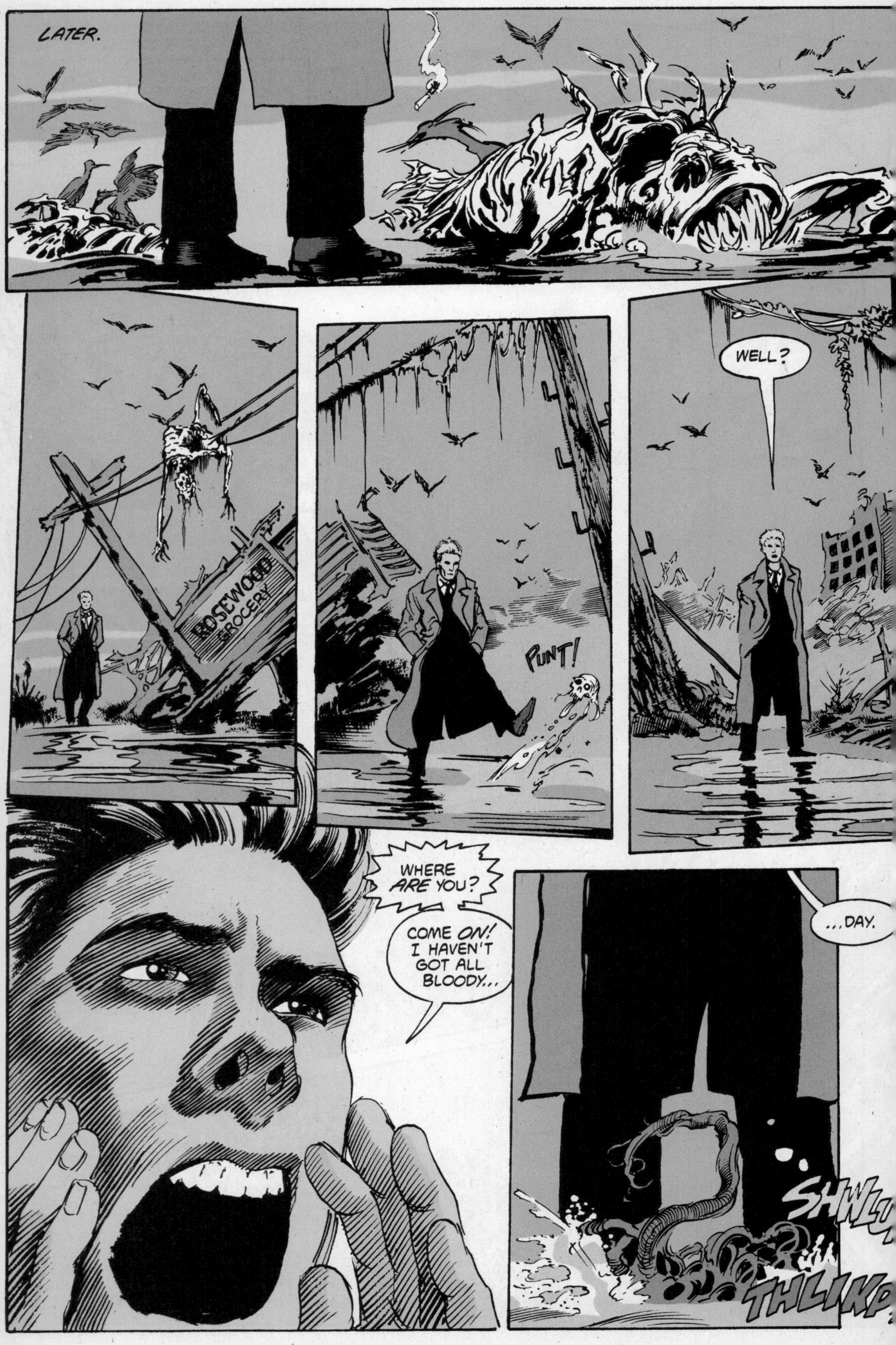
LATER.
ROSEWOOD GROCERY
PUNT!
WELL?
WHERE ARE YOU?
COME ON! I HAVEN'T GOT ALL BLOODY...
...DAY.
SHWLU
THLIKP

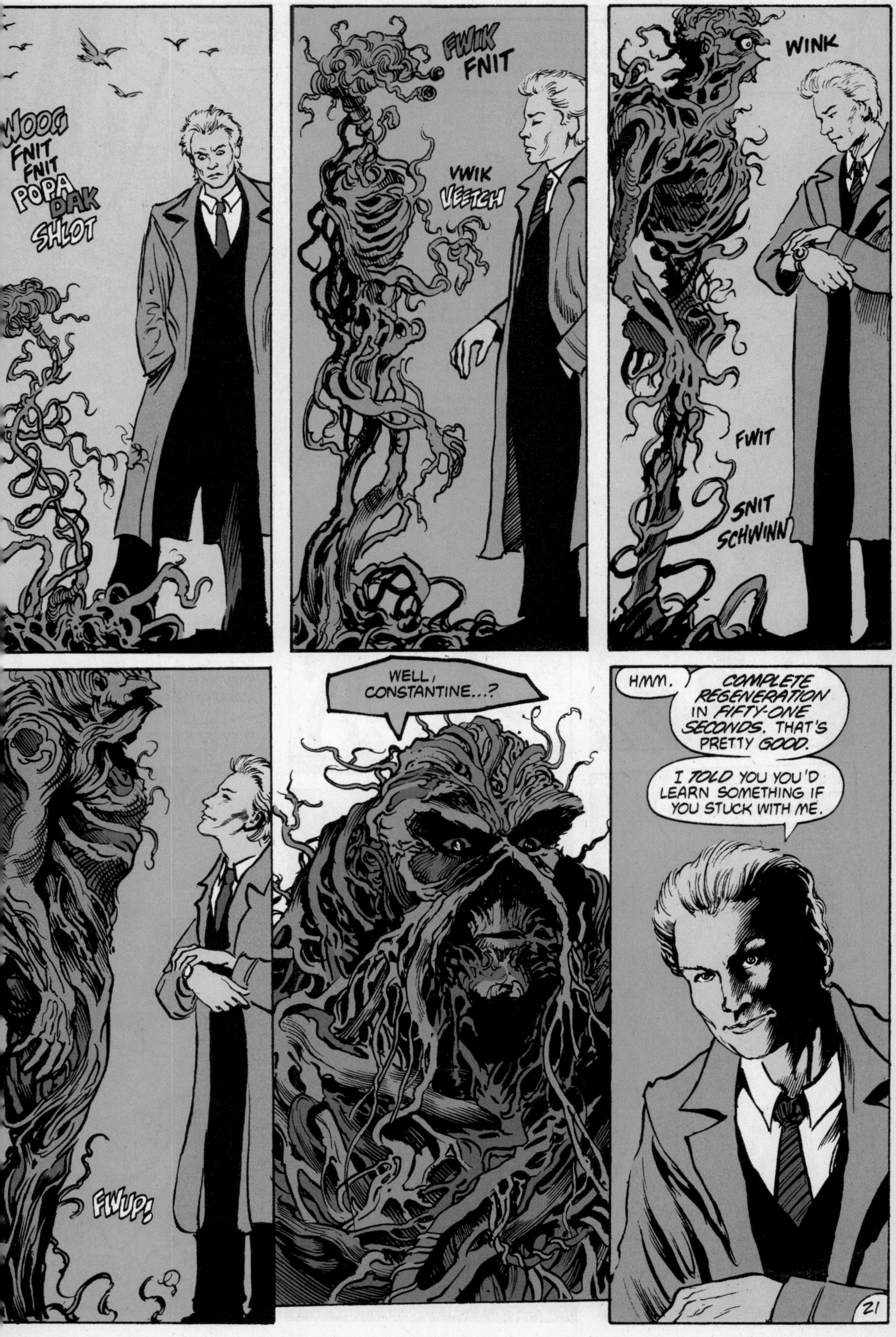
WOOG
FNIT
FNIT
POPA
DAK
SHLOT
FWIK
FNIT
VWIK
VEETCH
WINK
FWIT
SNIT
SCHWINN
FWUP!
WELL, CONSTANTINE...?
HMM.
COMPLETE REGENERATION IN FIFTY-ONE SECONDS. THAT'S PRETTY GOOD.
I TOLD YOU YOU'D LEARN SOMETHING IF YOU STUCK WITH ME.
21

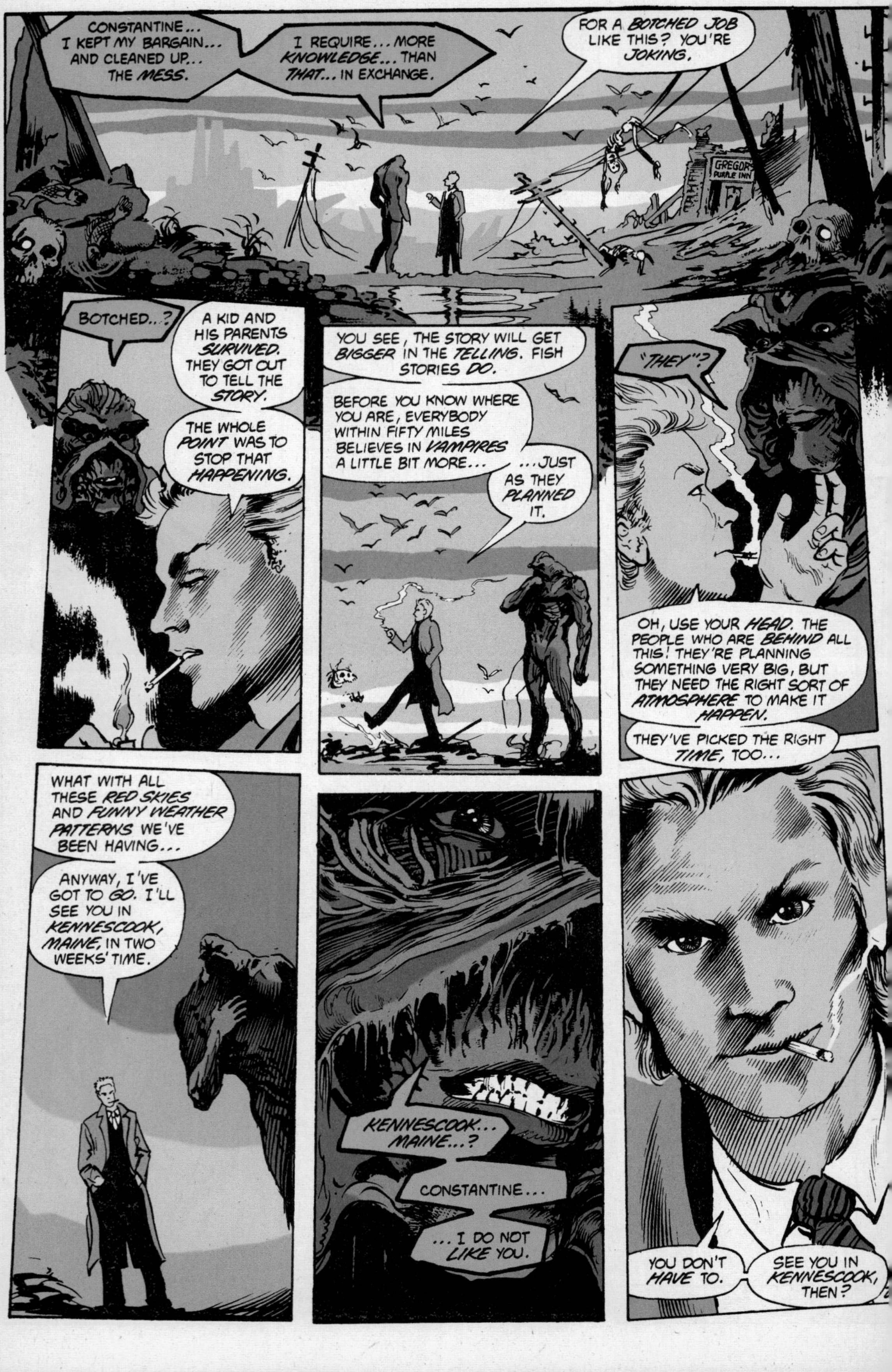
CONSTANTINE... I KEPT MY BARGAIN... AND CLEANED UP... THE MESS.
I REQUIRE... MORE KNOWLEDGE... THAN THAT... IN EXCHANGE.
FOR A BOTCHED JOB LIKE THIS? YOU'RE JOKING.
GREGOR'S PURPLE INN
BOTCHED...?
A KID AND HIS PARENTS SURVIVED. THEY GOT OUT TO TELL THE STORY.
THE WHOLE POINT WAS TO STOP THAT HAPPENING.
YOU SEE, THE STORY WILL GET BIGGER IN THE TELLING. FISH STORIES DO.
BEFORE YOU KNOW WHERE YOU ARE, EVERYBODY WITHIN FIFTY MILES BELIEVES IN VAMPIRES A LITTLE BIT MORE...
...JUST AS THEY PLANNED IT.
"THEY"?
OH, USE YOUR HEAD. THE PEOPLE WHO ARE BEHIND ALL THIS! THEY'RE PLANNING SOMETHING VERY BIG, BUT THEY NEED THE RIGHT SORT OF ATMOSPHERE TO MAKE IT HAPPEN.
THEY'VE PICKED THE RIGHT TIME, TOO...
WHAT WITH ALL THESE RED SKIES AND FUNNY WEATHER PATTERNS WE'VE BEEN HAVING...
ANYWAY, I'VE GOT TO GO. I'LL SEE YOU IN KENNESCOOK, MAINE, IN TWO WEEKS' TIME.
KENNESCOOK... MAINE...?
CONSTANTINE...
...I DO NOT LIKE YOU.
YOU DON'T HAVE TO.
SEE YOU IN KENNESCOOK, THEN?

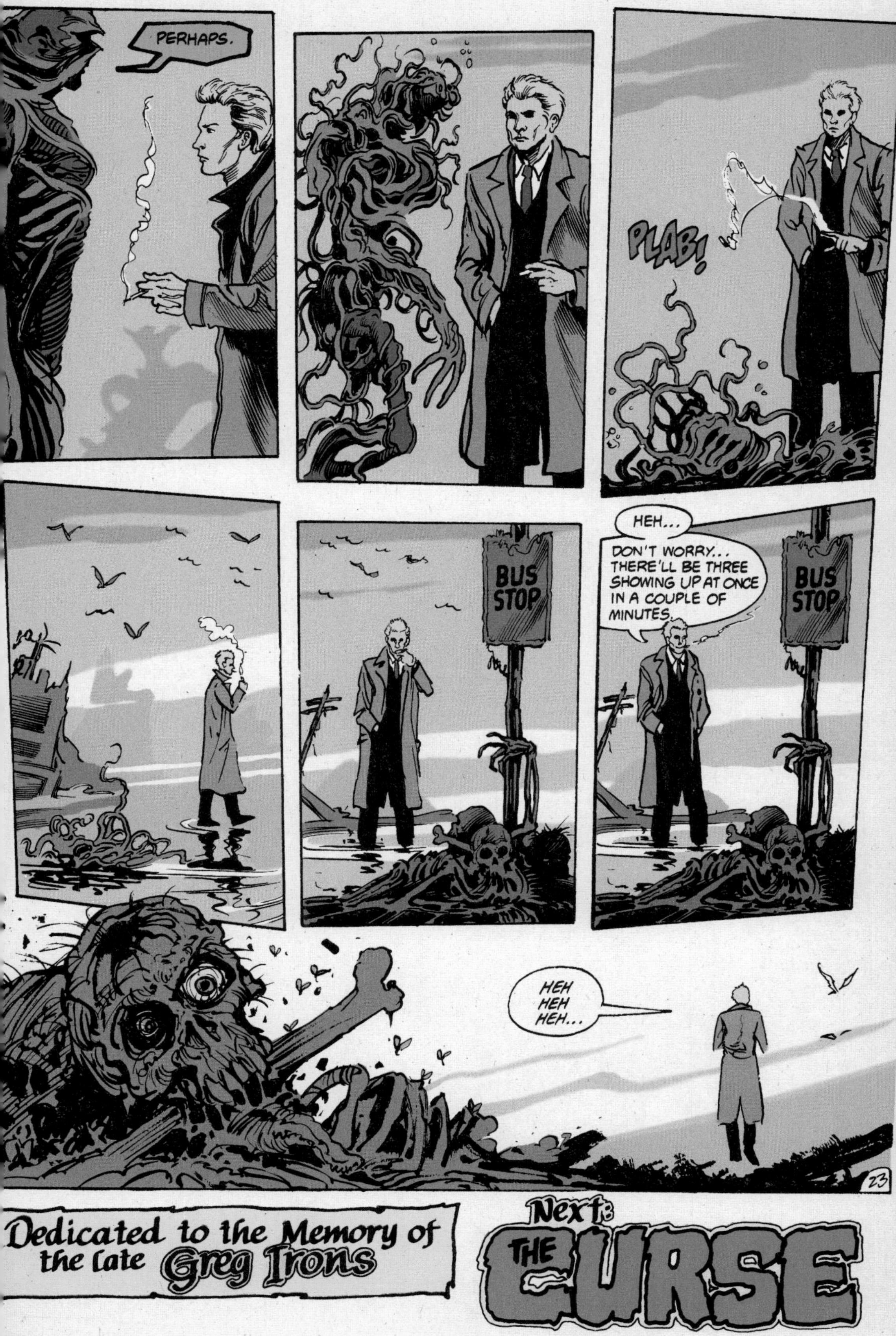
PERHAPS.
PLAB!
HEH...
DON'T WORRY... THERE'LL BE THREE SHOWING UP AT ONCE IN A COUPLE OF MINUTES.
BUS STOP
HEH HEH HEH...
23
Dedicated to the Memory of the late Greg Irons
Next: THE CURSE

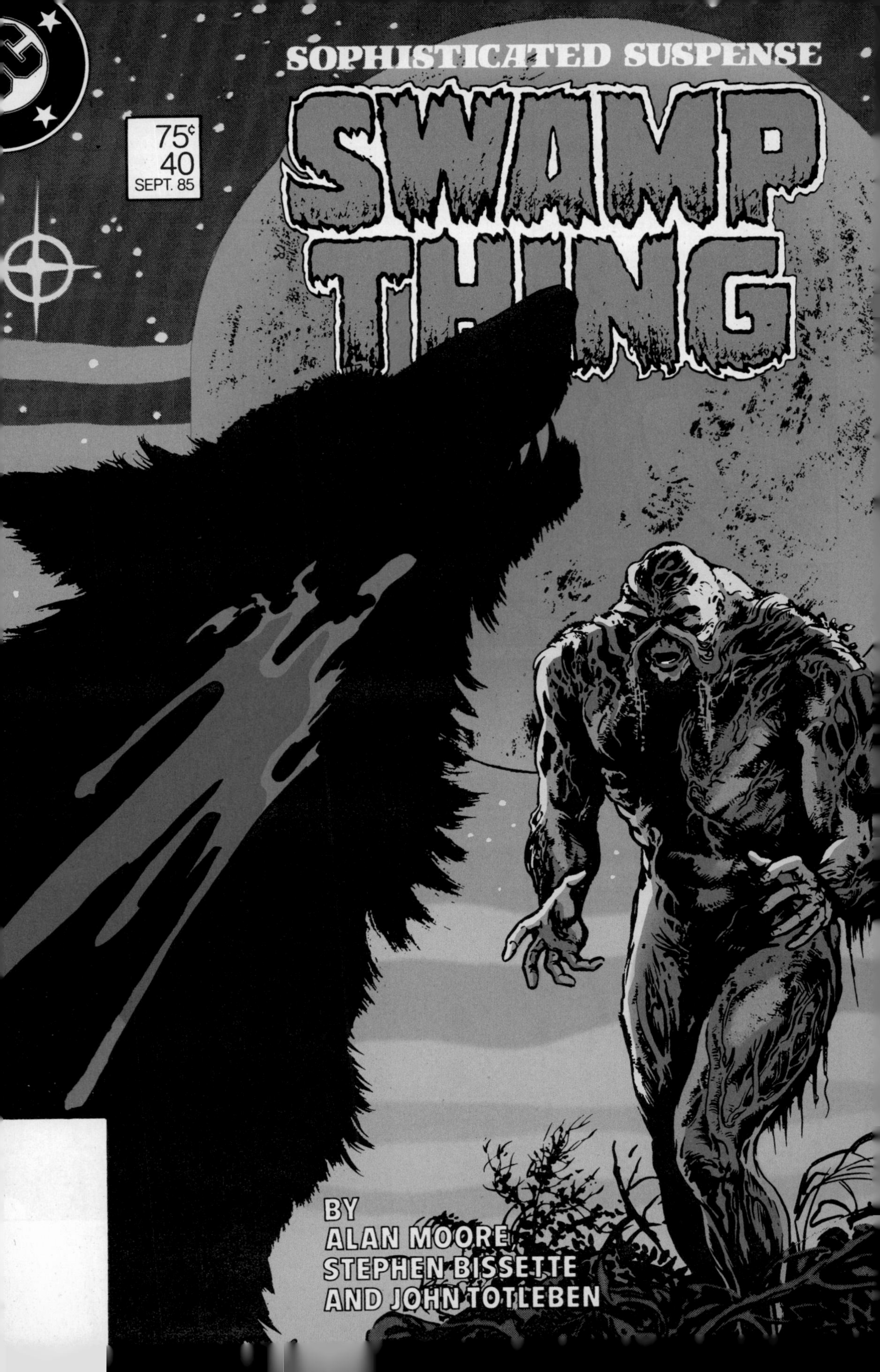
SOPHISTICATED SUSPENSE
SWAMP THING
75¢
40
SEPT. 85
BY
ALAN MOORE,
STEPHEN BISSETTE
AND JOHN TOTLEBEN

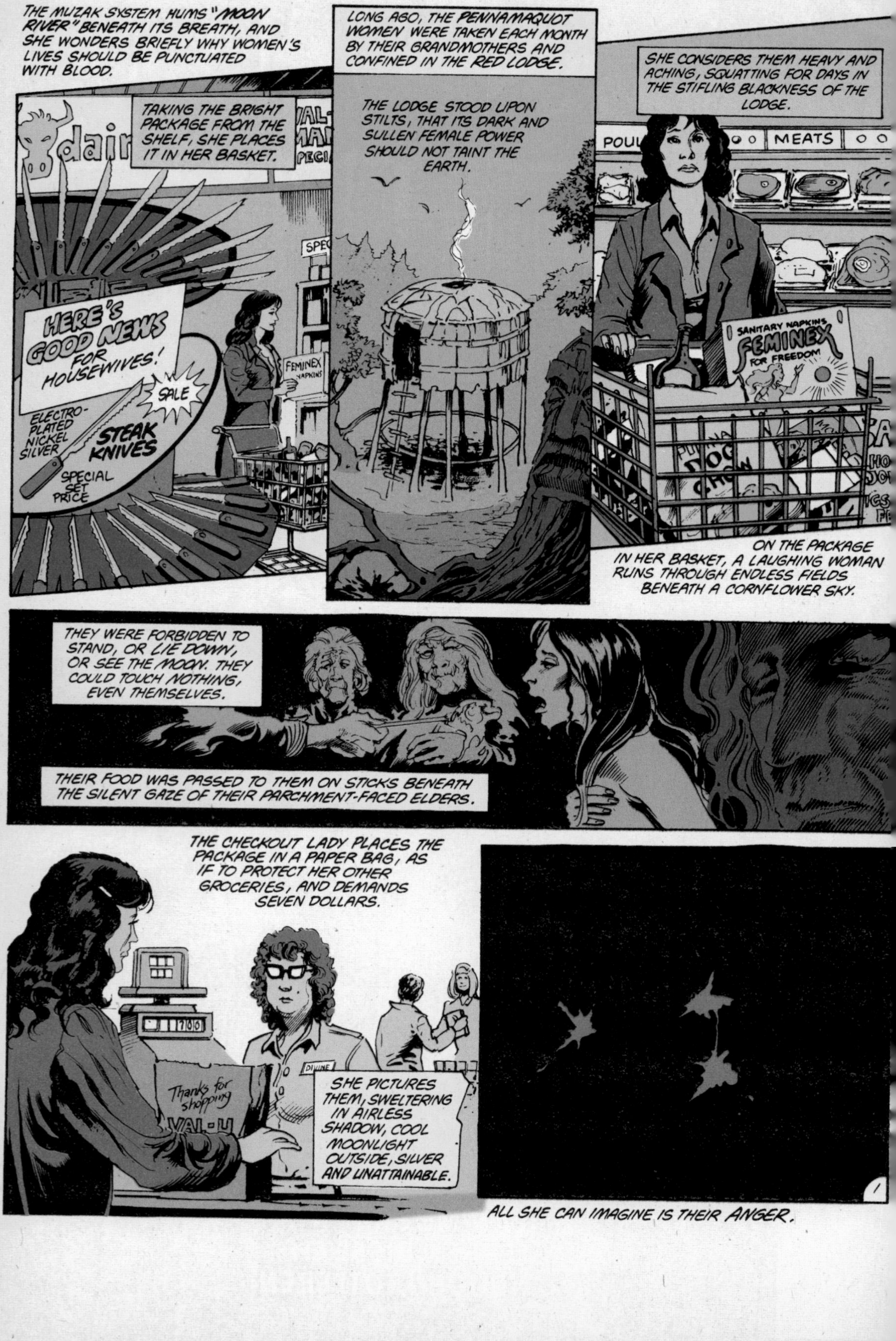
THE MUZAK SYSTEM HUMS "MOON RIVER" BENEATH ITS BREATH, AND SHE WONDERS BRIEFLY WHY WOMEN'S LIVES SHOULD BE PUNCTUATED WITH BLOOD.
TAKING THE BRIGHT PACKAGE FROM THE SHELF, SHE PLACES IT IN HER BASKET.
HERE'S GOOD NEWS FOR HOUSEWIVES!
SALE
ELECTRO-PLATED NICKEL SILVER
STEAK KNIVES
SPECIAL SET PRICE
FEMINEX NAPKINS
LONG AGO, THE PENNAMAQUOT WOMEN WERE TAKEN EACH MONTH BY THEIR GRANDMOTHERS AND CONFINED IN THE RED LODGE.
THE LODGE STOOD UPON STILTS, THAT ITS DARK AND SULLEN FEMALE POWER SHOULD NOT TAINT THE EARTH.
SHE CONSIDERS THEM HEAVY AND ACHING, SQUATTING FOR DAYS IN THE STIFLING BLACKNESS OF THE LODGE.
MEATS
SANITARY NAPKINS
FEMINEX
FOR FREEDOM
ON THE PACKAGE IN HER BASKET, A LAUGHING WOMAN RUNS THROUGH ENDLESS FIELDS BENEATH A CORNFLOWER SKY.
THEY WERE FORBIDDEN TO STAND, OR LIE DOWN, OR SEE THE MOON. THEY COULD TOUCH NOTHING, EVEN THEMSELVES.
THEIR FOOD WAS PASSED TO THEM ON STICKS BENEATH THE SILENT GAZE OF THEIR PARCHMENT-FACED ELDERS.
THE CHECKOUT LADY PLACES THE PACKAGE IN A PAPER BAG, AS IF TO PROTECT HER OTHER GROCERIES, AND DEMANDS SEVEN DOLLARS.
Thanks for shopping
VAL-U
DIVINE
SHE PICTURES THEM, SWELTERING IN AIRLESS SHADOW, COOL MOONLIGHT OUTSIDE, SILVER AND UNATTAINABLE.
1
ALL SHE CAN IMAGINE IS THEIR ANGER.

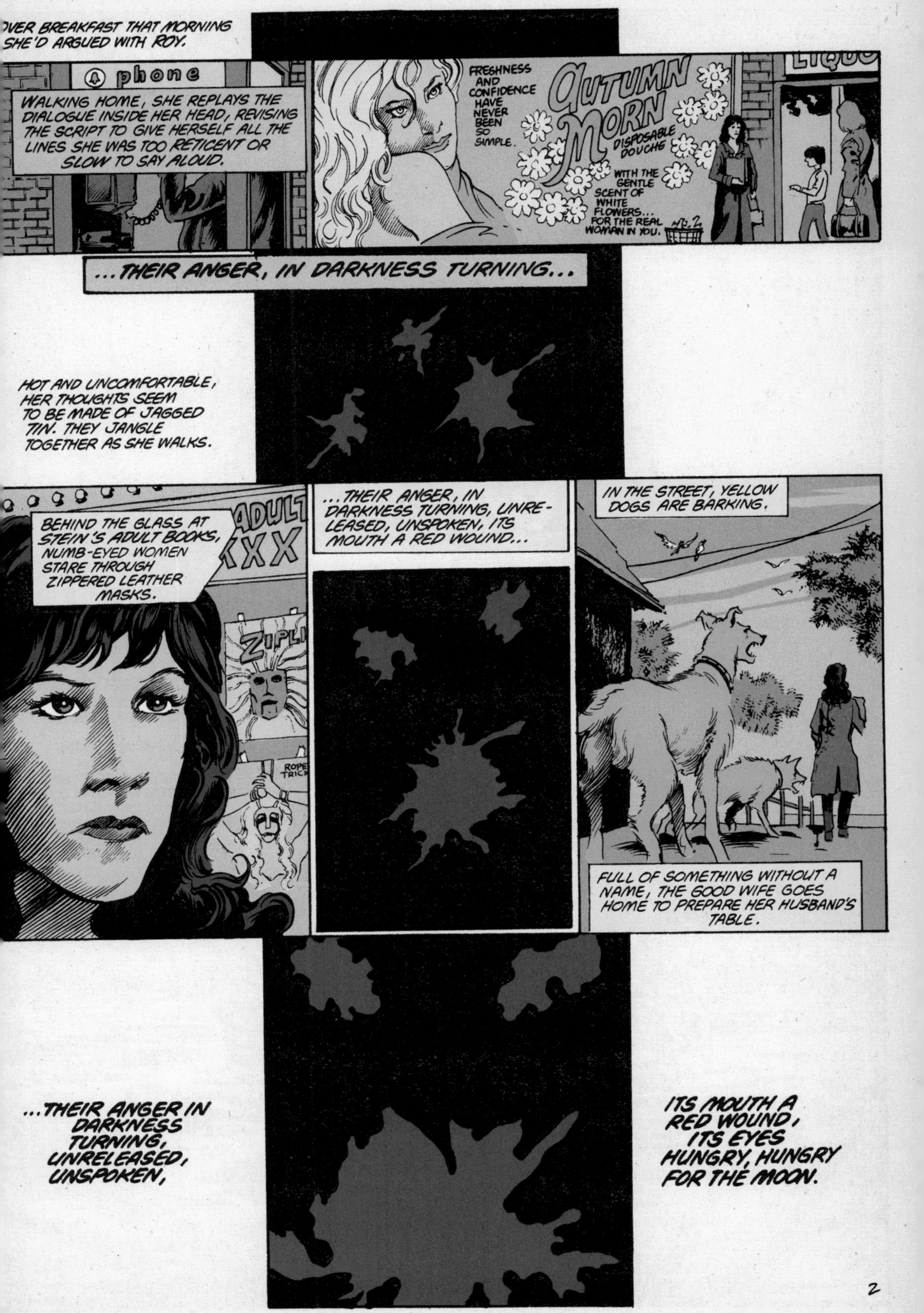
OVER BREAKFAST THAT MORNING SHE'D ARGUED WITH ROY.
phone
WALKING HOME, SHE REPLAYS THE DIALOGUE INSIDE HER HEAD, REVISING THE SCRIPT TO GIVE HERSELF ALL THE LINES SHE WAS TOO RETICENT OR SLOW TO SAY ALOUD.
FRESHNESS AND CONFIDENCE HAVE NEVER BEEN SO SIMPLE.
AUTUMN MORN
DISPOSABLE DOUCHE
WITH THE GENTLE SCENT OF WHITE FLOWERS... FOR THE REAL WOMAN IN YOU.
...THEIR ANGER, IN DARKNESS TURNING...
HOT AND UNCOMFORTABLE, HER THOUGHTS SEEM TO BE MADE OF JAGGED TIN. THEY JANGLE TOGETHER AS SHE WALKS.
ADULT XXX
BEHIND THE GLASS AT STEIN'S ADULT BOOKS, NUMB-EYED WOMEN STARE THROUGH ZIPPERED LEATHER MASKS.
...THEIR ANGER, IN DARKNESS TURNING, UNRELEASED, UNSPOKEN, ITS MOUTH A RED WOUND...
IN THE STREET, YELLOW DOGS ARE BARKING.
FULL OF SOMETHING WITHOUT A NAME, THE GOOD WIFE GOES HOME TO PREPARE HER HUSBAND'S TABLE.
...THEIR ANGER IN DARKNESS TURNING, UNRELEASED, UNSPOKEN,
ITS MOUTH A RED WOUND, ITS EYES HUNGRY, HUNGRY FOR THE MOON.
2

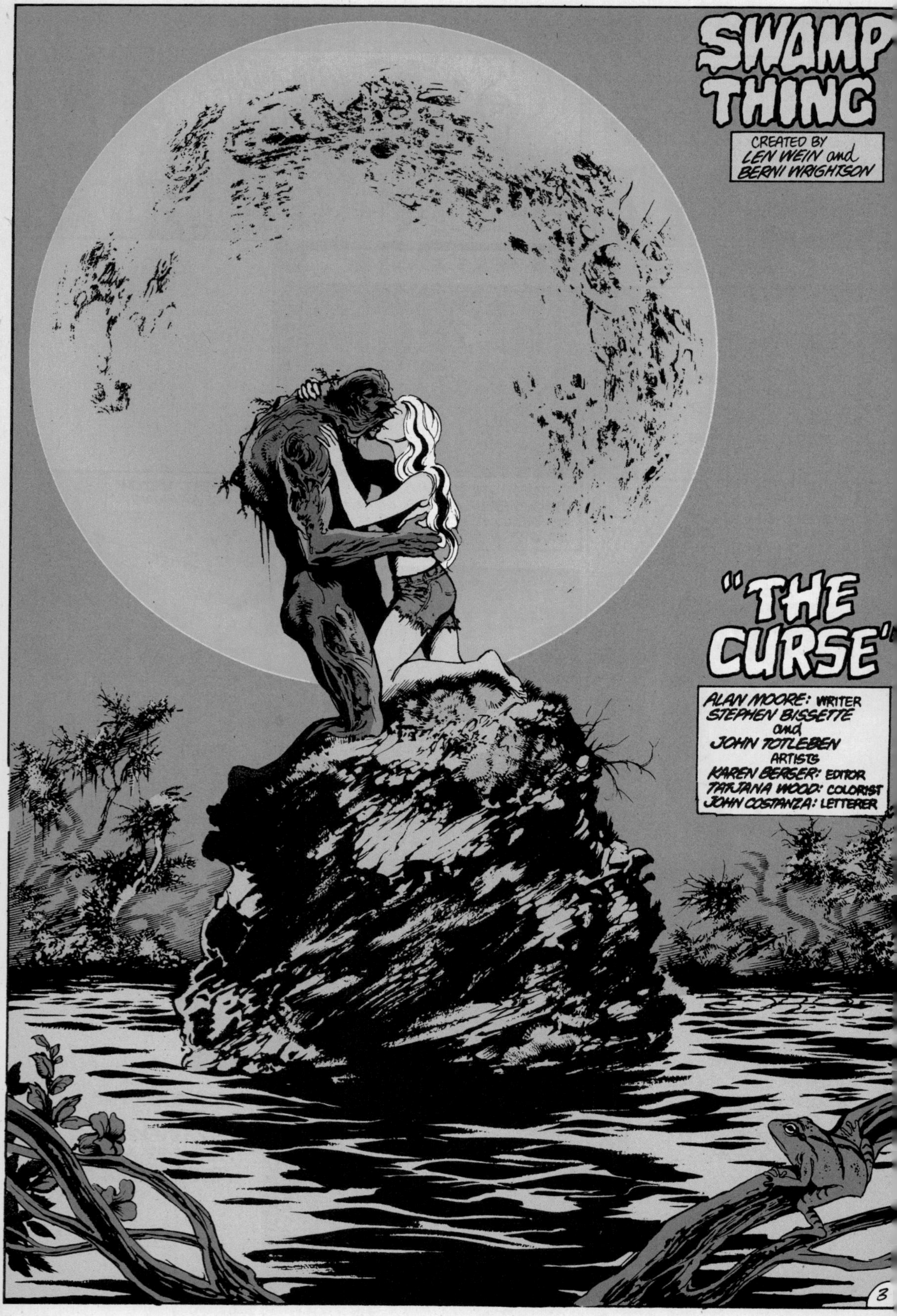
SWAMP THING
CREATED BY LEN WEIN and BERNI WRIGHTSON
"THE CURSE"
ALAN MOORE: WRITER
STEPHEN BISSETTE and JOHN TOTLEBEN ARTISTS
KAREN BERGER: EDITOR
TATJANA WOOD: COLORIST
JOHN COSTANZA: LETTERER
3

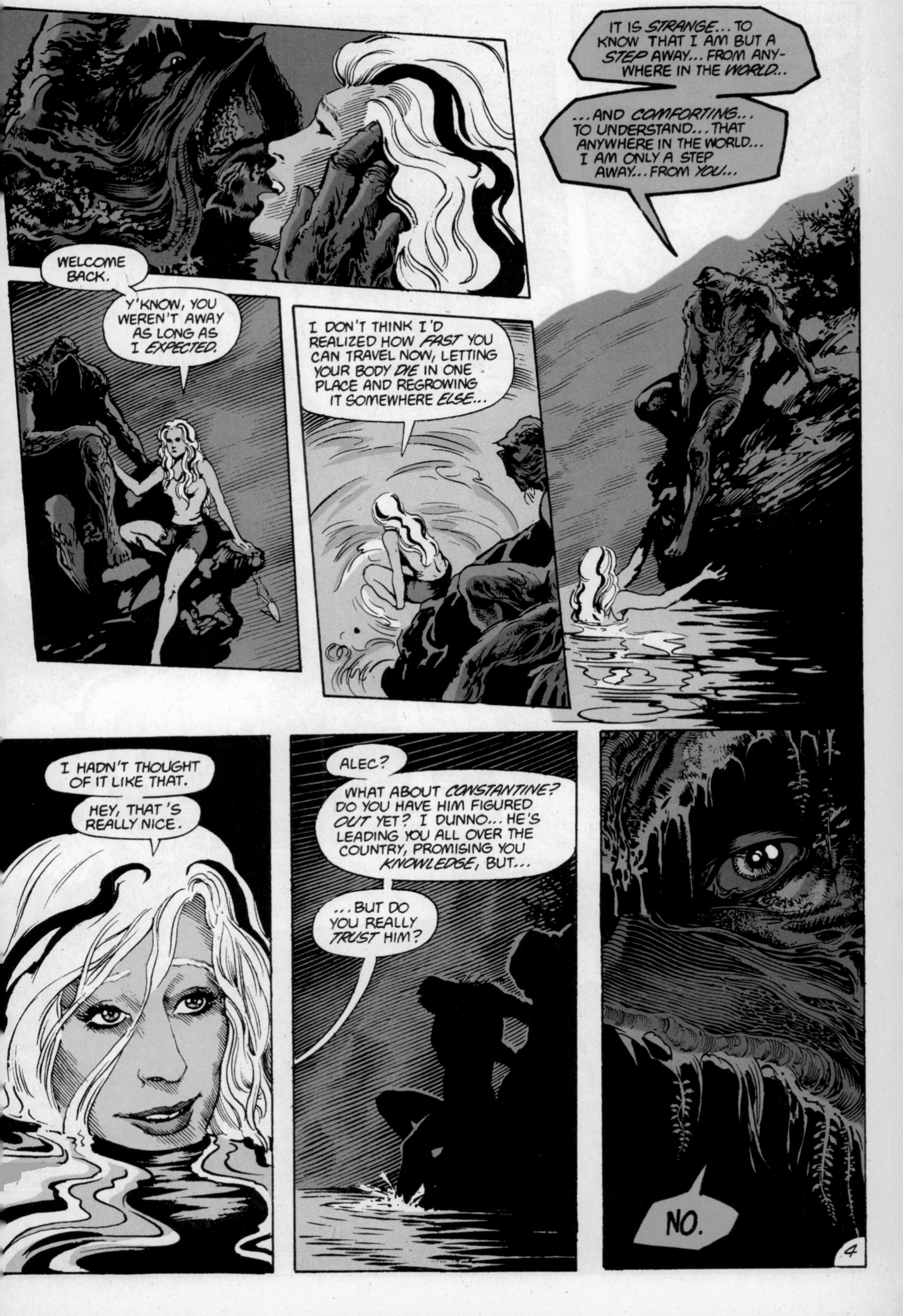
IT IS STRANGE... TO KNOW THAT I AM BUT A STEP AWAY... FROM ANYWHERE IN THE WORLD...
...AND COMFORTING... TO UNDERSTAND... THAT ANYWHERE IN THE WORLD... I AM ONLY A STEP AWAY... FROM YOU...
WELCOME BACK.
Y'KNOW, YOU WEREN'T AWAY AS LONG AS I EXPECTED.
I DON'T THINK I'D REALIZED HOW FAST YOU CAN TRAVEL NOW, LETTING YOUR BODY DIE IN ONE PLACE AND REGROWING IT SOMEWHERE ELSE...
I HADN'T THOUGHT OF IT LIKE THAT.
HEY, THAT'S REALLY NICE.
ALEC?
WHAT ABOUT CONSTANTINE? DO YOU HAVE HIM FIGURED OUT YET? I DUNNO... HE'S LEADING YOU ALL OVER THE COUNTRY, PROMISING YOU KNOWLEDGE, BUT...
...BUT DO YOU REALLY TRUST HIM?
NO.
4

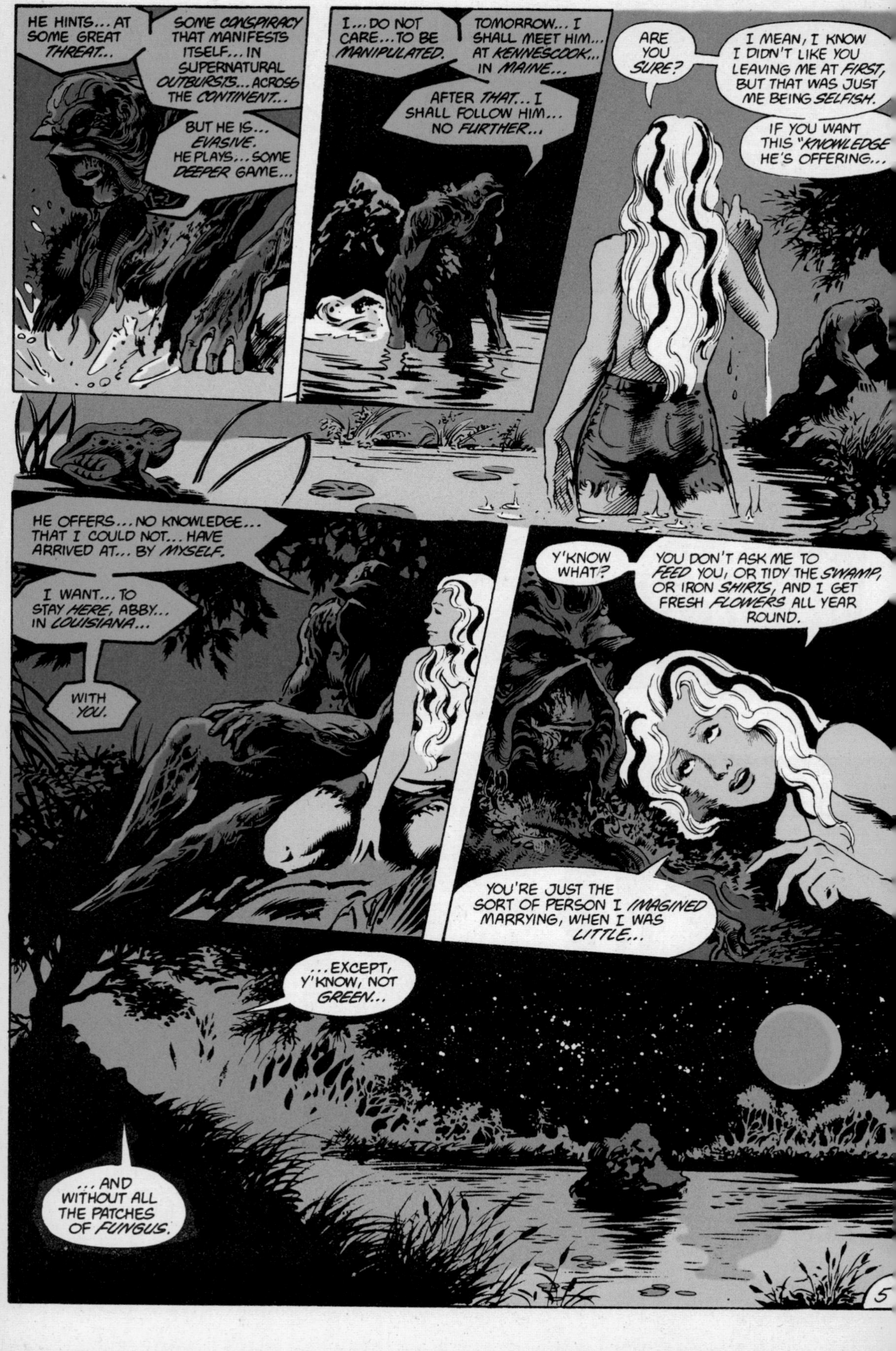
HE HINTS... AT SOME GREAT THREAT...
SOME CONSPIRACY THAT MANIFESTS ITSELF... IN SUPERNATURAL OUTBURSTS... ACROSS THE CONTINENT...
BUT HE IS... EVASIVE. HE PLAYS... SOME DEEPER GAME...
I... DO NOT CARE... TO BE MANIPULATED.
TOMORROW... I SHALL MEET HIM... AT KENNESCOOK... IN MAINE...
AFTER THAT... I SHALL FOLLOW HIM... NO FURTHER...
ARE YOU SURE?
I MEAN, I KNOW I DIDN'T LIKE YOU LEAVING ME AT FIRST, BUT THAT WAS JUST ME BEING SELFISH.
IF YOU WANT THIS "KNOWLEDGE HE'S OFFERING...
HE OFFERS... NO KNOWLEDGE... THAT I COULD NOT... HAVE ARRIVED AT... BY MYSELF.
I WANT... TO STAY HERE, ABBY... IN LOUISIANA...
WITH YOU.
Y'KNOW WHAT?
YOU DON'T ASK ME TO FEED YOU, OR TIDY THE SWAMP, OR IRON SHIRTS, AND I GET FRESH FLOWERS ALL YEAR ROUND.
YOU'RE JUST THE SORT OF PERSON I IMAGINED MARRYING, WHEN I WAS LITTLE...
...EXCEPT, Y'KNOW, NOT GREEN...
...AND WITHOUT ALL THE PATCHES OF FUNGUS.
5

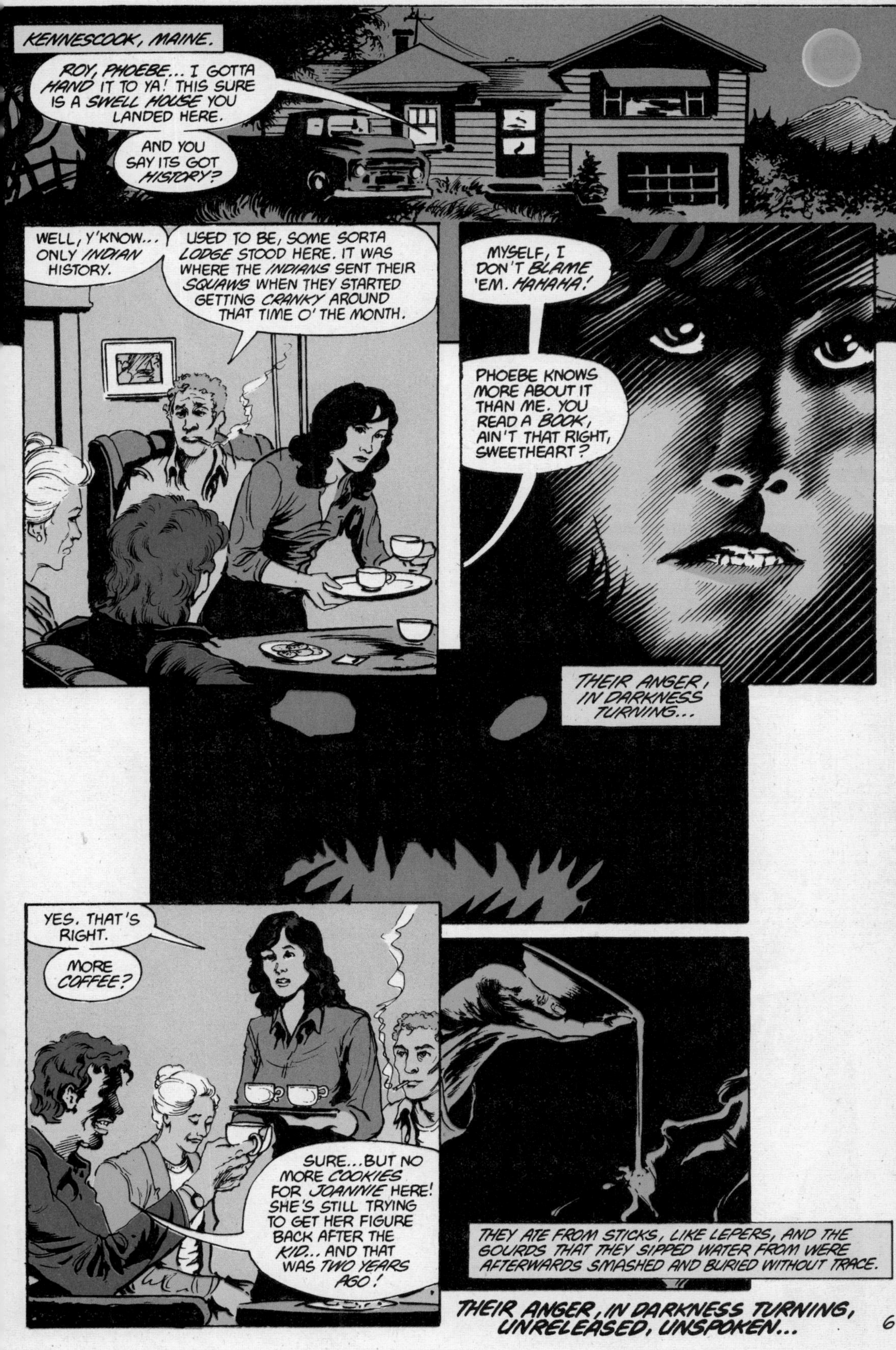
KENNESCOOK, MAINE.
ROY, PHOEBE... I GOTTA HAND IT TO YA! THIS SURE IS A SWELL HOUSE YOU LANDED HERE.
AND YOU SAY ITS GOT HISTORY?
WELL, Y'KNOW... ONLY INDIAN HISTORY.
USED TO BE, SOME SORTA LODGE STOOD HERE. IT WAS WHERE THE INDIANS SENT THEIR SQUAWS WHEN THEY STARTED GETTING CRANKY AROUND THAT TIME O' THE MONTH.
MYSELF, I DON'T BLAME 'EM. HAHAHA!
PHOEBE KNOWS MORE ABOUT IT THAN ME. YOU READ A BOOK, AIN'T THAT RIGHT, SWEETHEART?
THEIR ANGER, IN DARKNESS TURNING...
YES. THAT'S RIGHT.
MORE COFFEE?
SURE... BUT NO MORE COOKIES FOR JOANNIE HERE! SHE'S STILL TRYING TO GET HER FIGURE BACK AFTER THE KID... AND THAT WAS TWO YEARS AGO!
THEY ATE FROM STICKS, LIKE LEPERS, AND THE GOURDS THAT THEY SIPPED WATER FROM WERE AFTERWARDS SMASHED AND BURIED WITHOUT TRACE.
THEIR ANGER, IN DARKNESS TURNING, UNRELEASED, UNSPOKEN...
6

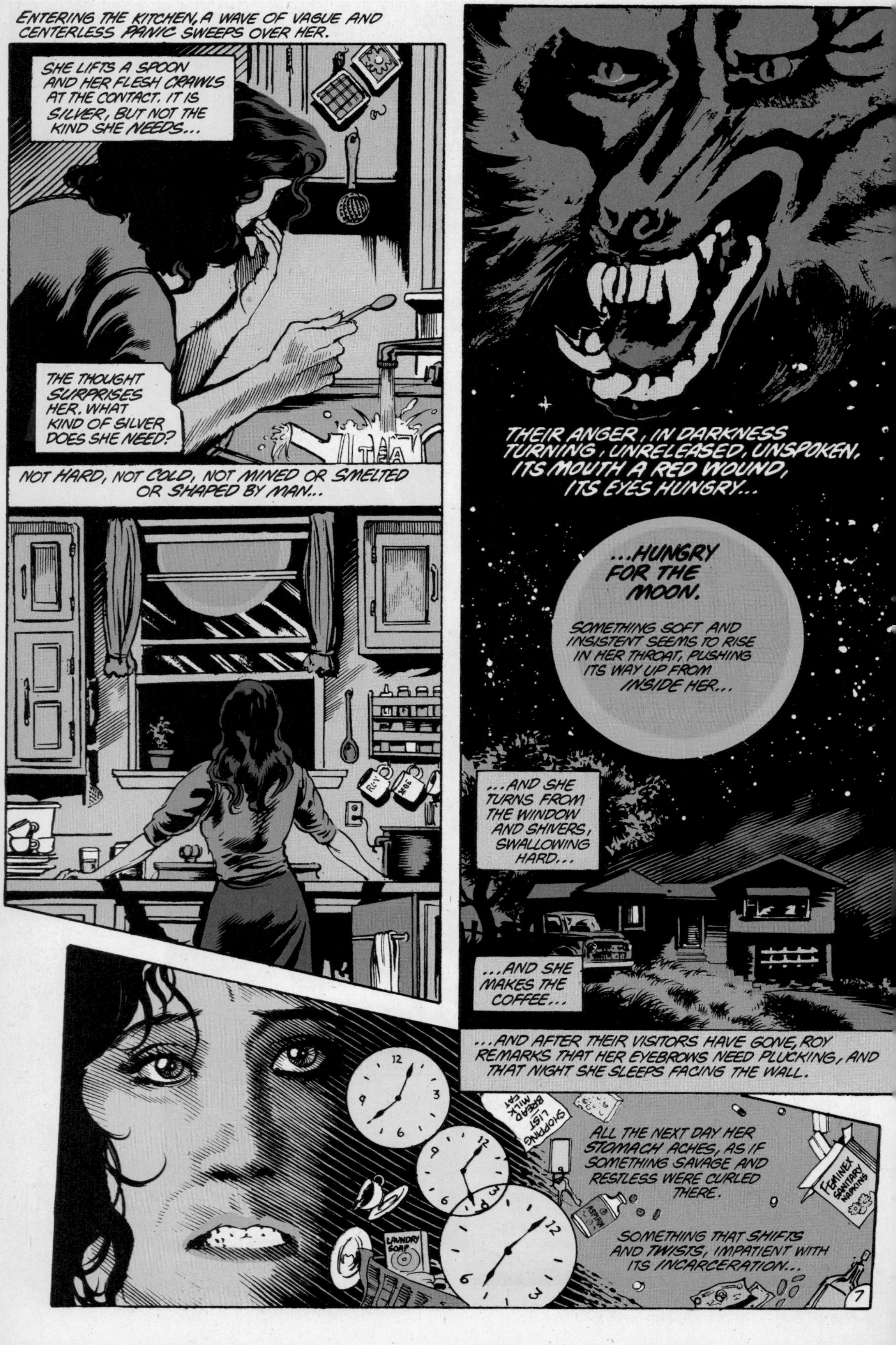
ENTERING THE KITCHEN, A WAVE OF VAGUE AND CENTERLESS PANIC SWEEPS OVER HER.
SHE LIFTS A SPOON AND HER FLESH CRAWLS AT THE CONTACT. IT IS SILVER, BUT NOT THE KIND SHE NEEDS...
THE THOUGHT SURPRISES HER. WHAT KIND OF SILVER DOES SHE NEED?
NOT HARD, NOT COLD, NOT MINED OR SMELTED OR SHAPED BY MAN...
THEIR ANGER, IN DARKNESS TURNING, UNRELEASED, UNSPOKEN. ITS MOUTH A RED WOUND, ITS EYES HUNGRY...
...HUNGRY FOR THE MOON.
SOMETHING SOFT AND INSISTENT SEEMS TO RISE IN HER THROAT, PUSHING ITS WAY UP FROM INSIDE HER...
ROY
...AND SHE TURNS FROM THE WINDOW AND SHIVERS, SWALLOWING HARD...
...AND SHE MAKES THE COFFEE...
...AND AFTER THEIR VISITORS HAVE GONE, ROY REMARKS THAT HER EYEBROWS NEED PLUCKING, AND THAT NIGHT SHE SLEEPS FACING THE WALL.
ALL THE NEXT DAY HER STOMACH ACHES, AS IF SOMETHING SAVAGE AND RESTLESS WERE CURLED THERE.
SOMETHING THAT SHIFTS AND TWISTS, IMPATIENT WITH ITS INCARCERATION...
7

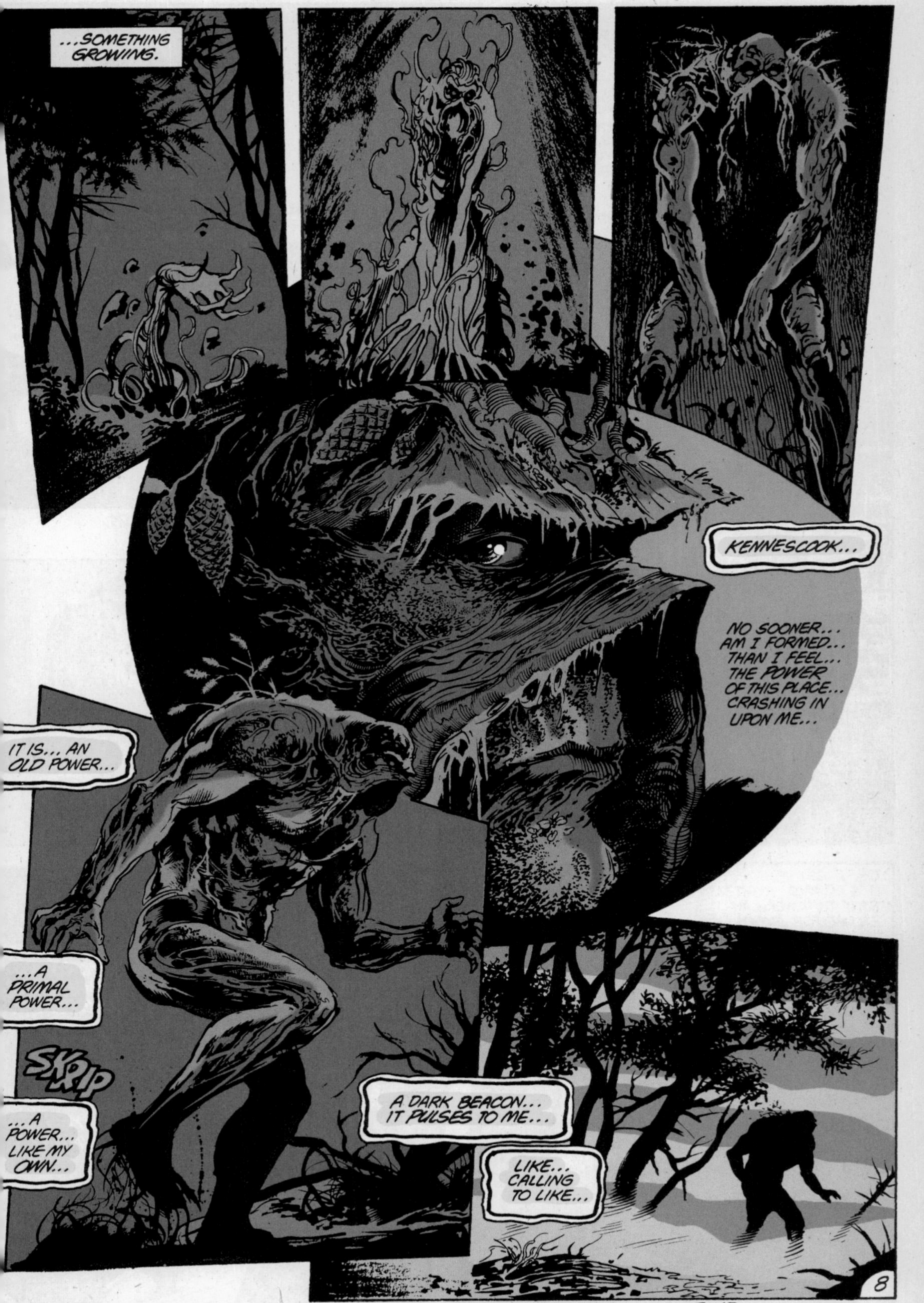
...SOMETHING GROWING.
KENNESCOOK...
NO SOONER... AM I FORMED... THAN I FEEL... THE POWER OF THIS PLACE... CRASHING IN UPON ME...
IT IS... AN OLD POWER...
...A PRIMAL POWER...
SKRIP
...A POWER... LIKE MY OWN...
A DARK BEACON... IT PULSES TO ME...
LIKE... CALLING TO LIKE...
8
IT WILL NOT... BE DIFFICULT... TO FIND...

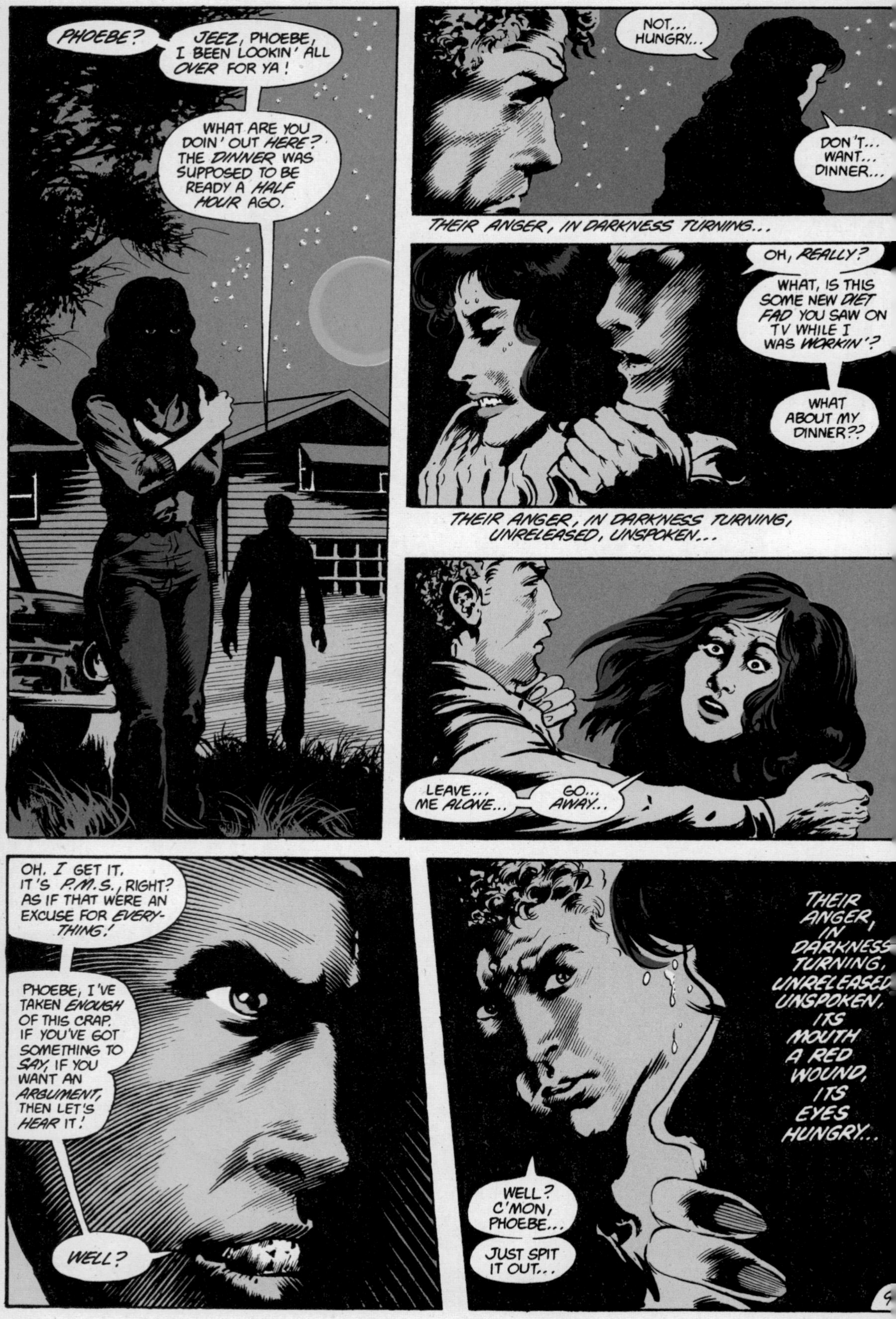
PHOEBE?
JEEZ, PHOEBE, I BEEN LOOKIN' ALL OVER FOR YA!
WHAT ARE YOU DOIN' OUT HERE? THE DINNER WAS SUPPOSED TO BE READY A HALF HOUR AGO.
NOT... HUNGRY...
DON'T... WANT... DINNER...
THEIR ANGER, IN DARKNESS TURNING...
OH, REALLY?
WHAT, IS THIS SOME NEW DIET FAD YOU SAW ON TV WHILE I WAS WORKIN'?
WHAT ABOUT MY DINNER??
THEIR ANGER, IN DARKNESS TURNING, UNRELEASED, UNSPOKEN...
LEAVE... ME ALONE...
GO... AWAY...
OH. I GET IT. IT'S P.M.S., RIGHT? AS IF THAT WERE AN EXCUSE FOR EVERYTHING!
PHOEBE, I'VE TAKEN ENOUGH OF THIS CRAP. IF YOU'VE GOT SOMETHING TO SAY, IF YOU WANT AN ARGUMENT, THEN LET'S HEAR IT!
WELL?
THEIR ANGER, IN DARKNESS TURNING, UNRELEASED UNSPOKEN, ITS MOUTH A RED WOUND, ITS EYES HUNGRY...
WELL? C'MON, PHOEBE...
JUST SPIT IT OUT...
9

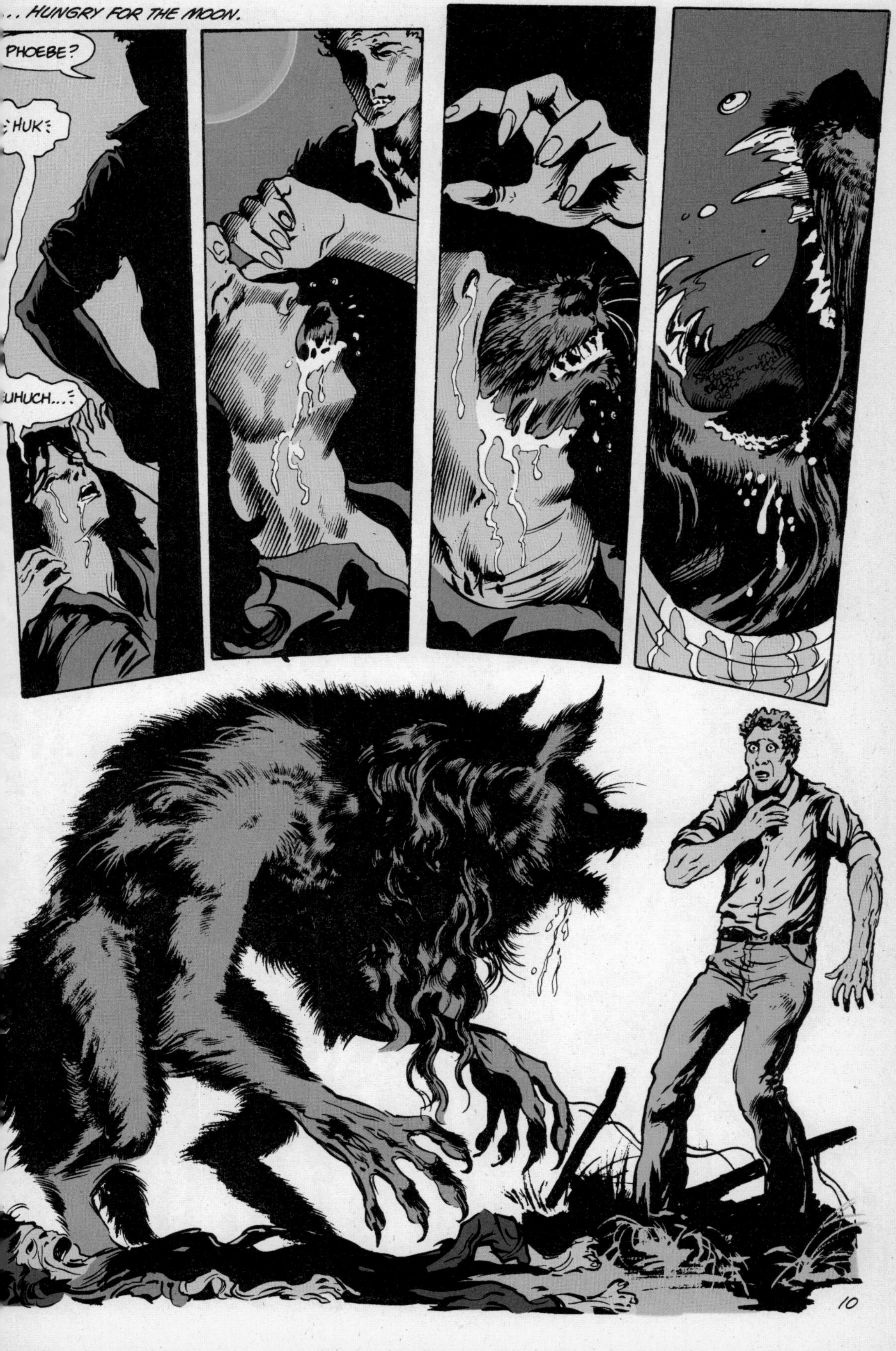
... HUNGRY FOR THE MOON.
PHOEBE?
HUK
UHUCH...
10

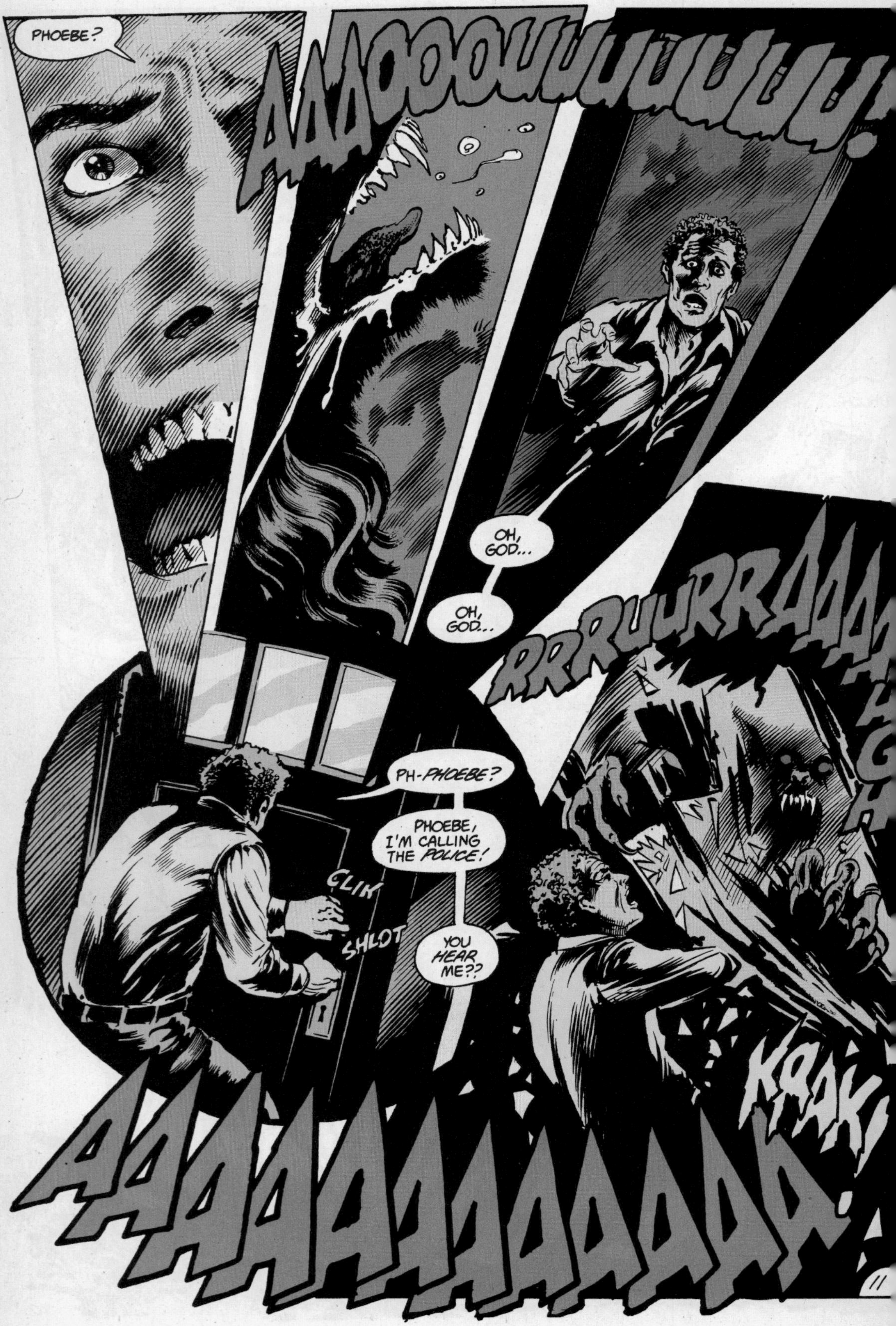
PHOEBE?
AAAOOOUUUUUUU!
OH, GOD...
OH, GOD...
RRRUURRAAA
PH-PHOEBE?
PHOEBE, I'M CALLING THE POLICE!
CLIK
SHLOT
YOU HEAR ME??
KRAK
AAAAAAAAAAAA!
11

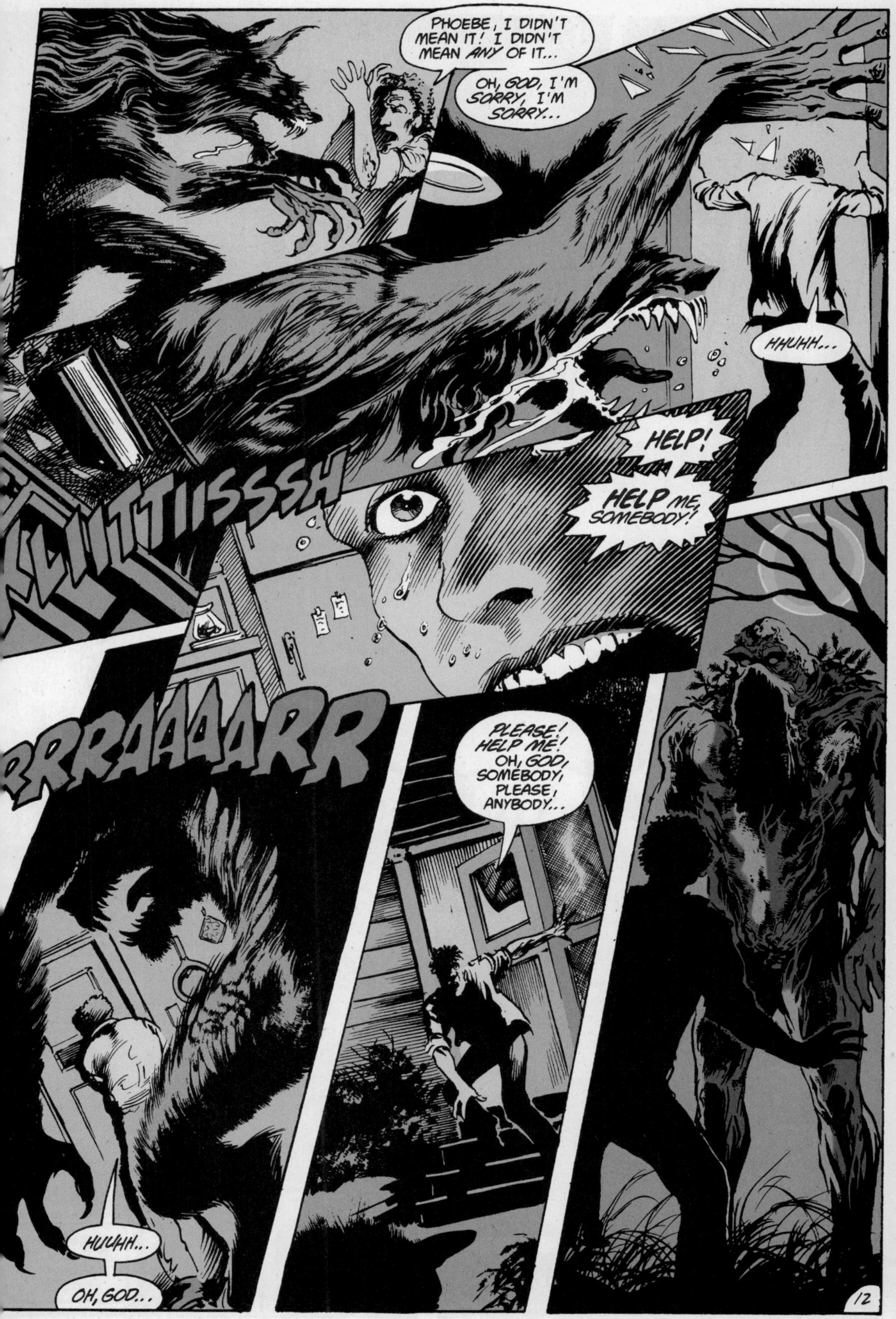
PHOEBE, I DIDN'T MEAN IT! I DIDN'T MEAN ANY OF IT...
OH, GOD, I'M SORRY, I'M SORRY...
HHUHH...
KLIITTIISSSH
HELP!
HELP ME, SOMEBODY!
RRRAAAARR
HUUHH...
OH, GOD...
PLEASE! HELP ME! OH, GOD, SOMEBODY, PLEASE, ANYBODY...
12

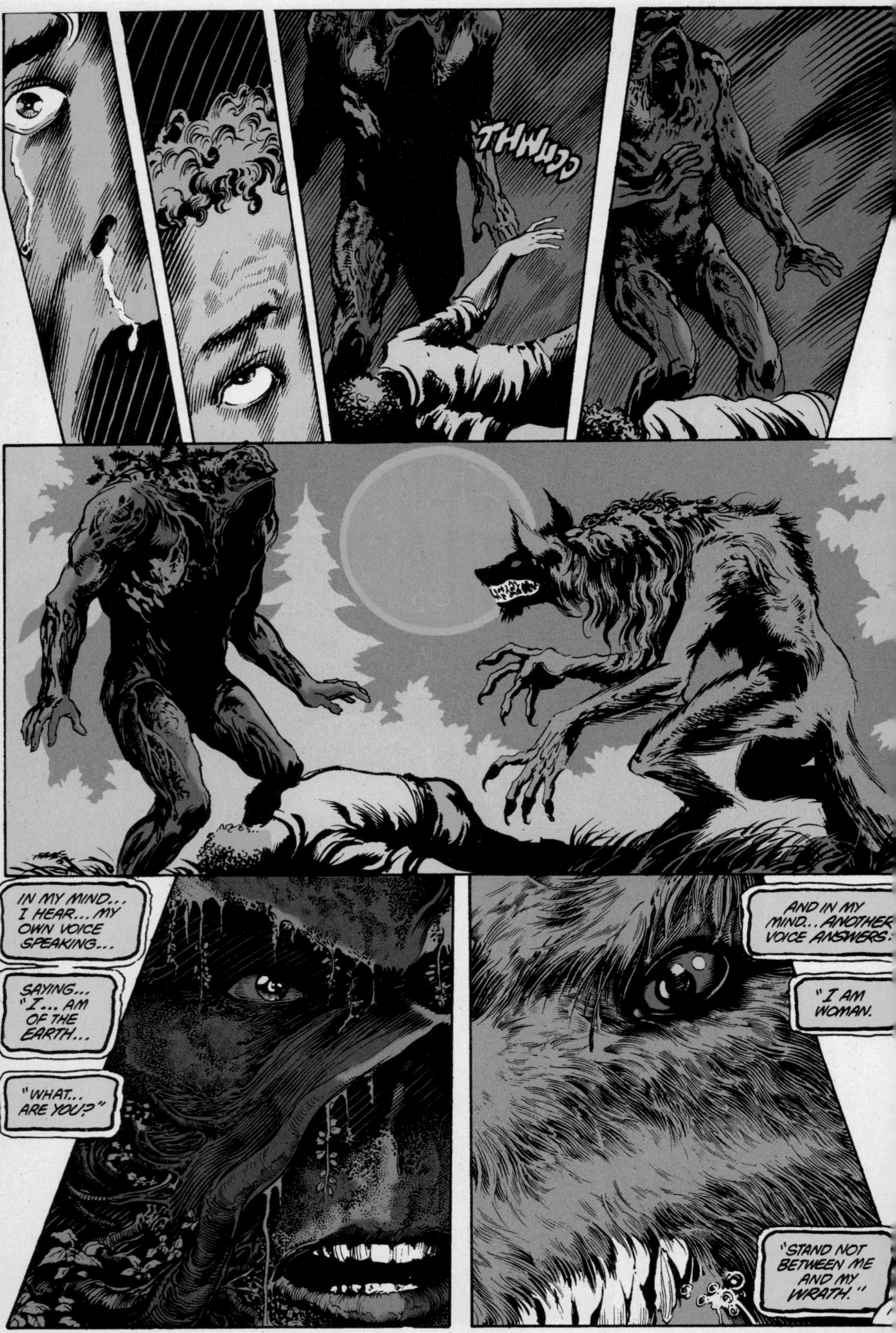
THWUCC
IN MY MIND... I HEAR... MY OWN VOICE SPEAKING...
SAYING... "I... AM OF THE EARTH...
"WHAT... ARE YOU?"
AND IN MY MIND... ANOTHER VOICE ANSWERS:
"I AM WOMAN.
"STAND NOT BETWEEN ME AND MY WRATH."

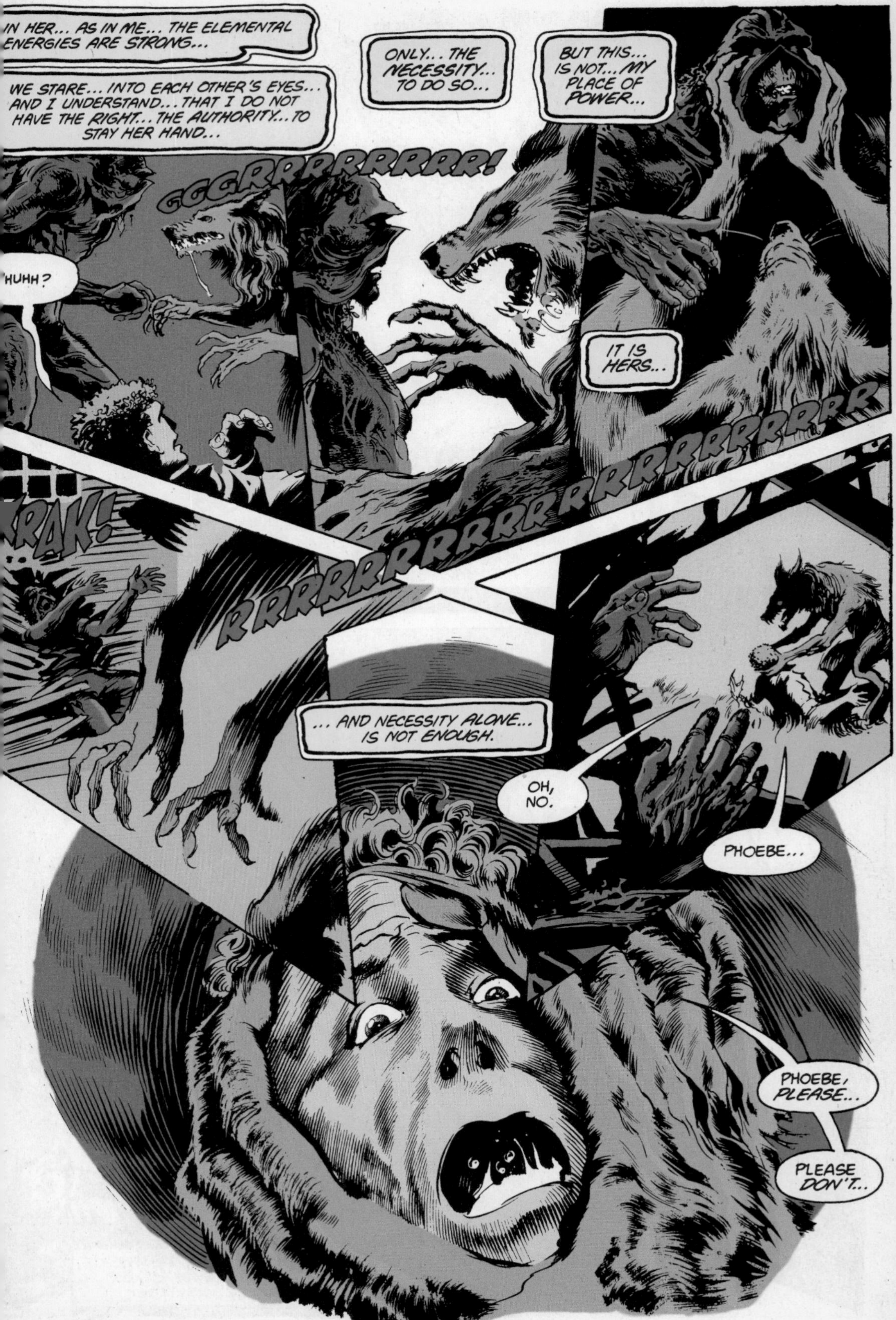
IN HER... AS IN ME... THE ELEMENTAL ENERGIES ARE STRONG...
WE STARE... INTO EACH OTHER'S EYES... AND I UNDERSTAND... THAT I DO NOT HAVE THE RIGHT... THE AUTHORITY... TO STAY HER HAND...
ONLY... THE NECESSITY... TO DO SO...
BUT THIS... IS NOT... MY PLACE OF POWER...
GGGRRRRRRRRR!
HUHH?
IT IS HERS...
KRAK!
RRRRRRRRRRRRRRRRRRRRRRRRRR
... AND NECESSITY ALONE... IS NOT ENOUGH.
OH, NO.
PHOEBE...
PHOEBE, PLEASE...
PLEASE DON'T...

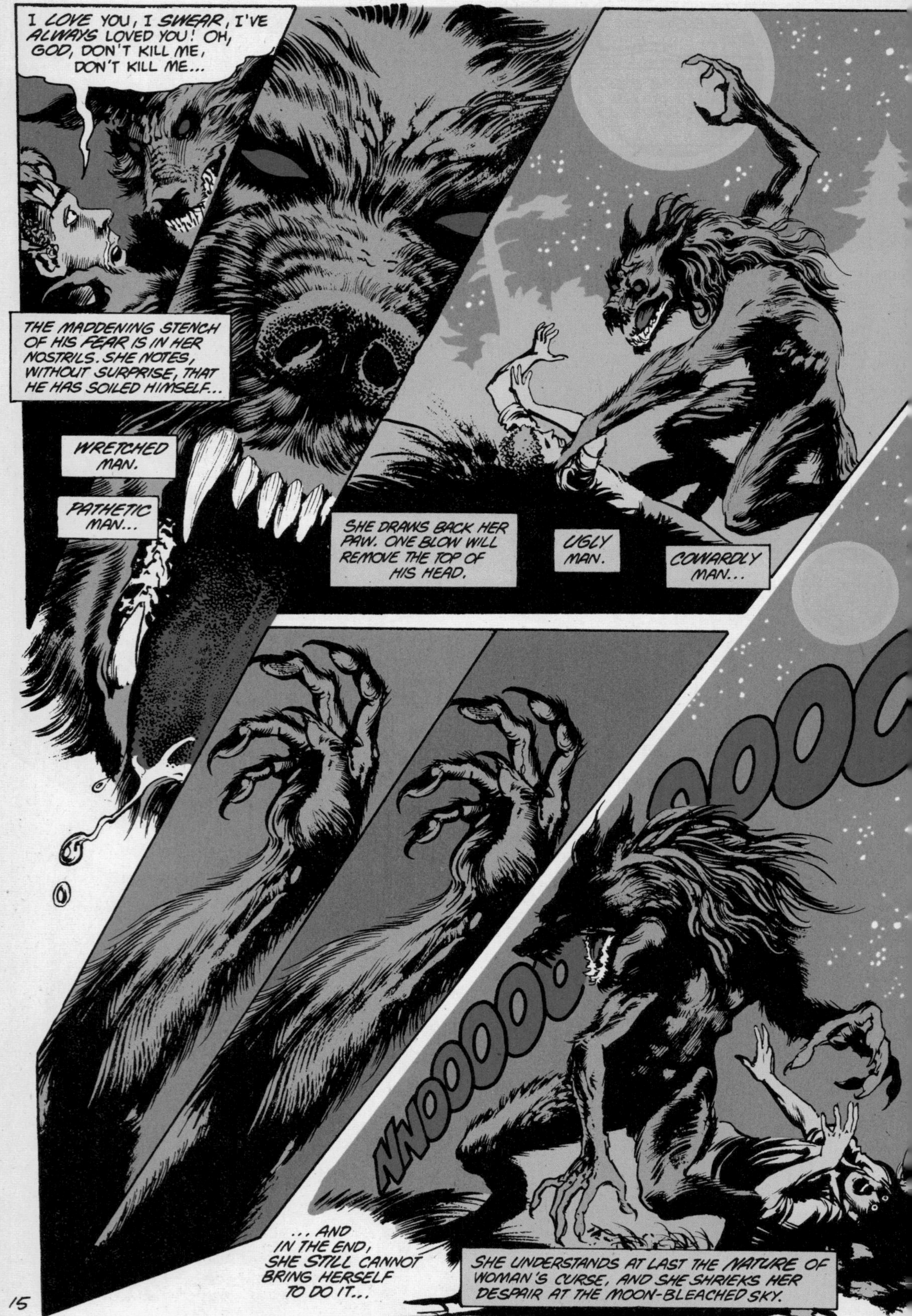
I LOVE YOU, I SWEAR, I'VE ALWAYS LOVED YOU! OH, GOD, DON'T KILL ME, DON'T KILL ME...
THE MADDENING STENCH OF HIS FEAR IS IN HER NOSTRILS. SHE NOTES, WITHOUT SURPRISE, THAT HE HAS SOILED HIMSELF...
WRETCHED MAN.
PATHETIC MAN...
SHE DRAWS BACK HER PAW. ONE BLOW WILL REMOVE THE TOP OF HIS HEAD.
UGLY MAN.
COWARDLY MAN...
NNOOOOOOOOOOOOO
... AND IN THE END, SHE STILL CANNOT BRING HERSELF TO DO IT...
SHE UNDERSTANDS AT LAST THE NATURE OF WOMAN'S CURSE, AND SHE SHRIEKS HER DESPAIR AT THE MOON-BLEACHED SKY.
15

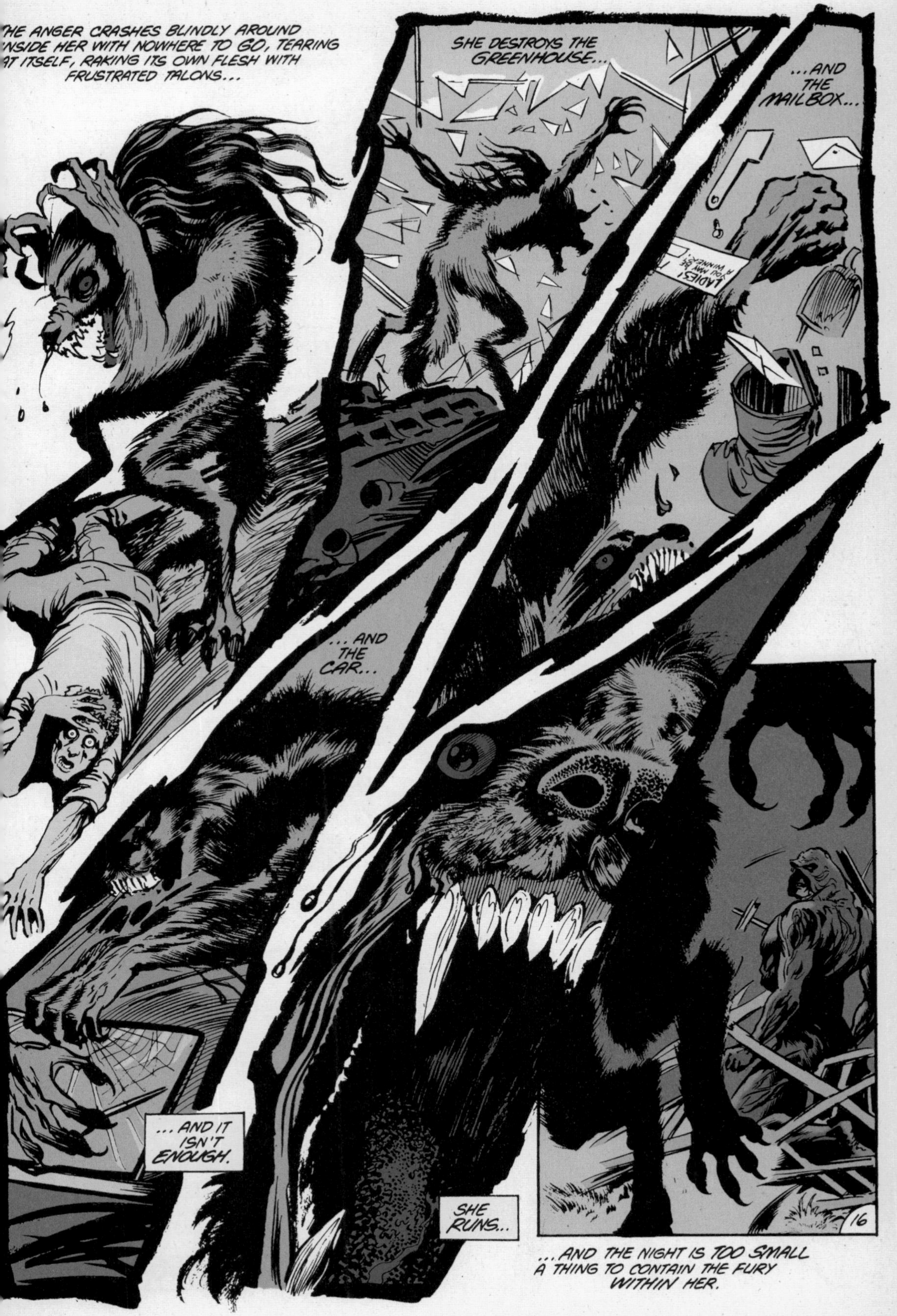
THE ANGER CRASHES BLINDLY AROUND INSIDE HER WITH NOWHERE TO GO, TEARING AT ITSELF, RAKING ITS OWN FLESH WITH FRUSTRATED TALONS...
SHE DESTROYS THE GREENHOUSE...
...AND THE MAILBOX...
LADIES! YOU MAY BE A WINNER!
...AND THE CAR...
...AND IT ISN'T ENOUGH.
SHE RUNS...
16
...AND THE NIGHT IS TOO SMALL A THING TO CONTAIN THE FURY WITHIN HER.

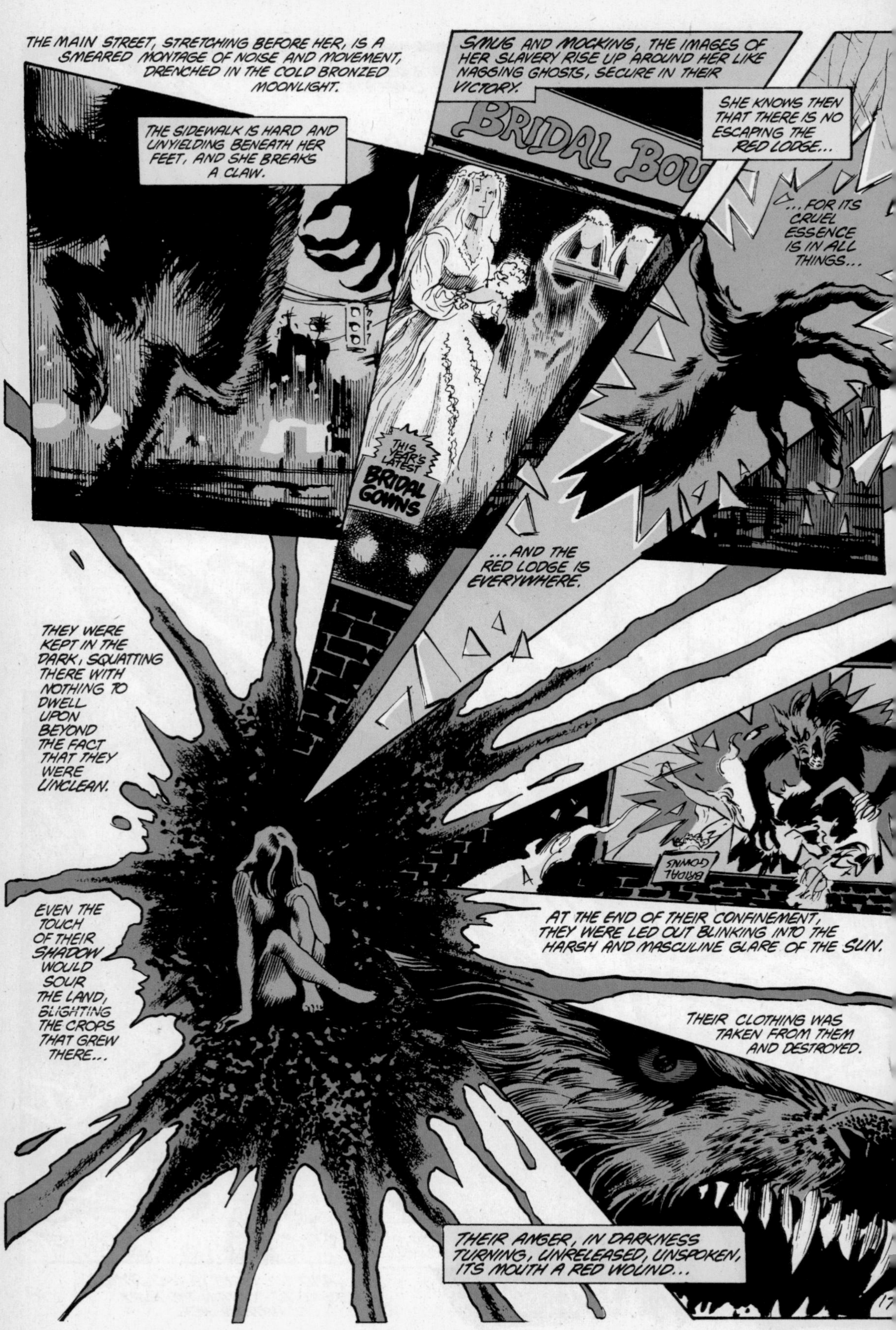
THE MAIN STREET, STRETCHING BEFORE HER, IS A SMEARED MONTAGE OF NOISE AND MOVEMENT, DRENCHED IN THE COLD BRONZED MOONLIGHT.
THE SIDEWALK IS HARD AND UNYIELDING BENEATH HER FEET, AND SHE BREAKS A CLAW.
SMUG AND MOCKING, THE IMAGES OF HER SLAVERY RISE UP AROUND HER LIKE NAGGING GHOSTS, SECURE IN THEIR VICTORY.
BRIDAL BOU
THIS YEAR'S LATEST BRIDAL GOWNS
SHE KNOWS THEN THAT THERE IS NO ESCAPING THE RED LODGE...
...FOR ITS CRUEL ESSENCE IS IN ALL THINGS...
...AND THE RED LODGE IS EVERYWHERE.
THEY WERE KEPT IN THE DARK, SQUATTING THERE WITH NOTHING TO DWELL UPON BEYOND THE FACT THAT THEY WERE UNCLEAN.
EVEN THE TOUCH OF THEIR SHADOW WOULD SOUR THE LAND, BLIGHTING THE CROPS THAT GREW THERE...
AT THE END OF THEIR CONFINEMENT, THEY WERE LED OUT BLINKING INTO THE HARSH AND MASCULINE GLARE OF THE SUN.
THEIR CLOTHING WAS TAKEN FROM THEM AND DESTROYED.
THEIR ANGER, IN DARKNESS TURNING, UNRELEASED, UNSPOKEN, ITS MOUTH A RED WOUND...
17

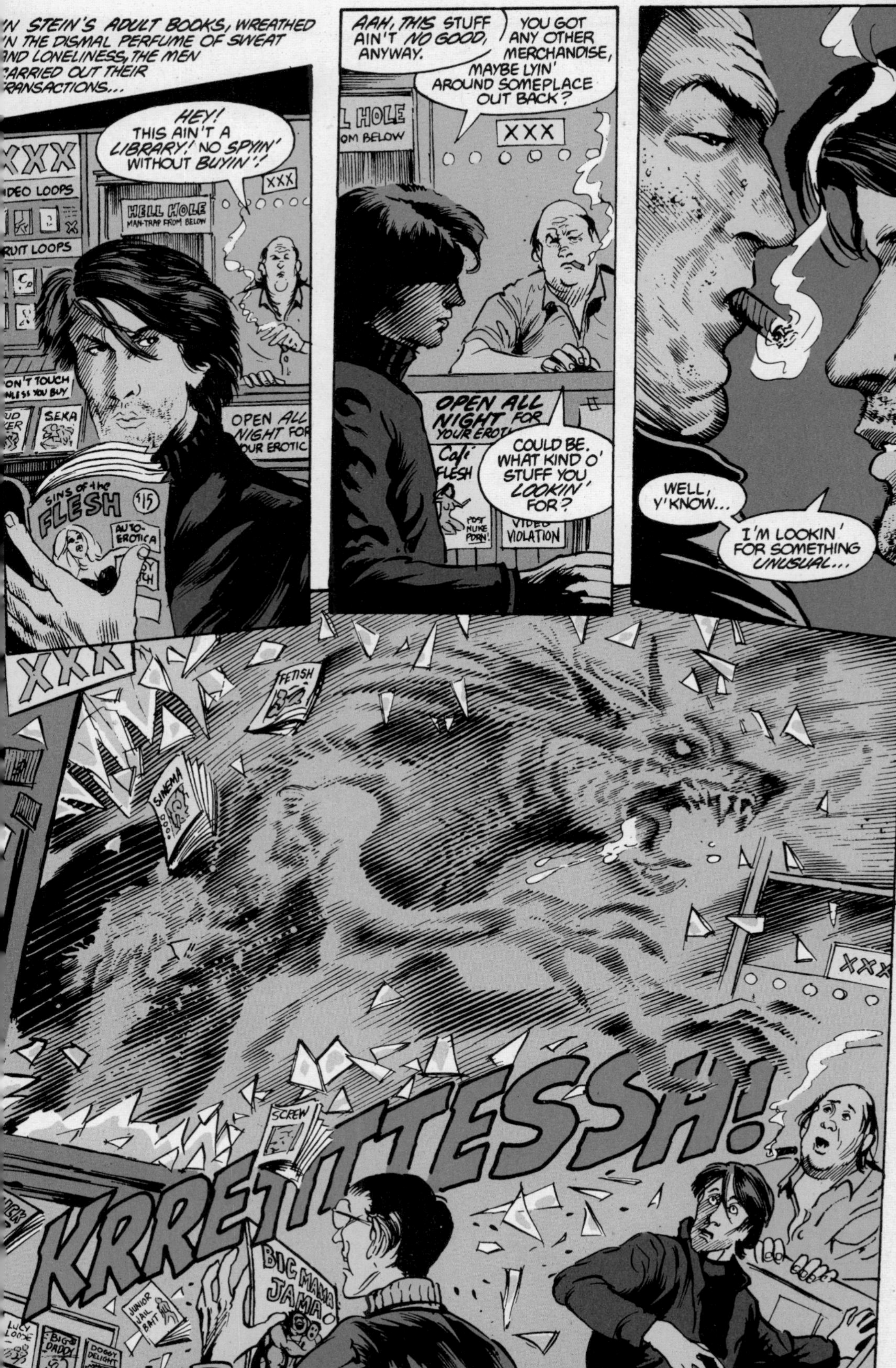

IN STEIN'S ADULT BOOKS, WREATHED IN THE DISMAL PERFUME OF SWEAT AND LONELINESS, THE MEN CARRIED OUT THEIR TRANSACTIONS...
HEY! THIS AIN'T A LIBRARY! NO SPYIN' WITHOUT BUYIN'!
XXX
VIDEO LOOPS
HELL HOLE
MAN-TRAP FROM BELOW
FRUIT LOOPS
DON'T TOUCH UNLESS YOU BUY
SEKA
OPEN ALL NIGHT FOR YOUR EROTIC
SINS OF THE FLESH $15
AUTO-EROTICA
AAH, THIS STUFF AIN'T NO GOOD, ANYWAY.
YOU GOT ANY OTHER MERCHANDISE, MAYBE LYIN' AROUND SOMEPLACE OUT BACK?
XXX
COULD BE. WHAT KIND O' STUFF YOU LOOKIN' FOR?
POST NUKE PORN!
VIDEO VIOLATION
WELL, Y'KNOW...
I'M LOOKIN' FOR SOMETHING UNUSUAL...
XXX
FETISH
SINEMA
KRRETTTTESSSH!
SCREW
BIG MAMA JAMA
JUNIOR JAIL BAIT
LUCY LOOSE
BIG DADDY
DOGGY DELIGHT

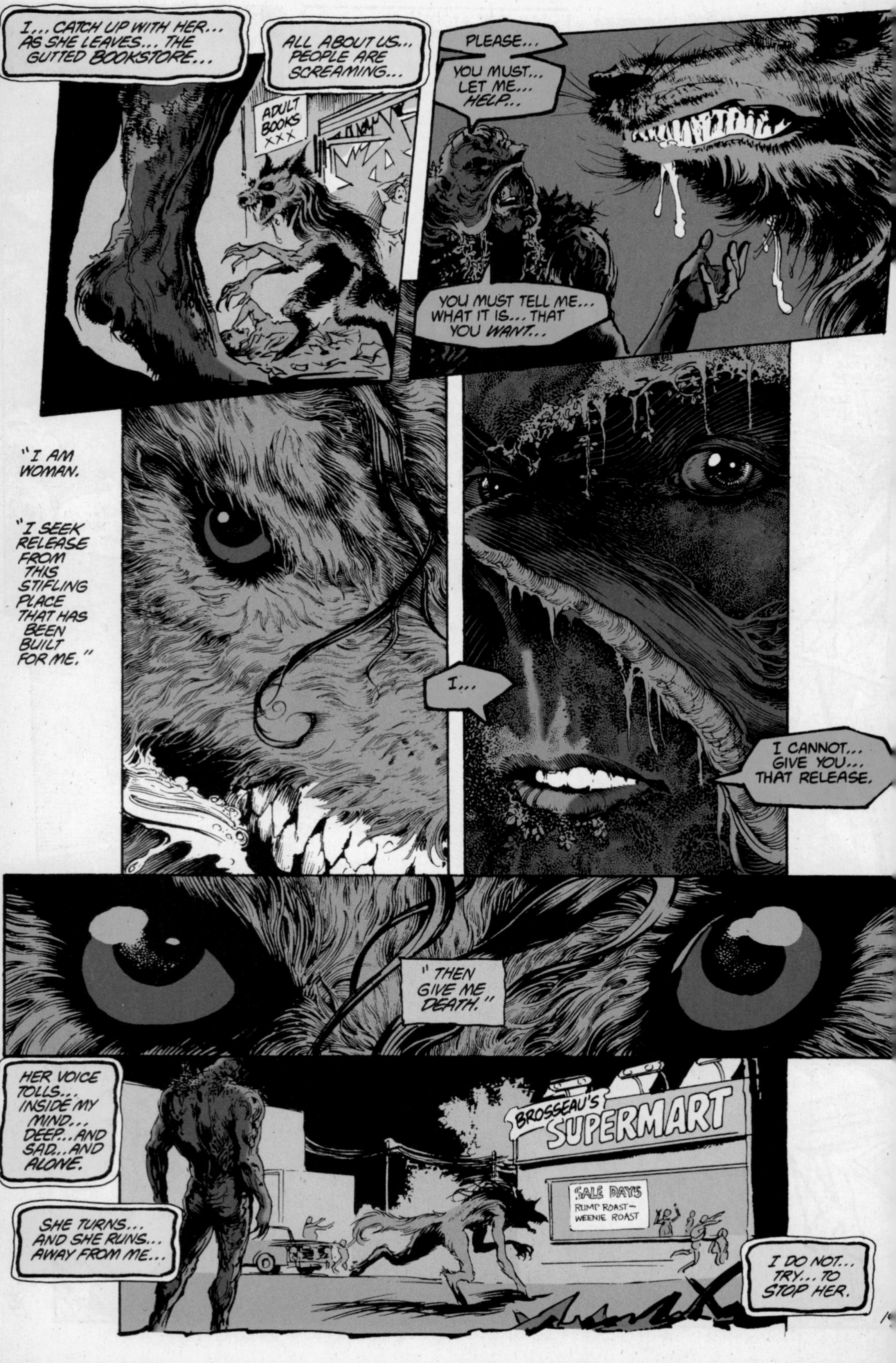
I... CATCH UP WITH HER... AS SHE LEAVES... THE GUTTED BOOKSTORE...
ALL ABOUT US... PEOPLE ARE SCREAMING...
ADULT BOOKS XXX
PLEASE...
YOU MUST... LET ME... HELP...
YOU MUST TELL ME... WHAT IT IS... THAT YOU WANT...
"I AM WOMAN.
"I SEEK RELEASE FROM THIS STIFLING PLACE THAT HAS BEEN BUILT FOR ME."
I...
I CANNOT... GIVE YOU... THAT RELEASE.
"THEN GIVE ME DEATH."
HER VOICE TOLLS... INSIDE MY MIND... DEEP... AND SAD... AND ALONE.
BROSSEAU'S SUPERMART
SALE DAYS
RUMP ROAST—
WEENIE ROAST
SHE TURNS... AND SHE RUNS... AWAY FROM ME...
I DO NOT... TRY... TO STOP HER.

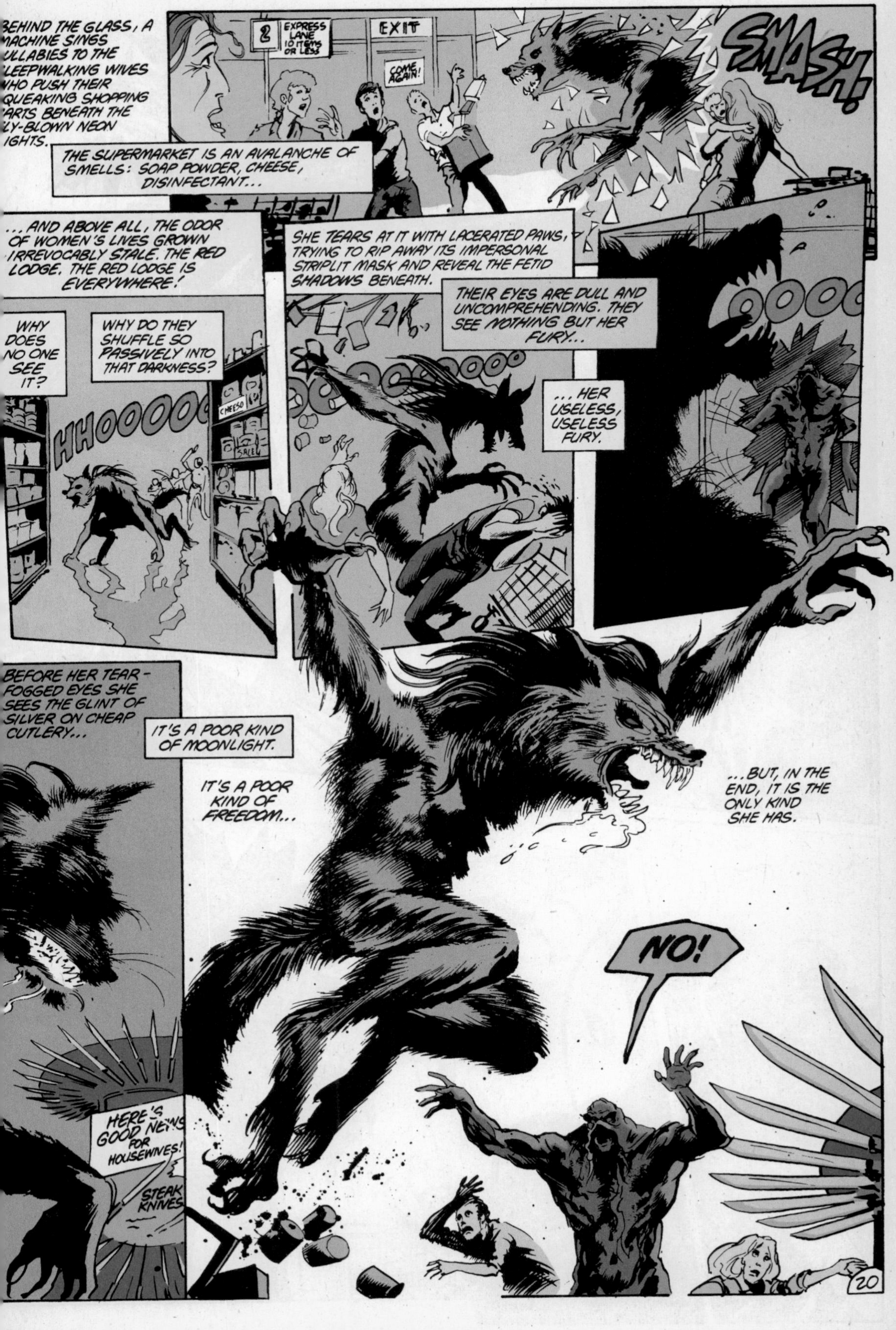
BEHIND THE GLASS, A MACHINE SINGS LULLABIES TO THE SLEEPWALKING WIVES WHO PUSH THEIR SQUEAKING SHOPPING CARTS BENEATH THE FLY-BLOWN NEON LIGHTS.
2 EXPRESS LANE 10 ITEMS OR LESS
EXIT
COME AGAIN!
SMASH!
THE SUPERMARKET IS AN AVALANCHE OF SMELLS: SOAP POWDER, CHEESE, DISINFECTANT...
...AND ABOVE ALL, THE ODOR OF WOMEN'S LIVES GROWN IRREVOCABLY STALE. THE RED LODGE. THE RED LODGE IS EVERYWHERE!
WHY DOES NO ONE SEE IT?
WHY DO THEY SHUFFLE SO PASSIVELY INTO THAT DARKNESS?
HHOOOOO
CHEESO
SALE
SHE TEARS AT IT WITH LACERATED PAWS, TRYING TO RIP AWAY ITS IMPERSONAL STRIPLIT MASK AND REVEAL THE FETID SHADOWS BENEATH.
THEIR EYES ARE DULL AND UNCOMPREHENDING. THEY SEE NOTHING BUT HER FURY...
...HER USELESS, USELESS FURY.
BEFORE HER TEAR-FOGGED EYES SHE SEES THE GLINT OF SILVER ON CHEAP CUTLERY...
IT'S A POOR KIND OF MOONLIGHT.
IT'S A POOR KIND OF FREEDOM...
...BUT, IN THE END, IT IS THE ONLY KIND SHE HAS.
NO!
HERE'S GOOD NEWS FOR HOUSEWIVES!
STEAK KNIVES
20

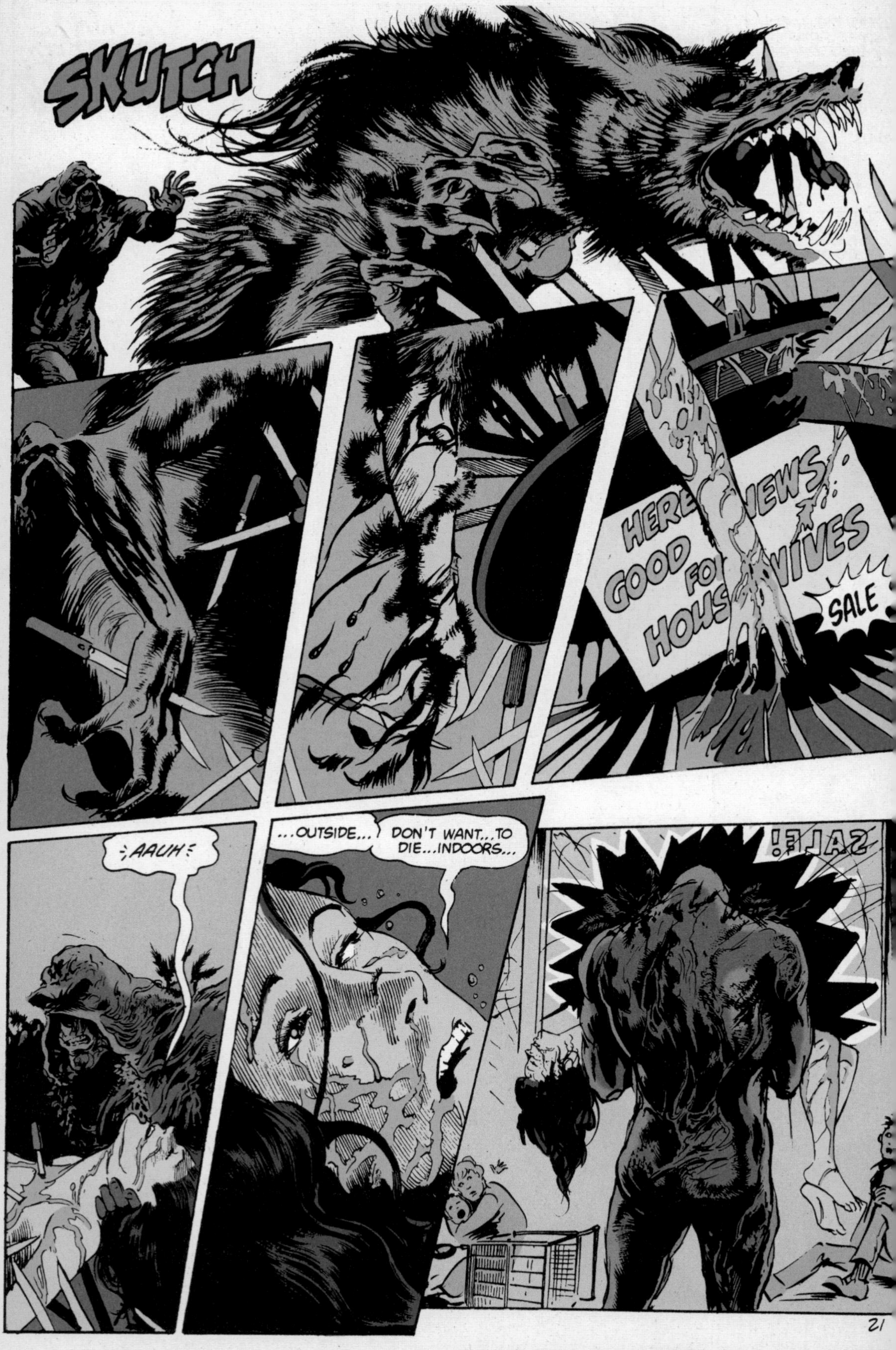
SKUTCH
HERE
NEWS
GOOD
FO
HOUS
VIVES
SALE
AAUH
...OUTSIDE...
DON'T WANT...TO DIE...INDOORS...
SALE!
21

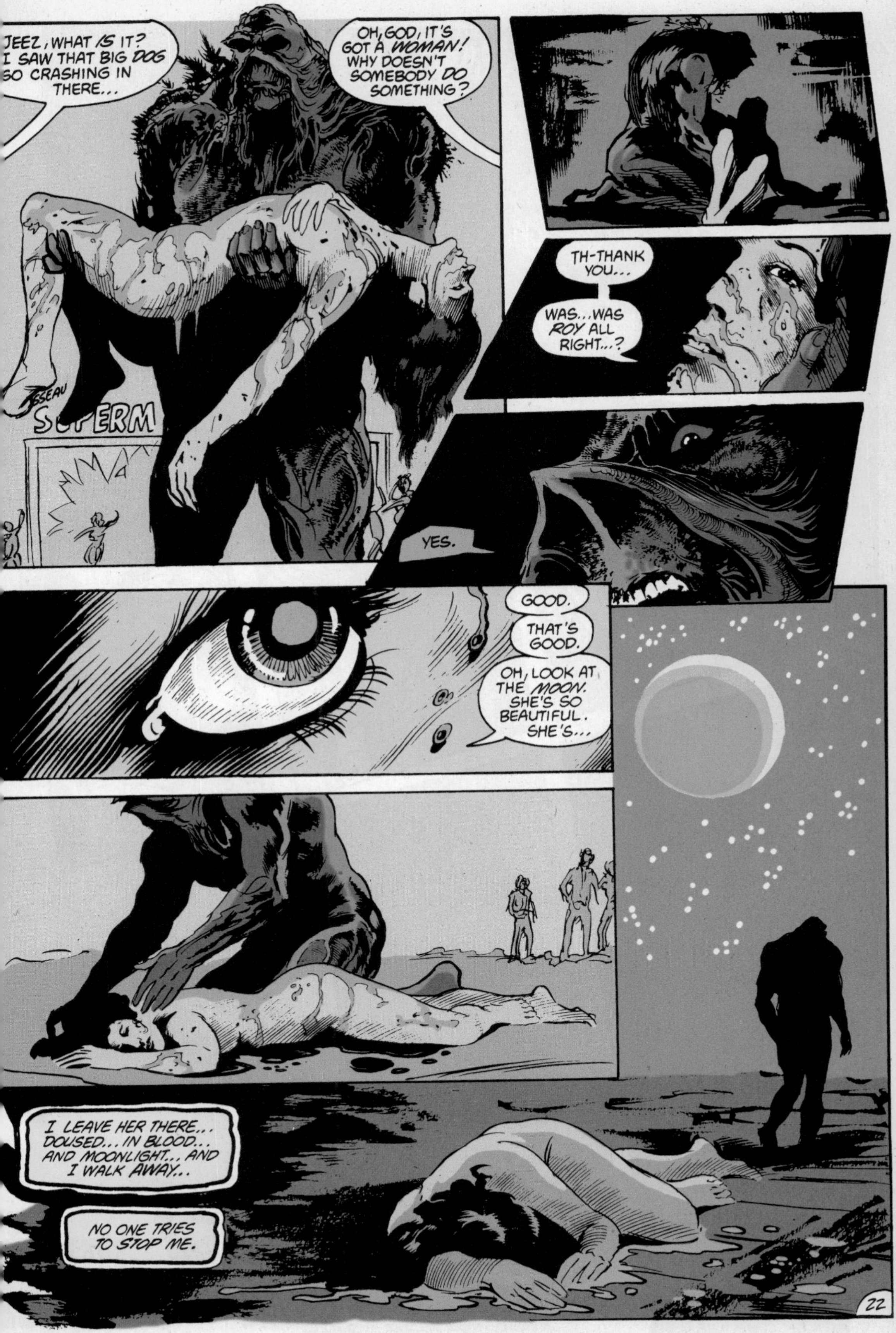
JEEZ, WHAT IS IT? I SAW THAT BIG DOG GO CRASHING IN THERE...
OH, GOD, IT'S GOT A WOMAN! WHY DOESN'T SOMEBODY DO SOMETHING?
SUPERM
TH-THANK YOU...
WAS...WAS ROY ALL RIGHT...?
YES.
GOOD.
THAT'S GOOD.
OH, LOOK AT THE MOON. SHE'S SO BEAUTIFUL. SHE'S...
I LEAVE HER THERE... DOUSED... IN BLOOD... AND MOONLIGHT... AND I WALK AWAY...
NO ONE TRIES TO STOP ME.
22

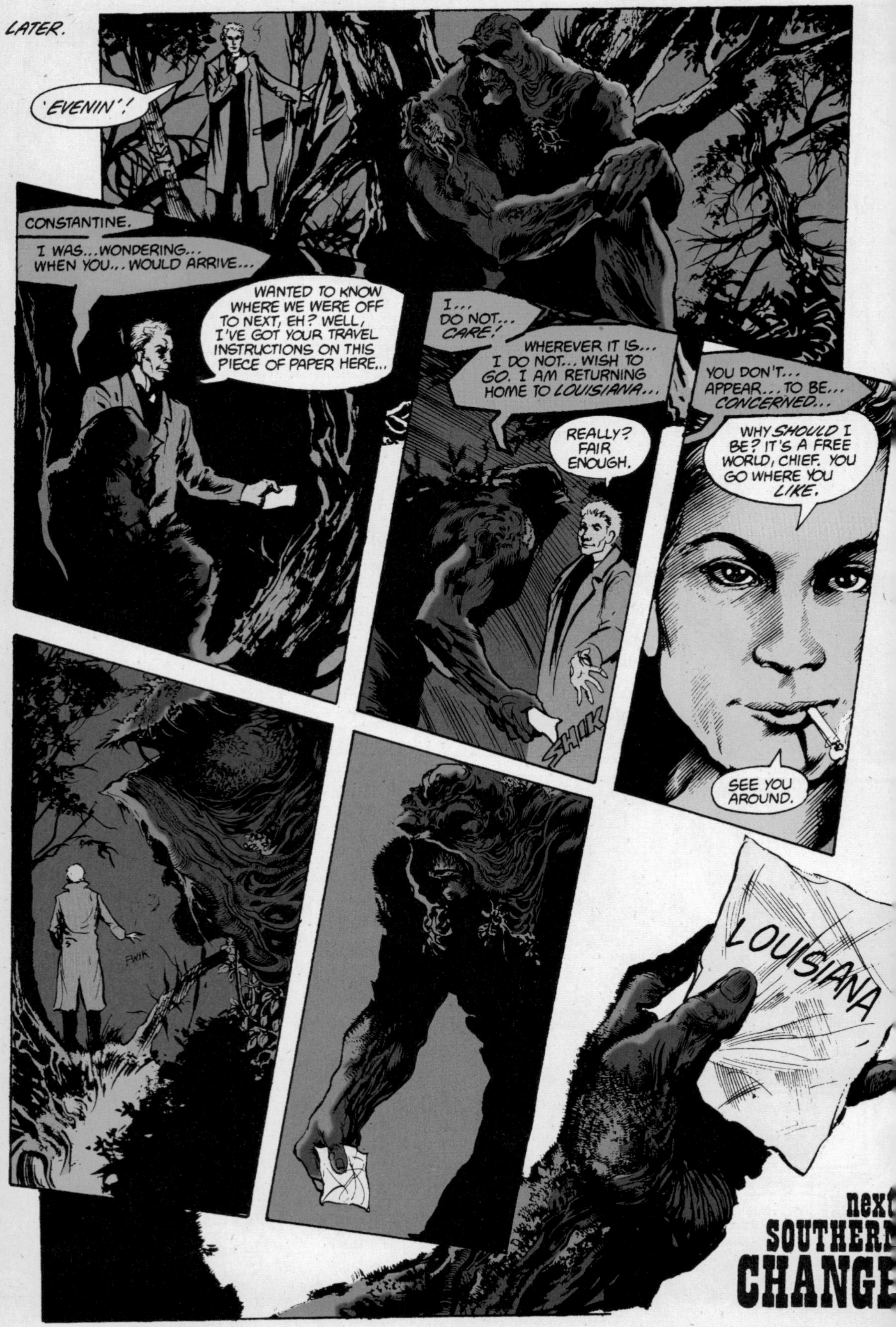
LATER.
'EVENIN'!
CONSTANTINE.
I WAS... WONDERING... WHEN YOU... WOULD ARRIVE...
WANTED TO KNOW WHERE WE WERE OFF TO NEXT, EH? WELL, I'VE GOT YOUR TRAVEL INSTRUCTIONS ON THIS PIECE OF PAPER HERE...
I... DO NOT... CARE!
WHEREVER IT IS... I DO NOT... WISH TO GO. I AM RETURNING HOME TO LOUISIANA...
REALLY? FAIR ENOUGH.
SHIK
YOU DON'T... APPEAR... TO BE... CONCERNED...
WHY SHOULD I BE? IT'S A FREE WORLD, CHIEF. YOU GO WHERE YOU LIKE.
SEE YOU AROUND.
FWIK
LOUISIANA
next
SOUTHERN
CHANGE

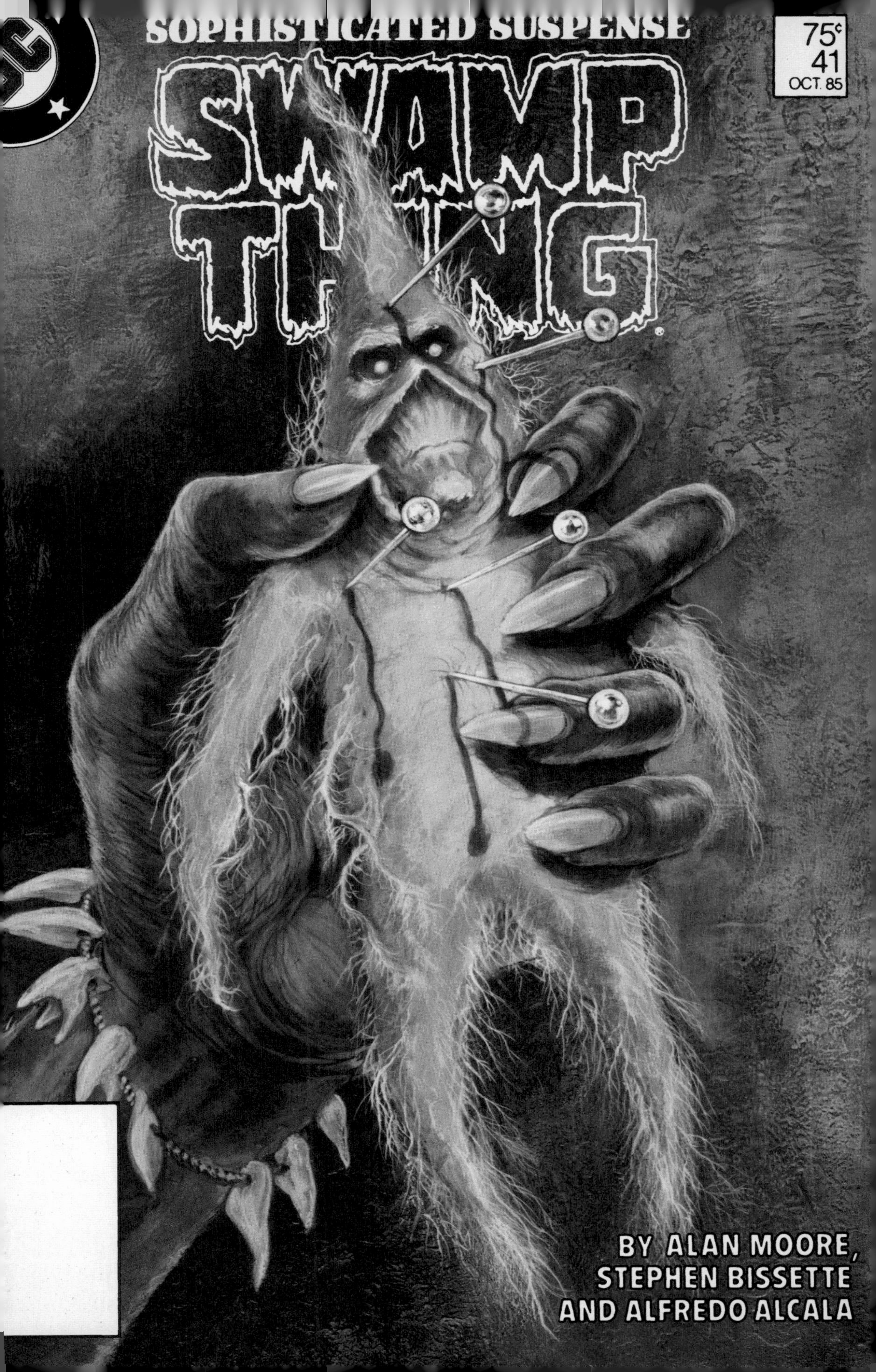
SOPHISTICATED SUSPENSE
SWAMP THING
75¢
41
OCT. 85
BY ALAN MOORE,
STEPHEN BISSETTE
AND ALFREDO ALCALA

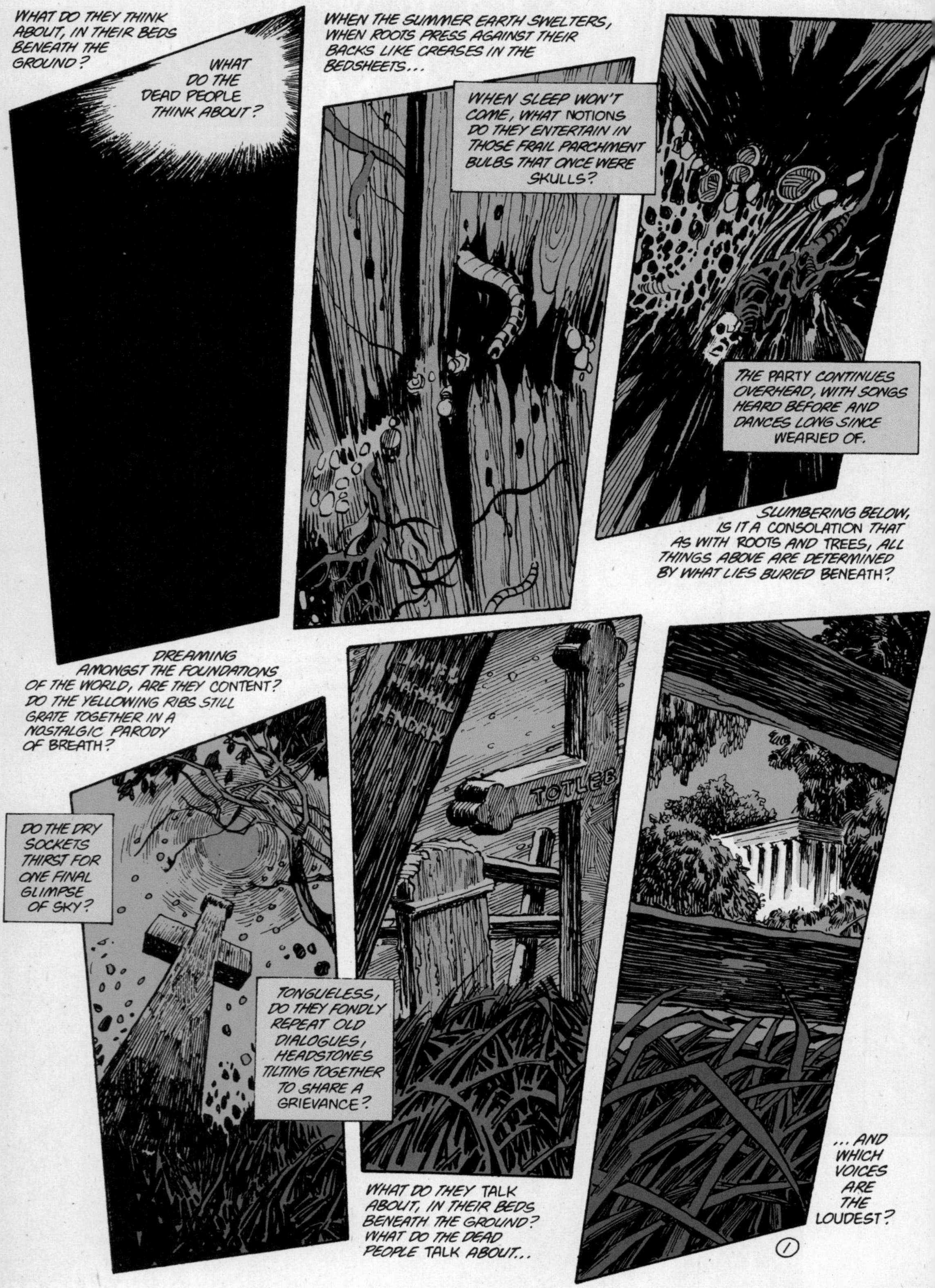
WHAT DO THEY THINK ABOUT, IN THEIR BEDS BENEATH THE GROUND?
WHAT DO THE DEAD PEOPLE THINK ABOUT?
WHEN THE SUMMER EARTH SWELTERS, WHEN ROOTS PRESS AGAINST THEIR BACKS LIKE CREASES IN THE BEDSHEETS...
WHEN SLEEP WON'T COME, WHAT NOTIONS DO THEY ENTERTAIN IN THOSE FRAIL PARCHMENT BULBS THAT ONCE WERE SKULLS?
THE PARTY CONTINUES OVERHEAD, WITH SONGS HEARD BEFORE AND DANCES LONG SINCE WEARIED OF.
SLUMBERING BELOW, IS IT A CONSOLATION THAT AS WITH ROOTS AND TREES, ALL THINGS ABOVE ARE DETERMINED BY WHAT LIES BURIED BENEATH?
DREAMING AMONGST THE FOUNDATIONS OF THE WORLD, ARE THEY CONTENT? DO THE YELLOWING RIBS STILL GRATE TOGETHER IN A NOSTALGIC PARODY OF BREATH?
DO THE DRY SOCKETS THIRST FOR ONE FINAL GLIMPSE OF SKY?
TONGUELESS, DO THEY FONDLY REPEAT OLD DIALOGUES, HEADSTONES TILTING TOGETHER TO SHARE A GRIEVANCE?
TOTLEB
WHAT DO THEY TALK ABOUT, IN THEIR BEDS BENEATH THE GROUND? WHAT DO THE DEAD PEOPLE TALK ABOUT...
...AND WHICH VOICES ARE THE LOUDEST?
1

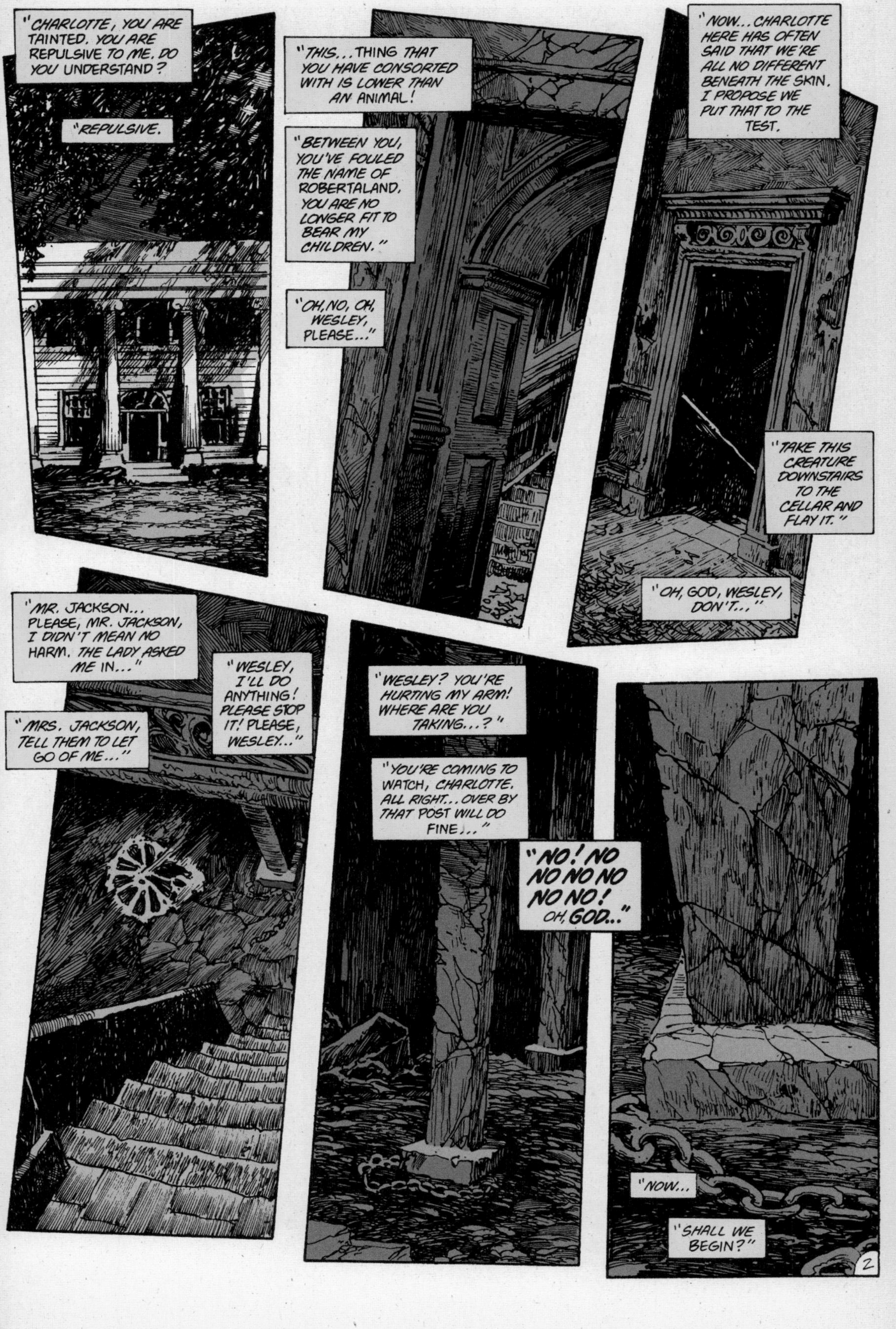
"CHARLOTTE, YOU ARE TAINTED. YOU ARE REPULSIVE TO ME. DO YOU UNDERSTAND?
"REPULSIVE.
"THIS... THING THAT YOU HAVE CONSORTED WITH IS LOWER THAN AN ANIMAL!
"BETWEEN YOU, YOU'VE FOULED THE NAME OF ROBERTALAND. YOU ARE NO LONGER FIT TO BEAR MY CHILDREN."
"OH, NO, OH, WESLEY, PLEASE..."
"NOW... CHARLOTTE HERE HAS OFTEN SAID THAT WE'RE ALL NO DIFFERENT BENEATH THE SKIN. I PROPOSE WE PUT THAT TO THE TEST.
"TAKE THIS CREATURE DOWNSTAIRS TO THE CELLAR AND FLAY IT."
"OH, GOD, WESLEY, DON'T..."
"MR. JACKSON... PLEASE, MR. JACKSON, I DIDN'T MEAN NO HARM. THE LADY ASKED ME IN..."
"MRS. JACKSON, TELL THEM TO LET GO OF ME..."
"WESLEY, I'LL DO ANYTHING! PLEASE STOP IT! PLEASE, WESLEY..."
"WESLEY? YOU'RE HURTING MY ARM! WHERE ARE YOU TAKING...?"
"YOU'RE COMING TO WATCH, CHARLOTTE. ALL RIGHT... OVER BY THAT POST WILL DO FINE..."
"NO! NO NO NO NO NO NO! OH, GOD..."
"NOW...
"SHALL WE BEGIN?"
2

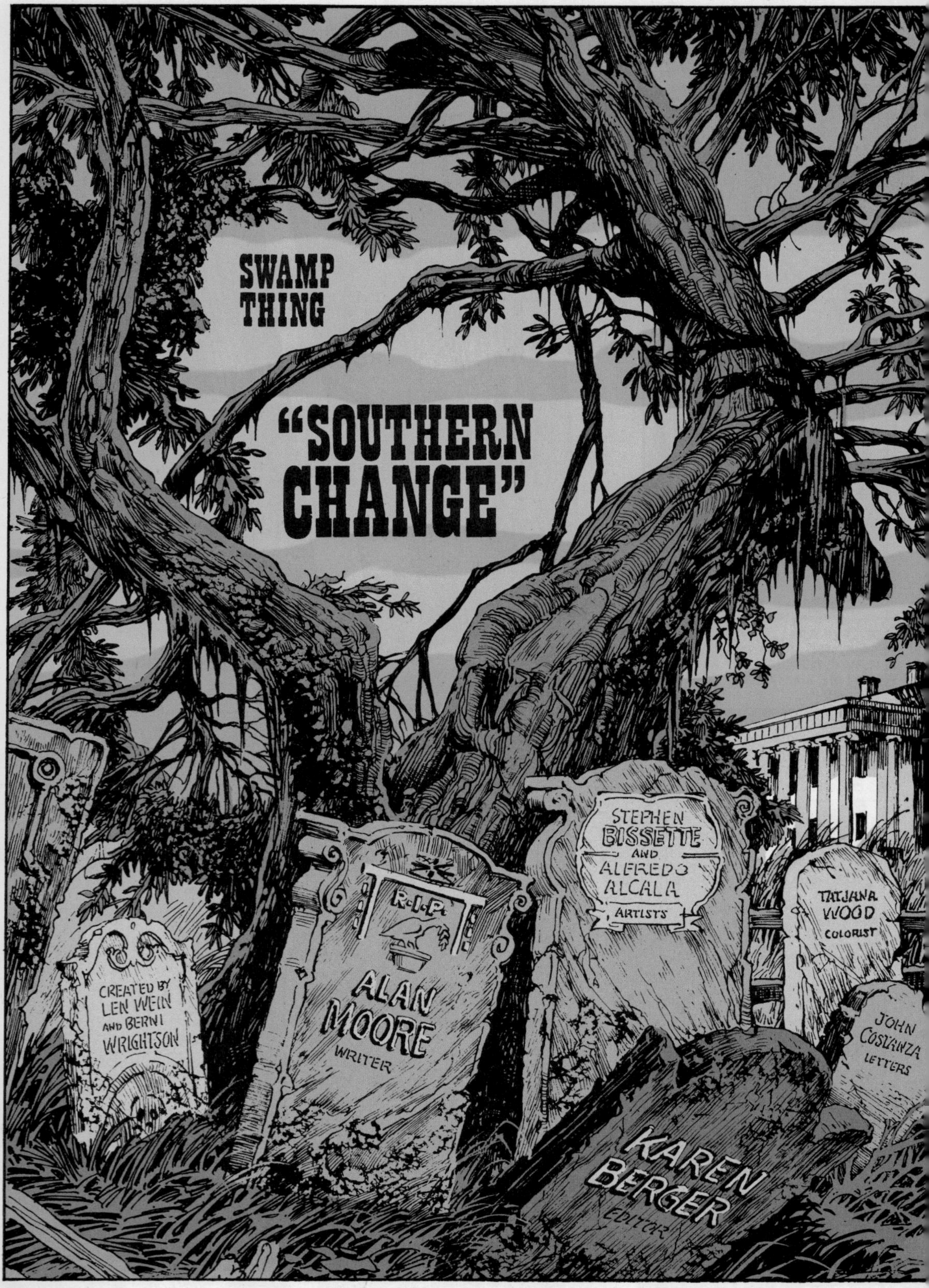
SWAMP THING
"SOUTHERN CHANGE"
CREATED BY LEN WEIN AND BERNI WRIGHTSON
R.I.P.
ALAN MOORE WRITER
STEPHEN BISSETTE AND ALFREDO ALCALA ARTISTS
TATJANA WOOD COLORIST
JOHN COSTANZA LETTERS
KAREN BERGER EDITOR

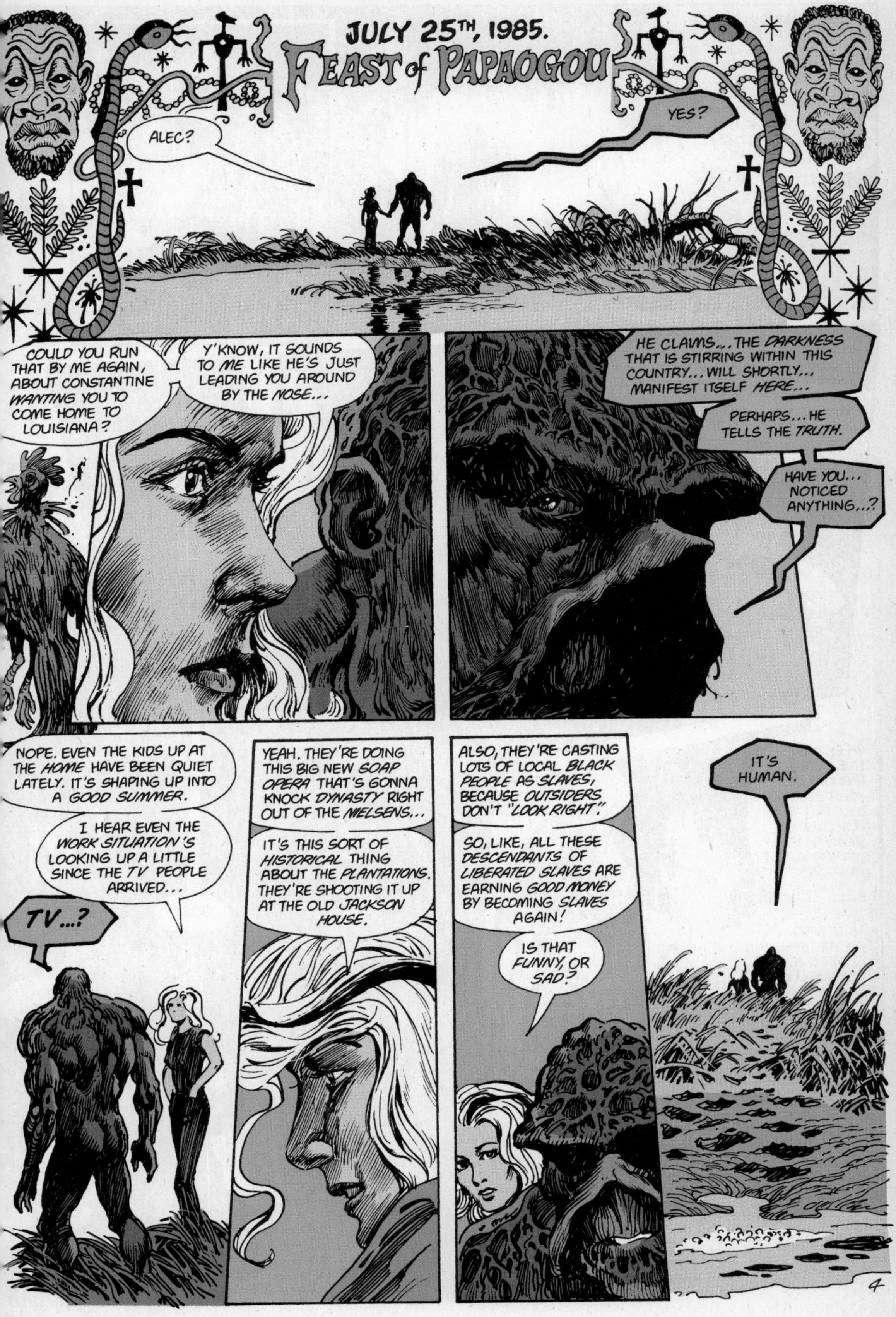
JULY 25TH, 1985.
FEAST of PAPAOGOU
ALEC?
YES?
COULD YOU RUN THAT BY ME AGAIN, ABOUT CONSTANTINE WANTING YOU TO COME HOME TO LOUISIANA?
Y'KNOW, IT SOUNDS TO ME LIKE HE'S JUST LEADING YOU AROUND BY THE NOSE...
HE CLAIMS... THE DARKNESS THAT IS STIRRING WITHIN THIS COUNTRY... WILL SHORTLY... MANIFEST ITSELF HERE...
PERHAPS... HE TELLS THE TRUTH.
HAVE YOU... NOTICED ANYTHING...?
NOPE. EVEN THE KIDS UP AT THE HOME HAVE BEEN QUIET LATELY. IT'S SHAPING UP INTO A GOOD SUMMER.
I HEAR EVEN THE WORK SITUATION'S LOOKING UP A LITTLE SINCE THE TV PEOPLE ARRIVED...
TV...?
YEAH. THEY'RE DOING THIS BIG NEW SOAP OPERA THAT'S GONNA KNOCK DYNASTY RIGHT OUT OF THE NIELSENS...
IT'S THIS SORT OF HISTORICAL THING ABOUT THE PLANTATIONS. THEY'RE SHOOTING IT UP AT THE OLD JACKSON HOUSE.
ALSO, THEY'RE CASTING LOTS OF LOCAL BLACK PEOPLE AS SLAVES, BECAUSE OUTSIDERS DON'T "LOOK RIGHT".
SO, LIKE, ALL THESE DESCENDANTS OF LIBERATED SLAVES ARE EARNING GOOD MONEY BY BECOMING SLAVES AGAIN!
IS THAT FUNNY, OR SAD?
IT'S HUMAN.
4

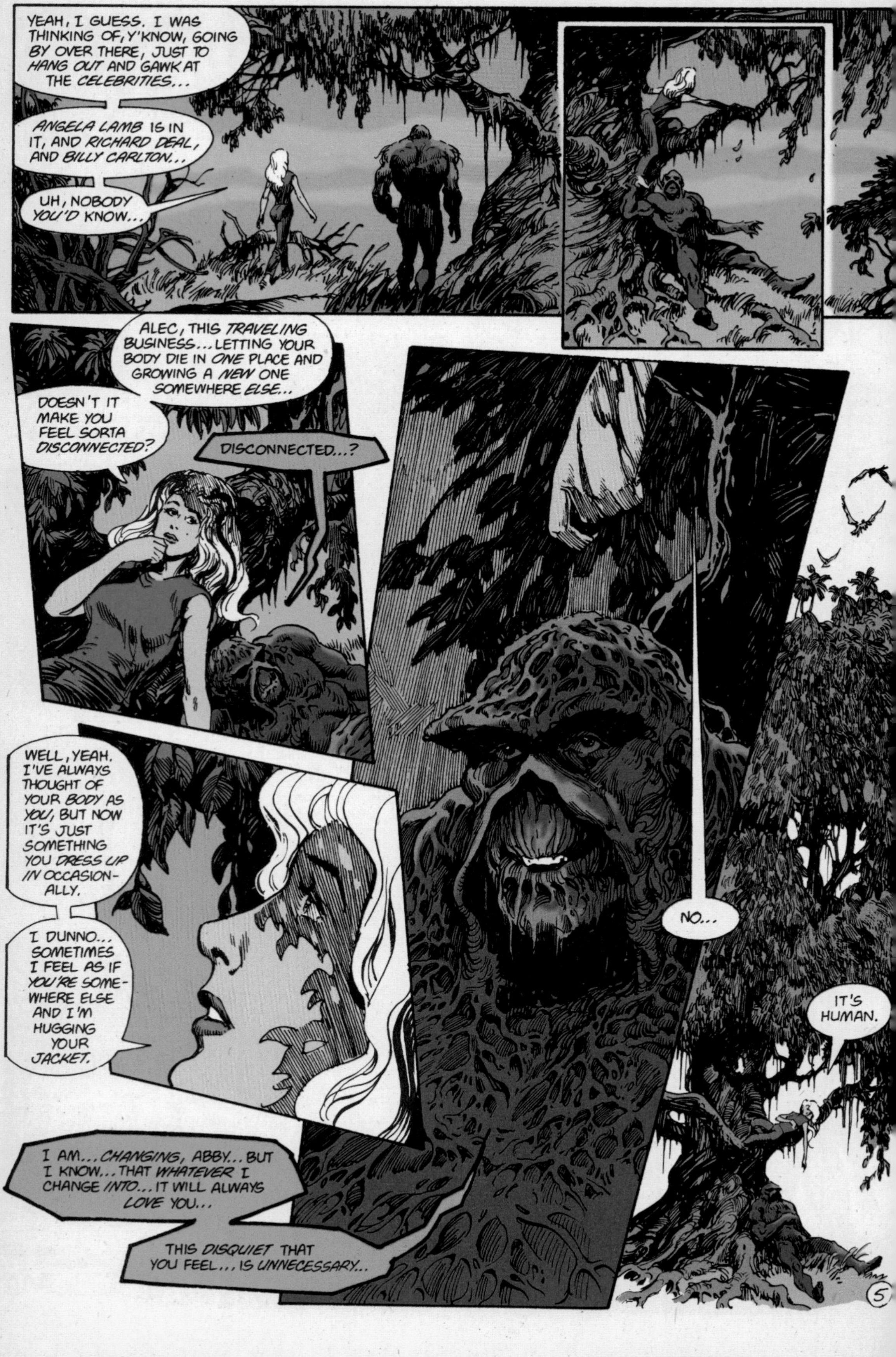
YEAH, I GUESS. I WAS THINKING OF, Y'KNOW, GOING BY OVER THERE, JUST TO HANG OUT AND GAWK AT THE CELEBRITIES...
ANGELA LAMB IS IN IT, AND RICHARD DEAL, AND BILLY CARLTON...
UH, NOBODY YOU'D KNOW...
ALEC, THIS TRAVELING BUSINESS... LETTING YOUR BODY DIE IN ONE PLACE AND GROWING A NEW ONE SOMEWHERE ELSE...
DOESN'T IT MAKE YOU FEEL SORTA DISCONNECTED?
DISCONNECTED...?
WELL, YEAH. I'VE ALWAYS THOUGHT OF YOUR BODY AS YOU, BUT NOW IT'S JUST SOMETHING YOU DRESS UP IN OCCASION-ALLY.
I DUNNO... SOMETIMES I FEEL AS IF YOU'RE SOME-WHERE ELSE AND I'M HUGGING YOUR JACKET.
NO...
IT'S HUMAN.
I AM... CHANGING, ABBY... BUT I KNOW... THAT WHATEVER I CHANGE INTO... IT WILL ALWAYS LOVE YOU...
THIS DISQUIET THAT YOU FEEL... IS UNNECESSARY...
5

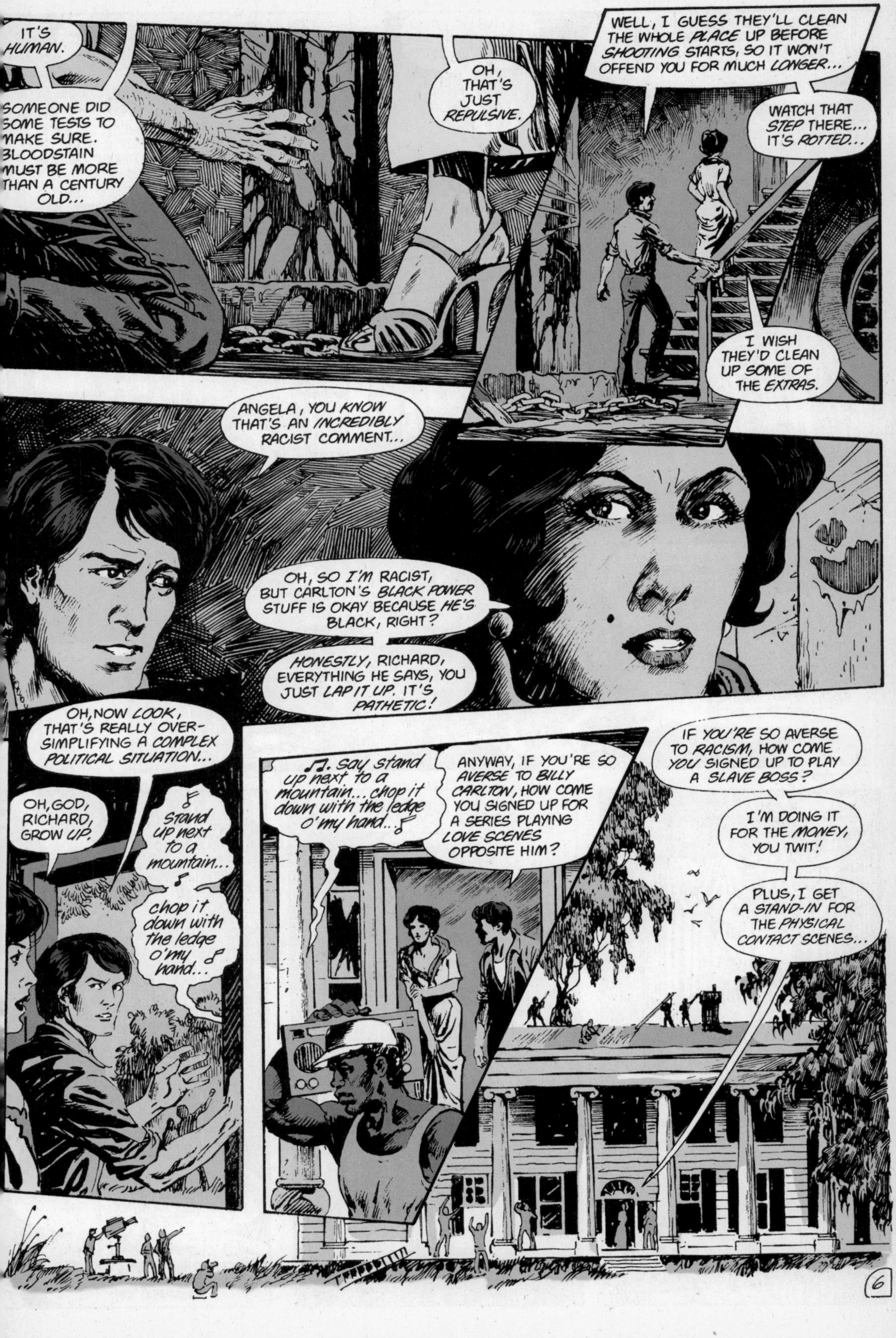
IT'S HUMAN.
SOMEONE DID SOME TESTS TO MAKE SURE. BLOODSTAIN MUST BE MORE THAN A CENTURY OLD...
OH, THAT'S JUST REPULSIVE.
WELL, I GUESS THEY'LL CLEAN THE WHOLE PLACE UP BEFORE SHOOTING STARTS, SO IT WON'T OFFEND YOU FOR MUCH LONGER...
WATCH THAT STEP THERE... IT'S ROTTED...
I WISH THEY'D CLEAN UP SOME OF THE EXTRAS.
ANGELA, YOU KNOW THAT'S AN INCREDIBLY RACIST COMMENT...
OH, SO I'M RACIST, BUT CARLTON'S BLACK POWER STUFF IS OKAY BECAUSE HE'S BLACK, RIGHT?
HONESTLY, RICHARD, EVERYTHING HE SAYS, YOU JUST LAP IT UP. IT'S PATHETIC!
OH, NOW LOOK, THAT'S REALLY OVER-SIMPLIFYING A COMPLEX POLITICAL SITUATION...
OH, GOD, RICHARD, GROW UP.
Stand up next to a mountain...
chop it down with the ledge o'my hand...
Say stand up next to a mountain... chop it down with the ledge o'my hand...
ANYWAY, IF YOU'RE SO AVERSE TO BILLY CARLTON, HOW COME YOU SIGNED UP FOR A SERIES PLAYING LOVE SCENES OPPOSITE HIM?
IF YOU'RE SO AVERSE TO RACISM, HOW COME YOU SIGNED UP TO PLAY A SLAVE BOSS?
I'M DOING IT FOR THE MONEY, YOU TWIT!
PLUS, I GET A STAND-IN FOR THE PHYSICAL CONTACT SCENES...
6

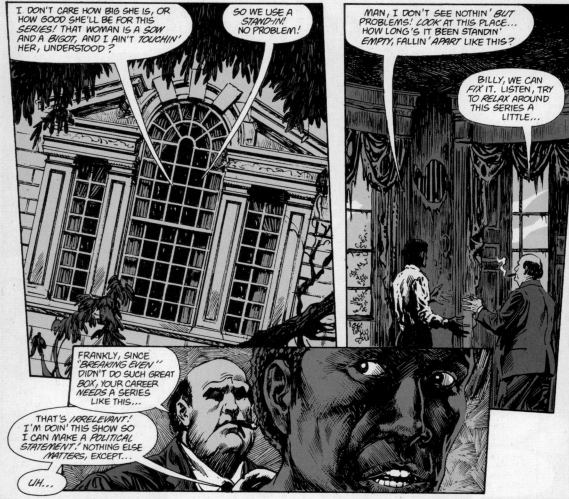

I DON'T CARE HOW BIG SHE IS, OR HOW GOOD SHE'LL BE FOR THIS *SERIES!* THAT WOMAN IS A *SOW* AND A *BIGOT,* AND I AIN'T *TOUCHIN'* HER, UNDERSTOOD?

SO WE USE A *STAND-IN!* NO PROBLEM!

MAN, I DON'T SEE NOTHIN' *BUT* PROBLEMS! LOOK AT THIS PLACE... HOW LONG'S IT BEEN STANDIN' *EMPTY,* FALLIN' *APART* LIKE THIS?

BILLY, WE CAN *FIX* IT. LISTEN, TRY TO *RELAX* AROUND THIS SERIES A LITTLE...

FRANKLY, SINCE "*BREAKING EVEN*" DIDN'T DO SUCH GREAT *BOX,* YOUR CAREER *NEEDS* A SERIES LIKE THIS...

THAT'S *IRRELEVANT!* I'M *DOIN'* THIS SHOW SO I CAN MAKE A *POLITICAL STATEMENT!* NOTHING ELSE MATTERS, EXCEPT...

UH...

BILLY?

HEY, BILLY, WHAT'S *WITH* YOU? YOU *SPACED OUT* OR SOMETHIN'?

LISTEN, AFTER "*BREAKING EVEN*" I THOUGHT WE HAD AN *AGREEMENT:* NO BLOW AROUND THE *SET,* RIGHT?

WHAT?

BILLY, BILLY, BILLY... WHY DO YOU *DO* THIS TO ME? COME ON... LET'S GET OUTSIDE IN THE *FRESH AIR.*

AND *LISTEN...* DON'T WORRY ABOUT THE *SERIES,* LIKE THE LADY *SAID,* "*TOMORROW IS ANOTHER DAY.*"

7

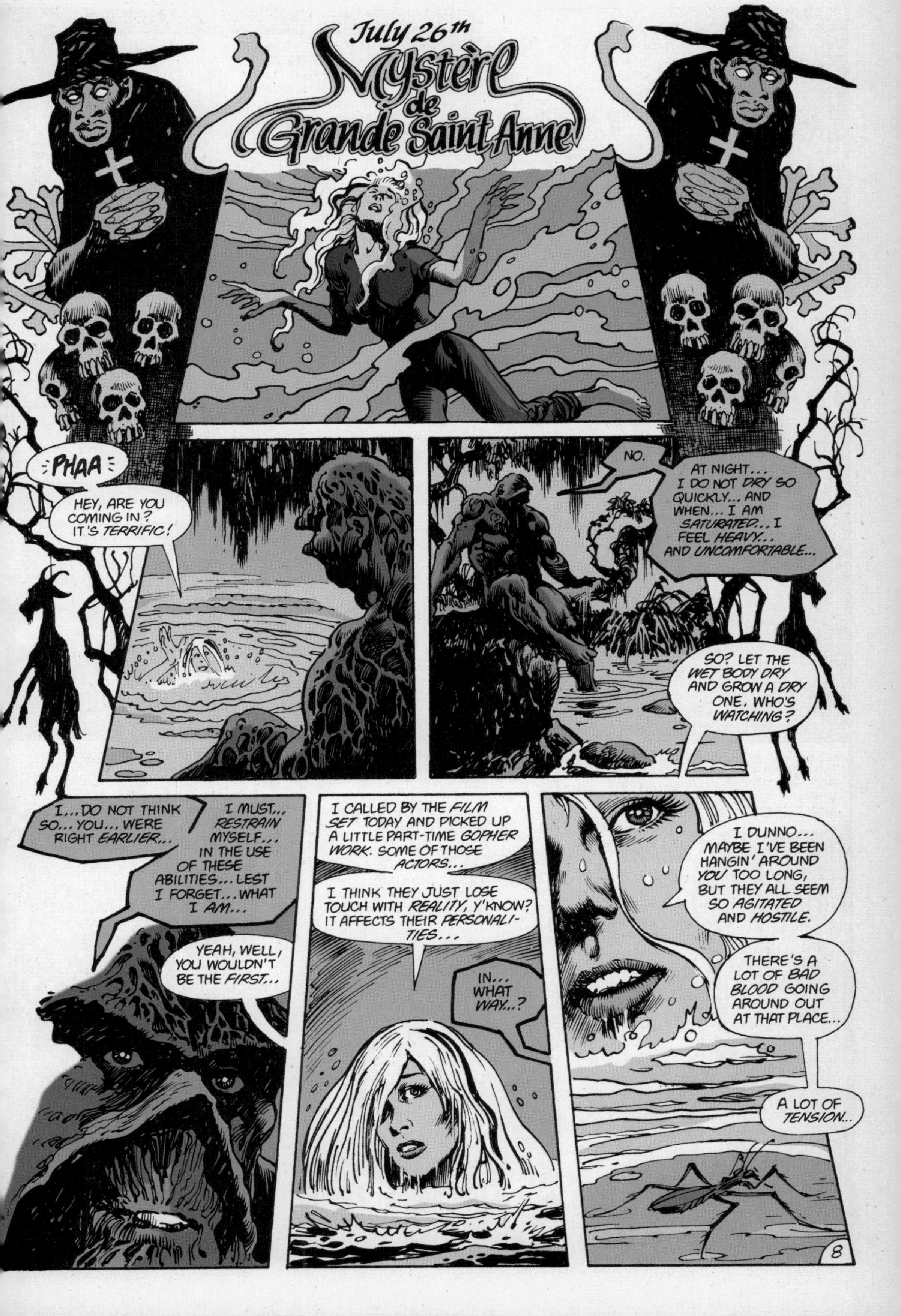
July 26th
Mystère de Grande Saint Anne
PHAA
HEY, ARE YOU COMING IN? IT'S TERRIFIC!
NO.
AT NIGHT... I DO NOT DRY SO QUICKLY... AND WHEN... I AM SATURATED... I FEEL HEAVY... AND UNCOMFORTABLE...
SO? LET THE WET BODY DRY AND GROW A DRY ONE, WHO'S WATCHING?
I... DO NOT THINK SO... YOU... WERE RIGHT EARLIER...
I MUST... RESTRAIN MYSELF... IN THE USE OF THESE ABILITIES... LEST I FORGET... WHAT I AM...
YEAH, WELL, YOU WOULDN'T BE THE FIRST...
I CALLED BY THE FILM SET TODAY AND PICKED UP A LITTLE PART-TIME GOPHER WORK. SOME OF THOSE ACTORS...
I THINK THEY JUST LOSE TOUCH WITH REALITY, Y'KNOW? IT AFFECTS THEIR PERSONALI-TIES...
IN... WHAT WAY...?
I DUNNO... MAYBE I'VE BEEN HANGIN' AROUND YOU TOO LONG, BUT THEY ALL SEEM SO AGITATED AND HOSTILE.
THERE'S A LOT OF BAD BLOOD GOING AROUND OUT AT THAT PLACE...
A LOT OF TENSION...
8

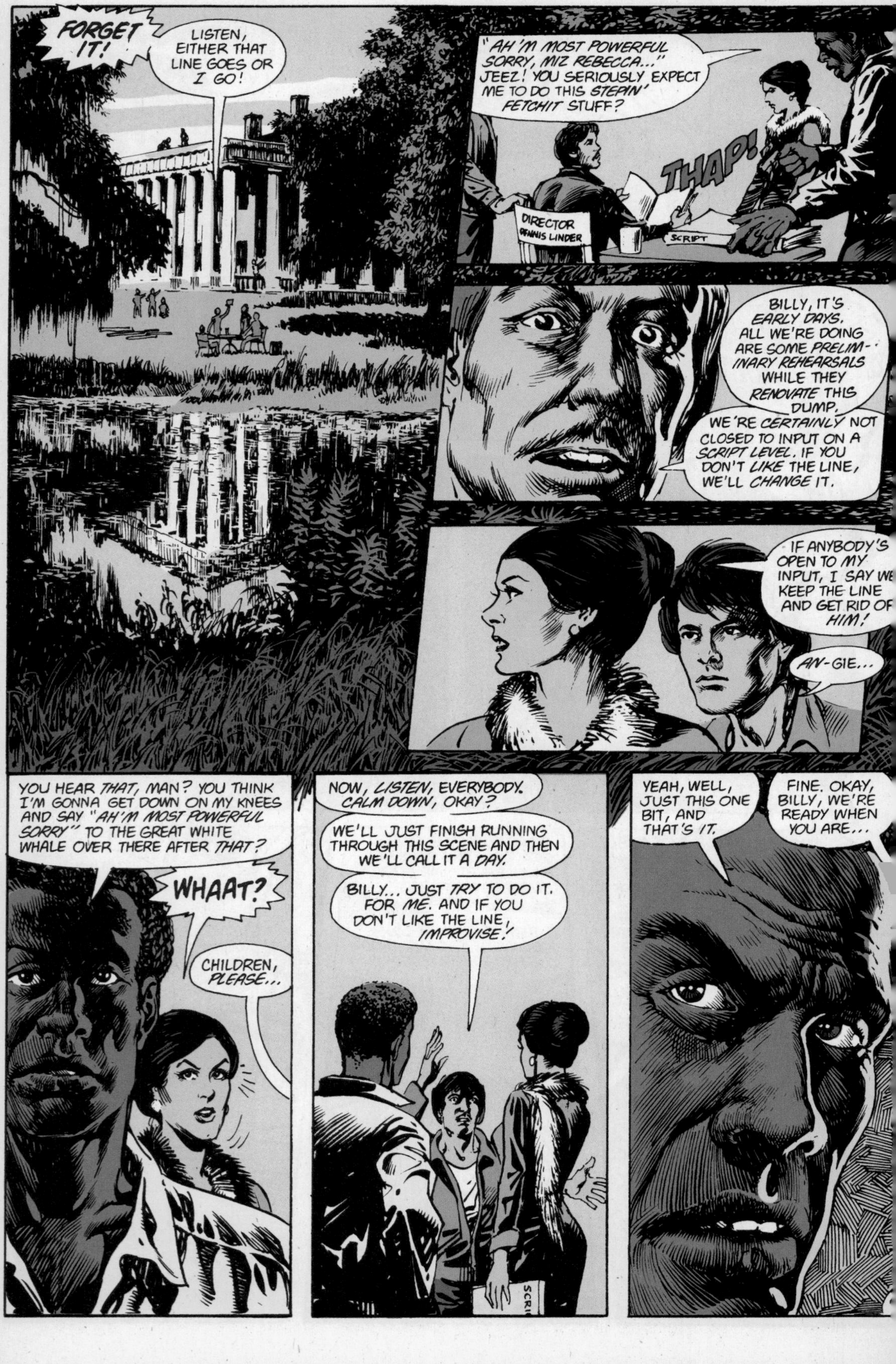
FORGET IT!
LISTEN, EITHER THAT LINE GOES OR I GO!
"AH'M MOST POWERFUL SORRY, MIZ REBECCA..." JEEZ! YOU SERIOUSLY EXPECT ME TO DO THIS STEPIN' FETCHIT STUFF?
THAP!
DIRECTOR DENNIS LINDER
SCRIPT
BILLY, IT'S EARLY DAYS. ALL WE'RE DOING ARE SOME PRELIMINARY REHEARSALS WHILE THEY RENOVATE THIS DUMP.
WE'RE CERTAINLY NOT CLOSED TO INPUT ON A SCRIPT LEVEL. IF YOU DON'T LIKE THE LINE, WE'LL CHANGE IT.
IF ANYBODY'S OPEN TO MY INPUT, I SAY WE KEEP THE LINE AND GET RID OF HIM!
AN-GIE...
YOU HEAR THAT, MAN? YOU THINK I'M GONNA GET DOWN ON MY KNEES AND SAY "AH'M MOST POWERFUL SORRY" TO THE GREAT WHITE WHALE OVER THERE AFTER THAT?
WHAAT?
CHILDREN, PLEASE...
NOW, LISTEN, EVERYBODY. CALM DOWN, OKAY?
WE'LL JUST FINISH RUNNING THROUGH THIS SCENE AND THEN WE'LL CALL IT A DAY.
BILLY... JUST TRY TO DO IT. FOR ME. AND IF YOU DON'T LIKE THE LINE, IMPROVISE!
YEAH, WELL, JUST THIS ONE BIT, AND THAT'S IT.
FINE. OKAY, BILLY, WE'RE READY WHEN YOU ARE...

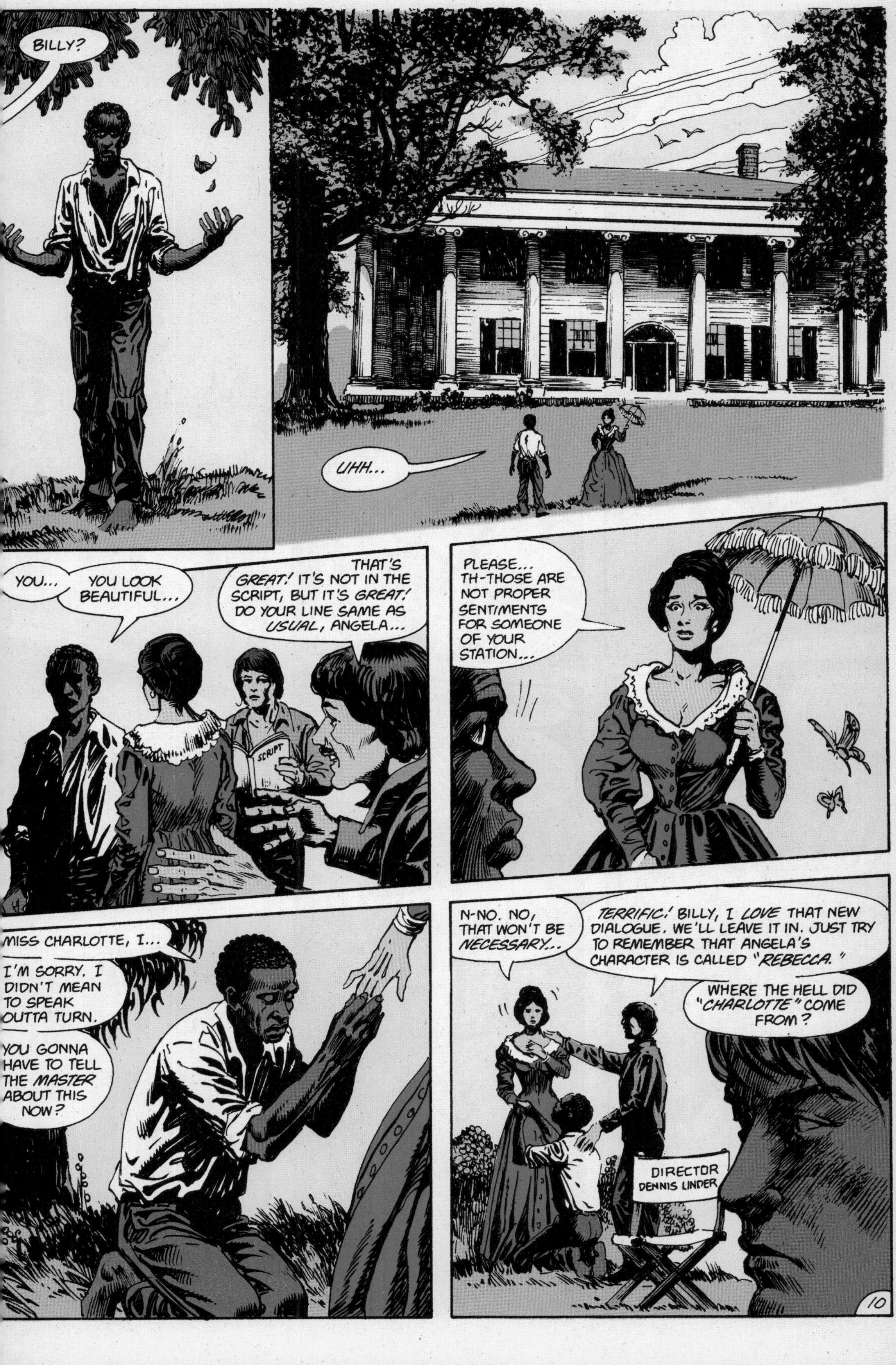
BILLY?
UHH...
YOU...
YOU LOOK BEAUTIFUL...
THAT'S GREAT! IT'S NOT IN THE SCRIPT, BUT IT'S GREAT! DO YOUR LINE SAME AS USUAL, ANGELA...
SCRIPT
PLEASE... TH-THOSE ARE NOT PROPER SENTIMENTS FOR SOMEONE OF YOUR STATION...
MISS CHARLOTTE, I...
I'M SORRY. I DIDN'T MEAN TO SPEAK OUTTA TURN.
YOU GONNA HAVE TO TELL THE MASTER ABOUT THIS NOW?
N-NO. NO, THAT WON'T BE NECESSARY...
TERRIFIC! BILLY, I LOVE THAT NEW DIALOGUE. WE'LL LEAVE IT IN. JUST TRY TO REMEMBER THAT ANGELA'S CHARACTER IS CALLED "REBECCA."
WHERE THE HELL DID "CHARLOTTE" COME FROM?
DIRECTOR
DENNIS LINDER
10

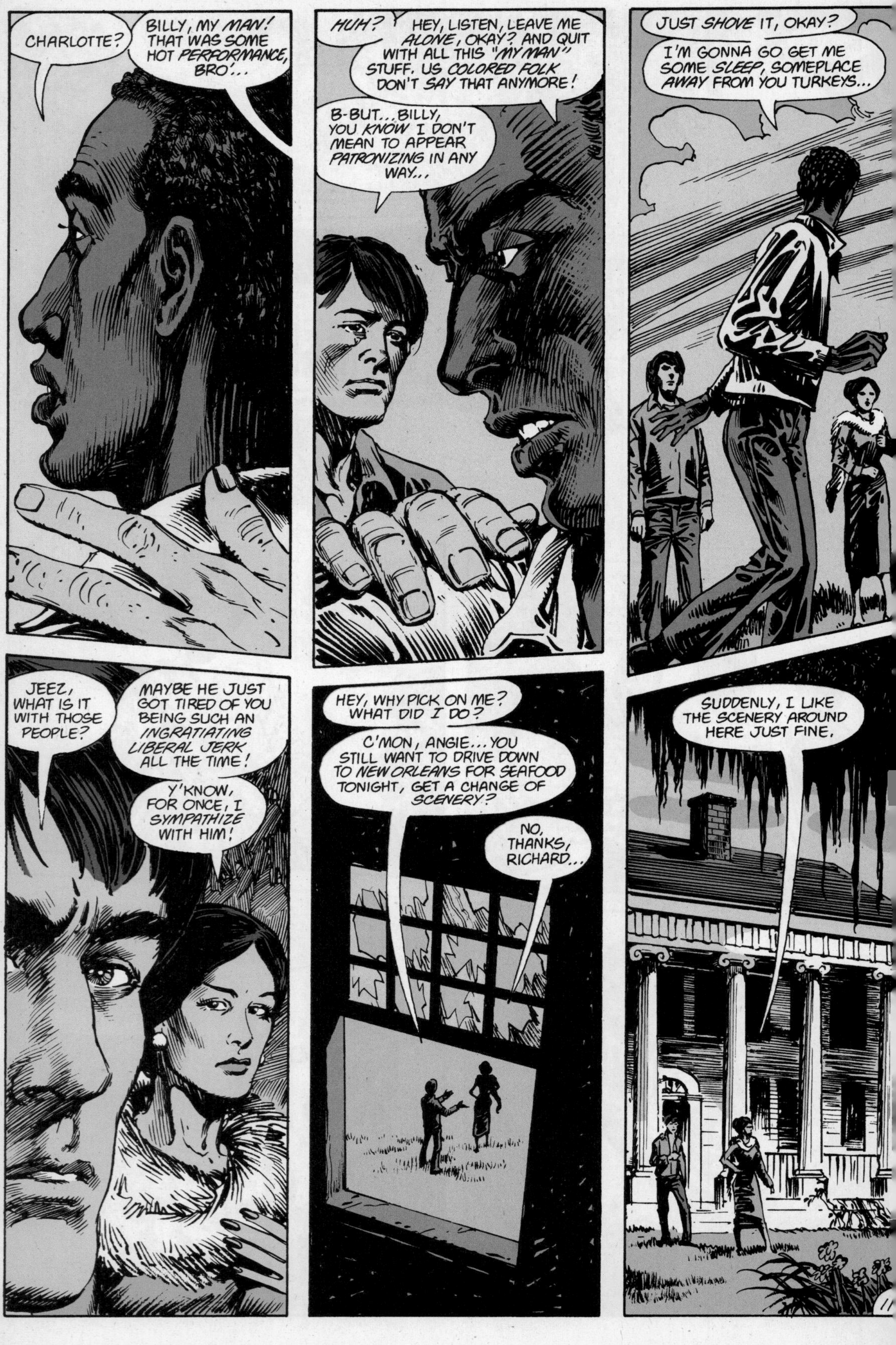
CHARLOTTE?
BILLY, MY MAN! THAT WAS SOME HOT PERFORMANCE, BRO'...
HUH?
HEY, LISTEN, LEAVE ME ALONE, OKAY? AND QUIT WITH ALL THIS "MY MAN" STUFF. US COLORED FOLK DON'T SAY THAT ANYMORE!
B-BUT... BILLY, YOU KNOW I DON'T MEAN TO APPEAR PATRONIZING IN ANY WAY...
JUST SHOVE IT, OKAY?
I'M GONNA GO GET ME SOME SLEEP, SOMEPLACE AWAY FROM YOU TURKEYS...
JEEZ, WHAT IS IT WITH THOSE PEOPLE?
MAYBE HE JUST GOT TIRED OF YOU BEING SUCH AN INGRATIATING LIBERAL JERK ALL THE TIME!
Y'KNOW, FOR ONCE, I SYMPATHIZE WITH HIM!
HEY, WHY PICK ON ME? WHAT DID I DO?
C'MON, ANGIE... YOU STILL WANT TO DRIVE DOWN TO NEW ORLEANS FOR SEAFOOD TONIGHT, GET A CHANGE OF SCENERY?
NO, THANKS, RICHARD...
SUDDENLY, I LIKE THE SCENERY AROUND HERE JUST FINE.
11

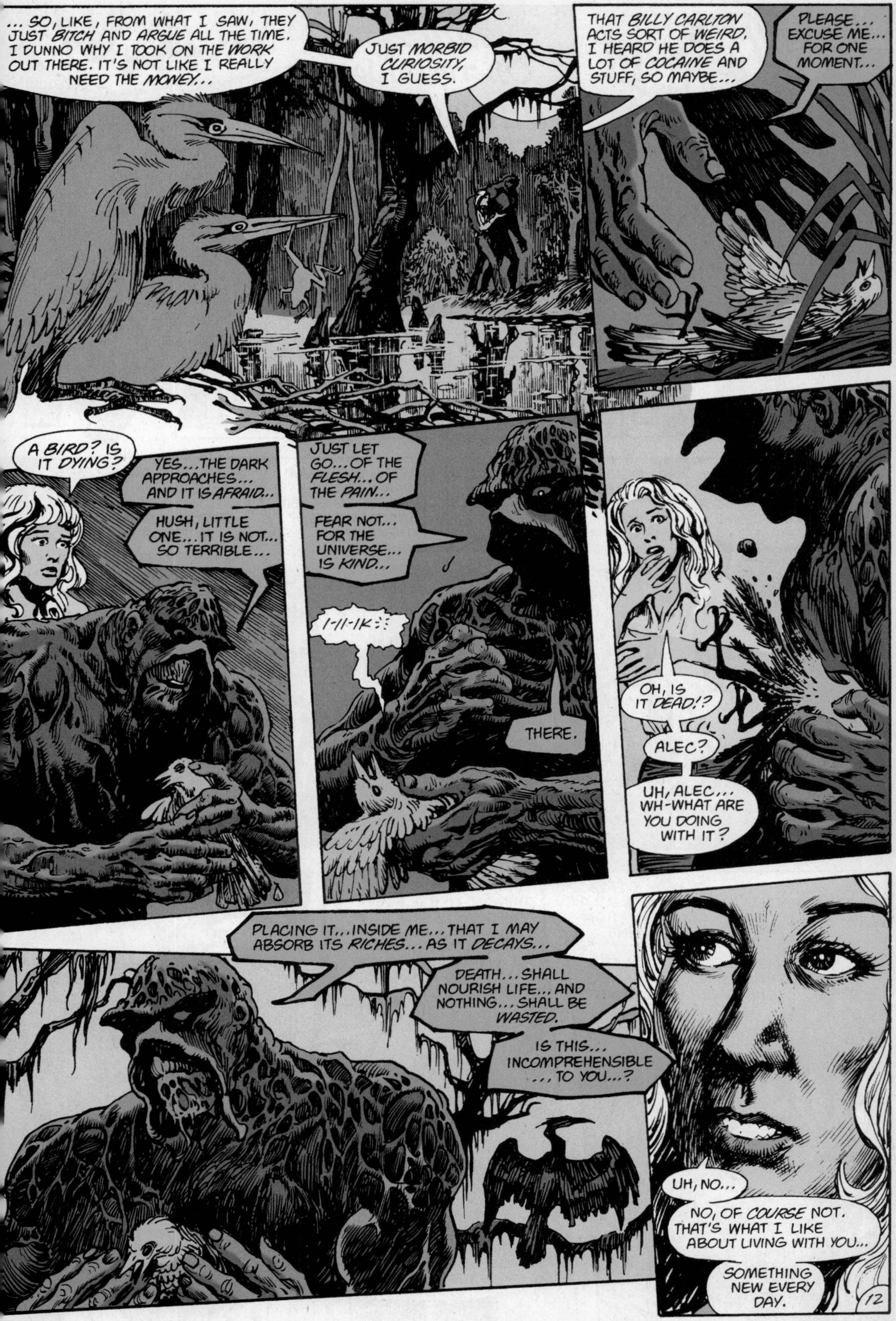
... SO, LIKE, FROM WHAT I SAW, THEY JUST BITCH AND ARGUE ALL THE TIME. I DUNNO WHY I TOOK ON THE WORK OUT THERE. IT'S NOT LIKE I REALLY NEED THE MONEY...
JUST MORBID CURIOSITY, I GUESS.
THAT BILLY CARLTON ACTS SORT OF WEIRD. I HEARD HE DOES A LOT OF COCAINE AND STUFF, SO MAYBE...
PLEASE... EXCUSE ME... FOR ONE MOMENT...
A BIRD? IS IT DYING?
YES... THE DARK APPROACHES... AND IT IS AFRAID...
HUSH, LITTLE ONE... IT IS NOT... SO TERRIBLE...
JUST LET GO... OF THE FLESH... OF THE PAIN...
FEAR NOT... FOR THE UNIVERSE... IS KIND...
I-II-IK
THERE.
OH, IS IT DEAD!?
ALEC?
UH, ALEC... WH-WHAT ARE YOU DOING WITH IT?
PLACING IT... INSIDE ME... THAT I MAY ABSORB ITS RICHES... AS IT DECAYS...
DEATH... SHALL NOURISH LIFE... AND NOTHING... SHALL BE WASTED.
IS THIS... INCOMPREHENSIBLE ...TO YOU...?
UH, NO...
NO, OF COURSE NOT. THAT'S WHAT I LIKE ABOUT LIVING WITH YOU...
SOMETHING NEW EVERY DAY.
12

July 29TH
Offering of food to
Mâitresse SilverinE
Offering of flowers to
Mâitresse Lorvana

HEY, WHAT'S WITH THE *EXTRAS?* WHERE DID ALL THE *FLOWERS* AND STUFF COME FROM?

GOD KNOWS. I GUESS IT'S SOMEBODY'S *BIRTHDAY.*

Y'KNOW, SOME OF THEM HAVE BEEN SLEEPING OUT HERE NIGHTS? YOU GO FIGURE.

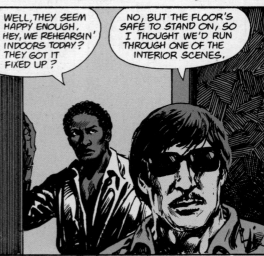

WELL, THEY SEEM HAPPY ENOUGH. HEY, WE REHEARSIN' INDOORS TODAY? THEY GOT IT FIXED UP?

NO, BUT THE FLOOR'S SAFE TO STAND ON, SO I THOUGHT WE'D RUN THROUGH ONE OF THE INTERIOR SCENES.

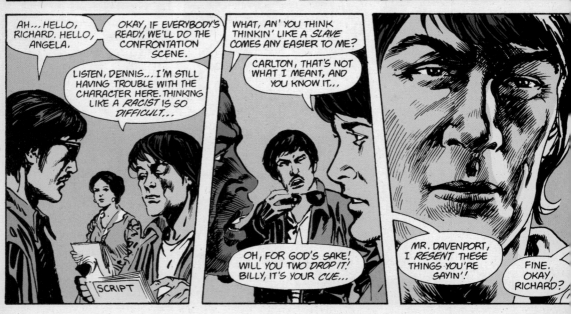

AH... HELLO, RICHARD. HELLO, ANGELA.

OKAY, IF EVERYBODY'S READY, WE'LL DO THE CONFRONTATION SCENE.

LISTEN, DENNIS... I'M STILL HAVING TROUBLE WITH THE CHARACTER HERE. THINKING LIKE A *RACIST* IS SO *DIFFICULT...*

WHAT, AN' YOU THINK THINKIN' LIKE A *SLAVE* COMES ANY EASIER TO ME?

CARLTON, THAT'S NOT WHAT I MEANT, AND YOU KNOW IT...

OH, FOR GOD'S SAKE! WILL YOU TWO *DROP* IT! BILLY, IT'S YOUR *CUE*...

MR. DAVENPORT, I *RESENT* THESE THINGS YOU'RE SAYIN'!

FINE. OKAY, RICHARD?

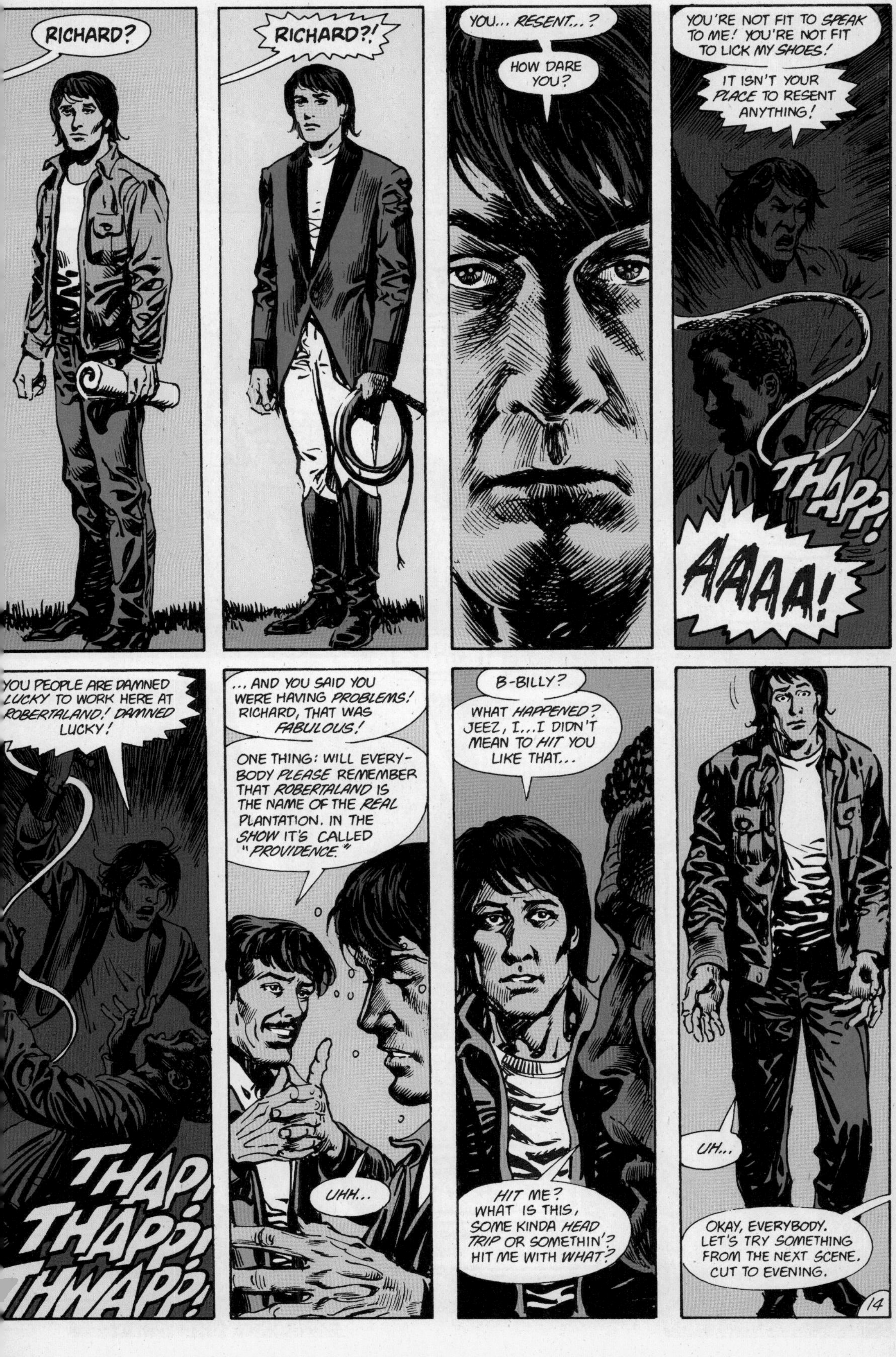
RICHARD?
RICHARD?!
YOU... RESENT...?
HOW DARE YOU?
YOU'RE NOT FIT TO SPEAK TO ME! YOU'RE NOT FIT TO LICK MY SHOES!
IT ISN'T YOUR PLACE TO RESENT ANYTHING!
THAPP!
AAAAA!
YOU PEOPLE ARE DAMNED LUCKY TO WORK HERE AT ROBERTALAND! DAMNED LUCKY!
THAP! THAPP! THWAPP!
...AND YOU SAID YOU WERE HAVING PROBLEMS! RICHARD, THAT WAS FABULOUS!
ONE THING: WILL EVERYBODY PLEASE REMEMBER THAT ROBERTALAND IS THE NAME OF THE REAL PLANTATION. IN THE SHOW IT'S CALLED "PROVIDENCE."
UHH...
B-BILLY?
WHAT HAPPENED? JEEZ, I...I DIDN'T MEAN TO HIT YOU LIKE THAT...
HIT ME? WHAT IS THIS, SOME KINDA HEAD TRIP OR SOMETHIN'? HIT ME WITH WHAT?
UH...
OKAY, EVERYBODY. LET'S TRY SOMETHING FROM THE NEXT SCENE. CUT TO EVENING.
14

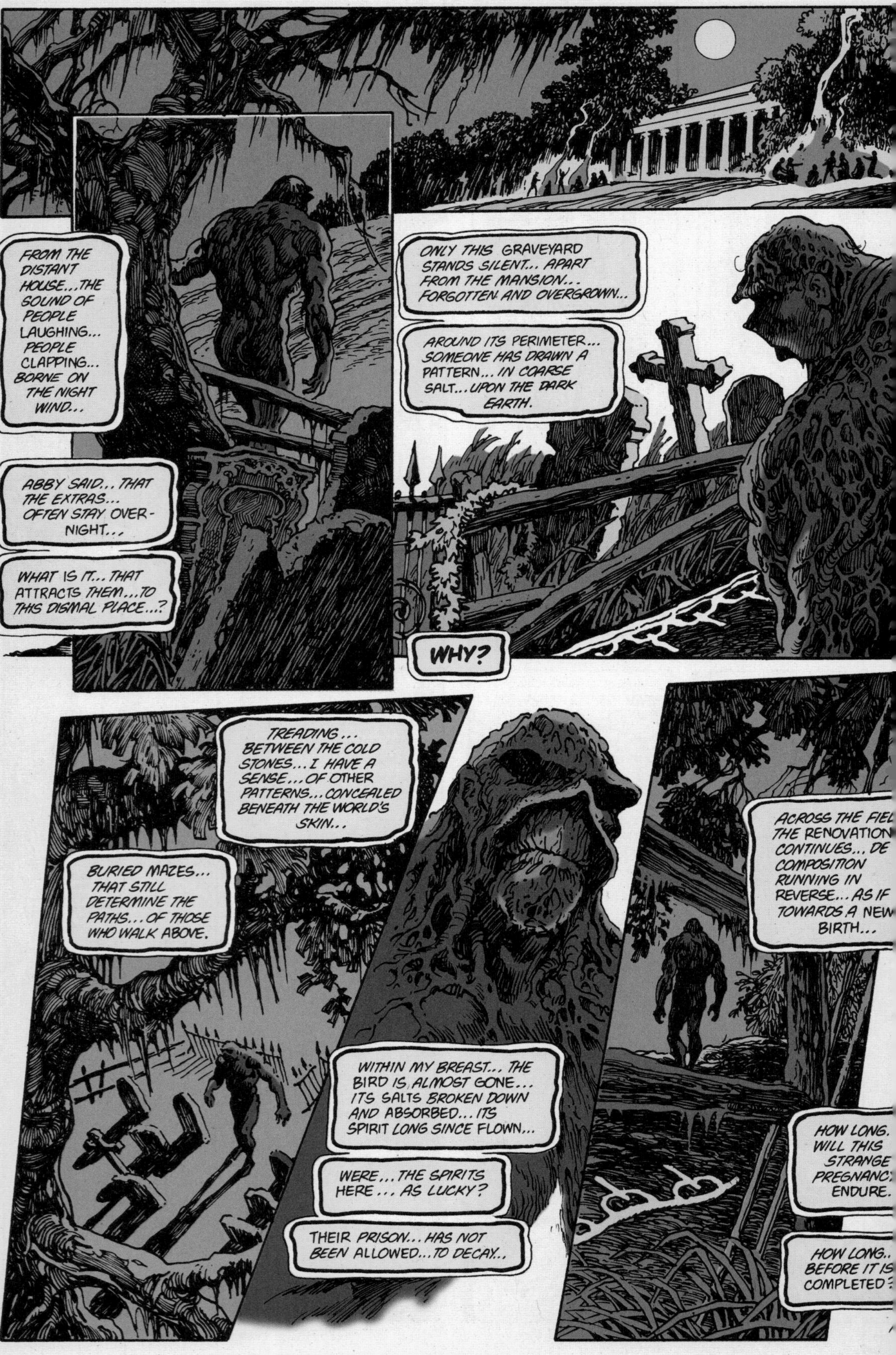
FROM THE DISTANT HOUSE... THE SOUND OF PEOPLE LAUGHING... PEOPLE CLAPPING... BORNE ON THE NIGHT WIND...
ABBY SAID... THAT THE EXTRAS... OFTEN STAY OVER-NIGHT...
WHAT IS IT... THAT ATTRACTS THEM... TO THIS DISMAL PLACE...?
ONLY THIS GRAVEYARD STANDS SILENT... APART FROM THE MANSION... FORGOTTEN AND OVERGROWN...
AROUND ITS PERIMETER... SOMEONE HAS DRAWN A PATTERN... IN COARSE SALT... UPON THE DARK EARTH.
WHY?
TREADING... BETWEEN THE COLD STONES... I HAVE A SENSE... OF OTHER PATTERNS... CONCEALED BENEATH THE WORLD'S SKIN...
BURIED MAZES... THAT STILL DETERMINE THE PATHS... OF THOSE WHO WALK ABOVE.
WITHIN MY BREAST... THE BIRD IS ALMOST GONE... ITS SALTS BROKEN DOWN AND ABSORBED... ITS SPIRIT LONG SINCE FLOWN...
WERE... THE SPIRITS HERE... AS LUCKY?
THEIR PRISON... HAS NOT BEEN ALLOWED... TO DECAY...
ACROSS THE FIEL THE RENOVATION CONTINUES... DE COMPOSITION RUNNING IN REVERSE... AS IF TOWARDS A NEW BIRTH...
HOW LONG. WILL THIS STRANGE PREGNANC ENDURE.
HOW LONG. BEFORE IT IS COMPLETED?

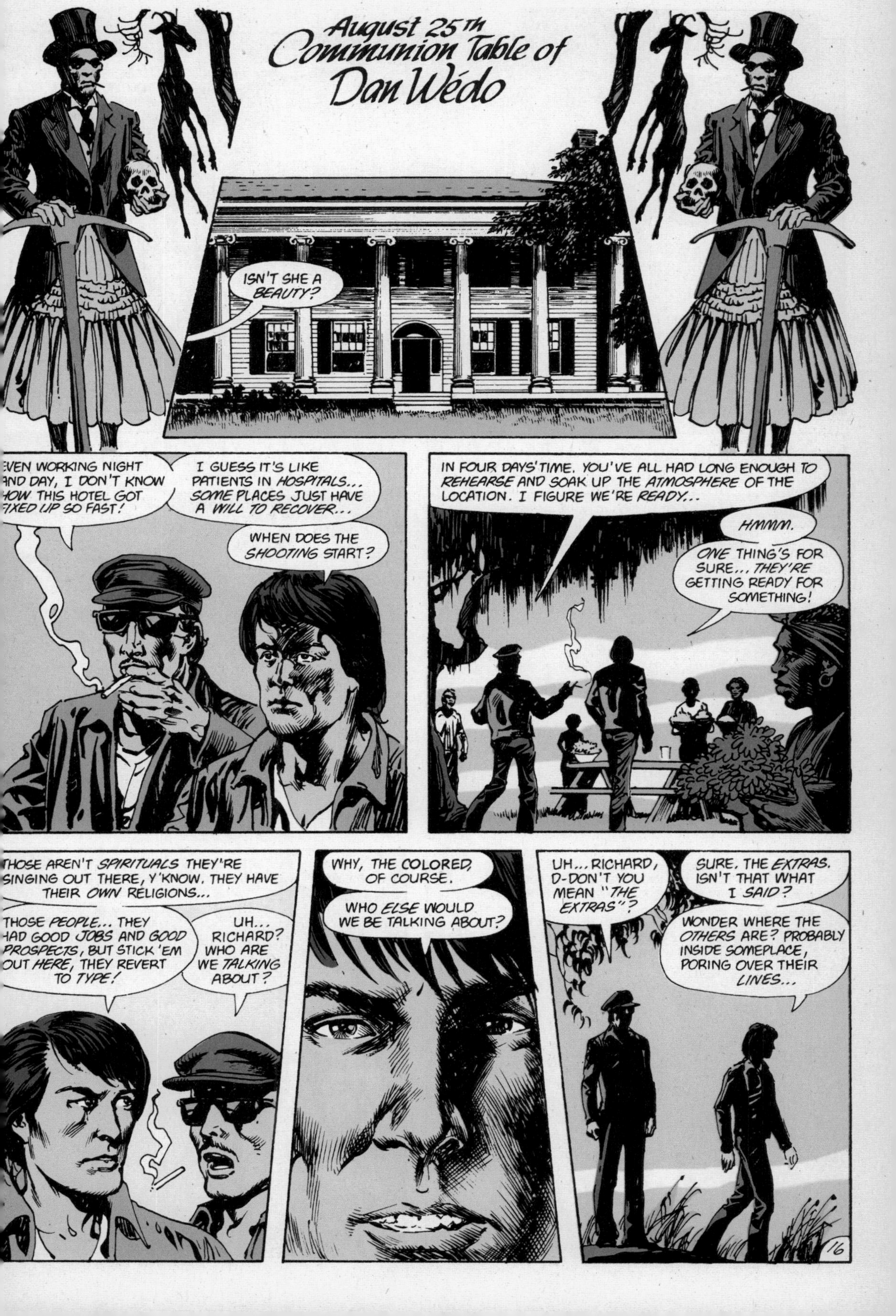
August 25th Communion Table of Dan Wédo
ISN'T SHE A BEAUTY?
EVEN WORKING NIGHT AND DAY, I DON'T KNOW HOW THIS HOTEL GOT FIXED UP SO FAST!
I GUESS IT'S LIKE PATIENTS IN HOSPITALS... SOME PLACES JUST HAVE A WILL TO RECOVER...
WHEN DOES THE SHOOTING START?
IN FOUR DAYS' TIME. YOU'VE ALL HAD LONG ENOUGH TO REHEARSE AND SOAK UP THE ATMOSPHERE OF THE LOCATION. I FIGURE WE'RE READY...
HMMM.
ONE THING'S FOR SURE... THEY'RE GETTING READY FOR SOMETHING!
THOSE AREN'T SPIRITUALS THEY'RE SINGING OUT THERE, Y'KNOW. THEY HAVE THEIR OWN RELIGIONS...
THOSE PEOPLE... THEY HAD GOOD JOBS AND GOOD PROSPECTS, BUT STICK 'EM OUT HERE, THEY REVERT TO TYPE!
UH... RICHARD? WHO ARE WE TALKING ABOUT?
WHY, THE COLORED, OF COURSE.
WHO ELSE WOULD WE BE TALKING ABOUT?
UH... RICHARD, D-DON'T YOU MEAN "THE EXTRAS"?
SURE. THE EXTRAS. ISN'T THAT WHAT I SAID?
WONDER WHERE THE OTHERS ARE? PROBABLY INSIDE SOMEPLACE, PORING OVER THEIR LINES...
16

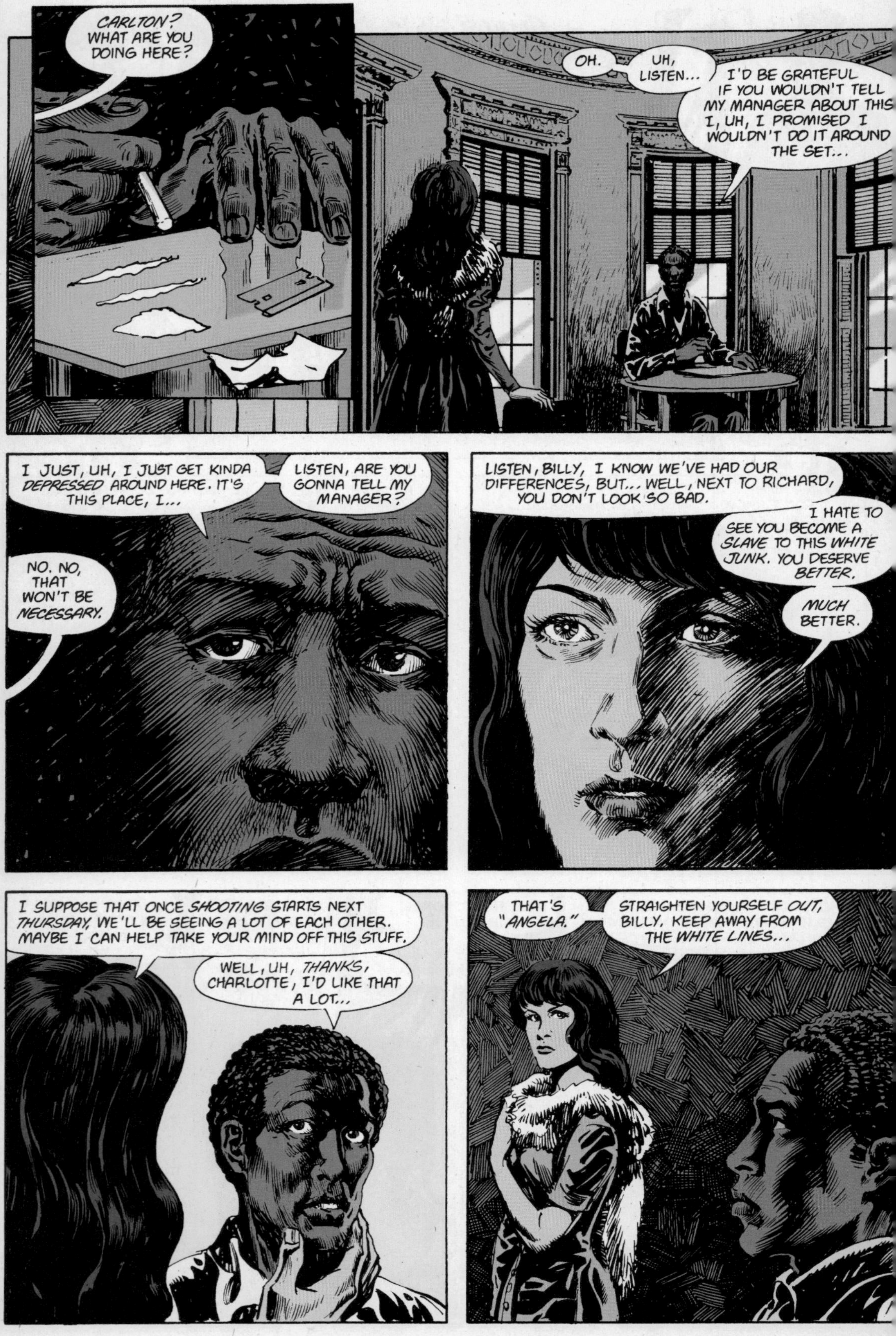
CARLTON? WHAT ARE YOU DOING HERE?
OH.
UH, LISTEN...
I'D BE GRATEFUL IF YOU WOULDN'T TELL MY MANAGER ABOUT THIS. I, UH, I PROMISED I WOULDN'T DO IT AROUND THE SET...
I JUST, UH, I JUST GET KINDA DEPRESSED AROUND HERE. IT'S THIS PLACE, I...
LISTEN, ARE YOU GONNA TELL MY MANAGER?
NO. NO, THAT WON'T BE NECESSARY.
LISTEN, BILLY, I KNOW WE'VE HAD OUR DIFFERENCES, BUT... WELL, NEXT TO RICHARD, YOU DON'T LOOK SO BAD.
I HATE TO SEE YOU BECOME A SLAVE TO THIS WHITE JUNK. YOU DESERVE BETTER.
MUCH BETTER.
I SUPPOSE THAT ONCE SHOOTING STARTS NEXT THURSDAY, WE'LL BE SEEING A LOT OF EACH OTHER. MAYBE I CAN HELP TAKE YOUR MIND OFF THIS STUFF.
WELL, UH, THANKS, CHARLOTTE, I'D LIKE THAT A LOT...
THAT'S "ANGELA."
STRAIGHTEN YOURSELF OUT, BILLY. KEEP AWAY FROM THE WHITE LINES...

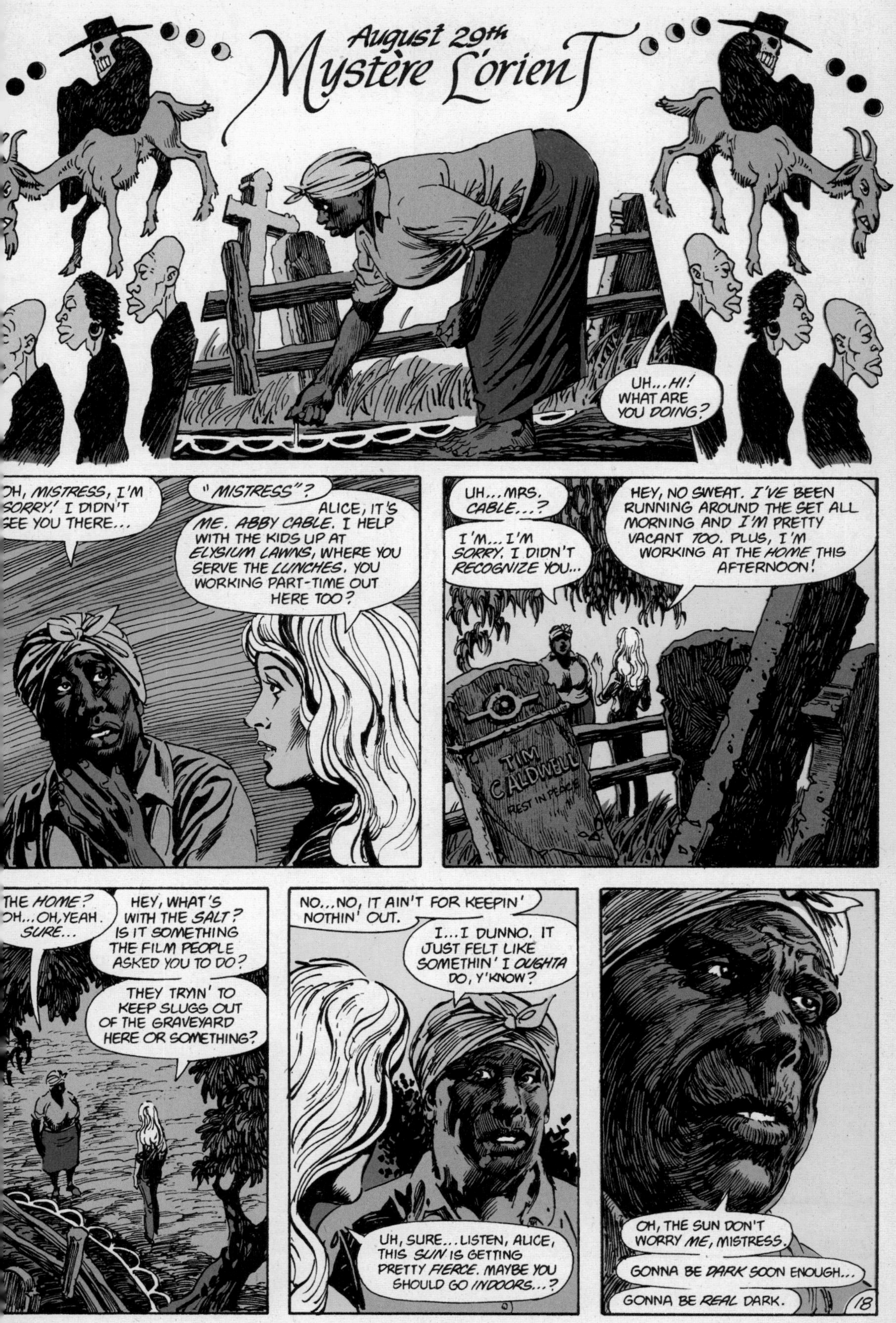
August 29th
Mystère L'orienT
UH...HI! WHAT ARE YOU DOING?
OH, MISTRESS, I'M SORRY! I DIDN'T SEE YOU THERE...
"MISTRESS"? ALICE, IT'S ME. ABBY CABLE. I HELP WITH THE KIDS UP AT ELYSIUM LAWNS, WHERE YOU SERVE THE LUNCHES. YOU WORKING PART-TIME OUT HERE TOO?
UH...MRS. CABLE...?
I'M... I'M SORRY. I DIDN'T RECOGNIZE YOU...
HEY, NO SWEAT. I'VE BEEN RUNNING AROUND THE SET ALL MORNING AND I'M PRETTY VACANT TOO. PLUS, I'M WORKING AT THE HOME THIS AFTERNOON!
TIM CALDWELL REST IN PEACE
THE HOME? OH...OH, YEAH. SURE...
HEY, WHAT'S WITH THE SALT? IS IT SOMETHING THE FILM PEOPLE ASKED YOU TO DO?
THEY TRYIN' TO KEEP SLUGS OUT OF THE GRAVEYARD HERE OR SOMETHING?
NO...NO, IT AIN'T FOR KEEPIN' NOTHIN' OUT.
I...I DUNNO. IT JUST FELT LIKE SOMETHIN' I OUGHTA DO, Y'KNOW?
UH, SURE... LISTEN, ALICE, THIS SUN IS GETTING PRETTY FIERCE. MAYBE YOU SHOULD GO INDOORS...?
OH, THE SUN DON'T WORRY ME, MISTRESS.
GONNA BE DARK SOON ENOUGH...
GONNA BE REAL DARK.
18

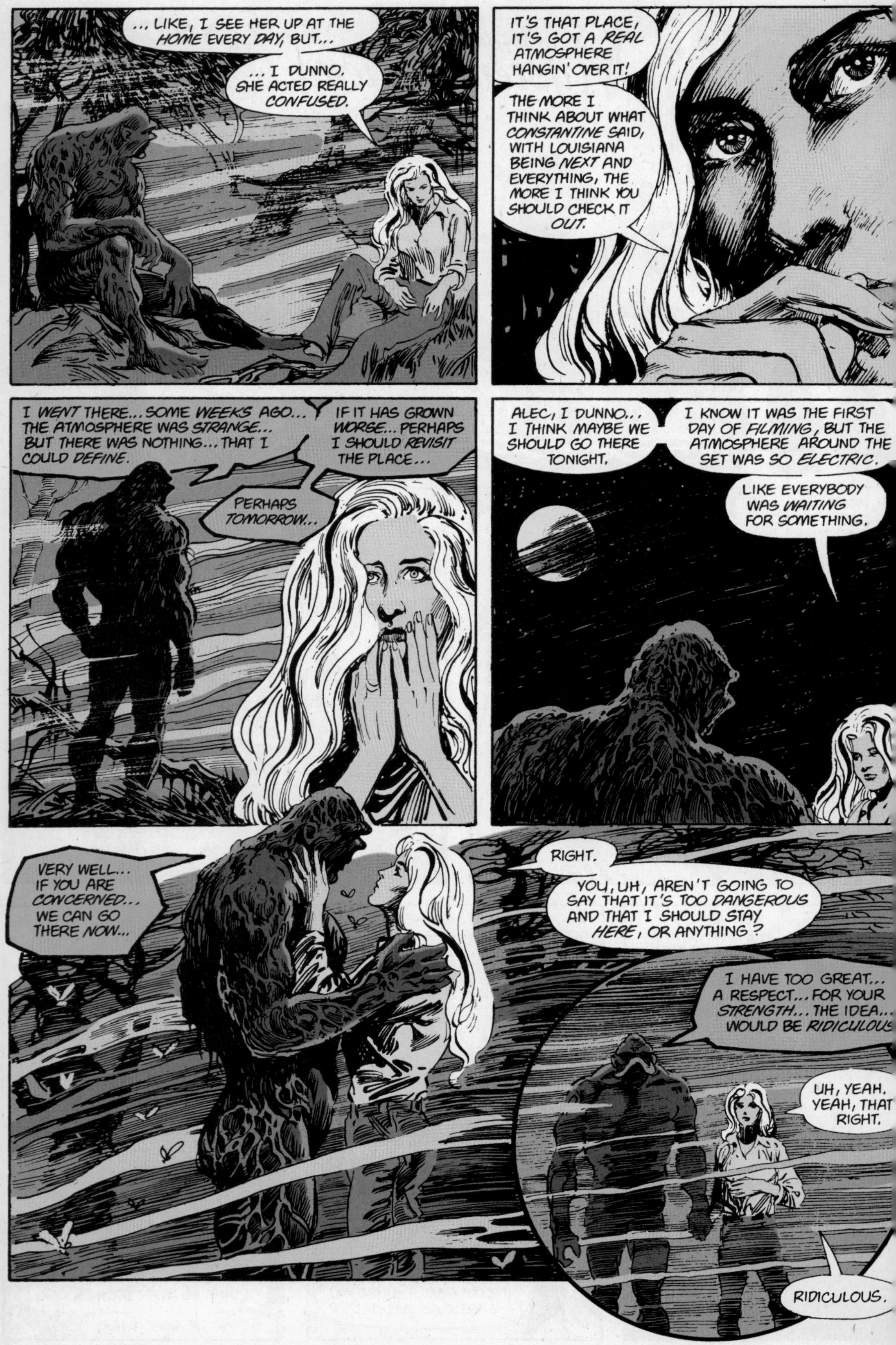
... LIKE, I SEE HER UP AT THE HOME EVERY DAY, BUT...
... I DUNNO. SHE ACTED REALLY CONFUSED.
IT'S THAT PLACE, IT'S GOT A REAL ATMOSPHERE HANGIN' OVER IT!
THE MORE I THINK ABOUT WHAT CONSTANTINE SAID, WITH LOUISIANA BEING NEXT AND EVERYTHING, THE MORE I THINK YOU SHOULD CHECK IT OUT.
I WENT THERE... SOME WEEKS AGO... THE ATMOSPHERE WAS STRANGE... BUT THERE WAS NOTHING... THAT I COULD DEFINE.
IF IT HAS GROWN WORSE... PERHAPS I SHOULD REVISIT THE PLACE...
PERHAPS TOMORROW...
ALEC, I DUNNO... I THINK MAYBE WE SHOULD GO THERE TONIGHT.
I KNOW IT WAS THE FIRST DAY OF FILMING, BUT THE ATMOSPHERE AROUND THE SET WAS SO ELECTRIC.
LIKE EVERYBODY WAS WAITING FOR SOMETHING.
VERY WELL... IF YOU ARE CONCERNED... WE CAN GO THERE NOW...
RIGHT.
YOU, UH, AREN'T GOING TO SAY THAT IT'S TOO DANGEROUS AND THAT I SHOULD STAY HERE, OR ANYTHING ?
I HAVE TOO GREAT... A RESPECT... FOR YOUR STRENGTH... THE IDEA... WOULD BE RIDICULOUS
UH, YEAH. YEAH, THAT RIGHT.
RIDICULOUS.

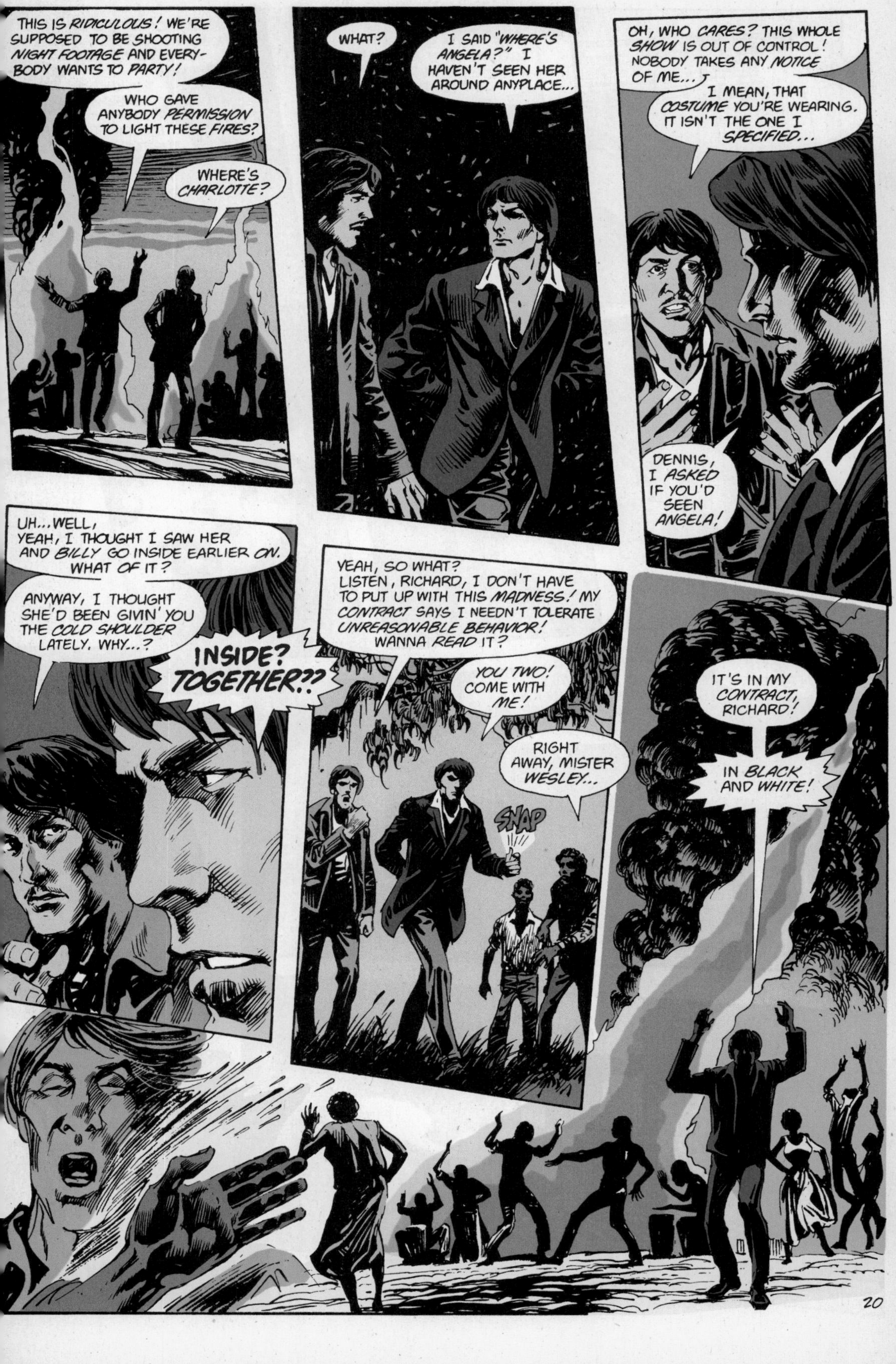
THIS IS RIDICULOUS! WE'RE SUPPOSED TO BE SHOOTING NIGHT FOOTAGE AND EVERYBODY WANTS TO PARTY!
WHO GAVE ANYBODY PERMISSION TO LIGHT THESE FIRES?
WHERE'S CHARLOTTE?
WHAT?
I SAID "WHERE'S ANGELA?" I HAVEN'T SEEN HER AROUND ANYPLACE...
OH, WHO CARES? THIS WHOLE SHOW IS OUT OF CONTROL! NOBODY TAKES ANY NOTICE OF ME...
I MEAN, THAT COSTUME YOU'RE WEARING. IT ISN'T THE ONE I SPECIFIED...
DENNIS, I ASKED IF YOU'D SEEN ANGELA!
UH...WELL, YEAH, I THOUGHT I SAW HER AND BILLY GO INSIDE EARLIER ON. WHAT OF IT?
ANYWAY, I THOUGHT SHE'D BEEN GIVIN' YOU THE COLD SHOULDER LATELY. WHY...?
INSIDE? TOGETHER??
YEAH, SO WHAT? LISTEN, RICHARD, I DON'T HAVE TO PUT UP WITH THIS MADNESS! MY CONTRACT SAYS I NEEDN'T TOLERATE UNREASONABLE BEHAVIOR! WANNA READ IT?
YOU TWO! COME WITH ME!
RIGHT AWAY, MISTER WESLEY...
SNAP
IT'S IN MY CONTRACT, RICHARD!
IN BLACK AND WHITE!

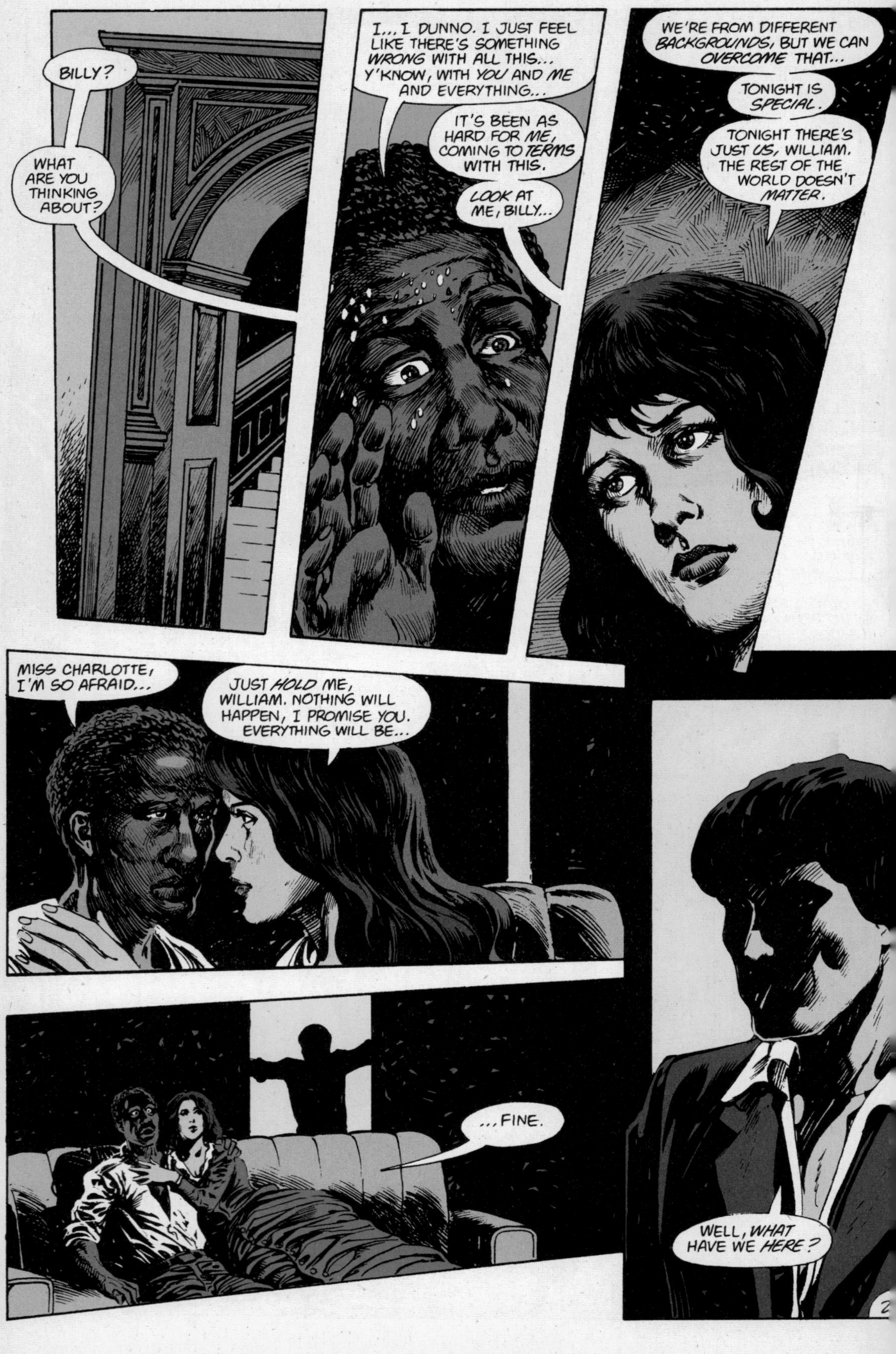
BILLY?
WHAT ARE YOU THINKING ABOUT?
I... I DUNNO. I JUST FEEL LIKE THERE'S SOMETHING WRONG WITH ALL THIS... Y'KNOW, WITH YOU AND ME AND EVERYTHING...
IT'S BEEN AS HARD FOR ME, COMING TO TERMS WITH THIS.
LOOK AT ME, BILLY...
WE'RE FROM DIFFERENT BACKGROUNDS, BUT WE CAN OVERCOME THAT...
TONIGHT IS SPECIAL.
TONIGHT THERE'S JUST US, WILLIAM. THE REST OF THE WORLD DOESN'T MATTER.
MISS CHARLOTTE, I'M SO AFRAID...
JUST HOLD ME, WILLIAM. NOTHING WILL HAPPEN, I PROMISE YOU. EVERYTHING WILL BE...
...FINE.
WELL, WHAT HAVE WE HERE?

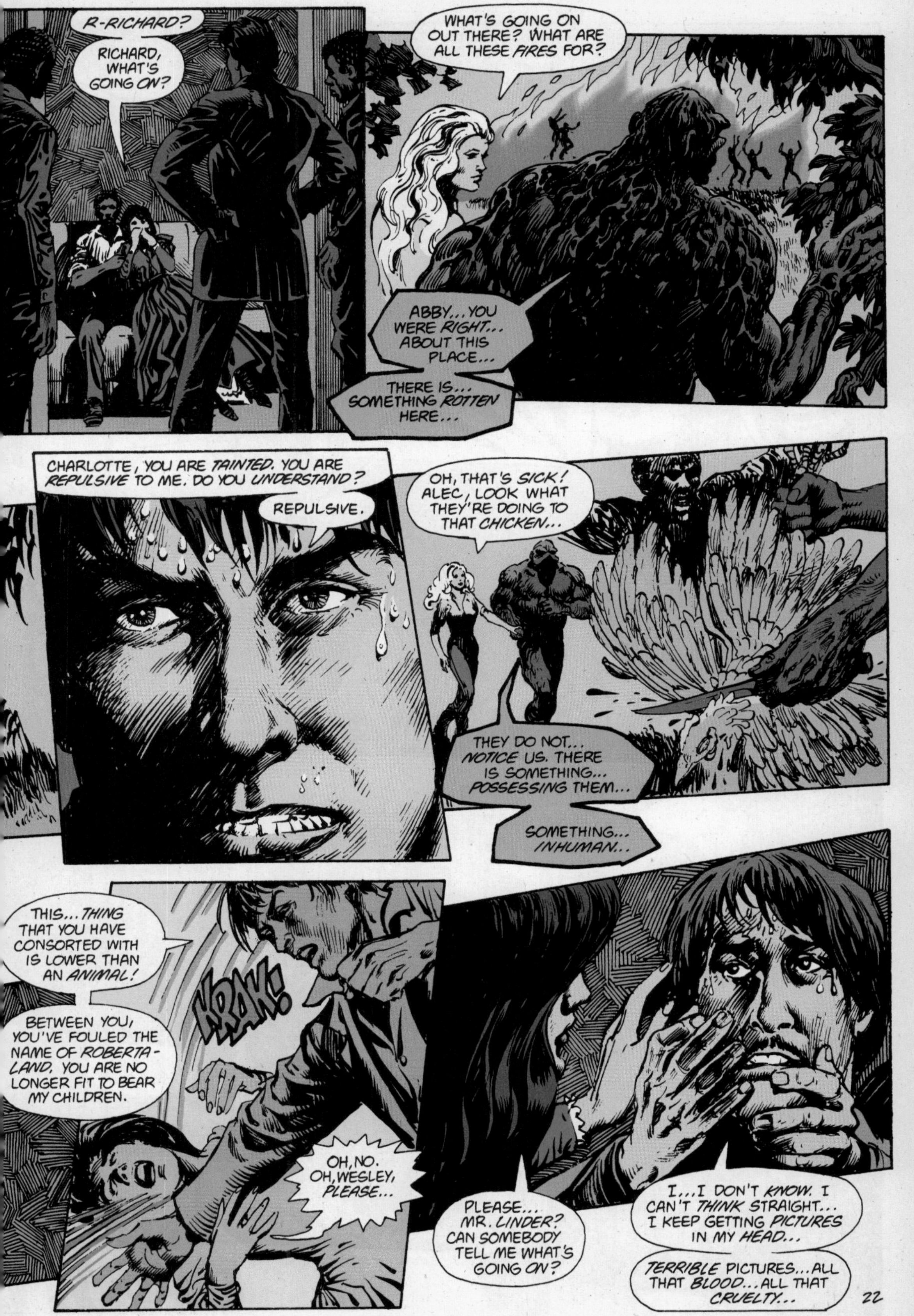
R-RICHARD?
RICHARD, WHAT'S GOING ON?
WHAT'S GOING ON OUT THERE? WHAT ARE ALL THESE FIRES FOR?
ABBY... YOU WERE RIGHT... ABOUT THIS PLACE...
THERE IS... SOMETHING ROTTEN HERE...
CHARLOTTE, YOU ARE TAINTED. YOU ARE REPULSIVE TO ME. DO YOU UNDERSTAND?
REPULSIVE.
OH, THAT'S SICK! ALEC, LOOK WHAT THEY'RE DOING TO THAT CHICKEN...
THEY DO NOT... NOTICE US. THERE IS SOMETHING... POSSESSING THEM...
SOMETHING... INHUMAN...
THIS... THING THAT YOU HAVE CONSORTED WITH IS LOWER THAN AN ANIMAL!
KRAK!
BETWEEN YOU, YOU'VE FOULED THE NAME OF ROBERTA-LAND. YOU ARE NO LONGER FIT TO BEAR MY CHILDREN.
OH, NO. OH, WESLEY, PLEASE...
PLEASE... MR. LINDER? CAN SOMEBODY TELL ME WHAT'S GOING ON?
I... I DON'T KNOW. I CAN'T THINK STRAIGHT... I KEEP GETTING PICTURES IN MY HEAD...
TERRIBLE PICTURES... ALL THAT BLOOD... ALL THAT CRUELTY...
22

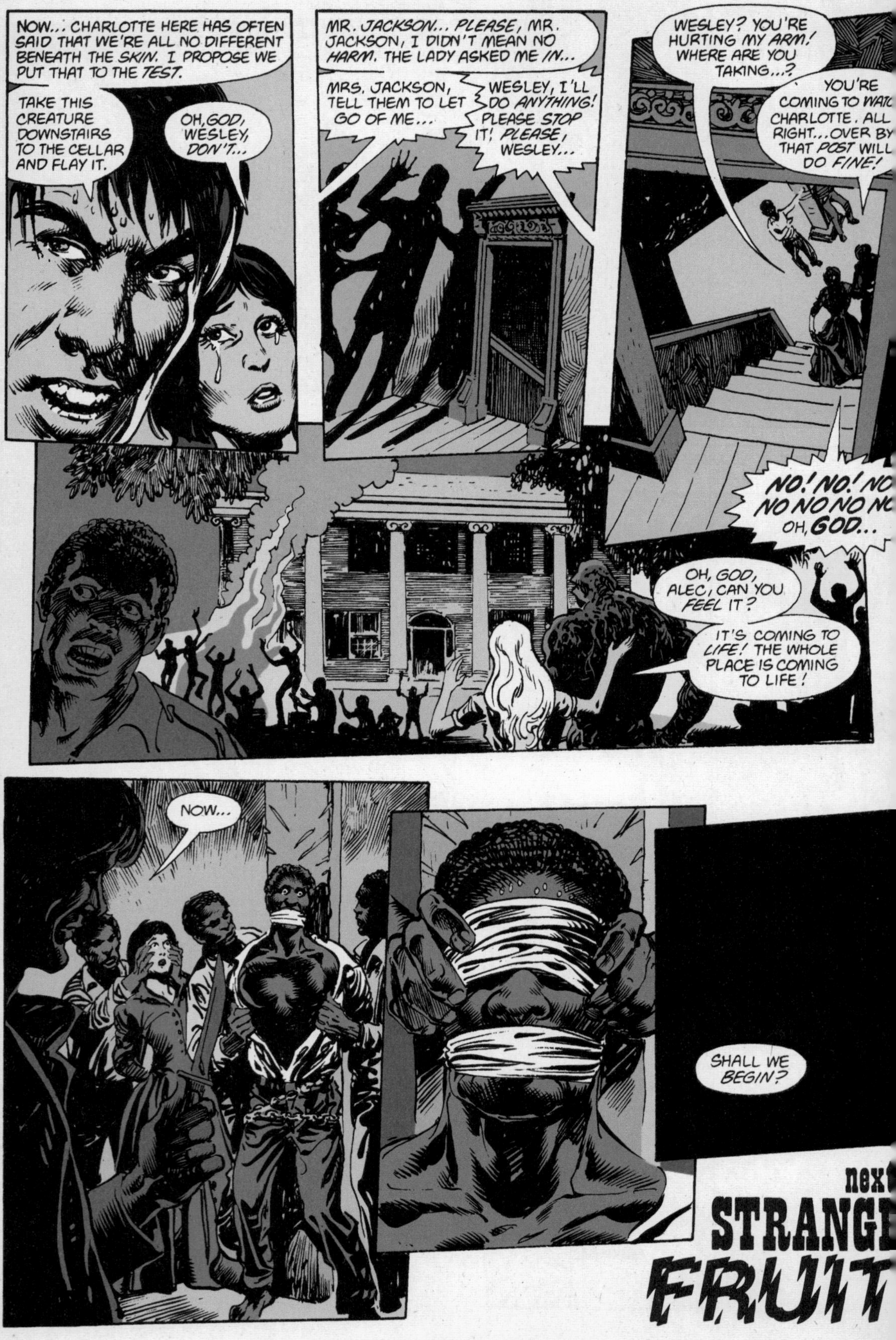
NOW... CHARLOTTE HERE HAS OFTEN SAID THAT WE'RE ALL NO DIFFERENT BENEATH THE SKIN. I PROPOSE WE PUT THAT TO THE TEST.
TAKE THIS CREATURE DOWNSTAIRS TO THE CELLAR AND FLAY IT.
OH, GOD, WESLEY, DON'T...
MR. JACKSON... PLEASE, MR. JACKSON, I DIDN'T MEAN NO HARM. THE LADY ASKED ME IN...
MRS. JACKSON, TELL THEM TO LET GO OF ME...
WESLEY, I'LL DO ANYTHING! PLEASE STOP IT! PLEASE, WESLEY...
WESLEY? YOU'RE HURTING MY ARM! WHERE ARE YOU TAKING...?
NO! NO! NO NO NO NO OH, GOD...
OH, GOD, ALEC, CAN YOU FEEL IT?
IT'S COMING TO LIFE! THE WHOLE PLACE IS COMING TO LIFE!
NOW...
SHALL WE BEGIN?

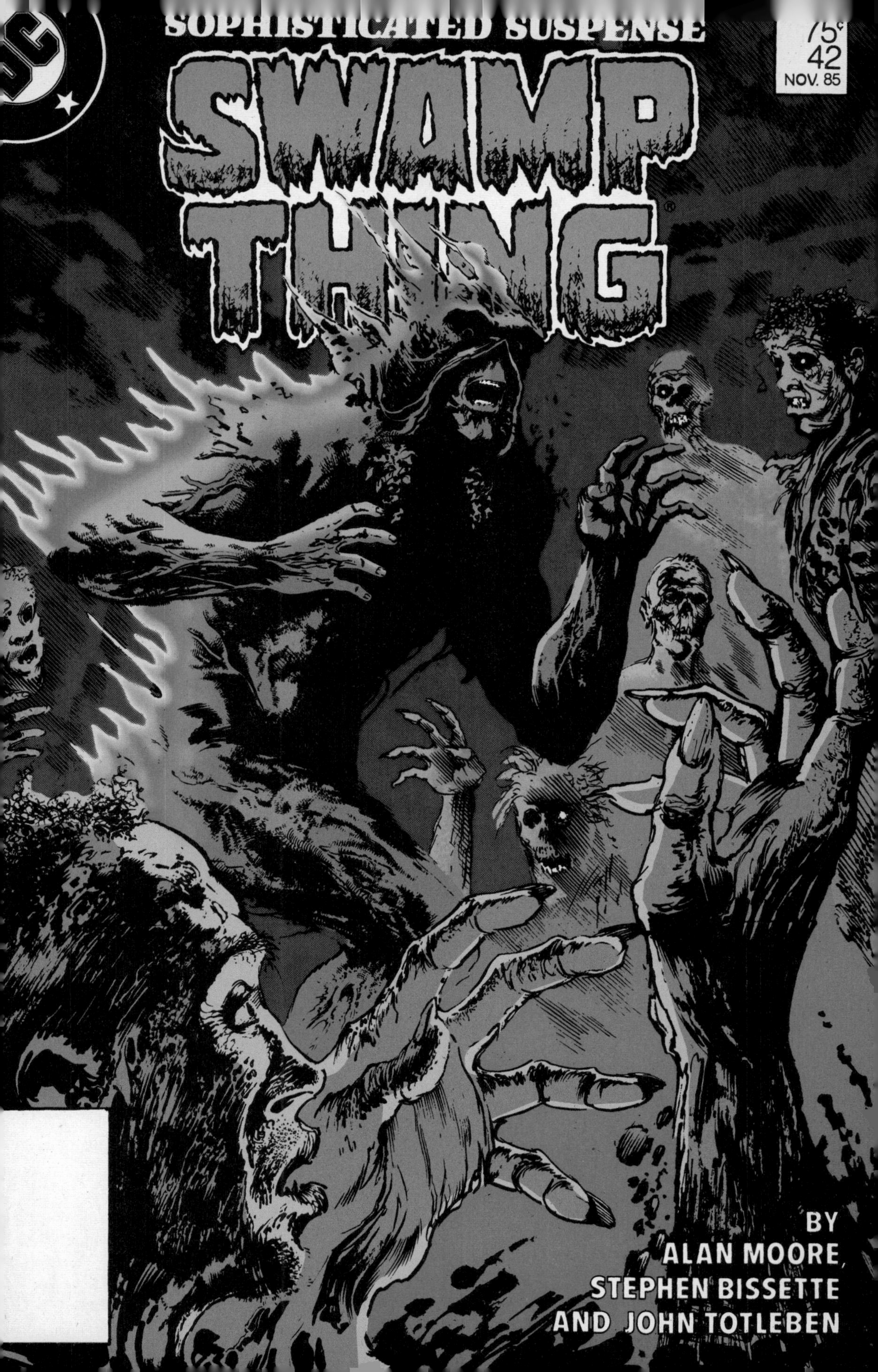
SOPHISTICATED SUSPENSE
SWAMP THING
75¢
42
NOV. 85
BY
ALAN MOORE,
STEPHEN BISSETTE
AND JOHN TOTLEBEN

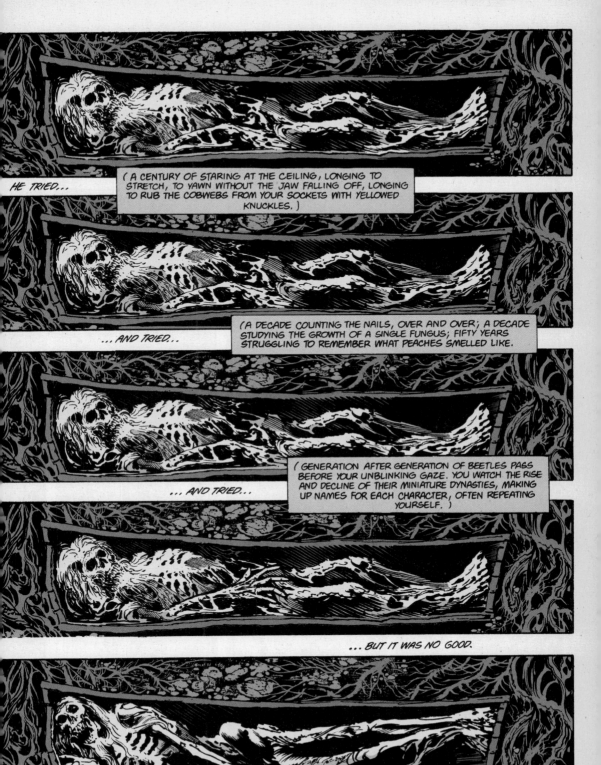

HE TRIED...

(A CENTURY OF STARING AT THE CEILING, LONGING TO STRETCH, TO YAWN WITHOUT THE JAW FALLING OFF, LONGING TO RUB THE COBWEBS FROM YOUR SOCKETS WITH YELLOWED KNUCKLES.)

...AND TRIED...

(A DECADE COUNTING THE NAILS, OVER AND OVER; A DECADE STUDYING THE GROWTH OF A SINGLE FUNGUS; FIFTY YEARS STRUGGLING TO REMEMBER WHAT PEACHES SMELLED LIKE.

... AND TRIED...

(GENERATION AFTER GENERATION OF BEETLES PASS BEFORE YOUR UNBLINKING GAZE. YOU WATCH THE RISE AND DECLINE OF THEIR MINIATURE DYNASTIES, MAKING UP NAMES FOR EACH CHARACTER, OFTEN REPEATING YOURSELF.)

... BUT IT WAS NO GOOD.

HE COULDN'T SLEEP.

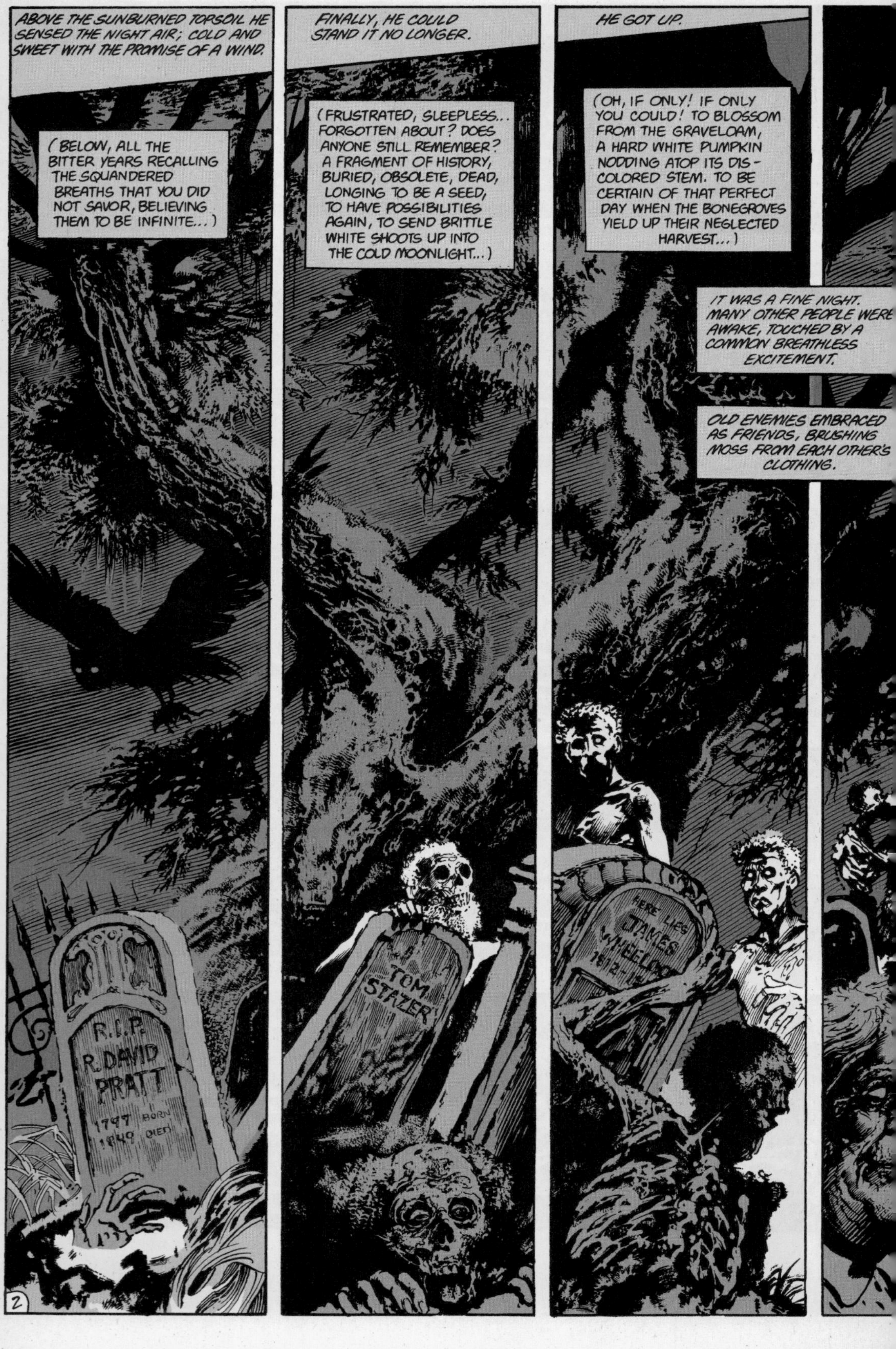
ABOVE THE SUNBURNED TOPSOIL HE SENSED THE NIGHT AIR; COLD AND SWEET WITH THE PROMISE OF A WIND.
(BELOW, ALL THE BITTER YEARS RECALLING THE SQUANDERED BREATHS THAT YOU DID NOT SAVOR, BELIEVING THEM TO BE INFINITE...)
R.I.P.
R. DAVID PRATT
1797 BORN
1840 DIED
2
FINALLY, HE COULD STAND IT NO LONGER.
(FRUSTRATED, SLEEPLESS... FORGOTTEN ABOUT? DOES ANYONE STILL REMEMBER? A FRAGMENT OF HISTORY, BURIED, OBSOLETE, DEAD, LONGING TO BE A SEED, TO HAVE POSSIBILITIES AGAIN, TO SEND BRITTLE WHITE SHOOTS UP INTO THE COLD MOONLIGHT...)
TOM STAZER
HE GOT UP.
(OH, IF ONLY! IF ONLY YOU COULD! TO BLOSSOM FROM THE GRAVELOAM, A HARD WHITE PUMPKIN NODDING ATOP ITS DIS-COLORED STEM. TO BE CERTAIN OF THAT PERFECT DAY WHEN THE BONEGROVES YIELD UP THEIR NEGLECTED HARVEST...)
HERE LIES
JAMES
IT WAS A FINE NIGHT. MANY OTHER PEOPLE WERE AWAKE, TOUCHED BY A COMMON BREATHLESS EXCITEMENT.
OLD ENEMIES EMBRACED AS FRIENDS, BRUSHING MOSS FROM EACH OTHER'S CLOTHING.

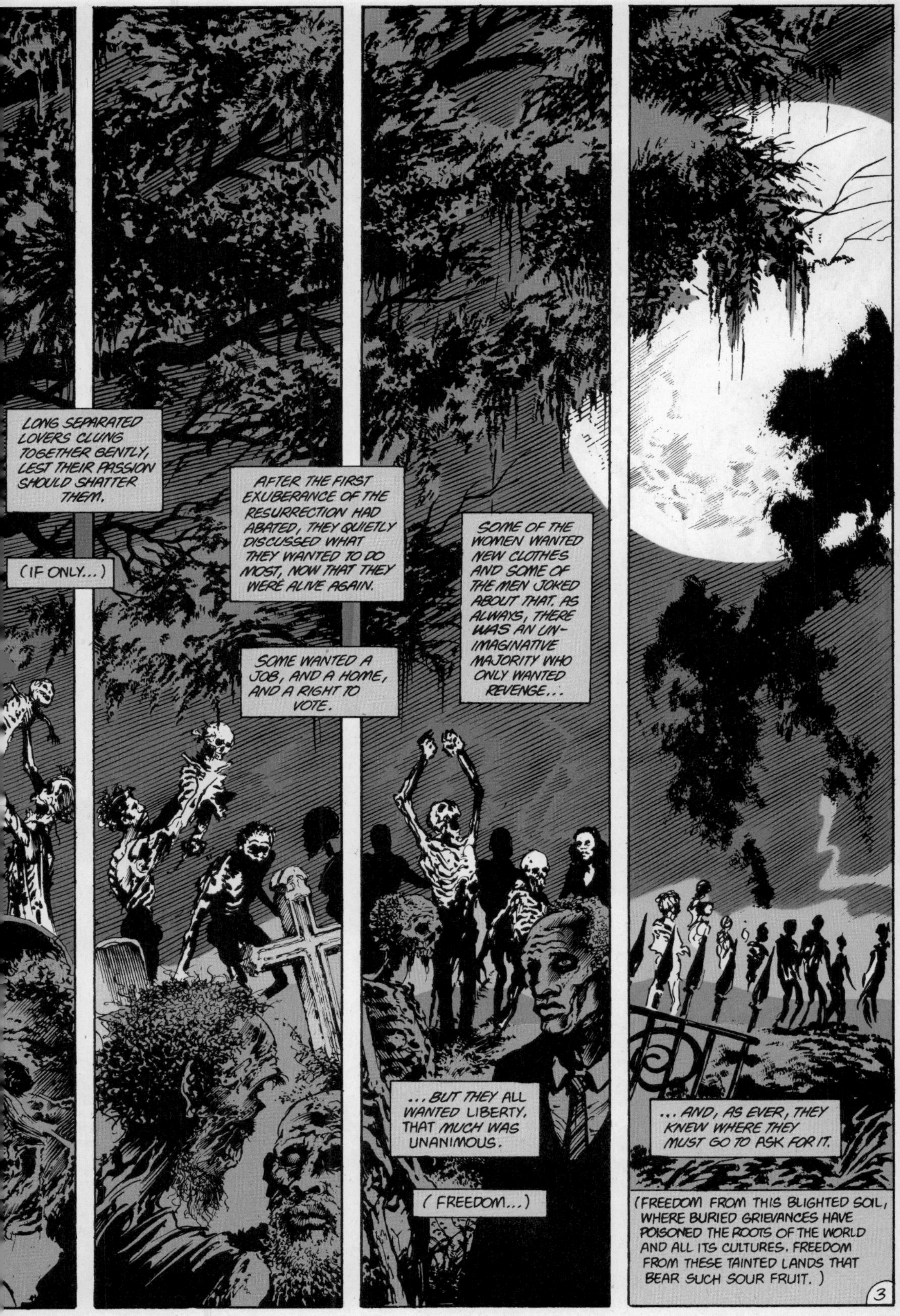
LONG SEPARATED LOVERS CLUNG TOGETHER GENTLY, LEST THEIR PASSION SHOULD SHATTER THEM.
(IF ONLY...)
AFTER THE FIRST EXUBERANCE OF THE RESURRECTION HAD ABATED, THEY QUIETLY DISCUSSED WHAT THEY WANTED TO DO MOST, NOW THAT THEY WERE ALIVE AGAIN.
SOME WANTED A JOB, AND A HOME, AND A RIGHT TO VOTE.
SOME OF THE WOMEN WANTED NEW CLOTHES AND SOME OF THE MEN JOKED ABOUT THAT. AS ALWAYS, THERE WAS AN UNIMAGINATIVE MAJORITY WHO ONLY WANTED REVENGE...
...BUT THEY ALL WANTED LIBERTY. THAT MUCH WAS UNANIMOUS.
(FREEDOM...)
...AND, AS EVER, THEY KNEW WHERE THEY MUST GO TO ASK FOR IT.
(FREEDOM FROM THIS BLIGHTED SOIL, WHERE BURIED GRIEVANCES HAVE POISONED THE ROOTS OF THE WORLD AND ALL ITS CULTURES. FREEDOM FROM THESE TAINTED LANDS THAT BEAR SUCH SOUR FRUIT.)
3

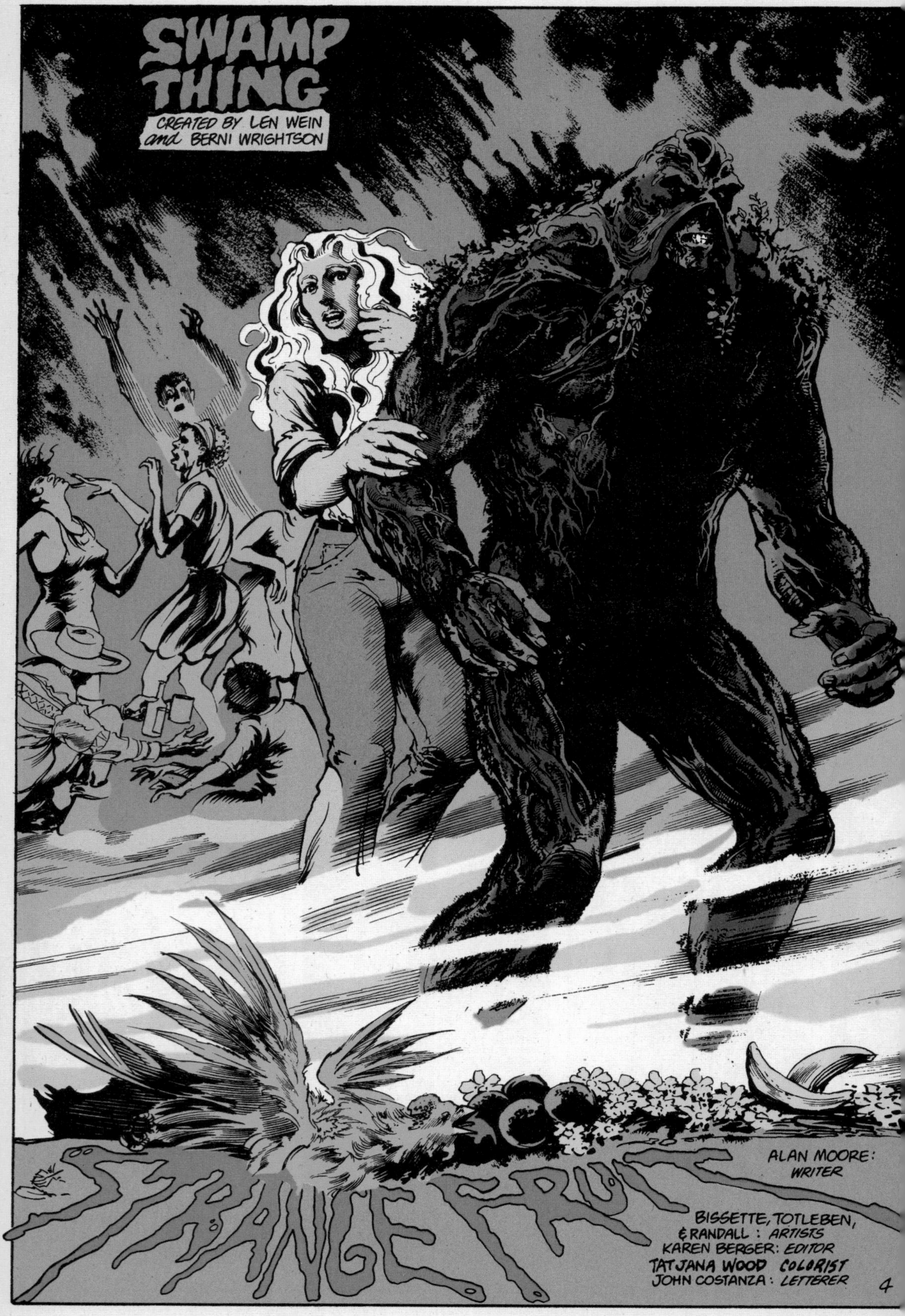
SWAMP THING
CREATED BY LEN WEIN and BERNI WRIGHTSON
STRANGE FRUIT
ALAN MOORE: WRITER
BISSETTE, TOTLEBEN, & RANDALL : ARTISTS
KAREN BERGER: EDITOR
TATJANA WOOD COLORIST
JOHN COSTANZA : LETTERER
4

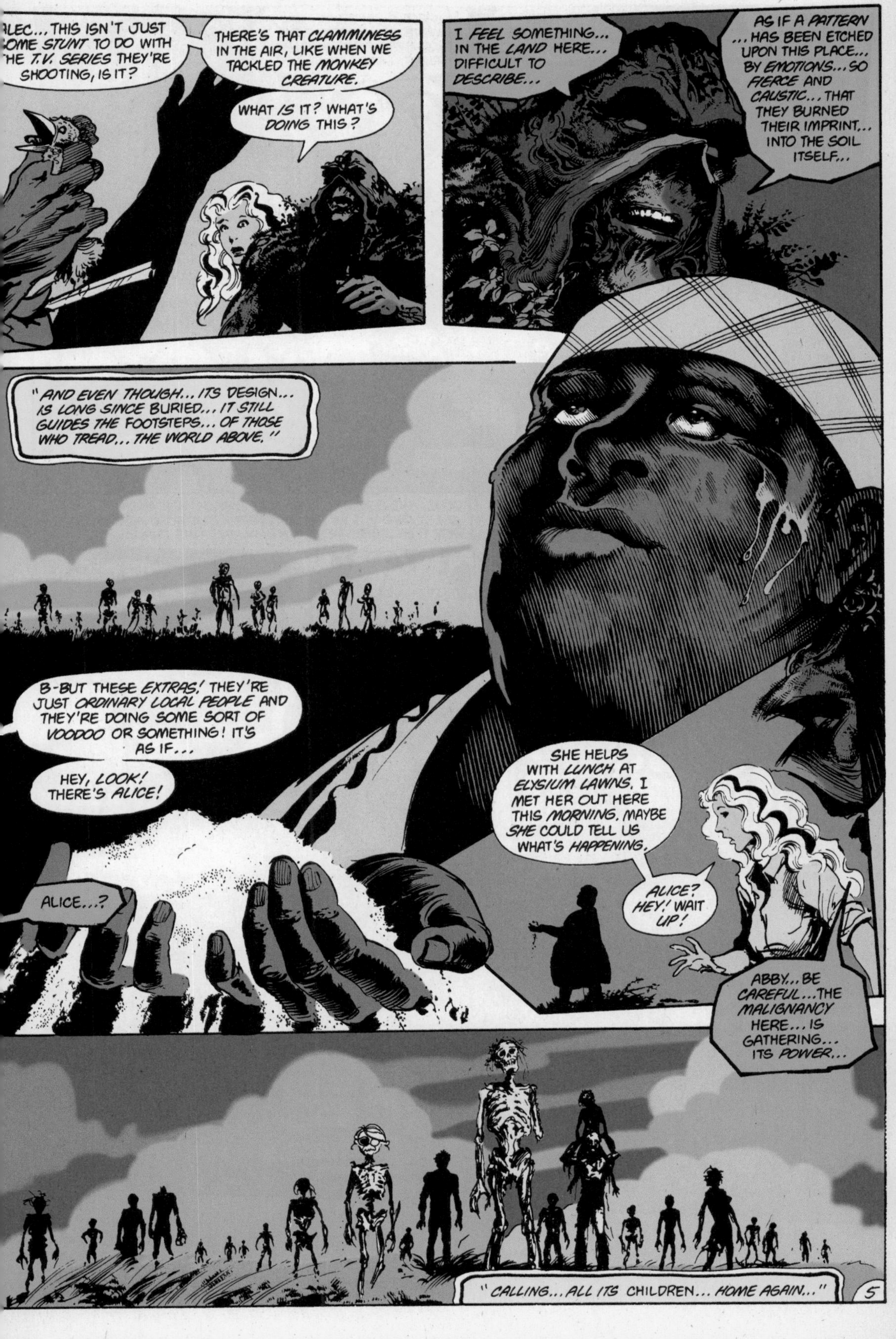
ALEC... THIS ISN'T JUST SOME STUNT TO DO WITH THE T.V. SERIES THEY'RE SHOOTING, IS IT?
THERE'S THAT CLAMMINESS IN THE AIR, LIKE WHEN WE TACKLED THE MONKEY CREATURE.
WHAT IS IT? WHAT'S DOING THIS?
I FEEL SOMETHING... IN THE LAND HERE... DIFFICULT TO DESCRIBE...
AS IF A PATTERN... HAS BEEN ETCHED UPON THIS PLACE... BY EMOTIONS... SO FIERCE AND CAUSTIC... THAT THEY BURNED THEIR IMPRINT... INTO THE SOIL ITSELF...
"AND EVEN THOUGH... ITS DESIGN... IS LONG SINCE BURIED... IT STILL GUIDES THE FOOTSTEPS... OF THOSE WHO TREAD... THE WORLD ABOVE."
B-BUT THESE EXTRAS! THEY'RE JUST ORDINARY LOCAL PEOPLE AND THEY'RE DOING SOME SORT OF VOODOO OR SOMETHING! IT'S AS IF...
HEY, LOOK! THERE'S ALICE!
SHE HELPS WITH LUNCH AT ELYSIUM LAWNS. I MET HER OUT HERE THIS MORNING. MAYBE SHE COULD TELL US WHAT'S HAPPENING.
ALICE...?
ALICE? HEY! WAIT UP!
ABBY... BE CAREFUL... THE MALIGNANCY HERE... IS GATHERING... ITS POWER...
"CALLING... ALL ITS CHILDREN... HOME AGAIN..."
5

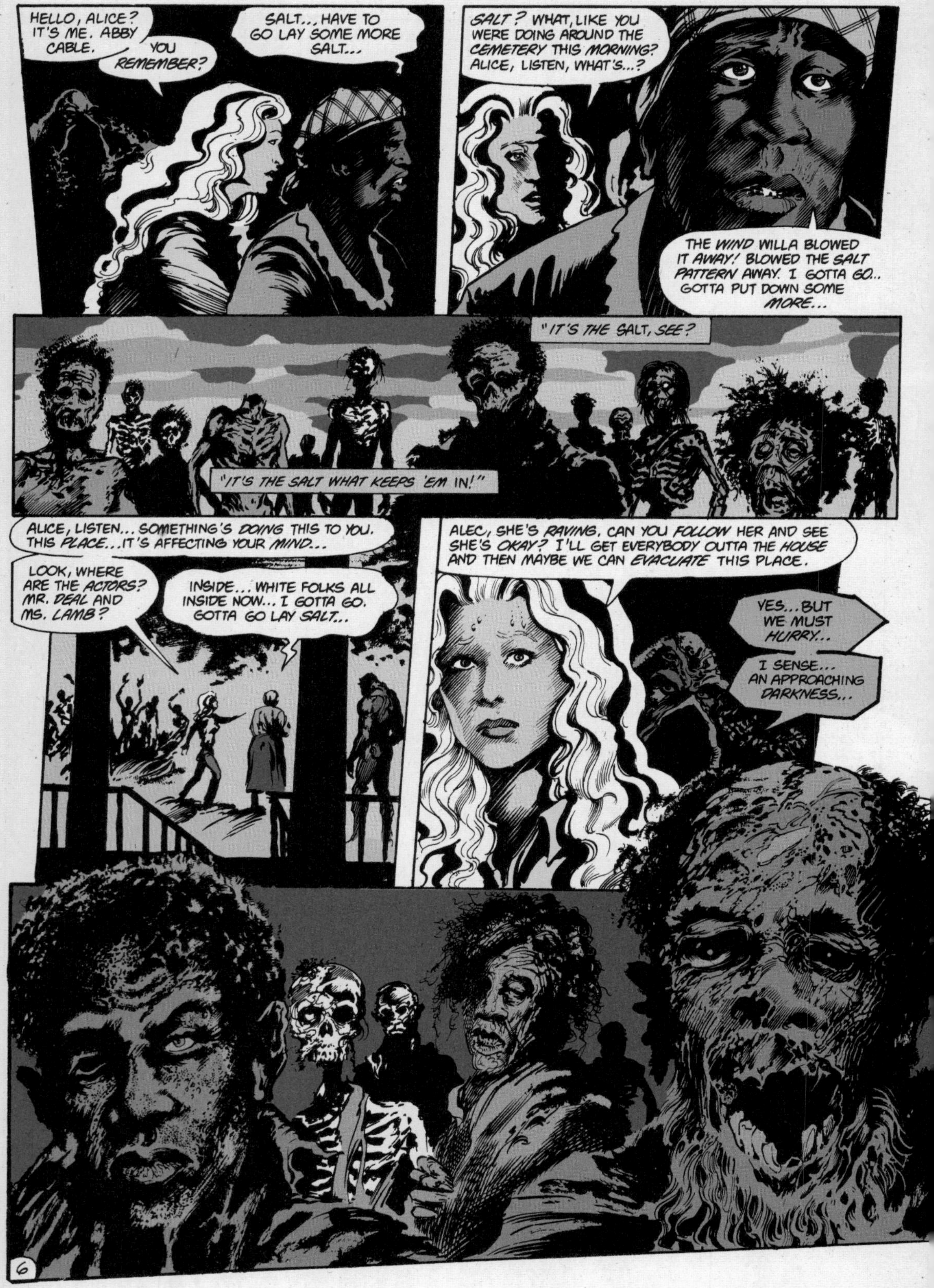
HELLO, ALICE? IT'S ME. ABBY CABLE.
YOU REMEMBER?
SALT... HAVE TO GO LAY SOME MORE SALT...
SALT? WHAT, LIKE YOU WERE DOING AROUND THE CEMETERY THIS MORNING? ALICE, LISTEN, WHAT'S...?
THE WIND WILLA BLOWED IT AWAY! BLOWED THE SALT PATTERN AWAY. I GOTTA GO... GOTTA PUT DOWN SOME MORE...
"IT'S THE SALT, SEE?
"IT'S THE SALT WHAT KEEPS 'EM IN!"
ALICE, LISTEN... SOMETHING'S DOING THIS TO YOU. THIS PLACE... IT'S AFFECTING YOUR MIND...
LOOK, WHERE ARE THE ACTORS? MR. DEAL AND MS. LAMB?
INSIDE... WHITE FOLKS ALL INSIDE NOW... I GOTTA GO. GOTTA GO LAY SALT...
ALEC, SHE'S RAVING. CAN YOU FOLLOW HER AND SEE SHE'S OKAY? I'LL GET EVERYBODY OUTTA THE HOUSE AND THEN MAYBE WE CAN EVACUATE THIS PLACE.
YES... BUT WE MUST HURRY...
I SENSE... AN APPROACHING DARKNESS...
6

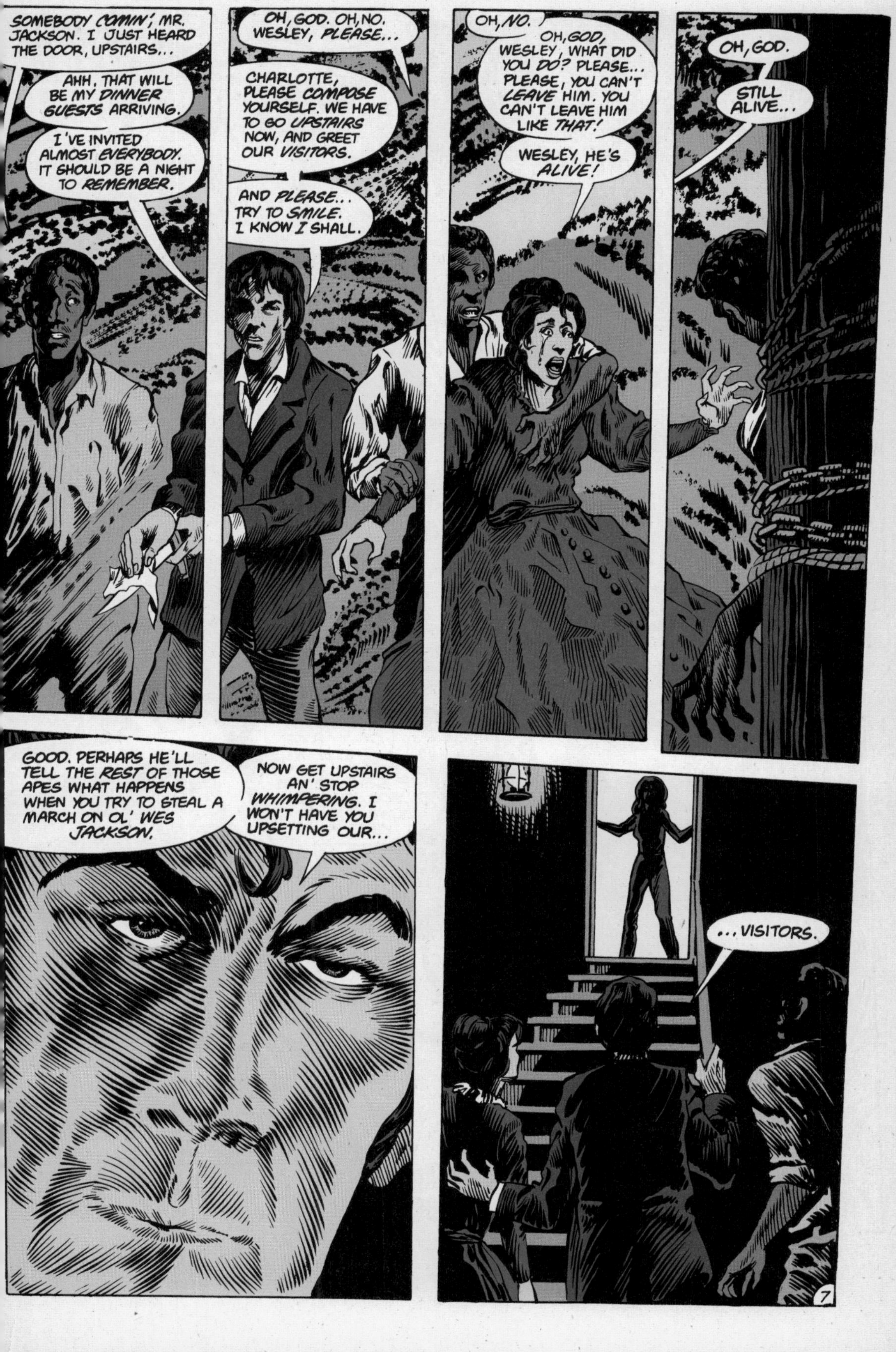
SOMEBODY COMIN', MR. JACKSON. I JUST HEARD THE DOOR, UPSTAIRS...
AHH, THAT WILL BE MY DINNER GUESTS ARRIVING.
I'VE INVITED ALMOST EVERYBODY. IT SHOULD BE A NIGHT TO REMEMBER.
OH, GOD. OH, NO. WESLEY, PLEASE...
CHARLOTTE, PLEASE COMPOSE YOURSELF. WE HAVE TO GO UPSTAIRS NOW, AND GREET OUR VISITORS.
AND PLEASE... TRY TO SMILE. I KNOW I SHALL.
OH, NO.
OH, GOD, WESLEY, WHAT DID YOU DO? PLEASE... PLEASE, YOU CAN'T LEAVE HIM. YOU CAN'T LEAVE HIM LIKE THAT!
WESLEY, HE'S ALIVE!
OH, GOD.
STILL ALIVE...
GOOD. PERHAPS HE'LL TELL THE REST OF THOSE APES WHAT HAPPENS WHEN YOU TRY TO STEAL A MARCH ON OL' WES JACKSON.
NOW GET UPSTAIRS AN' STOP WHIMPERING. I WON'T HAVE YOU UPSETTING OUR...
...VISITORS.
7

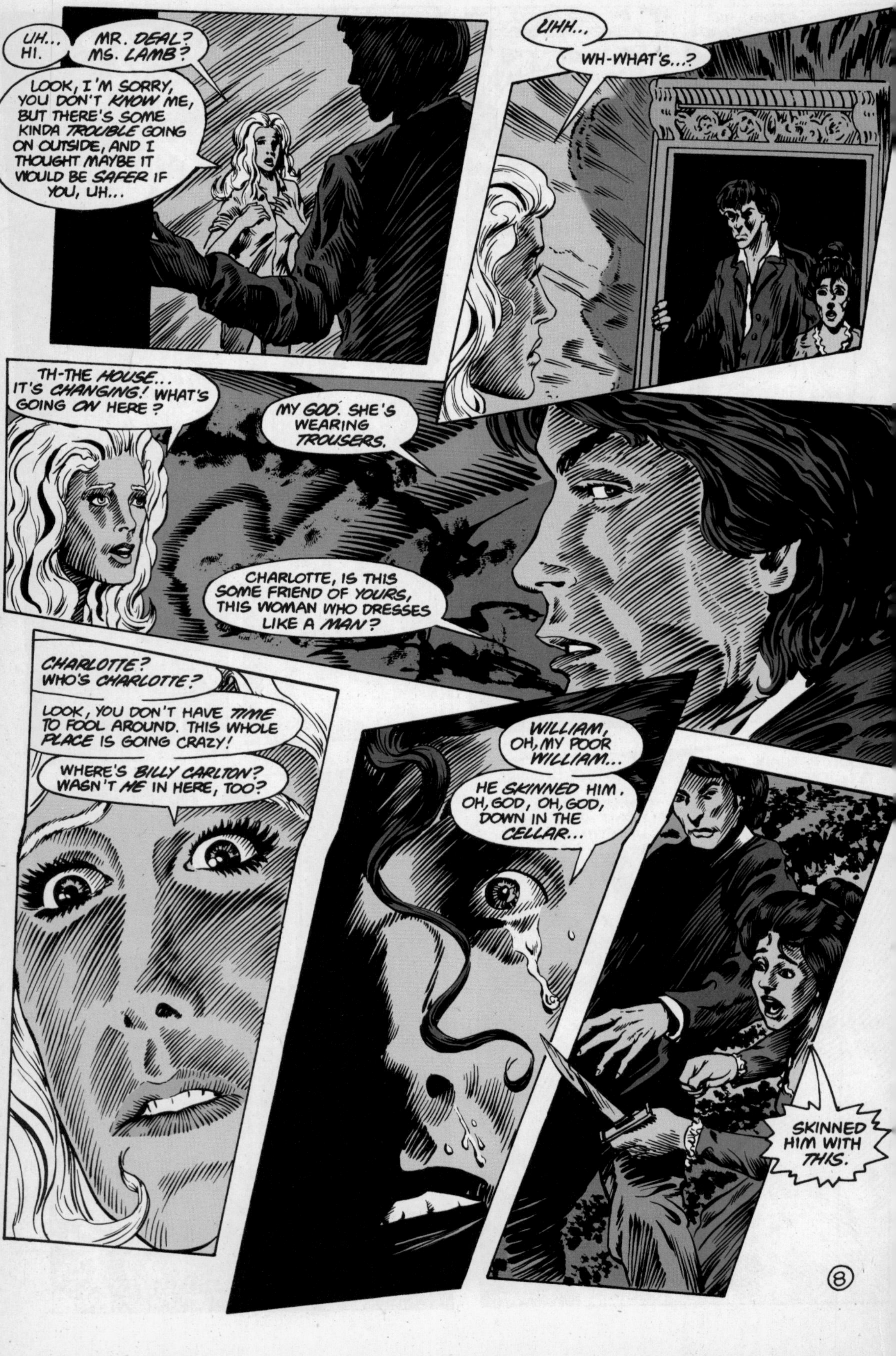
UH... HI.
MR. DEAL? MS. LAMB?
LOOK, I'M SORRY, YOU DON'T KNOW ME, BUT THERE'S SOME KINDA TROUBLE GOING ON OUTSIDE, AND I THOUGHT MAYBE IT WOULD BE SAFER IF YOU, UH...
UHH...
WH-WHAT'S...?
TH-THE HOUSE... IT'S CHANGING! WHAT'S GOING ON HERE?
MY GOD. SHE'S WEARING TROUSERS.
CHARLOTTE, IS THIS SOME FRIEND OF YOURS, THIS WOMAN WHO DRESSES LIKE A MAN?
CHARLOTTE? WHO'S CHARLOTTE?
LOOK, YOU DON'T HAVE TIME TO FOOL AROUND. THIS WHOLE PLACE IS GOING CRAZY!
WHERE'S BILLY CARLTON? WASN'T HE IN HERE, TOO?
WILLIAM, OH, MY POOR WILLIAM...
HE SKINNED HIM. OH, GOD, OH, GOD, DOWN IN THE CELLAR...
SKINNED HIM WITH THIS.
8

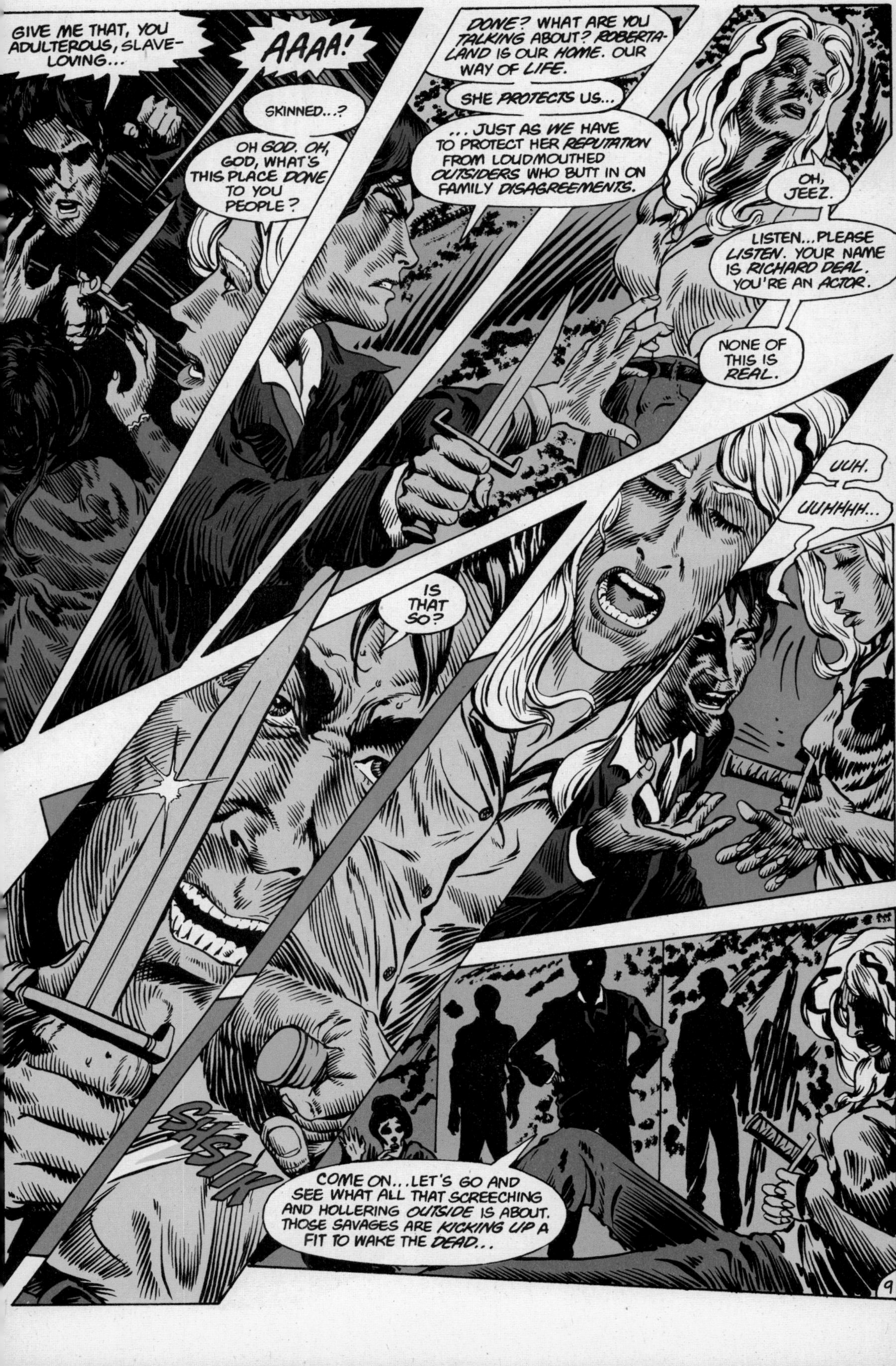
GIVE ME THAT, YOU ADULTEROUS, SLAVE-LOVING...
AAAA!
SKINNED...?
OH GOD. OH, GOD, WHAT'S THIS PLACE DONE TO YOU PEOPLE?
DONE? WHAT ARE YOU TALKING ABOUT? ROBERTA-LAND IS OUR HOME. OUR WAY OF LIFE.
SHE PROTECTS US...
...JUST AS WE HAVE TO PROTECT HER REPUTATION FROM LOUDMOUTHED OUTSIDERS WHO BUTT IN ON FAMILY DISAGREEMENTS.
OH, JEEZ.
LISTEN...PLEASE LISTEN. YOUR NAME IS RICHARD DEAL. YOU'RE AN ACTOR.
NONE OF THIS IS REAL.
IS THAT SO?
UUH.
UUHHHH...
SHSHK
COME ON...LET'S GO AND SEE WHAT ALL THAT SCREECHING AND HOLLERING OUTSIDE IS ABOUT. THOSE SAVAGES ARE KICKING UP A FIT TO WAKE THE DEAD...
9

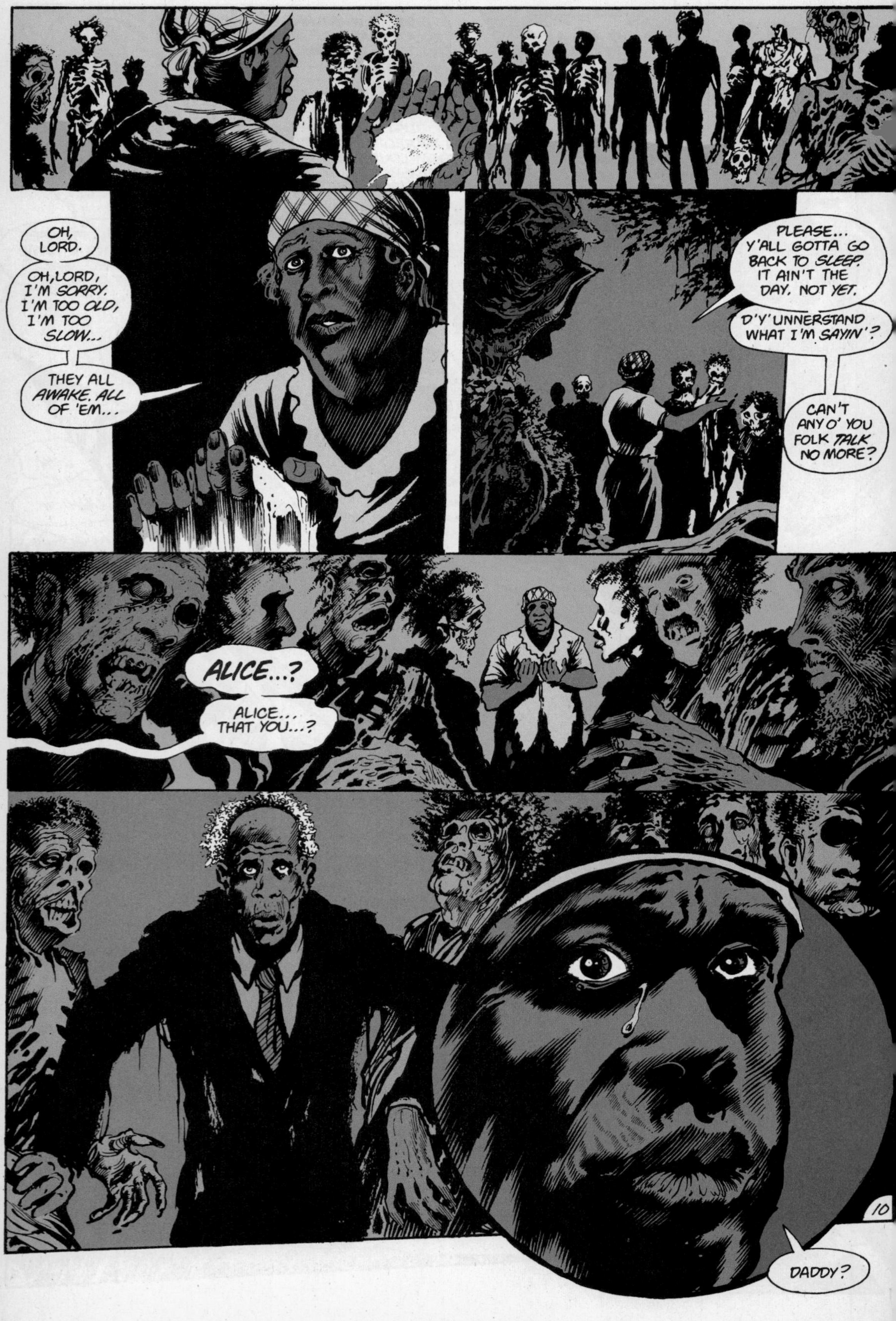
OH, LORD.
OH, LORD, I'M SORRY. I'M TOO OLD, I'M TOO SLOW...
THEY ALL AWAKE. ALL OF 'EM...
PLEASE... Y'ALL GOTTA GO BACK TO SLEEP. IT AIN'T THE DAY. NOT YET.
D'Y'UNNERSTAND WHAT I'M SAYIN'?
CAN'T ANY O' YOU FOLK TALK NO MORE?
ALICE...?
ALICE... THAT YOU...?
10
DADDY?

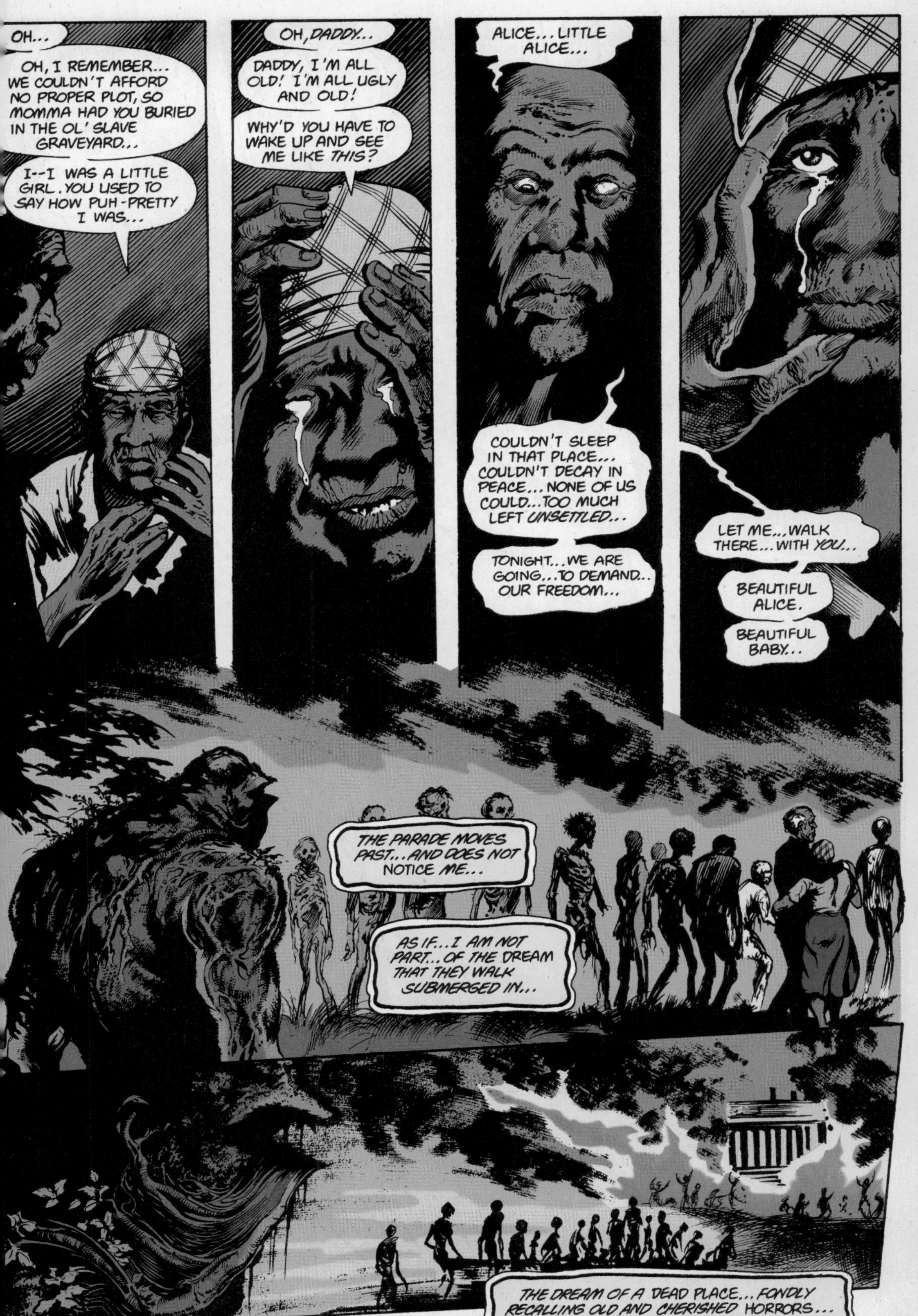
OH...
OH, I REMEMBER... WE COULDN'T AFFORD NO PROPER PLOT, SO MOMMA HAD YOU BURIED IN THE OL' SLAVE GRAVEYARD...
I--I WAS A LITTLE GIRL. YOU USED TO SAY HOW PUH-PRETTY I WAS...
OH, DADDY...
DADDY, I'M ALL OLD! I'M ALL UGLY AND OLD!
WHY'D YOU HAVE TO WAKE UP AND SEE ME LIKE THIS?
ALICE... LITTLE ALICE...
COULDN'T SLEEP IN THAT PLACE... COULDN'T DECAY IN PEACE... NONE OF US COULD... TOO MUCH LEFT UNSETTLED...
TONIGHT... WE ARE GOING... TO DEMAND... OUR FREEDOM...
LET ME... WALK THERE... WITH YOU...
BEAUTIFUL ALICE.
BEAUTIFUL BABY...
THE PARADE MOVES PAST... AND DOES NOT NOTICE ME...
AS IF... I AM NOT PART... OF THE DREAM THAT THEY WALK SUBMERGED IN...
THE DREAM OF A DEAD PLACE... FONDLY RECALLING OLD AND CHERISHED HORRORS...

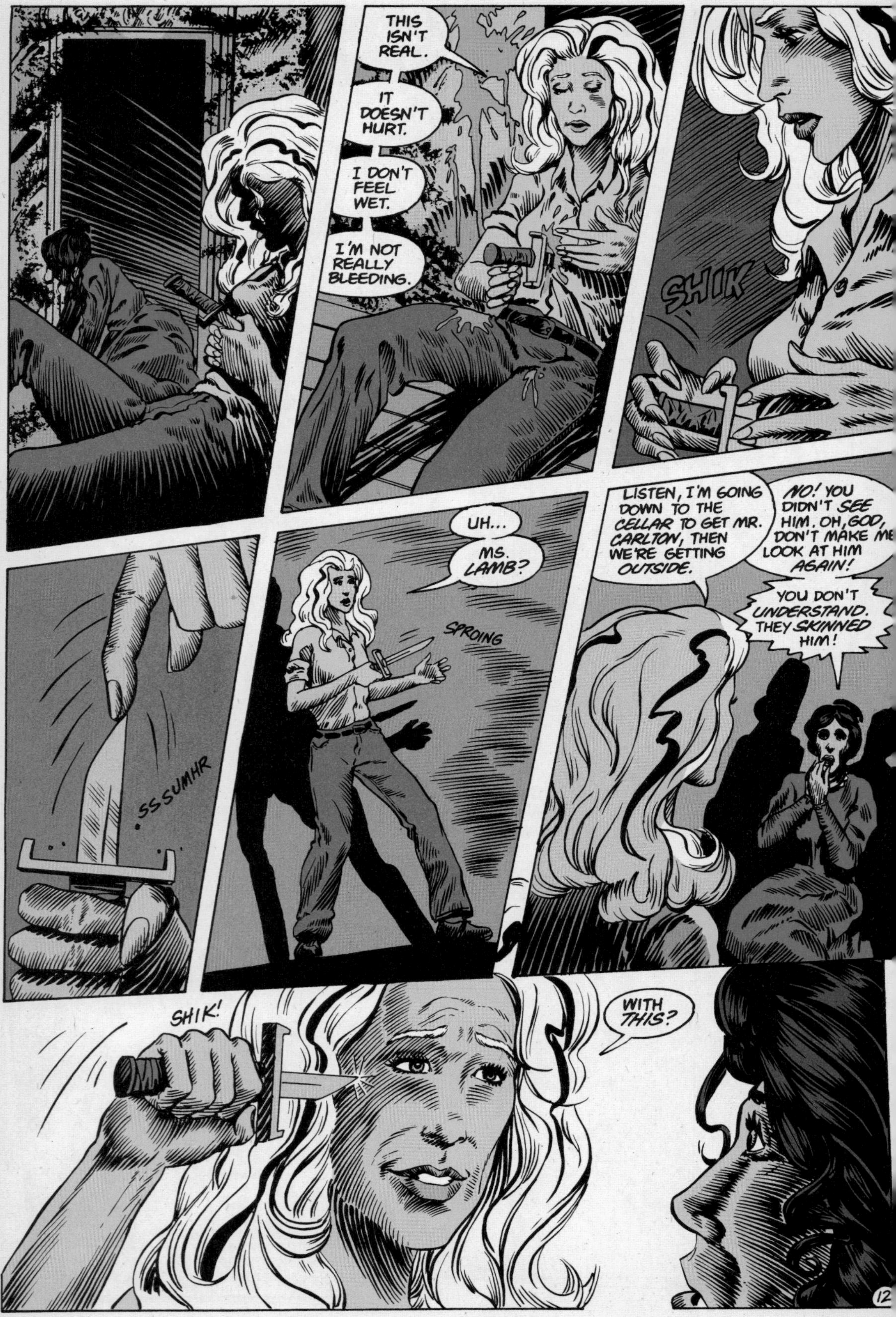

THIS ISN'T REAL.
IT DOESN'T HURT.
I DON'T FEEL WET.
I'M NOT REALLY BLEEDING.
SHIK
UH...
MS. LAMB?
SPROING
LISTEN, I'M GOING DOWN TO THE CELLAR TO GET MR. CARLTON, THEN WE'RE GETTING OUTSIDE.
NO! YOU DIDN'T SEE HIM. OH, GOD, DON'T MAKE ME LOOK AT HIM AGAIN!
YOU DON'T UNDERSTAND. THEY SKINNED HIM!
SSSUMHR
SHIK!
WITH THIS?
12

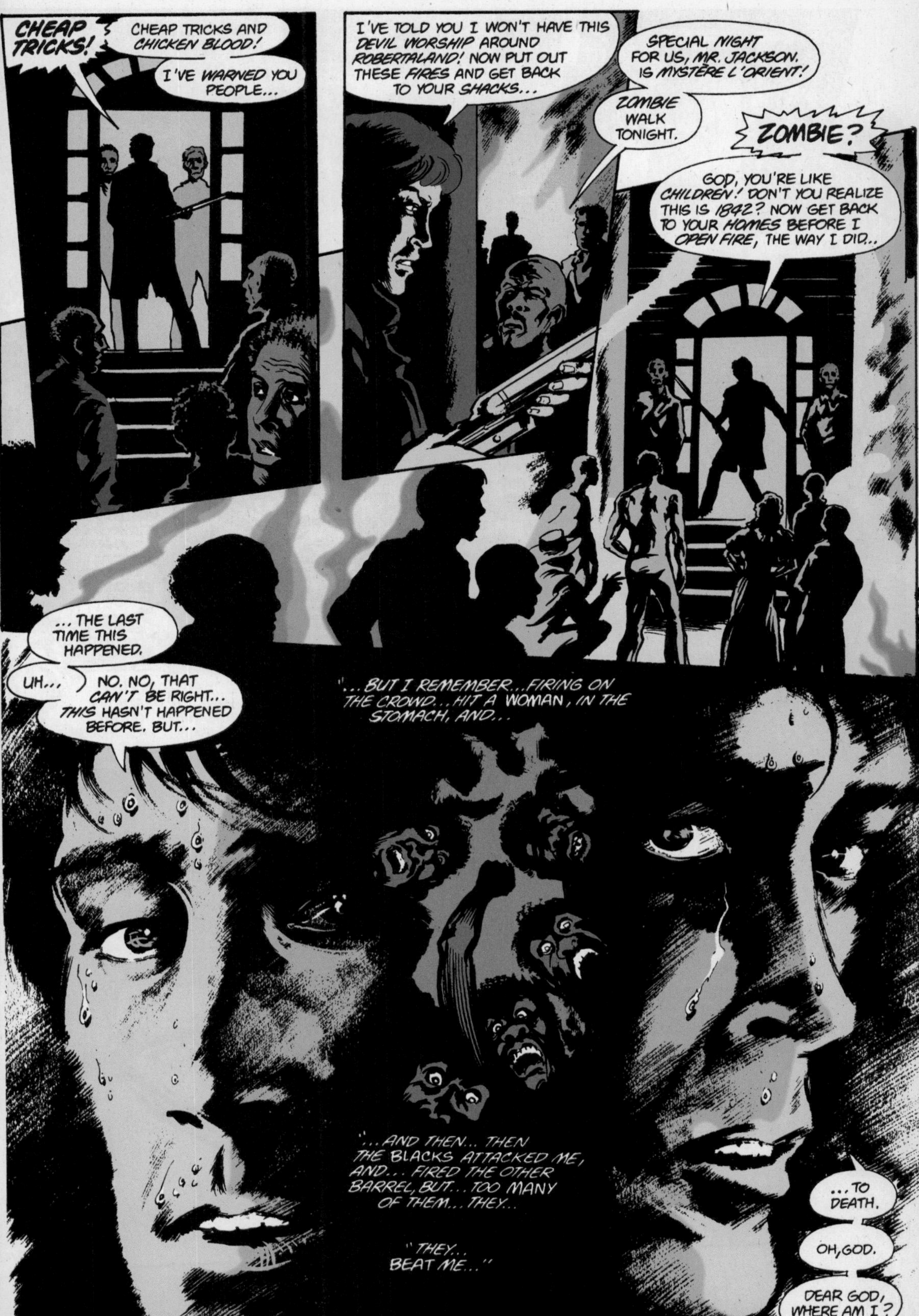
CHEAP TRICKS!
CHEAP TRICKS AND CHICKEN BLOOD!
I'VE WARNED YOU PEOPLE...
I'VE TOLD YOU I WON'T HAVE THIS DEVIL WORSHIP AROUND ROBERTALAND! NOW PUT OUT THESE FIRES AND GET BACK TO YOUR SHACKS...
SPECIAL NIGHT FOR US, MR. JACKSON. IS MYSTÈRE L'ORIENT!
ZOMBIE WALK TONIGHT.
ZOMBIE?
GOD, YOU'RE LIKE CHILDREN! DON'T YOU REALIZE THIS IS 1842? NOW GET BACK TO YOUR HOMES BEFORE I OPEN FIRE, THE WAY I DID...
... THE LAST TIME THIS HAPPENED.
UH...
NO. NO, THAT CAN'T BE RIGHT... THIS HASN'T HAPPENED BEFORE. BUT...
"... BUT I REMEMBER... FIRING ON THE CROWD... HIT A WOMAN, IN THE STOMACH, AND...
"... AND THEN... THEN THE BLACKS ATTACKED ME, AND... FIRED THE OTHER BARREL, BUT... TOO MANY OF THEM... THEY...
"THEY... BEAT ME..."
... TO DEATH.
OH, GOD.
DEAR GOD, WHERE AM I?
13

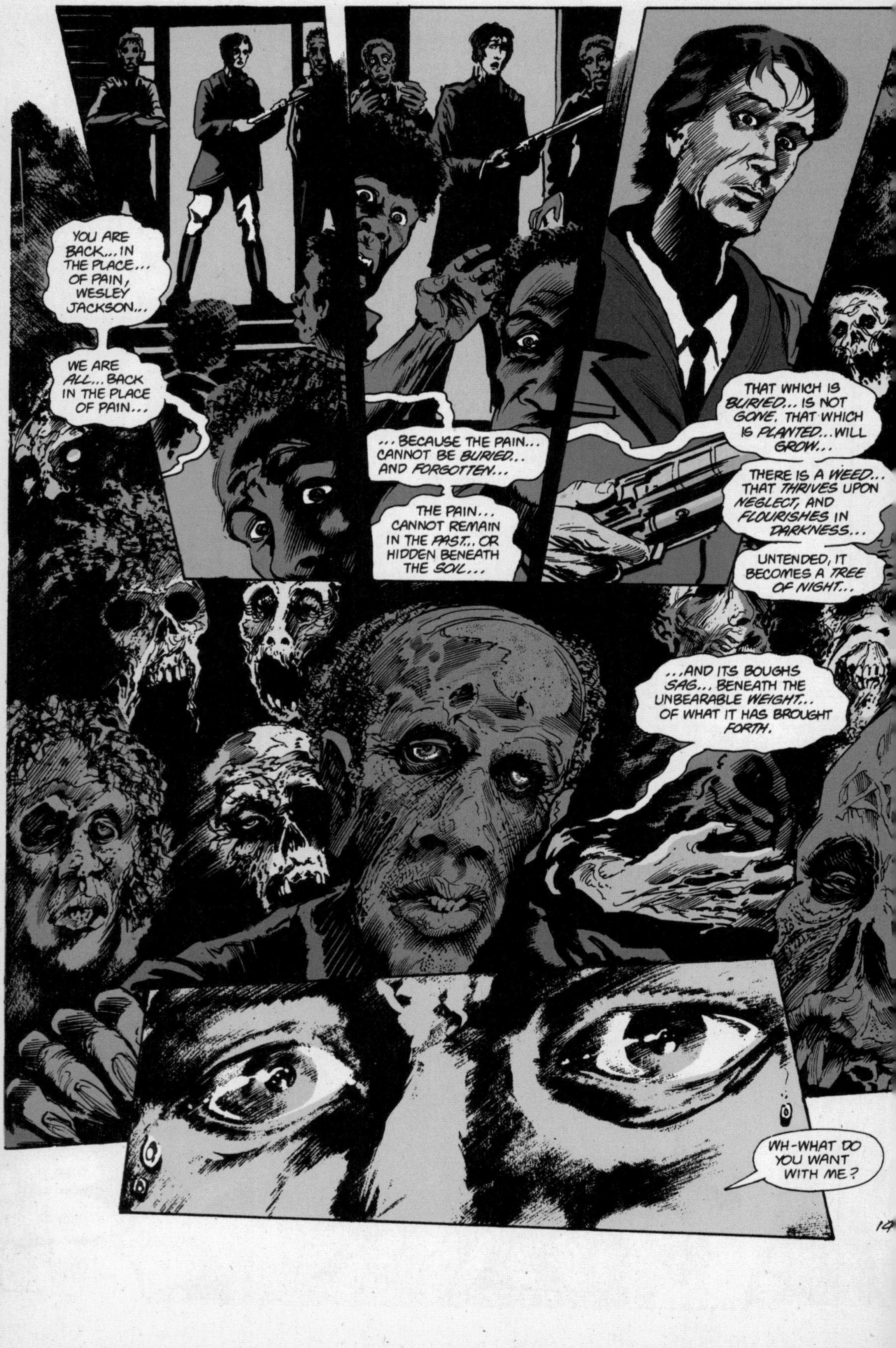
YOU ARE BACK... IN THE PLACE... OF PAIN, WESLEY JACKSON...
WE ARE ALL... BACK IN THE PLACE OF PAIN...
...BECAUSE THE PAIN... CANNOT BE BURIED... AND FORGOTTEN...
THE PAIN... CANNOT REMAIN IN THE PAST... OR HIDDEN BENEATH THE SOIL...
THAT WHICH IS BURIED... IS NOT GONE. THAT WHICH IS PLANTED... WILL GROW...
THERE IS A WEED... THAT THRIVES UPON NEGLECT, AND FLOURISHES IN DARKNESS...
UNTENDED, IT BECOMES A TREE OF NIGHT...
...AND ITS BOUGHS SAG... BENEATH THE UNBEARABLE WEIGHT... OF WHAT IT HAS BROUGHT FORTH.
WH-WHAT DO YOU WANT WITH ME?
14

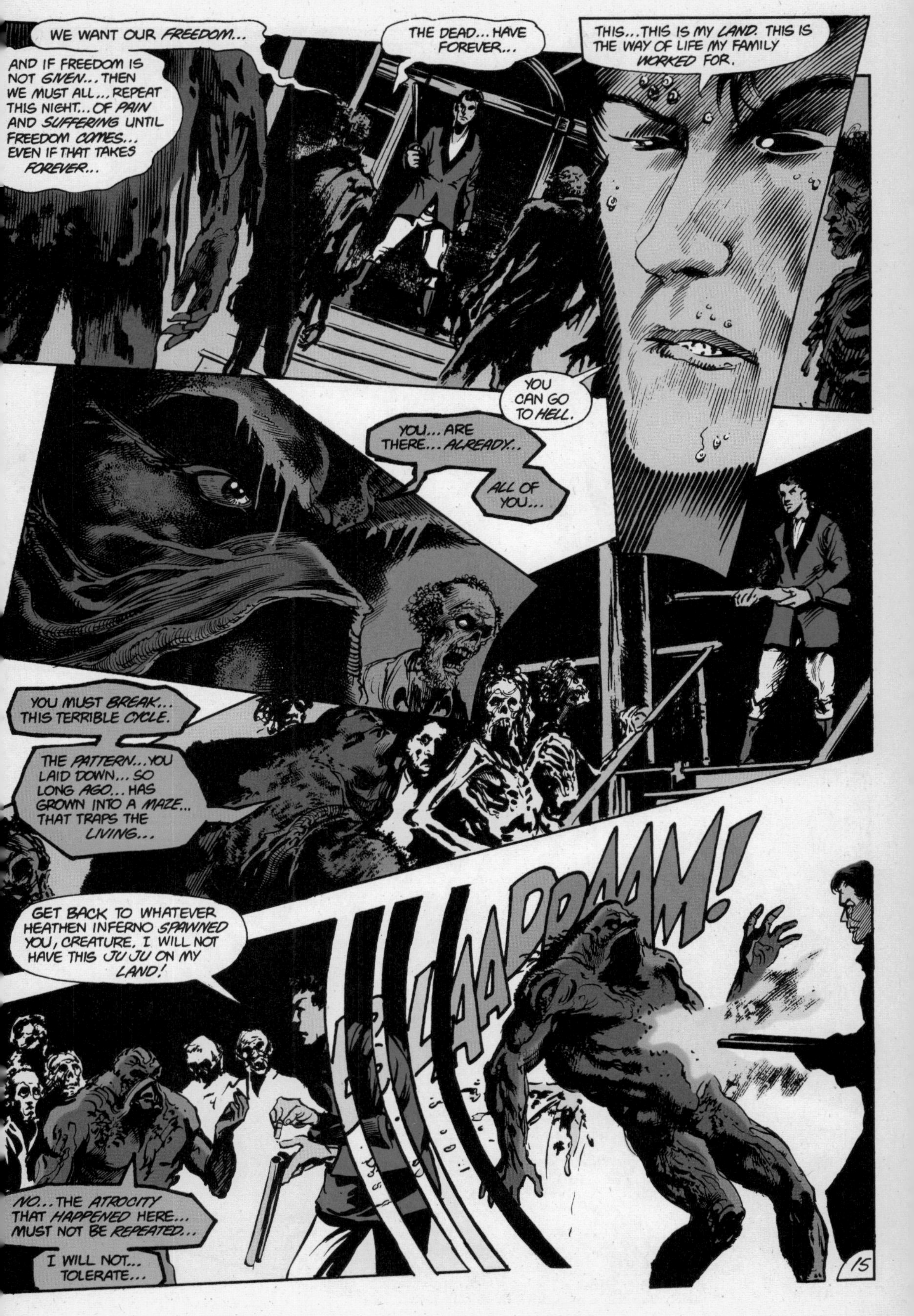
WE WANT OUR FREEDOM...
AND IF FREEDOM IS NOT GIVEN... THEN WE MUST ALL... REPEAT THIS NIGHT... OF PAIN AND SUFFERING UNTIL FREEDOM COMES... EVEN IF THAT TAKES FOREVER...
THE DEAD... HAVE FOREVER...
THIS... THIS IS MY LAND. THIS IS THE WAY OF LIFE MY FAMILY WORKED FOR.
YOU CAN GO TO HELL.
YOU... ARE THERE... ALREADY...
ALL OF YOU...
YOU MUST BREAK... THIS TERRIBLE CYCLE.
THE PATTERN... YOU LAID DOWN... SO LONG AGO... HAS GROWN INTO A MAZE... THAT TRAPS THE LIVING...
GET BACK TO WHATEVER HEATHEN INFERNO SPAWNED YOU, CREATURE. I WILL NOT HAVE THIS JU JU ON MY LAND!
WHADDAAM!
NO... THE ATROCITY THAT HAPPENED HERE... MUST NOT BE REPEATED...
I WILL NOT... TOLERATE...
15

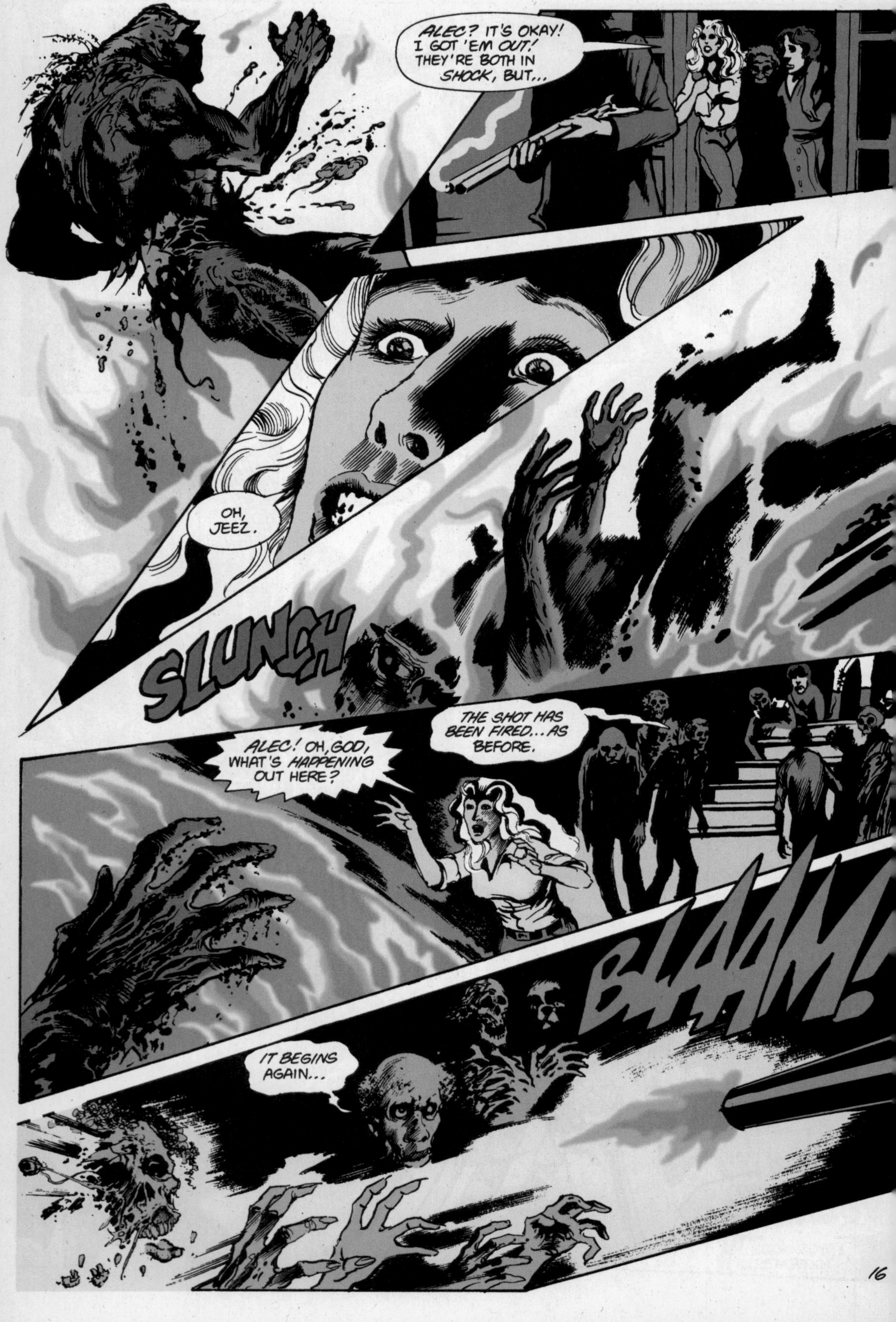
ALEC? IT'S OKAY! I GOT 'EM OUT! THEY'RE BOTH IN SHOCK, BUT...
OH, JEEZ.
SLUNCH
ALEC! OH, GOD, WHAT'S HAPPENING OUT HERE?
THE SHOT HAS BEEN FIRED... AS BEFORE.
BLAAM!
IT BEGINS AGAIN...
16

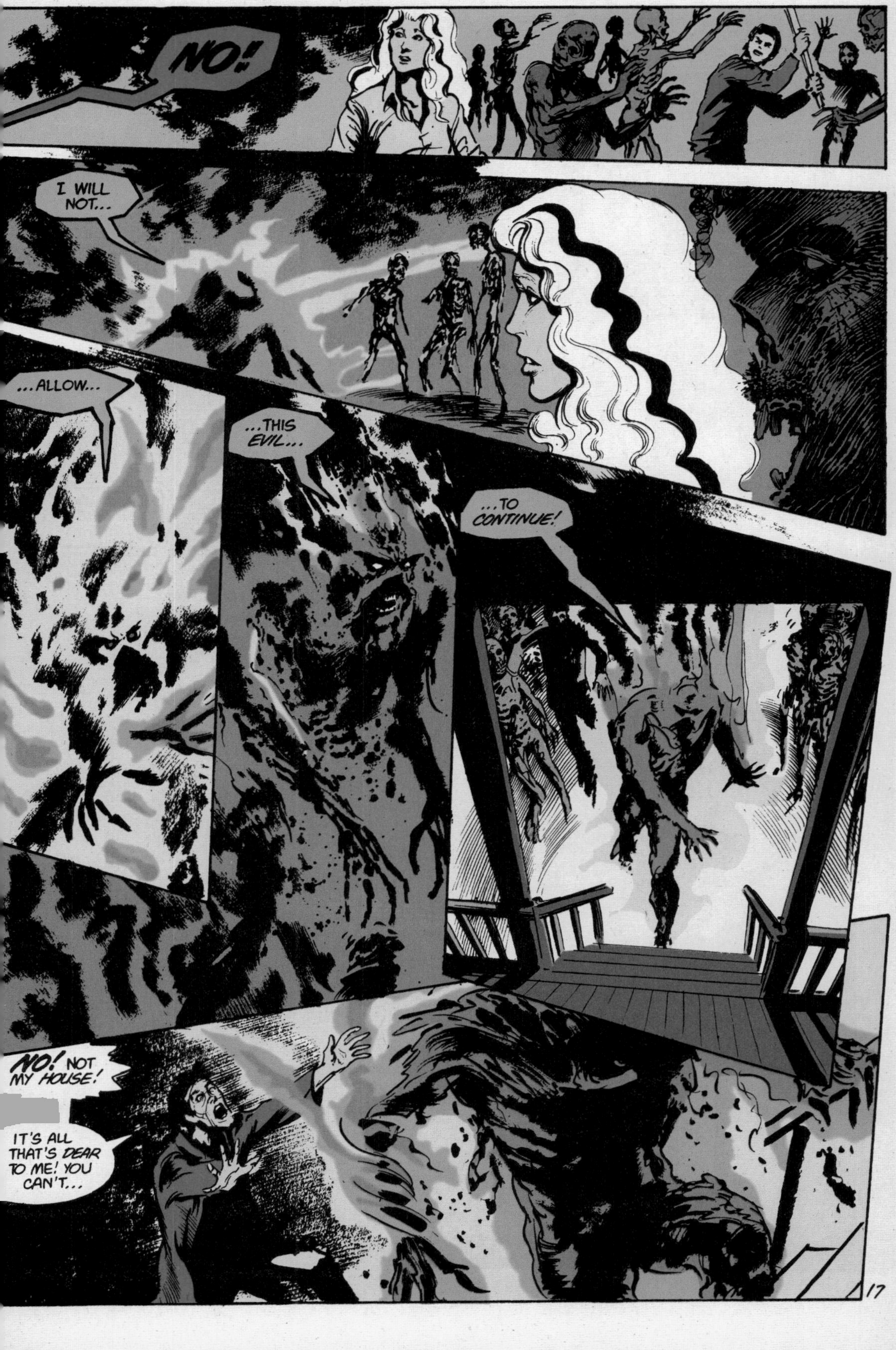
NO!
I WILL NOT...
...ALLOW...
...THIS EVIL...
...TO CONTINUE!
NO! NOT MY HOUSE!
IT'S ALL THAT'S DEAR TO ME! YOU CAN'T...
17

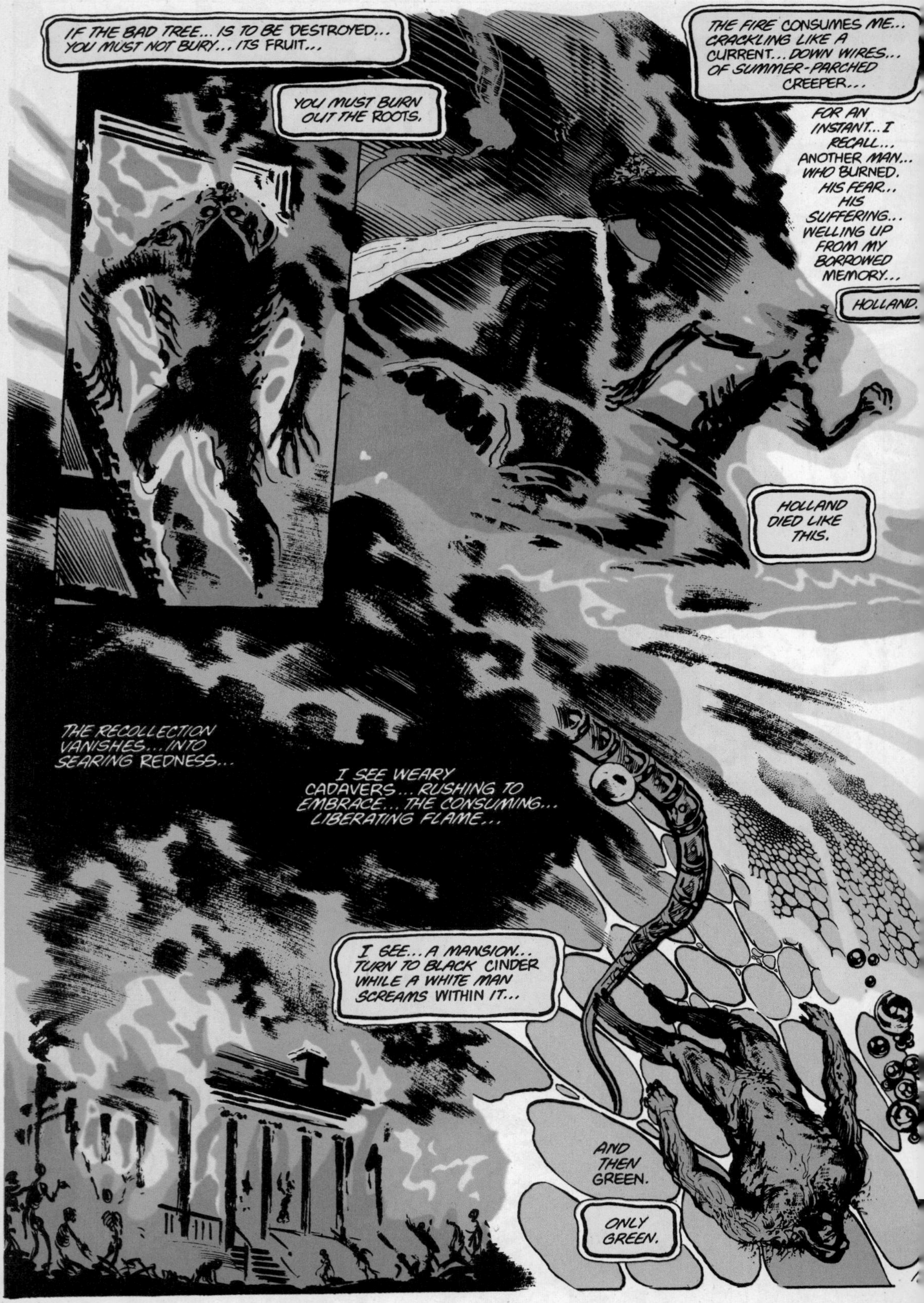
IF THE BAD TREE... IS TO BE DESTROYED... YOU MUST NOT BURY... ITS FRUIT...
YOU MUST BURN OUT THE ROOTS.
THE FIRE CONSUMES ME... CRACKLING LIKE A CURRENT... DOWN WIRES... OF SUMMER-PARCHED CREEPER...
FOR AN INSTANT... I RECALL... ANOTHER MAN... WHO BURNED. HIS FEAR... HIS SUFFERING... WELLING UP FROM MY BORROWED MEMORY...
HOLLAND.
HOLLAND DIED LIKE THIS.
THE RECOLLECTION VANISHES... INTO SEARING REDNESS...
I SEE WEARY CADAVERS... RUSHING TO EMBRACE... THE CONSUMING... LIBERATING FLAME...
I SEE... A MANSION... TURN TO BLACK CINDER WHILE A WHITE MAN SCREAMS WITHIN IT...
AND THEN GREEN.
ONLY GREEN.

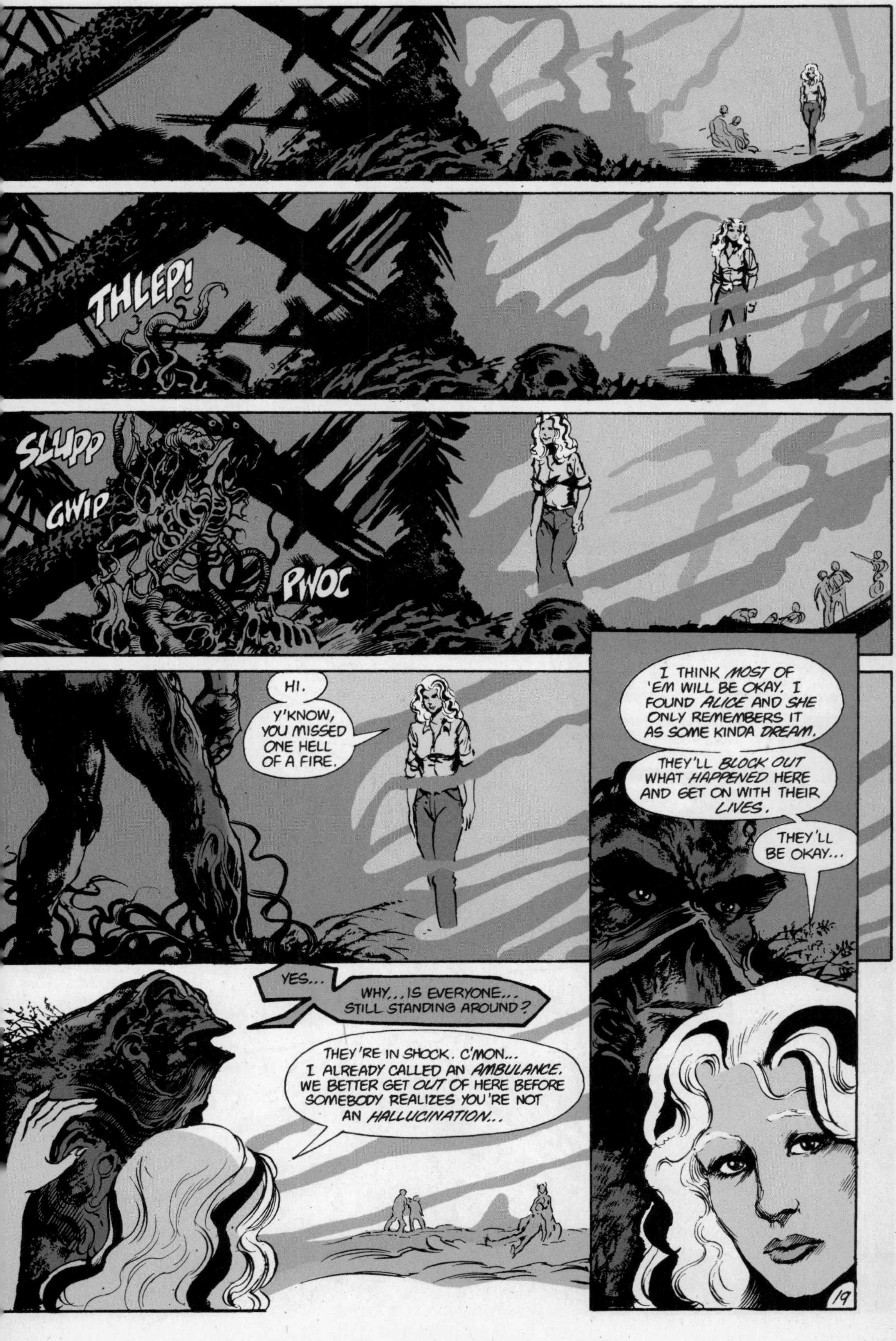
THLEP!
SLUPP
GWIP
PWOC
HI.
Y'KNOW, YOU MISSED ONE HELL OF A FIRE.
I THINK MOST OF 'EM WILL BE OKAY. I FOUND ALICE AND SHE ONLY REMEMBERS IT AS SOME KINDA DREAM.
THEY'LL BLOCK OUT WHAT HAPPENED HERE AND GET ON WITH THEIR LIVES.
THEY'LL BE OKAY...
YES...
WHY... IS EVERYONE... STILL STANDING AROUND?
THEY'RE IN SHOCK. C'MON... I ALREADY CALLED AN AMBULANCE. WE BETTER GET OUT OF HERE BEFORE SOMEBODY REALIZES YOU'RE NOT AN HALLUCINATION...
19

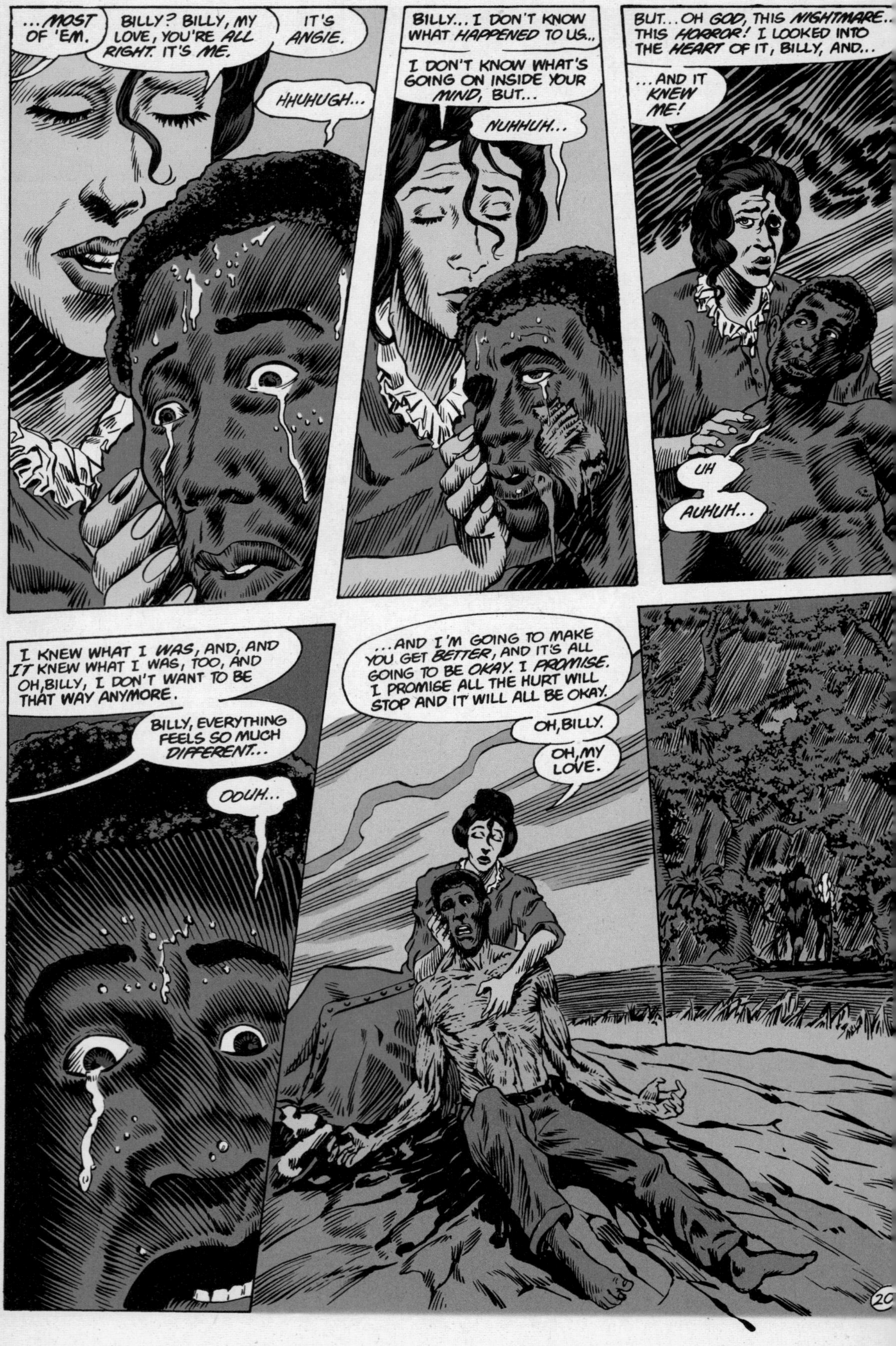
...MOST OF 'EM.
BILLY? BILLY, MY LOVE, YOU'RE ALL RIGHT. IT'S ME.
IT'S ANGIE.
HHUHUGH...
BILLY... I DON'T KNOW WHAT HAPPENED TO US...
I DON'T KNOW WHAT'S GOING ON INSIDE YOUR MIND, BUT...
NUHHUH...
BUT... OH GOD, THIS NIGHTMARE... THIS HORROR! I LOOKED INTO THE HEART OF IT, BILLY, AND...
...AND IT KNEW ME!
UH
AUHUH...
I KNEW WHAT I WAS, AND, AND IT KNEW WHAT I WAS, TOO, AND OH, BILLY, I DON'T WANT TO BE THAT WAY ANYMORE.
BILLY, EVERYTHING FEELS SO MUCH DIFFERENT...
OOUH...
...AND I'M GOING TO MAKE YOU GET BETTER, AND IT'S ALL GOING TO BE OKAY. I PROMISE. I PROMISE ALL THE HURT WILL STOP AND IT WILL ALL BE OKAY.
OH, BILLY.
OH, MY LOVE.
20

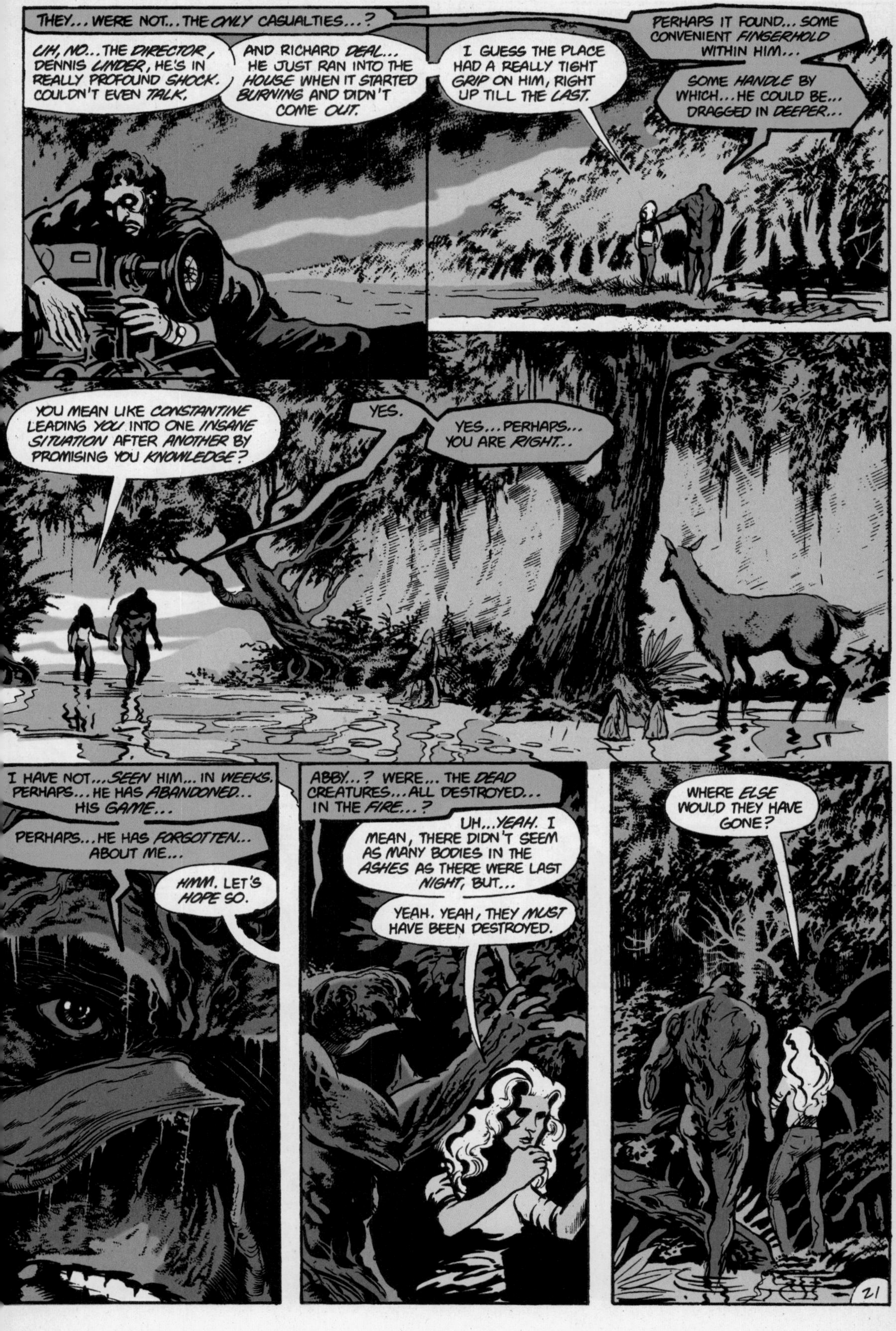
THEY... WERE NOT... THE ONLY CASUALTIES...?
UH, NO... THE DIRECTOR, DENNIS LINDER, HE'S IN REALLY PROFOUND SHOCK. COULDN'T EVEN TALK.
AND RICHARD DEAL... HE JUST RAN INTO THE HOUSE WHEN IT STARTED BURNING AND DIDN'T COME OUT.
I GUESS THE PLACE HAD A REALLY TIGHT GRIP ON HIM, RIGHT UP TILL THE LAST.
PERHAPS IT FOUND... SOME CONVENIENT FINGERHOLD WITHIN HIM...
SOME HANDLE BY WHICH... HE COULD BE... DRAGGED IN DEEPER...
YOU MEAN LIKE CONSTANTINE LEADING YOU INTO ONE INSANE SITUATION AFTER ANOTHER BY PROMISING YOU KNOWLEDGE?
YES.
YES... PERHAPS... YOU ARE RIGHT...
I HAVE NOT... SEEN HIM... IN WEEKS. PERHAPS... HE HAS ABANDONED... HIS GAME...
PERHAPS... HE HAS FORGOTTEN... ABOUT ME...
HMM. LET'S HOPE SO.
ABBY...? WERE... THE DEAD CREATURES... ALL DESTROYED... IN THE FIRE...?
UH,... YEAH. I MEAN, THERE DIDN'T SEEM AS MANY BODIES IN THE ASHES AS THERE WERE LAST NIGHT, BUT...
YEAH. YEAH, THEY MUST HAVE BEEN DESTROYED.
WHERE ELSE WOULD THEY HAVE GONE?
21

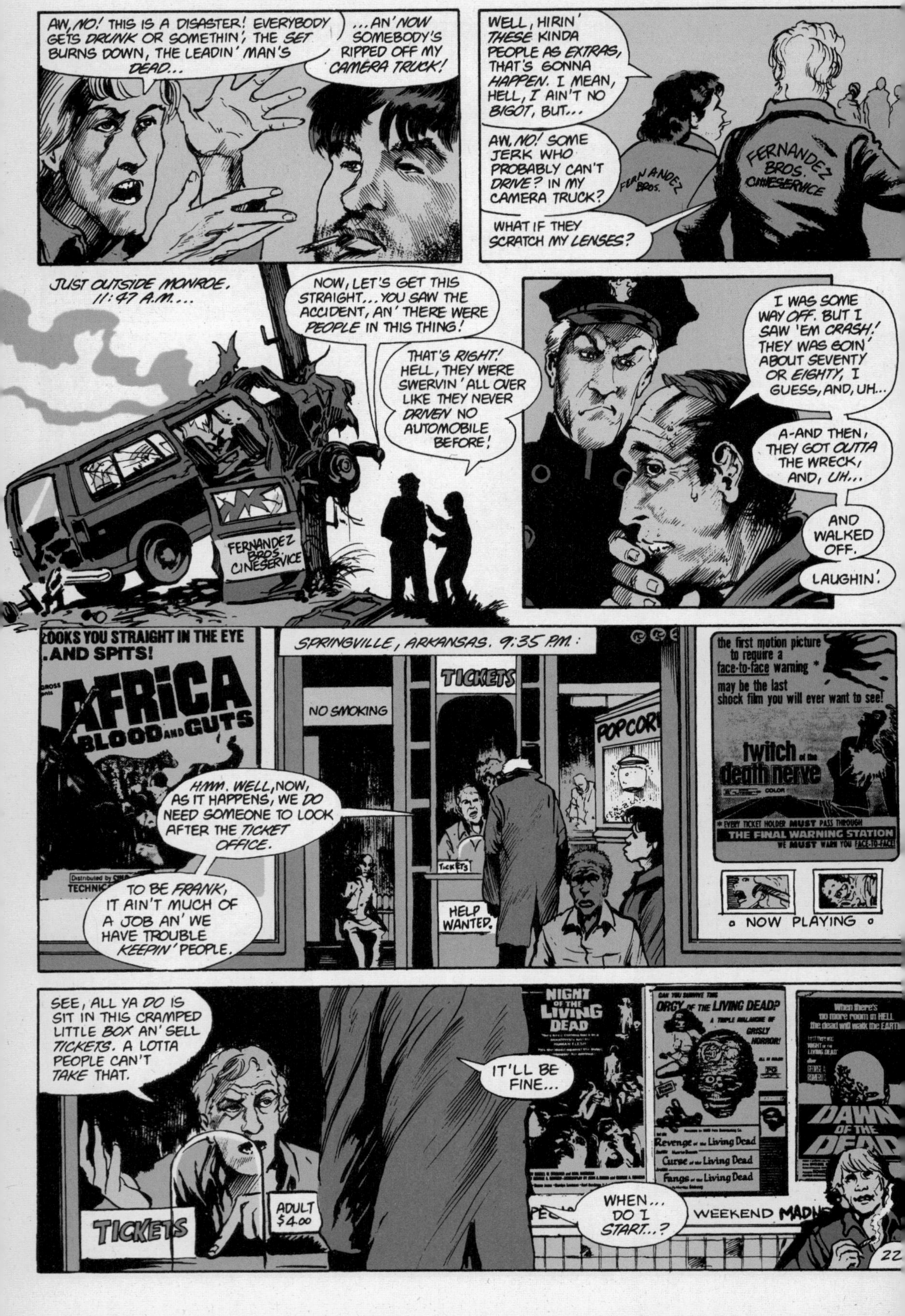
AW, NO! THIS IS A DISASTER! EVERYBODY GETS DRUNK OR SOMETHIN', THE SET BURNS DOWN, THE LEADIN' MAN'S DEAD...
...AN' NOW SOMEBODY'S RIPPED OFF MY CAMERA TRUCK!
WELL, HIRIN' THESE KINDA PEOPLE AS EXTRAS, THAT'S GONNA HAPPEN. I MEAN, HELL, I AIN'T NO BIGOT, BUT...
AW, NO! SOME JERK WHO PROBABLY CAN'T DRIVE? IN MY CAMERA TRUCK?
WHAT IF THEY SCRATCH MY LENSES?
FERNANDEZ BROS.
FERNANDEZ BROS. CINESERVICE
JUST OUTSIDE MONROE. 11:47 A.M...
NOW, LET'S GET THIS STRAIGHT... YOU SAW THE ACCIDENT, AN' THERE WERE PEOPLE IN THIS THING!
THAT'S RIGHT! HELL, THEY WERE SWERVIN' ALL OVER LIKE THEY NEVER DRIVEN NO AUTOMOBILE BEFORE!
FERNANDEZ BROS. CINESERVICE
I WAS SOME WAY OFF. BUT I SAW 'EM CRASH! THEY WAS GOIN' ABOUT SEVENTY OR EIGHTY, I GUESS, AND, UH...
A-AND THEN, THEY GOT OUTTA THE WRECK, AND, UH...
AND WALKED OFF.
LAUGHIN'.
LOOKS YOU STRAIGHT IN THE EYE ...AND SPITS!
AFRICA BLOOD AND GUTS
SPRINGVILLE, ARKANSAS. 9:35 P.M.:
TICKETS
NO SMOKING
POPCORN
the first motion picture to require a face-to-face warning * may be the last shock film you will ever want to see!
twitch of the death nerve
COLOR
* EVERY TICKET HOLDER MUST PASS THROUGH THE FINAL WARNING STATION WE MUST WARN YOU FACE-TO-FACE!
HMM. WELL, NOW, AS IT HAPPENS, WE DO NEED SOMEONE TO LOOK AFTER THE TICKET OFFICE.
TO BE FRANK, IT AIN'T MUCH OF A JOB AN' WE HAVE TROUBLE KEEPIN' PEOPLE.
TICKETS
HELP WANTED.
NOW PLAYING
SEE, ALL YA DO IS SIT IN THIS CRAMPED LITTLE BOX AN' SELL TICKETS. A LOTTA PEOPLE CAN'T TAKE THAT.
IT'LL BE FINE...
NIGHT OF THE LIVING DEAD
CAN YOU SURVIVE THIS ORGY OF THE LIVING DEAD? A TRIPLE AVALANCHE OF GRISLY HORROR!
Revenge of the Living Dead
Curse of the Living Dead
Fangs of the Living Dead
When there's no more room in HELL the dead will walk the EARTH
DAWN OF THE DEAD
ADULT $4.00
TICKETS
WHEN... DO I START...?
WEEKEND MADN
22

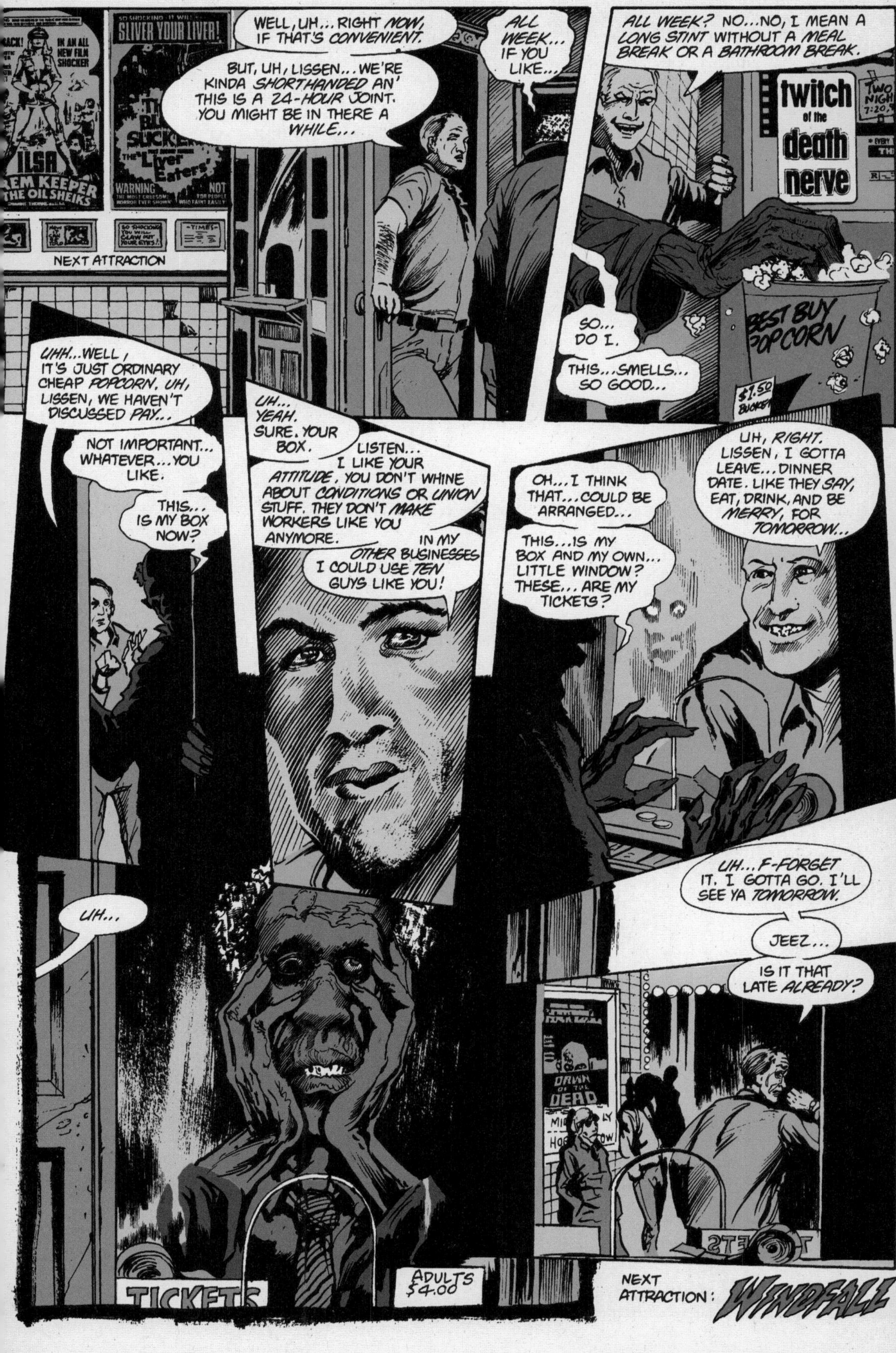
SLIVER YOUR LIVER!
ILSA
THE OIL SHEIKS
NEXT ATTRACTION
WELL, UH... RIGHT NOW, IF THAT'S CONVENIENT.
BUT, UH, LISSEN... WE'RE KINDA SHORTHANDED AN' THIS IS A 24-HOUR JOINT. YOU MIGHT BE IN THERE A WHILE...
ALL WEEK... IF YOU LIKE...
ALL WEEK? NO...NO, I MEAN A LONG STINT WITHOUT A MEAL BREAK OR A BATHROOM BREAK.
twitch of the death nerve
SO... DO I.
THIS... SMELLS... SO GOOD...
BEST BUY POPCORN
$1.50
UHH...WELL, IT'S JUST ORDINARY CHEAP POPCORN. UH, LISSEN, WE HAVEN'T DISCUSSED PAY...
NOT IMPORTANT... WHATEVER... YOU LIKE.
THIS... IS MY BOX NOW?
UH... YEAH. SURE. YOUR BOX.
LISTEN... I LIKE YOUR ATTITUDE. YOU DON'T WHINE ABOUT CONDITIONS OR UNION STUFF. THEY DON'T MAKE WORKERS LIKE YOU ANYMORE.
IN MY OTHER BUSINESSES I COULD USE TEN GUYS LIKE YOU!
OH... I THINK THAT... COULD BE ARRANGED...
THIS... IS MY BOX AND MY OWN... LITTLE WINDOW? THESE... ARE MY TICKETS?
UH, RIGHT. LISSEN, I GOTTA LEAVE... DINNER DATE. LIKE THEY SAY, EAT, DRINK, AND BE MERRY, FOR TOMORROW...
UH...
UH... F-FORGET IT. I GOTTA GO. I'LL SEE YA TOMORROW.
JEEZ...
IS IT THAT LATE ALREADY?
DAWN OF THE DEAD
TICKETS
ADULTS $4.00
NEXT ATTRACTION: WINDFALL

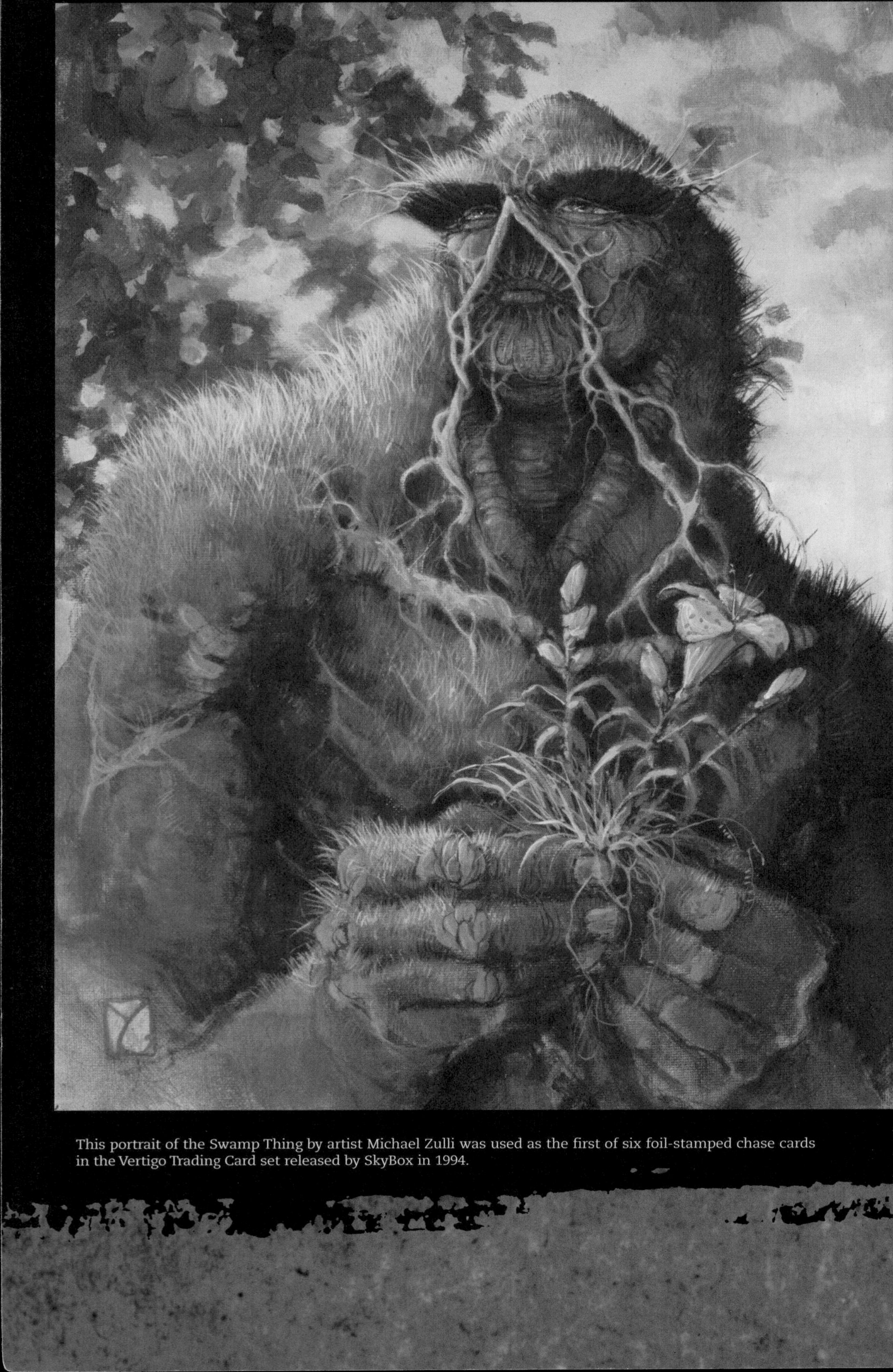

This portrait of the Swamp Thing by artist Michael Zulli was used as the first of six foil-stamped chase cards in the Vertigo Trading Card set released by SkyBox in 1994.

ALAN MOORE is perhaps the most acclaimed writer in the graphic story medium, having garnered countless awards for works such as *Watchmen*, *V For Vendetta*, *From Hell*, *Miracleman* and *Swamp Thing*. He is also the mastermind behind the America's Best Comics line, through which he has created (along with many talented illustrators) *The League of Extraordinary Gentlemen*, *Promethea*, *Tom Strong*, *Tomorrow Stories* and *Top 10*. As one of the medium's most important innovators since the early 1980s, Moore has influenced an entire generation of comics creators, and his work continues to inspire an ever-growing audience. He resides in central England.

Following his multi-award-winning tenure on *Swamp Thing*, Joe Kubert School pioneer class graduate **STEPHEN R. BISSETTE** went on to co-found, edit, and co-publish the controversial and Eisner Award-winning horror anthology *Taboo*, collaborate with Alan Moore, Rick Veitch, Chester Brown, Dave Gibbons and John Totleben on the Image series *1963*, and create and self-publish four issues of *S.R. Bissette's Tyrant*. He has also been on the faculty of the Center for Cartoon Studies in White River Junction, Vermont since its opening in 2005. Bissette's film criticism, articles and short fiction have appeared in over two dozen periodicals and anthologies, and his original novella *Aliens: Tribes* won a Bram Stoker Award in 1993. Most recently he penned the short story "Copper" for the zombie anthology *The New Dead*, co-authored *Prince of Stories: The Many Worlds of Neil Gaiman*, and provided characteristically memorable illustrations for *The Vermont Monster Guide*.

After a childhood in Erie, Pennsylvania spent consuming a steady diet of comics, monster magazines and monster movies, **JOHN TOTLEBEN** went to the Joe Kubert School of Cartoon and Graphic Art where he met Stephen Bissette. Together they worked on *Bizarre Adventures* followed by *Swamp Thing*, which they drew for almost three years. Totleben is best known for his illustrative work on Alan Moore's *Miracleman*. His other credits include *1963*, *Vermillion* and *The Dreaming*.

RICK VEITCH worked in the underground comics scene before attending the Joe Kubert School of Cartoon and Graphic Art. After graduating, he worked with Stephen Bissette on *Bizarre Adventures* before creating and illustrating *The One*, the innovative Epic Comics miniseries. In addition to writing and drawing an acclaimed run on *Swamp Thing*, he is the creator/cartoonist of *Brat Pack*, *Maximortal* and the dream-based *Rare Bit Fiends*, and a contributing artist on *1963*. He is also the writer and artist of the miniseries *Greyshirt: Indigo Sunset* from America's Best Comics, and the creator of the critically acclaimed graphic novel *Can't Get No* and the spectacularly satirical series *Army@Love* from Vertigo.

ALFREDO ALCALA's graceful, moody inks helped maintain the style on *Swamp Thing* through many penciller changes. DC first employed Alcala's talents in its horror and war comics such as *Ghosts*, *Unexpected*, and *Weird War Tales*. Later he moved on to titles including *All-Star Squadron*, *Savage Sword of Conan*, *Batman*, *Swamp Thing* and countless others for both DC and Marvel. After a long battle with cancer, Alcala passed away in April, 2000.

RON RANDALL has been working professionally as an illustrator and storyteller for over twenty years. He has worked for all the major American comic publishers, including DC, Marvel, Dark Horse and Image, as well as commercial clients such as Disney, Nike, SeaWorld and Sony.

TATJANA WOOD switched careers from dressmaking to comics coloring in the late 1960s and quickly established herself as one of the top colorists in the field, winning two Shazam awards in the early 1970s.

Over his long and prolific career, **JOHN COSTANZA** has lettered a huge number of comics and has won numerous awards along the way. A cartoonist in his own right, Costanza has also contributed stories and art to a variety of titles, beginning in the late 1960s and continuing right through to the new millennium.